PROBLEM SOLVING SURVIVAL GUIDE
VOLUME 1: CHAPTERS 1-13

INTERMEDIATE ACCOUNTING
SIXTH CANADIAN EDITION

Marilyn F. Hunt, M.A., C.P.A.
University of Central Florida
Orlando, Florida

Donald E. Kieso, Ph.D., C.P.A.
KPMG Peat Marwick Emeritus Professor of Accountancy
Northern Illinois University
DeKalb, Illinois

Jerry J. Weygandt, Ph.D., C.P.A.
Arthur Andersen Alumni Professor of Accounting
University of Wisconsin
Madison, Wisconsin

Terry D. Warfield, Ph.D., C.P.A.
University of Wisconsin
Madison, Wisconsin

Canadian Edition prepared by:
Hilary M. Becker, M.B.A., C.G.A.
Carleton University
Ottawa, Ontario

WILEY

JOHN WILEY AND SONS CANADA, LTD

National Library of Canada Cataloguing in Publication Data

Becker, Hilary
      Problem solving survival guide vol. 1 to accompany
Intermediate accounting, 6th Canadian edition

Supplement to: Kieso, Donald E. Intermediate accounting.
ISBN 0-470-83165-0

      1.   Accounting—Problems, exercises, etc. I. Kieso, Donald E.
Intermediate accounting. II. Title.

HF5635.I573 2001 Suppl. 1   657'.044   C2001-902468-1

Production Credits
Publisher: John Horne
Publishing Services Director: Karen Bryan
Editorial Manager: Karen Staudinger
Sr. Marketing Manager: Janine Daoust
New Media Editor: Elsa Passera
Publishing Services/Permissions Co-ordinator: Michelle Love
Cover Design: Ian Koo
Cover Photo: Grant V. Faint/Image Bank
Printing and Binding: Tri-Graphic Printing Limited

Printed and Bound in Canada
10 9 8 7 6 5 4 3 2 1

John Wiley and Sons Canada Ltd
22 Worcester Road
Etobicoke, Ontario M9W 1L1

Visit our website at www.wiley.com/canada

CONTENTS

PREFACE: To the Student

The purpose of this problem solving tutorial is to help you to improve your success rate in solving accounting homework assignments and in answering accounting exam questions. For each chapter we provide you with:

OVERVIEW	To briefly introduce the chapter topics and their importance.
STUDY OBJECTIVES	To provide you with a learning framework. Explanations of these objectives also provide you with a summary of the major points covered in the chapter.
TIPS	To alert you to common pitfalls and misconceptions and to remind you of important terminology, concepts, and relationships that are relevant to answering specific questions or solving certain problems. To help you to understand the intricacies of a problematic situation and to tell you what to do in similar circumstances.
EXERCISES	To provide you with a selection of problems which are representative of homework assignments which an intermediate accounting student may encounter.
MULTIPLE CHOICE	To provide you with a selection of multiple-choice questions which are representative of common exam questions covering topics in the chapter.
PURPOSES	To identify the essence of each question or exercise and to link them to learning objectives.
SOLUTIONS	To show you the appropriate solution for each exercise and multiple-choice question presented.
EXPLANATIONS	To give you the details of how selected solutions were derived and to explain why things are done as shown.
APPROACHES	To coach you on the particular model, computational format, or other strategy to be used to solve particular problems. To teach you how to analyse and solve multiple-choice questions.

This book will be a welcome teaching/learning aid because it provides you with the opportunity to solve accounting problems in addition to the ones assigned by your instructor without having to rely on your teacher for solutions. Many of the exercises and questions contained herein are very similar to items in your intermediate accounting textbook; the difference is, the ones in this book are accompanied with detailed clearly-laid out solutions.

The use of the multiple choice questions in this volume and the related suggestions on how to approach them can easily increase your ability (and confidence in your ability) to deal with exam questions of this variety.

HOW TO STUDY ACCOUNTING

The successful study of accounting requires a different approach than most other subjects. In addition to reading a chapter, applying the material through the completion of exercises or problems is necessary to develop a true and lasting understanding of the concepts introduced in the text chapter. The study of accounting principles is a combination of theory and practice; theory describes what to do and why, and practice is the application of guidelines to actual situations. We use illustrations to demonstrate how theory works and we use theory to explain whey something is done in practice. Therefore, it is impossible to separate the two in the study of accounting.

Learning accounting is a cumulative process. It is difficult to master Chapter 4 until you are thoroughly familiar with Chapters 1-3, and so on. Therefore, it is imperative that you keep up with class assignments. And because accounting is a technical subject, you must pay particular attention to terminology.

Accounting is the language of business. It is an exciting subject that provides a challenge for most business majors. Your ultimate success in life may well depend on your ability to grasp financial data. The effort you expend now will provide rewards for years to come.

We encourage you to follow the four steps for study outlined below to give yourself the best possible chance for a successful learning experience and to make the most efficient use of your time. These steps provide a system of study for each new chapter in your text.

Step 1
- Scan the study objectives in the text.
- Scan the chapter (or chapter section) rather quickly.
- Glance over the questions at the end of the chapter.

The first step will give you an overview of the material to be mastered.

Step 2
- Read the assigned pages slowly.
- Use the marginal notes to review and to locate topics within each chapter.
- Study carefully and mark for later attention any portions not clearly understood.
- Pay particular attention to examples and illustrations.
- Try to formulate tentative answers to end-of-chapter questions.

During this phase, you will be filling in the "outline" you formed in Step 1. Most of the details will fall into place during this part of your study. The remaining steps are necessary, however, for a keen understanding of the subject.

Step 3
- Carefully read the **Overview**, **Learning Objectives**, and **Tips** sections of this *Problem Solving Survival Guide* volume.

- Do the **Exercises** and **Cases** in the *Problem Solving Survival Guide* that pertain to the same learning objectives as your homework assignments. Review the relevant **Illustrations** in this book.
- Do the **Multiple-Choice Type Questions** in the *Problem Solving Survival Guide* that pertain to the same study objectives as your homework assignments.
- Refer back to the sections of the chapter in the text that you marked as unclear if any. It is likely that any confusion or questions on your part will have been cleared up through your work in the *Problem Solving Survival Guide*. If a section remains unclear, carefully reread it and rework relevant pages of the *Problem Solving Survival Guide*.
- Repeat this process for each assigned topic area.

Step 4 • Write out formal answers to homework assignments in the text.

This step is crucial because you find out whether you can independently apply the material you have been studying to fresh situations. You may find it necessary to go back to the text and/or the *Problem Solving Survival Guide* to restudy certain sections. This is common and merely shows that the study assignments are working for you.

Additional comments pertaining to Step 3 and your usage of this *Problem Solving Survival Guide* volume are as follows:

- The **Learning Objectives** and **Tips** sections, along with **Illustrations** will aid your understanding and retention of the material. **Exercises** provide examples of application of the text material. These should be very valuable in giving you guidance in completing homework assignments which are often similar in nature and content.

- The **Approach** stated for an exercise or question is likely the most valuable feature of this *Problem Solving Survival Guide* volume because it tells you how to **think** through the situation at hand. This thought process can then be used for similar situations. It is impossible to illustrate every situation you may encounter. You can, however, handle new situations by simply applying what you know and making modifications where appropriate. Many students make the mistake of attempting to memorize their way through an accounting book. That too is an impossible feat. **Do not rely on memorization**. If this material is going to be useful to you, you must think about what you are reading and always be thinking of **why** things are as they are. If you know the reasoning for a particular accounting treatment, it will be much easier to remember that treatment and reconstruct it even weeks after your initial study of it.

- **Explanations** are provided for exercise and questions. These are very detailed so that you will thorough understand what is being done and why.

These details will serve you well when you complete your homework assignments.

- Always make an honest effort to solve the exercises and answer the questions contained in this *Problem Solving Survival Guide* volume **before** you look at the solutions. Answering the questions on your own will maximize the benefits you can expect to reap from this book.

- The **Multiple-Choice Type Questions** are self-tests to give you immediate feedback on how well you understand the material. Study the **Approaches** suggested for answering these questions in the *Problem Solving Survival Guide*. Practice them when answering the multiple choice questions in the text. Apply them when taking examinations. By doing so, you will learn to calmly, methodically, and successfully process examination questions. This will definitely improve your exam scores when you work an **Exercise** or **Case** in the *Problem Solving Survival Guide* or in the text, always read the instructions **before** you read all of the given data. This allows you to determine what you are to accomplish. Therefore, as you now tread through the data, you can begin to process it because you can determine its significance and relevance. If you read the data before the instructions, you are likely to waste your time because you will have to reread the facts once you find out what you are to do with them. Also, more importantly, you are likely to begin to anticipate what the problem is about, which will often cause you to do things other than what is requested in the questions.

Good luck and best wishes for a positive learning experience!

CHAPTER 1

THE CANADIAN FINANCIAL REPORTING ENVIRONMENT

OVERVIEW

Accounting is the language of business. As such, accountants collect and communicate economic information about business enterprises or other entities to a wide variety of persons. To be useful, financial statements must be clearly understandable and comparable so that users may compare the performance of one business with the performance of the same business for a prior period or with the performance of another similar business. Therefore, all general purpose financial statements should be prepared in accordance with the same uniform guidelines. In this chapter, we will examine the history and sources of current financial accounting standards (generally accepted accounting principles).

SUMMARY OF LEARNING OBJECTIVES

1. **Describe the essential characteristics of accounting.** The essential characteristics of accounting are: (1) identification, measurement, and communication of financial information about (2) economic entities to (3) interested persons.

2. **Identify the major financial statements and other means of financial reporting.** The financial statements most frequently provided are (1) the balance sheet, (2) the income statement, (3) the statement of cash flows, and (4) the statement of owners' or shareholders' equity. Financial reporting other than financial statements may take various forms. Examples include the president's letter or supplementary schedules in the corporate annual report, prospectuses, reports filed with government agencies, news releases, management's forecasts, and descriptions of an enterprise's social or environmental impact.

3. **Explain how accounting assists in the efficient use of scarce resources.** Accounting provides reliable, relevant, and timely information to managers, investors, and creditors so that resources are allocated to the most efficient enterprises. Accounting also provides measurements of efficiency (profitability) and financial soundness.

4. **Explain the meaning of stakeholders and identify the key stakeholders in financial reporting.** Stakeholders are parties that have something at stake in the financial reporting environment, e.g., salary, job, investment, and reputation. Key stakeholders are investors, creditors, analysts, managers, employees, customers, suppliers, industry groups, unions, government departments and ministers, the public in general (e.g., consumer groups), regulatory agencies, other companies, standard setters, auditors, lawyers, and others.

5. **Identify the objective of financial reporting.** According to the *CICA Handbook,* the objective of financial statements is to communicate information that is useful to investors, members, contributors, creditors, and other users in making their resource allocation decisions and/or assessing management stewardship. Consequently, financial statements provide information about:

    (a)   An entity's economic resources, obligations, and equity/net assets;

    (b)   Changes in an entity's economic resources, obligation and equity/net assets; and

    (c)   The economic performance of the entity.

6.   **Explain the notion of management bias with respect to financial reporting.** Management bias implies that the financial statements are not neutral—that the preparers of the financial information are presenting the information in a manner that may overemphasize the positive and de-emphasize the negative.

7.   **Understand the importance of user needs in the financial reporting process.** The financial reporting process is based on ensuring that users receive decision-relevant information. This is a challenge as different users have different knowledge levels and needs. Management bias may render financial information less useful.

8.   **Explain the need for accounting standards.** The accounting profession has attempted to develop a set of standards that is generally accepted and universally practised. Without this set of standards, each enterprise would have to develop its own standards, and readers of financial statements would have to familiarize themselves with every company's peculiar accounting reporting practices. As a result, it would be almost impossible to prepare statements that could be compared.

9.   **Identify the major entities that influence the standard-setting process and explain how they influence financial reporting.** The **CICA AcSB** is the main standard-setting body in Canada. It derives its mandate from the **CBCA** as well as provincial acts of incorporation. Public companies are required to follow **GAAP** in order to access capital markets. This is monitored by provincial securities commissions. **FASB** and the **IASC** are also important as they influence Canadian standard setting. Canada is committed to international harmonization of GAAP.

10.   **Explain the meaning of "generally accepted accounting principles."** Generally accepted accounting principles are those principles that have substantial authoritative support, such as *CICA Handbook,* or that over time have been accepted as appropriate because of its universal application.

11.   **Explain the significance of professional judgement in applying GAAP.** Professional judgement plays an important role in Canadian GAAP since much of GAAP is based on general principles, which need to be interpreted.

12.   **Understand issues related to ethics and financial accounting.** Financial accountants in the performance of their professional duties are called on for moral discernment and ethical decision-making. Decisions are more difficult because a public consensus has not emerged to formulate a comprehensive ethical system that provides guidelines in making ethical judgements.

13.   **Identify some of the challenges facing accounting.** Globalization, leading to a requirement for international harmonization of standards; Increased technology, resulting in the need for more timely information; Move to a new economy, resulting in a focus on measuring and reporting non-traditional assets that create value; Increased requirement for accountability, resulting in creation of new measurement and reporting models that look at business reporting as a whole.

TIPS ON CHAPTER TOPICS

TIPS: The accounting profession has adopted a common set of standards and procedures called **generally accepted accounting principles** (often referred to as **GAAP**). The term "generally accepted" can mean either that an authoritative accounting rule-making body has established a principle of reporting in a given area or that over time a given practice has been accepted as appropriate because of its universal application.

TIP: Because most business owners (shareholders of corporations) are not involved with the operation of the business, the **stewardship function**—measuring and reporting data to absentee owners—has emerged as a critical role for accounting. This situation greatly increases the need for accounting standards.

TIP: The financial statements most frequently provided by an entity (often called the **basic financial statements** or **general purpose financial statements**) are: (1) the income statement, (2) the statement of owners' equity (or statement of shareholders' equity), (3) the balance sheet, and (4) the statement of cash flows. In addition, note disclosures and other supporting schedules are an integral part of the financial statements.

TIP: The primary focus of this textbook concerns the development of two types of financial information which are governed by generally accepted accounting principles: (1) the basic financial statements and (2) the related note disclosures.

TIP: The terms **principles** and **standards** are used interchangeably in practice and throughout this book.

TIP: The **accrual basis of accounting** is used in preparing the basic financial statements. The accrual basis provides for (1) reporting revenues in the period they are earned (which may not be the same period in which the related cash is received), and (2) reporting expenses in the period they are incurred (which may not be the same period in which the related cash is paid).

TIP: Accounting is a constantly changing and evolving entity, which continues to change to meet the needs and demands of the users, thus the principles of GAAP will continue to evolve over time.

TIP: Potential management bias may play a key role in the development and choice of accounting principles chosen by management. These should always be kept in mind when analysing a set of financial statements. This may take the form of overstating assets/revenues or understating liabilities/expenses.

TIP: There exists over 150 different GAAPs around the world. Each country has their own GAAP to meet the unique needs (objectives) and conditions of that country or group of countries. GAAP of one country may or may not be the same for the same situation. Harmonization of GAAP principles is a main focus of many accounting standard setters to eliminate barriers and improve comparability.

> **TIP:** The *CICA Handbook* is the primary authoritative source of accounting **recommendations** in Canada. The secondary sources include other Canadian companies and professional judgement.
>
> **TIP:** The "Balanced Scorecard" links internal and external reporting to evaluate the strategic objectives of a company by evaluating financial, customer, internal processes and learning and growth.

CASE 1-1

Purpose: (L.O.10) This case will review the meaning of generally accepted accounting principles and their significance.

All publicly-held companies must have their annual financial statements audited by an independent accountant. In accordance with generally accepted auditing standards (which you will study in an auditing class), the auditor expresses an opinion regarding the fairness of the financial statements, which are to be in conformity with generally accepted accounting principles.

Instructions

(a)   Define generally accepted accounting principles and explain their significance to an auditor of financial statements.

(b)   What is meant by the GAAP Hierarchy.

Solution to Case 1-2

(a)   The accounting profession has adopted a common set of standards and procedures called **generally accepted accounting principles** (often referred to as GAAP). The word "principles" refers to methods or procedures or standards. The phrase "generally accepted" means having "substantial authoritative support." A method has substantial authoritative support if it has been approved by a rule-making body or if it has gained acceptance over time because of its universal application.

(b)   The meaning of generally accepted accounting principles is defined by *CICA Handbook,* Section 1000, par. 60. "The term generally accepted accounting principles encompasses not only specific rules, practices and procedures relating to particular circumstances but also broad principles and conventions of general application, including the underlying concepts described in this Section. Specifically, generally accepted accounting principles comprise the Accounting Recommendations in the Handbook and, when a matter is not covered by a Recommendation, other accounting principles that either:

    (a)   are generally accepted by virtue of their use in similar circumstances by a significant number of entities in Canada; or

    (b)   are consistent with the Recommendations in the *Handbook* and are developed through the exercise of professional judgement, including consultation with other informed accountants where appropriate, and the application of the concepts described in this Section. In exercising professional judgement, established principles for analogous situations dealt with in the Handbook would be taken into account and reference would be made to:

(i)   other relevant matters dealt with in the Handbook;

(ii)   practice in similar circumstances;

(iii)   Accounting Guidelines;

(iv)   Abstracts of Issues Discussed by the CICA Emerging Issues Committee;

(v)   International Accounting Standards published by the International Accounting Standards Committee;

(vi)   standards published by bodies authorized to establish financial accounting standards in other jurisdictions;

(vii)   CICA research studies; and

(viii) other sources of accounting literature such as textbooks and journals.

The relative importance of these various sources is a matter of professional judgement in the circumstances."

ANALYSIS OF MULTIPLE-CHOICE TYPE QUESTIONS

QUESTION

1.   (L.O.1) The process of identifying, measuring, analysing, and communicating financial information needed by management to plan, evaluate, and control an organization's operations is called:

a.   financial accounting.

b.   managerial accounting.

c.   tax accounting.

d.   auditing.

Approach and Explanation: Define each answer selection. Select the answer item for which your definition matches the stem of the question. **Financial accounting** is the process that culminates in the preparation of financial reports on the enterprise as a whole for use by parties both internal and external to the enterprise. (Users of these financial reports include investors, creditors, managers, unions, and government agencies.) **Managerial accounting** is the process of identifying, measuring, analysing, and communicating financial information needed by management to plan, evaluate, and control an organization's operations. (These reports are only for the use of parties internal to the enterprise.) **Tax accounting** usually refers to tax planning, advising on tax matters, and/or preparing tax returns. **Auditing** refers to the examination of financial statements by a certified accountant (CA or CGA depending on jurisdiction) in order to express an opinion on their fairness. An auditor attests to the fairness of financial statements and their conformity to generally accepted accounting principles. (Solution = b.)

QUESTION

2.   (L.O.5) One objective of financial reporting is to provide:

a.   information about the investors in the business entity.

b.   information about the liquidation values of the resources held by the enterprise.

c.   information that is useful in resource allocation decisions.

d.   information that will attract new customers.

Approach and Explanation: Before you read the possible answers, mentally list the objectives of financial reporting or write down the key words of each objective. Then carefully read the suggested answers. As you read an answer choice, note whether it is a match to an item in your list or not. The objectives of financial reporting are to communicate information that is useful to investors, members, contributors, creditors, and other users in making their resource allocation decisions and/or assessing management stewardship. Consequently, financial statements provide information about:

(a)   An entity's economic resources, obligations, and equity/net assets;
(b)   Changes in an entity's economic resources, obligation and equity/net assets; and
(c)   The economic performance of the entity. (Solution = c.)

QUESTION
3.   (L.O.6) The measuring and reporting of data to absentee owners of a corporation is referred to as management's:
    a.   fiduciary responsibility.
    b.   stewardship function.
    c.   accounting standard-setting function.
    d.   audit function.

Explanation: Management's responsibility to manage assets with care and trust is its **fiduciary responsibility**. Management does not set accounting standards. Audits are conducted by independent accountants, not management. The **stewardship function** involves measuring and reporting data to absentee owners. (Solution = b.)

QUESTION
4.   (L.O.7) The most significant current source of generally accepted accounting principles in the nongovernmental sector is the:
    a.   Securities Commissions and Stock Exchanges.
    b.   FASB.
    c.   IASC.
    d.   CICA.

Explanation: The mission of the the AcSB of the CICA is to develop and maintain GAAP in Canada. The Securities and Stock Exchanges have an influence on the standard setting, and control the stock exchanges. FASB is the primary standard setting organization in the United States (CICA counterpart in the U.S.), while the IASC is an international organization involved in harmonization of accounting principles. (Solution = d.)

QUESTION
5.   (L.O.3) Accounting assists in the efficient use of scare resources by providing information that is:
    I.   Timely.
    II.   Reliable.
    III.   Relevant.
    a.   1 only.
    b.   I and II.
    c.   I and III
    d.   All of the above.

Explanation: Think about how accounting information can be used to provide information to aid in the decision-making of scarce resources. An effective process of capital allocation promotes productivity, encourages innovation, and provides an efficient and liquid market for buying and selling securities and debt. Unreliable and irrelevant information can lead to poor capital allocation. To be useful, information must be relevant to the decision-maker, it must be received in a timely manner and it must be reliable. (Solution = d.)

QUESTION
6. (L.O.4) Management bias can occur by all of the following except:
   a. Increasing reported revenues.
   b. Decreasing reported expenses.
   c. Increasing reported debt.
   d. Increasing reported assets.

Explanation: Management is responsible for the preparation of the financial statements of an enterprise. Companies that are trying to present their company in the best light will tend to use more aggressive accounting methods, which will tend to overstate revenues/assets and understate expenses/liabilities, hence increasing reported debt would be considered more conservative. (Solution = c.)

QUESTION
7. (L.O.9) All of the following organizations are directly involved in the development of financial accounting standards (GAAP) in Canada, except the:
   a. Canadian Customs and Revenue Agency (CCRA).
   b. Accounting Standards Board (AcSB).
   c. Canadian Institute of Chartered Accountants (CICA).
   d. Provincial Securities Commissions (SEC).

Explanation: The Canadian Customs and Revenue Agency (CCRA) is responsible for federal income tax rules and administration. Although the CCRA influences accounting practice, they are not directly involved in the development of accounting standards (for financial statements) as are the other organizations listed. (Solution = a.)

QUESTION
8. (L.O.9) Which of the following steps is not typical in the evolution of an addition or amendment to the *CICA Handbook*.
   a. Task force established to study the issue.
   b. Topic identified and placed on the boards agenda.
   c. Exposure draft produced and posted on CICA website.
   d. Discussion with government for final approval of addition or amendment.

Explanation: Think about the steps involved in the process of the evolution of an addition or amendment:
   i. topics identified and placed on Board's agenda.
   ii. Task force established to study issue.
   iii. Research and analysis conducted.
   iv. Exposure Draft produced and posted for comment on CICA website.
   v. Board evaluates responses and changes exposure draft, if necessary. Final standard issued.

The CICA has the responsibility in Canada for the development and maintenance of GAAP. It does not have to consult with the government prior to final approval of an addition or amendment to Canadian GAAP. (Solution = d).

CHAPTER 2

CONCEPTUAL FRAMEWORK
UNDERLYING FINANCIAL REPORTING

OVERVIEW

Financial statements are needed for decision-making. In order to make informed decisions, a financial statement user must understand both the financial information conveyed and how it is derived. To be useful, financial statements must be clearly understandable and comparable so that users may compare the performance of one business with the performance of the same business for a prior period or with the performance of another similar business. Therefore the financial statements need relevant and reliable information, and all general purpose financial statements should be prepared in accordance with the same uniform guidelines. In this chapter, we will examine basic accounting principles.

SUMMARY OF LEARNING OBJECTIVES

1. **Describe the usefulness of a conceptual framework.** A conceptual framework is needed to (1) build on and relate to an established body of concepts and objectives, (2) provide a framework for solving new and emerging practical problems, (3) increase financial statement users' understanding of and confidence in financial reporting, and (4) enhance comparability among companies' financial statements.

2. **Describe the main components of the conceptual framework for financial reporting.** The first level deals with objectives of financial reporting. The second level includes the qualitative characteristics of useful information and elements of financial statements. The third level includes assumptions, principles and constraints.

3. **Understand the objectives of financial reporting.** The objectives of financial reporting are to provide information that is useful to those making investment and credit decisions.

4. **Identify the qualitative characteristics of accounting information.** The overriding criterion by which accounting choices can be judged is decision usefulness; that is, providing information that is most useful for decision-making. Understandability relevance, reliability, comparability, and consistency are the qualities that make accounting information useful for decision-making.

5. **Define the basic elements of financial statements.** The basic elements of financial statements are (1) assets, (2) liabilities, (3) equity, (4) revenues, (5) expenses, (6) gains, and (7) losses. These seven elements are defined on page 32 of the text.

6. **Describe the basic assumptions of accounting.** Four basic assumptions underlying the financial accounting structure are (1) **Economic entity:** the assumption that the activity of a business enterprise can be kept separate and distinct from its owners and any other business unit. (2) **Going concern:** the assumption that the business enterprise will have a long life. (3) **Monetary unit:** the assumption that money is the common denominator by which economic activity is conducted, and that the monetary unit provides an appropriate basis for measurement and analysis. (4) **Periodicity:** the assumption that the economic activities of an enterprise can be divided into artificial time periods.

7.   **Explain the application of the basic principles of accounting.** (1) **Historical cost principle:** Existing GAAP requires that most assets and liabilities be accounted for and reported on the basis of acquisition price. (2) **Revenue recognition:** Revenue is generally recognized when (a) earned and (b) measurable and collectible (realizable). (3) **Matching principle:** Expenses are recognized when the work (service) or the product actually makes its contribution to revenue. (4) **Full disclosure principle:** Accountants follow the general practice of providing information that is important enough to influence the judgement and decisions of an informed user.

8.   **Describe the impact that constraints have on reporting accounting information.** The constraints and their impact are: (1) **Cost-benefit relationship:** The costs of providing the information must be weighed against the benefits that can be derived from using the information. (2) **Materiality:** Sound and acceptable standards should be followed if the amount involved is significant when compared with the other revenues and expenses, assets and liabilities, or net income of the entity. (3) **Industry practices:** Follow the general practices in the firm's industry, which sometimes requires departure from basic theory. (4) **Conservatism:** When in doubt, choose the solution that will be least likely to overstate net assets and net income.

TIPS ON CHAPTER TOPICS

TIP: Although it can sometimes be confusing, accountants often use the terms **assumptions**, **concepts**, **principles**, **conventions**, **constraints**, and **standards** interchangeably. Regardless of the particular term used, they are all a part of GAAP (generally accepted accounting principles).

TIP: The revenue recognition principle is applied before the matching principle is applied. The revenue recognition principle gives guidance in determining what revenues to recognize in a given period. The matching principle then gives guidance as to what expenses to recognize during the period. According to the **revenue recognition principle**, revenues are to be recognized in the period earned. Per the **matching principle**, expenses are to be recognized in the same period as the revenues they helped generate.

TIP: The term **recognition** refers to the process of formally recording or incorporating an item in the accounts and financial statements of an entity.

TIP: Accounting assumptions underlie the more detailed accounting principles or standards. These assumptions include the economic entity assumption, the going concern assumption, the monetary unit assumption, and the periodicity assumption. They are the foundation for the basic principles that include the historical cost principle, the revenue recognition principle, the matching principle, and the full disclosure principle. For example, the historical cost principle and the matching principle would not be appropriate if it were not for the going concern assumption. If an entity is not expected to continue in business, then plant assets would be reported on the balance sheet at their liquidation or net realizable value (estimated selling price less estimated cost of disposal) rather than at their cost, and amortization of these assets would not be appropriate.

TIP: There are three common bases of expense recognition: (1) cause and effect, (matched against revenue in the period), (2) systematic and rational allocation, and (3) immediate expense recognition. You should be able to explain and give examples for each of these. (See **Case 2-3.**)

ILLUSTRATION 2-1
A CONCEPTUAL FRAMEWORK FOR FINANCIAL REPORTING
(L.O. 2 THROUGH 8)

Recognition and Measurement Concepts

ASSUMPTIONS
1. Economic entity
2. Going concern
3. Monetary unit
4. Periodicity

PRINCIPLES
1. Historical cost
2. Revenue recognition
3. Matching
4. Full disclosure

CONSTRAINTS
1. Cost-benefit
2. Materiality
3. Industry practices

Third Level:
"The how"—
implementation

QUALITATIVE CHARACTERISTICS
A. Understandability
B. Relevance
   (1) Predictive value
   (2) Feedback value
   (3) Timeliness
C. Reliability
   (1) Verifiability
   (2) Representational
      faithfulness
   (3) Neutrality (conservatism
      when uncertain)
D. Comparability
E. Consistency

ELEMENTS
1. Assets
2. Liabilities
3. Equity
4. Revenues
5. Expenses
6. Gains
7. Losses

Second Level:
Bridge between
first and third
levels.

OBJECTIVES
Provide information:
1. Useful in investment
   and credit decisions
2. Useful in making resource
   allocation decisions
3. Useful in assessing
   management steward-
   ship

First Level:
"The Why"—
goals and
purposes of
accounting.

At the first level, the **objectives** identify the goals and purposes of financial accounting and are the building blocks for the conceptual framework. At the second level are the **qualitative characteristics** that make financial accounting information useful and the **elements** of financial statements (assets, liabilities, and so on). At the final, or third level, are the **measurement and recognition concepts** that accountants use in establishing and applying financial accounting standards. These concepts include assumptions, principles, and constraints that describe the present reporting environment.

CASE 2-1

Purpose: (L.O. 4) This exercise is designed to review the qualitative characteristics that make accounting information useful for decision-making purposes.

The qualitative characteristics that make accounting information useful for decision-making are as follows:

Understandability	Verifiability
Relevance	Representational faithfulness
Reliability	Neutrality
Predictive value	Comparability
Feedback value	Consistency
Timeliness	

Instructions
Fill in the blank to identify the appropriate qualitative characteristic(s) being described in each of the statements below. A qualitative characteristic may be used more than once.

_____   1. Two qualitative characteristics that make accounting information useful for decision-making purposes.

_____   2. Information that is capable of making a difference in a decision is said to have this qualitative characteristic.

_____   3. Information that is verifiable and reasonably free of error and bias is said to have this primary qualitative characteristic.

_____   4. Two qualitative characteristics that are related to both relevance and reliability.

_____   5. An entity is to apply the same accounting methods to similar events for successive accounting periods; that is, when an entity selects one method from a list of alternative acceptable methods, that same method is used period after period.

_____   6. Information is measured and reported in a similar manner for different enterprises.

_____   7. Neutrality is an ingredient of this qualitative characteristic of accounting information.

_____   8. Requires that information cannot be selected to favour one set of interested parties over another.

9. Predictive value is an ingredient of this qualitative characteristic of information.

10. When information provides a basis for forecasting annual earnings for future periods, it is said to have this qualitative characteristic of accounting information.

11. Quality of information that confirms or corrects users' prior expectations.

12. Information must be available to decision makers before it loses its capacity to influence their decisions.

13. Imperative for providing comparisons of a single firm from period to period.

14. Qualitative characteristic being employed when companies in the same industry are using the same accounting principles.

15. A company cannot suppress information just because such disclosure is embarrassing or damaging to the entity.

16. The amounts and descriptions in financial statements agree with the elements or events that these amounts and descriptions purport to represent.

17. Independent measurers, using the same measurement methods, obtain similar results.

18. The numbers and descriptions in financial statements represent what really existed or happened.

19. Requires information to be free of personal bias.

20. Requires a high degree of consensus among individuals on a given measurement.

21. Financial information is a tool and, like most tools, cannot be much direct help to those who are unable or unwilling to use it or who misuse it.

Solution to Case 2-1

1. Relevance and reliability
2. Relevance
3. Reliability
4. Comparability and consistency
5. Consistency
6. Comparability
7. Reliability
8. Neutrality
9. Relevance
10. Predictive value
11. Feedback value
12. Timeliness
13. Consistency
14. Comparability
15. Neutrality
16. Representational faithfulness
17. Verifiability
18. Representational faithfulness
19. Neutrality
20. Verifiability
21. Understandability

Approach: Before beginning to fill in the 21 blanks required, visualize the diagram for the hierarchy of accounting qualities (**Illustration 2-1**). Also, take a few minutes to individually consider the characteristics listed and think of the key phrases involved in describing those items. Such as:

- **Understandability:** information provided by financial reporting should be comprehensible to those who have a reasonable understanding of business and economic activities and are willing to study the information with reasonable diligence.
- **Relevance:** capable of making a difference in a decision.
- **Reliability:** users can depend on information to be verifiable, reasonably free of error and bias, and to represent what it purports to represent.
- **Predictive value:** helps users make predictions about the outcome of past, present, and future events.
- **Feedback value:** helps to confirm or correct prior expectations.
- **Timeliness:** information must be available to decision makers before it loses its capacity to influence their decisions.
- **Verifiability:** is demonstrated when a high degree of consensus can be secured among independent measurers using the same measurement methods.
- **Representational faithfulness:** correspondence or agreement between the accounting numbers and descriptions and the resources or events that these numbers and descriptions purport to represent.
- **Neutrality:** information is not to be selected to favour one set of interested parties over another and is to be free from bias towards a predetermined result.
- **Comparability:** information that has been measured and reported in a similar manner for different enterprises is considered comparable.
- **Consistency:** a company is to apply the same methods to similar accountable events from period to period.

ILLUSTRATION 2-2
ELEMENTS OF FINANCIAL STATEMENTS (L.O. 5)

Assets: Probable future economic benefits obtained or controlled by a particular entity as a result of past transactions or events.

Liabilities: Probable future sacrifices of economic benefits arising from present duty or responsibility to others, as a result of past transactions or events, where there is little or no discretion to avoid the obligation.

Equity/Net Assets: Residual interest in the assets of an entity that remains after deducting its liabilities. In a business enterprise, the equity is the ownership interest.

Revenues: Increases in economic resources, either by inflows or other enhancements of assets of an entity or settlement of its liabilities resulting from ordinary activities of the entity.

Expenses: Decreases in economic resources, either by outflows or reductions of assets or incurrence of liabilities resulting from an entity's ordinary revenue-generating activities.

Gains: Increases in equity (net assets) from peripheral or incidental transactions of an entity and from all other transactions and other events and circumstances affecting the entity during a period except those that result from revenues or investments by owners.

Losses: Decreases in equity (net assets) from peripheral or incidental transactions of an entity and from all other transactions and other events and circumstances affecting the entity during a period except those that result from expenses or distributions to owners.

ILLUSTRATION 2-3
BASIC ACCOUNTING ASSUMPTIONS, PRINCIPLES, AND CONSTRAINTS (L.O. 6, 7, and 8)

Economic entity assumption: States that economic events can be identified with a particular unit of accountability. The activities of an accounting entity can be and should be kept separate and distinct from its owners and all other accounting entities. The entity concept does not necessarily refer to a legal entity.

Going concern assumption: Assumes that the enterprise will continue in operation long enough to carry out its existing objectives and commitments. It assumes the entity will continue in operation long enough to recover the cost of its assets. This assumption serves as a basis for basic principles such as the historical cost principle. Because of this assumption, liquidation values of assets are not relevant.

Monetary unit assumption: States that only transaction data capable of being expressed in terms of money should be included in the accounting records of the economic entity. All transactions and events can be measured in terms of a common denominator—units of money. A corollary is the added assumption that the unit of measure remains constant from one period to the next (some people call the corollary the "stable dollar assumption").

Periodicity assumption: Assumes that the economic life of a business can be divided into artificial time periods. Although some companies choose to subdivide the business life into months or quarters, others report financial statements only for an annual period.

Historical cost principle: States that assets should initially be recorded and subsequently accounted for at acquisition cost. The principle also states that cost is measured by the fair market value (cash equivalent value) of the consideration given or the fair market value (cash equivalent value) of the consideration received, whichever is the more objectively determinable. In addition, the cost of an asset includes all costs necessary to acquire the item and get it in the place and condition for its intended use.

Revenue recognition principle: Dictates that revenue should be recognized when (1) **realized** or **realizable** and (2) **earned**. Revenues are **realized** when products (goods or services, merchandise, or other assets) are exchanged for cash or claims to cash. Revenues are **realizable** when assets received or held are readily convertible into cash or claims to cash. Assets are readily convertible when they are saleable or interchangeable in an active market at readily determinable prices without significant additional cost. Revenues are considered **earned** when the entity has substantially accomplished what it must do to be entitled to the benefits represented by the revenues. The revenue generating process for most entities includes a number of steps. As a result, revenue is **earned** when the "critical point" in the earnings process is reached. This critical point is different for different circumstances as the following examples illustrate. Examples are: (1) when a sale is involved, the point of sale is the critical event, (2) when long-term construction contracts are involved, progress toward completion is the critical event, (3) when products are saleable in an active market at readily determinable prices without significant additional cost, the completion of production is the critical event, and (4) when uncertainty about the collection of receivables exists for credit sales of goods

ILLUSTRATION 2-3 (Continued)

and services, the receipt of cash is the critical event. In example (1), the sales basis is used for revenue recognition. In example (2), the percentage-of-completion method is appropriate for revenue recognition. In example (3), recognition of revenue at the end of production is justified. In example (4), the instalment method is used.

Matching principle: Dictates that expenses be matched with revenues whenever it is reasonable and practical to do so, "let the expense follow the revenue". Expenses (efforts) are recognized in the same period as the related revenue (accomplishment) is recognized. Thus, a factory worker's wages are not recognized as an expense when cash is paid or when the work is performed, or when the product is produced; they are recognized as an expense when the labour (service) or the product actually makes its contribution to the revenue generating process (which is when the related product is sold).

Full disclosure principle: Dictates that information should be provided when the information is important enough to influence the judgement and decisions of an informed user. An entity is to disclose through the data contained in the financial statements and the information in the notes that accompany the statements all information necessary to make the statements not misleading. To be recognized in the main body of the financial statements, an item should meet the definition of one of the basic elements, be measurable with sufficient certainty, and be relevant and reliable. The notes to financial statements generally amplify or explain the items presented in the body of the statements. Information in the notes does not have to be quantifiable, nor does it need to qualify as an element. A trade-off exists between sufficient detail and sufficient condensation.

Cost-benefit relationship: States that the costs of providing the information must be weighed against the benefits that can be derived from using the information. In order to justify requiring a particular measurement or disclosure, the benefits perceived to be derived from it must exceed the costs perceived to be associated with the measurement or disclosure. When the perceived costs exceed the perceived benefits, a measurement or disclosure may be foregone based on its lack of practicality.

Materiality constraint: Dictates that an immaterial item need not be given strict accounting treatment; it can be given expedient treatment. An item is material if its inclusion or omission would influence or change the judgement of a reasonable person. The point involved here is one of relative size and importance. If the amount involved is significant when compared with other revenues and expenses, assets and liabilities, or net income of the entity, it is a material item and generally acceptable standards should be followed. If the amount is so small that it is quite unimportant when compared with other items, strict treatment is of less importance. The nature of an item may also affect the judgement of its materiality. A misclassification affecting cash has a lower threshold of materiality than the same dollar amount of a misclassification affecting plant assets.

ILLUSTRATION 2-3 (Continued)

Industry practices constraint: States that the peculiar nature of some industries and business concerns sometimes requires departure from what would normally be considered good accounting practice. For example, current assets usually appear first on a balance sheet; however, for a public utility, it is an acceptable industry practice to report plant assets (noncurrent items) first on the balance sheet to highlight the entity's capital-intensive nature.

TIP: Accounting constraints are justifications for departure from the basic accounting principles in certain situations. They are sometimes referred to as "exception principles." For example, the cost of an item that will benefit operations for five years should be initially recorded as an asset and amortized (expensed) over the related five-year period as dictated by the matching principle. However, if the item is a recycling container that cost $20, the amount is deemed to be insignificant and the whole amount is handled with expedience—that is, it is expensed in the period the container is acquired. This departure from the matching principle is justified by the materiality constraint. For another example, if the market value (replacement value) of inventory is below the cost of inventory, the inventory is to be reported at the market value (the lower value). Thus, there is a departure from the historical cost principle with the justification being the conservatism constraint.

CASE 2-2

Purpose: (L.O. 6, 7, 8) This exercise will test your comprehension of the essence and significance of basic accounting assumptions, principles, and constraints.

Instructions
For each of the following statements, identify (by letter) the basic accounting assumption, principle or constraint that is **most directly** related to the given phrase. Each code letter may be used more than once.

Assumptions, Principles, and Constraints

a. Economic entity assumption	g. Matching principle
b. Going concern assumption	h. Full disclosure principle
c. Monetary unit assumption	i. Cost-benefit relationship
d. Periodicity assumption	j. Materiality constraint
e. Historical cost principle	k. Industry practices constraint
f. Revenue recognition principle	

TIP: Before you begin to read and answer the items listed, it would be helpful to briefly think about what you know about each of the assumptions, principles, and constraints. An explanation of each appears in **Illustration 2-3**.

Statements

_____ 1. Revenue should be recognized when it is earned, which is usually at the point of sale.

_____ 2. All information necessary to ensure that the financial statements are not misleading should be reported.

_____ 3. This concept eliminates the "liquidation concept" in viewing business affairs.

_____ 4. Measurement of the standing and progress of entities should be made at regular intervals rather than at the end of the business's life.

_____ 5. Although an item such as a wastebasket may be of service for eight years, the total cost of the item may be expensed when it is purchased, because the amount is too insignificant to warrant the strict treatment of depreciation over the eight years.

_____ 6. The recorded amount of an acquired item should be the fair market value of what was given or the fair market value of what was received in the exchange, whichever can be more objectively determined.

_____ 7. There must be complete and understandable reporting on financial statements.

_____ 8. The president of a business should not loan his spouse the company's credit card for personal gasoline purchases.

_____ 9. Expenses should be recognized in the same period that the related revenues are recognized.

_____ 10. This concept is often exemplified by numerous notes to the financial statements.

_____ 11. If revenue is deferred to a future period, the related costs of generating that revenue should be deferred to the same future period.

_____ 12. This concept includes a set of rules concerning when to recognize revenue and how to measure its amount.

_____ 13. All transactions and events are expressed in terms of a common denominator.

_____ 14. It is assumed that an organization will remain in business long enough to recover the cost of its assets.

_____ 15. Changes in the purchasing power of the dollar are so small from one period to the next that they are ignored in preparing the basic financial statements.

_____ 16. Items whose amounts are very small relative to other amounts on the financial statements may be accounted for in the most expedient manner, rather than requiring strict accounting treatment under GAAP.

_____ 17. The cost of an item should be measured by the amount of the resources expended to acquire it.

_____ 18. Accruals and deferrals are often necessary in order to report expenses in the proper time periods.

_____ 19. Each accounting unit is considered separate and distinct from all other accounting units.

_____ 20. An accountant assumes that a business will continue indefinitely.

_____ 21. Assets which have appreciated in value are not reported at their current worth subsequent to acquisition because of this principle.

_____ 22. Amortization of a long-term tangible asset is based on the asset's original acquisition cost rather than the asset's current market value.

_____ 23. If an item will not affect any business decisions, it need not be separately reported in the financial statements.

_____ 24. In order to justify requiring a particular measurement or disclosure, the benefits perceived to be derived from it must exceed the costs expected to be associated with it.

_____ 25. Externally acquired intangible assets are capitalized and amortized over the periods benefited.

_____ 26. Repair tools are expensed when purchased even though they may be of use for more than one period.

_____ 27. Brokerage firms use market value for purposes of valuation of all marketable securities. Changes in those market values are recognized in the income statement in the periods the changes occur.

_____ 28. All significant post-balance sheet events are reported in the notes to the financial statements.

_____ 29. Revenue for a retail establishment is recorded at the point of sale.

_____ 30. All important aspects of bond indentures (contracts) are presented in the financial statements.

_____ 31. Reporting must be done at defined time intervals. The time intervals are of equal length.

_____ 32. An allowance for doubtful (uncollectible) accounts is established.

_____ 33. All payments out of petty cash are charged to Miscellaneous Expense, even though some expenditures will benefit the following period. (Do not use conservatism.)

_____ 34. A company charges its sales commission costs to expense in the same period that the sale is made.

_____ 35. When the liquidation of an enterprise looks imminent, this assumption is inapplicable and thus, the historical cost principle does not apply. Rather, assets are reported at their net realizable values.

_____ 36. The initial note to financial statements is usually a summary of significant accounting policies.

Solution to Case 2-2

1.	f	11.	g	21.	e	31.	d	
2.	h	12.	f	22.	e*	32.	g	
3.	b	13.	c	23.	j	33.	j	
4.	d	14.	b	24.	i	34.	g	
5.	j	15.	c	25.	g	35.	b	*An argument could be
6.	e	16.	j	26.	j	36.	h	made for answer "g."
7.	h	17.	e	27.	k			
8.	a	18.	g	28.	h			
9.	g	19.	a	29.	f			
10.	h	20.	b	30.	h			

CASE 2-3

Purpose: (L.O. 7) This case is designed to review the three methods of matching expenses with revenues and examples of each.

An unexpired cost represents probable future benefits and hence is accounted for as an asset. An expired cost represents an expiration of benefits and hence is accounted for as an expense or a loss. There are three common bases of expense recognition: (1) cause and effect, (2) systematic and rational allocation, and (3) immediate recognition.

Instructions
Describe each of the three bases of expense recognition and give a few examples of each for a retail establishment.

Solution to Case 2-3

1. **Cause and effect:** When there is a direct association between the expiration of a cost and a particular revenue transaction, the expense recognition should accompany the revenue recognition; that is, the cost is expensed in the same time period that the related specific revenue is recognized.

   Examples: Cost of goods sold, sales commissions, transportation-out.

2.   **Systematic and rational allocation:** This basis is used when, although a cost benefits the revenue generating process of two or more accounting periods, the cost cannot be related to particular revenue transactions. Even though a close cause-and-effect relationship between revenue and cost cannot be determined, this relationship is assumed to exist. The cost is thus initially accounted for as an asset and then allocated to the periods benefited (as an expense) in a systematic and rational manner. The allocation method used should appear reasonable to an unbiased observer and should be consistently applied from period to period.

> *Examples:*   Amortization of plant assets, amortization of intangibles, amortization of prepaids (such as rent and insurance).

3.   **Immediate recognition:** This basis is used for costs that fall in the following categories:
(a)   Their incurrence during the period provides no discernible future benefits.
(b)   They must be incurred each accounting period, and no build-up of expected future benefits occurs.
(c)   By their nature, they relate to current revenues even though they cannot be directly associated with any specific revenues.
(d)   The amount of cost to be deferred can be measured only in an arbitrary manner or great uncertainty exists regarding the realization of future benefits.
(e)   Uncertainty exists regarding whether allocating them to current and future periods will serve any useful purpose.
(f)   They are measures of asset costs recorded in prior periods from which no future benefits are now discernible.

> *Examples:*   Sales salaries, office salaries, utilities, repairs, advertising, accounting and legal, research and development, postage, write-off of worthless patent.

TIP: Costs incurred by a manufacturing company are often classified into two groups: product costs and period costs. **Product costs** such as material, labour, and manufacturing overhead attach to the product and are carried into future periods (as a balance in inventory) if the product remains unsold at the end of the current period, and, therefore, the revenue recognition is deferred to the period of sale. Product costs are expensed in the period of sale in accordance with the cause and effect basis of expense recognition. **Period costs** such as officers' salaries and other administrative expenses are charged off immediately, even though benefits associated with these costs may occur in the future, because no direct relationship between cost and revenue can be determined and it is highly uncertain what, if any, benefits relate to the future.

TIP: For a manufacturing company, amortization of the office building is determined and expensed based on a systematic and rational allocation. On the other hand, amortization of factory machinery is a component of manufacturing overhead; thus, it is an element of product cost. The amount of amortization that pertains to the products produced during a period is first determined by use of the selected amortization method. The amount of amortization that ends up being reflected as an expense on the income statement for the same period depends on the number of products sold (not produced) during the period; it is included as a part of cost of goods sold expense.

ANALYSIS OF MULTIPLE-CHOICE TYPE QUESTIONS

QUESTION

1.   (L.O. 3) The objectives of financial reporting include all of the following *except* to provide information that:

a.   is useful to the Canadian Custom and Revenue Agency in allocating the tax burden to the business community.
b.   is useful to those making investment and credit decisions.
c.   is helpful in assessing future cash flows.
d.   identifies the economic resources (assets), the claims to those resources (liabilities), and the changes in those resources and claims.

Explanation: Financial reporting is for the use of investors, potential investors, management, and other interested parties. It is not for the CCRA. The information required to be reported to the CCRA is provided by the reporting entity on tax forms and is referred to as income tax accounting as opposed to financial reporting. (Solution = a)

QUESTION

2.   (L.O. 4) According to *The Conceptual Framework for Financial Reporting*, timeliness is an ingredient of:

	Relevance	Reliability
a.	Yes	Yes
b.	Yes	No
c.	No	No
d.	No	Yes

Approach and Explanation: In answering this question, read the stem and answer "Yes" (true) or "No" (false) when completing the statement with the word **relevance**. Then reread the stem and answer "Yes" or "No" when completing the statement with the word **reliability**. Then look for the corresponding combination of "Yes" and "No" to select your answer. In the diagram of the hierarchy of accounting qualities, timeliness is linked to relevance and not reliability. Therefore, we want to respond "Yes" to the relevance column and "No" to the reliability column. (Solution = b.)

QUESTION

3.   (L.O. 4) According to *The Conceptual Framework for Financial Reporting*, neutrality is an ingredient of the qualitative characteristics of:

	Relevance	Reliability
a.	Yes	Yes
b.	Yes	No
c.	No	No
d.	No	Yes

Approach and Explanation: In answering this question, read the stem and answer "Yes" (true) or "No" (false) when completing the statement with the word **relevance.** Then reread the stem and answer "Yes" or "No" when completing the statement with the word **reliability.** Then look for the corresponding combination of "Yes" and "No" to select your answer. In the diagram of the hierarchy of accounting qualities, neutrality is linked to reliability and not relevance. Therefore, we want to respond "No" to the relevance column and "Yes" to the reliability column. (Solution = d.)

QUESTION

4.   (L.O. 4) If the LIFO inventory method was used last period, it should be used for the current and following periods because of:
   a.   materiality.
   b.   verifiability.
   c.   timeliness.
   d.   consistency.

Approach and Explanation: In reading the stem of the question, cover up the answer selections. Anticipate the correct answer by attempting to complete the statement given. This process should yield the answer of "consistency." If you cannot think of the word to complete the statement, then take each answer selection and write down what each means. You should then be able to match up the question with answer selection "d."

Selection "d" is correct because consistency is a qualitative characteristic of accounting information. To be useful, financial statements should reflect consistent application of generally accepted accounting principles. This means that a company should apply the same methods to similar accountable events from period to period. Selection "a" is incorrect because materiality refers to a constraint whereby an item is to be given strict accounting treatment unless it is insignificant. Selection "b" is incorrect because verifiability refers to an ingredient of reliability (it is demonstrated when a high degree of consensus can be secured among independent measurers using the same measurement methods). Selection "c" is incorrect because timeliness is an ingredient of relevance which indicates that for information to be relevant, it must be prepared on a timely basis. (Solution = d.)

QUESTION

5.   (L.O. 5) Which of the following transactions does not represent a gain to the organization:
   a.   a bookstore selling a computer for a profit.
   b.   a consulting company selling a block of land it was holding for future expansion.
   c.   the Ottawa Senators selling season tickets.
   d.   a lawyer selling a pair of theatre tickets for more than she paid for them.

Approach and Explanation: Define or explain "gain" before you read the answer selections. Select the answer that best fits your description. The CICA defines a gain as an increase in equity from a peripheral or incidental transaction. Ask yourself whether the revenue earned in each situation would be in the normal course of business for the enterprise or is this an incidental or peripheral transaction. Bookstores are not in the business of regularly selling computers. Land held for expansion would not represent a normal transaction for a consulting firm and a lawyer does not regularly sell theatre tickets as a scalper. The Ottawa Senators however would try to sell season tickets in the normal course of business. (Solution = c.)

QUESTION

6.   (L.O. 5) Which of the following does not represent a liability to the organization.

   a.   Salaries earned for work performed last week by employees

   b.   Money received by Northern Air in advance of a flight to take place next week.

   c.   Inventory purchased but not paid for.

   d.   Owner of a company decides to buy a car next week and goes to the lot to pick out the car she wants.

Approach and Explanation: Define the term liability. Compare your definition of liability against the possible choices available. A liability represents a probable future sacrifice of economic benefits arising from a present duty or responsibility to others, as a result of a past transaction or event, where there is little or no discretion to avoid the obligation. In all cases, this will probably represent a future sacrifice to the organization of economic benefits (monetary in a, c, and d, and a service to be provided in b). Situation a, b and c all represent past transactions, while d represents an event which has not yet taken place as she has not purchased the vehicle and certainly has the ability to change her mind, thus there is the possibility to avoid the transaction. (Solution = d.)

QUESTION

7.   (L.O. 6) The assumption that an enterprise will remain in business indefinitely and will not liquidate in the near future is called the:

   a.   economic entity assumption.

   b.   going concern assumption.

   c.   monetary unit assumption.

   d.   periodicity assumption.

Approach and Explanation: Read the stem (while covering up the answer selections) and attempt to complete the statement. Compare your attempt with the selections. Hopefully, you anticipated the correct answer. If your attempt does not match any of the selections given, take each selection and write down the key words in the definitions of the term. This process should lead you to the correct response.

Answer selection "b" is correct because the going concern assumption implies that an enterprise will continue in business and will not liquidate within the foreseeable future. Selection "a" is incorrect because the economic entity assumption indicates that the activities of an accounting entity should be kept separate and distinct from all other accounting entities. Selection "c" is incorrect because the monetary unit assumption indicates that all transactions and events can be measured in terms of a common denominator—units of money. Selection "d" is incorrect because the periodicity assumption indicates that the economic activities of an enterprise can be divided into equally spaced artificial time periods. (Solution = b.)

QUESTION

    8.   (L.O. 7) Pluto Magazine Company sells space to advertisers. The company requires an advertiser to pay for services one month before publication. Advertising revenue should be recognized when:

         a.   an advertiser places an order.
         b.   a bill is sent to an advertiser.
         c.   the related cash is received.
         d.   the related ad is published.

Approach and Explanation: Read the last sentence of the stem. We want to know the point at which revenue should be recognized. Write down what you know from the revenue recognition principle. Revenue is generally recognized when (1) realized or realizable, and (2) earned. Read the stem and think of how to apply the revenue recognition principle to the facts given. At the points when an order is placed and a bill is sent to an advertiser, revenue has neither been realized nor earned. At the point when the cash is received in advance of the publication, the revenue is realized but not earned. The revenue is earned when the related ad is published and, thus, should be recognized then. (Solution = d.)

QUESTION

    9.   (L.O. 7) The historical cost principle provides that:

         a.   items whose costs are insignificant compared to other amounts on the financial statements may be accounted for in the most expedient manner.
         b.   assets and equities be expressed in terms of a common denominator.
         c.   the recorded amount of an acquired item should be the fair market value of what is given or the fair market value of what is received in the exchange, whichever is more objectively determinable.
         d.   the expenses of generating revenue should be recognized in the same period that the related revenue is recognized.

Approach and Explanation: Briefly define the historical cost principle before you read the answer selections. See **Illustration 2-3**. Answer selection "a" describes the materiality constraint. Selection "b" describes the monetary unit assumption. Selection "d" relates to the matching principle. (Solution = c.)

QUESTION

    10.   (L.O. 7) If revenue is received in the current period, but it is not earned until a future period, the related expenses of generating the revenue should *not* be recognized until that future period. This guideline is an application of the:

         a.   revenue recognition principle.
         b.   full disclosure principle.
         c.   matching principle.
         d.   conservatism constraint.

Explanation: The revenue recognition principle dictates that revenue be recognized (recorded and reported) in the period it is realized (or realizable) and earned. The matching principle dictates that expenses be recognized in the same period as the revenue which they helped to generate is recognized. Thus, if revenue is deferred, the related expenses should also be deferred. (Solution = c.)

QUESTION
11.   (L.O. 7) The process of reporting an item in the financial statements of an enterprise is:
a.   recognition.
b.   realization.
c.   allocation.
d.   incorporation.

Explanation: The term recognition refers to the process of formally recording or incorporating an item in the accounts and financial statements of an entity. An item that gets recorded in the accounts eventually gets reported in the financial statements of the enterprise. Realization is the process of converting noncash resources and rights into money and is most precisely used in accounting and financial reporting to refer to sales of assets for cash or claims to cash. The term allocation refers to the process or result of allocating (assigning costs or systematically spreading costs). The term incorporation refers to the process of establishing a business in the corporate form of organization. (Solution = a.)

QUESTION
12.   (L.O. 7) Revenue is to be recognized when it is realized (or realizable) and earned. This statement refers to the:
a.   revenue recognition principle.
b.   matching principle.
c.   going concern assumption.
d.   consistency concept.

Approach and Explanation: Briefly define each of the answer selections. Choose the item for which your definition most closely agrees with the stem of the question. See **Illustration 2-3.** The revenue recognition principle dictates that revenue be recognized (recorded and reported) in the period it is realized (or realizable) and earned. The matching principle dictates that expenses be recognized in the same period as the revenue which they helped to generate is recognized. The going concern assumption implies that an enterprise will continue in business indefinitely. The consistency concept or characteristic dictates that for financial information to be useful, an entity is to apply the same accounting methods to similar events for successive accounting periods. (Solution = a.)

QUESTION
13.   (L.O. 8) In matters of doubt and great uncertainty, accounting issues should be resolved by choosing the alternative that has the least favourable effect on net income, assets, and owners' equity. This guidance comes from the:
a.   materiality constraint.
b.   industry practices constraint.
c.   conservatism constraint.
d.   full disclosure principle.

Approach and Explanation: Briefly define each of the answer selections. Choose the item for which your definition most closely agrees with the stem of the question. See **Illustration 2-4**. In matters of doubt and uncertainty, the accountant is conservative and chooses the accounting alternative that is the least likely to cause an overstatement of net income, assets, and owners' equity. (Solution = c.)

QUESTION

14.   (L.O. 8) When an entity charges the entire cost of an electric pencil sharpener to expense in the period when it was purchased even though the appliance has an estimated life of five years, we have an application of the:

a.   matching principle.

b.   materiality constraint.

c.   historical cost principle.

d.   conservatism constraint.

Explanation: When an item benefits operations of more than one period, the matching principle will dictate that the cost of the item be allocated (spread) systematically over the periods benefited.   However, the materiality constraint dictates that an immaterial item need not be given strict accounting treatment; it can be given expedient treatment. The cost of a pencil sharpener would obviously be small and thus immaterial. Consequently, the materiality constraint is justification for departure from the matching principle in accounting for the cost of the pencil sharpener. (Solution = b.)

CHAPTER 3

THE ACCOUNTING INFORMATION SYSTEM

OVERVIEW

Accounting information must be accumulated and summarized before it can be communicated and analysed. In this chapter, we will discuss the steps involved in the accounting cycle. We will emphasize the subject of adjusting entries. Throughout an accounting period, cash receipts and cash disbursements are recorded. At the end of the accounting period, adjusting entries are required so that revenues and expenses are reflected on the accrual basis of accounting. Adjusting entries are simply entries required to bring account balances up to date. The failure to record proper adjustments will cause errors on both the income statement and the balance sheet.

SUMMARY OF LEARNING OBJECTIVES

1. **Understand basic accounting terminology.** It is important to understand the following 11 terms: (1) Event, (2) Transaction, (3) Account, (4) Permanent and Temporary accounts, (5) Ledger, (6) Journal, (7) Posting, (8) Trial balances, (9) Adjusting entries, (10) Financial statements, and (11) Closing entries.

2. **Explain double-entry rules.** The left side of an account is the debit side; the right side is the credit side. All asset and expense accounts are increased on the left or debit side and decreased on the right or credit side. Conversely, all liability and revenue accounts are increased on the right or credit side and decreased on the left or debit side. Shareholders' equity accounts, Common Shares and Retained Earnings, are increased on the credit side, whereas Dividends is increased on the debit side.

3. **Identify steps in the accounting cycle.** The basic steps in the accounting cycle are (1) identification and measurement of transactions and other events, (2) journalization, (3) posting, (4) unadjusted trial balance, (5) adjustments, (6) adjusted trial balance, (7) statement presentation, and (8) closing.

4. **Record transactions in journals, post to ledger accounts, and prepare a trial balance.** The simplest journal form is a chronological listing of transactions and events expressed in terms of debits and credits to particular accounts. The items entered in a general journal must be transferred (posted) to the general ledger. An unadjusted trial balance should be prepared at the end of a given period after the entries have been recorded in the journal and posted to the ledger.

5. **Explain the reasons for preparing adjusting entries.** Adjustments are necessary to achieve a proper matching of revenues and expenses so as to determine net income for the current period and to achieve an accurate statement of end-of-the period balances in assets, liabilities, and owners' equity accounts.

6. **Prepare closing entries.** In the closing process, all of the revenue and expense account balances (income statement items) are transferred to a clearing account called Income Summary, which is used only at the end of the fiscal year. Revenues and expenses are matched in the Income Summary account. The net result of this matching, which represents the net income or net loss for the period, is then transferred to an owners' equity account (Retained Earnings for a corporation and capital accounts for proprietorships and partnerships.)

7.   **Explain how inventory accounts are adjusted at year-end.** Under a perpetual inventory system, the balance in the Inventory account at the end of the period should represent the ending inventory amount. When the inventory records are maintained on a periodic inventory system, a Purchases account is used; the Inventory account is unchanged during the period. The Inventory account represents the beginning inventory amount throughout the period. At the end of the accounting period, the Inventory account must be adjusted by closing-out the beginning inventory amount and recording the ending inventory amount.

8.   **Prepare a 10-column work sheet.** The 10-column work sheet provides columns for the first trial balance, adjustments, adjusted trial balance, income statement, and balance sheet. The work sheet does not replace the financial statements. Instead, it is the accountant's informal device for accumulating and sorting information needed for the financial statements.

*9.   **Identify adjusting entries that may be reversed.** Reversing entries are most often used to reverse two types of adjusting entries: accrued revenues and accrued expenses. Prepayments may also be reversed if the initial entry to record the transaction is made to an expense or revenue account.

*10. **Differentiate the cash basis of accounting from the accrual basis of accounting.** Accrual basis accounting provides information about cash inflows and outflows associated with earnings activities as soon as these cash flows can be estimated with an acceptable degree of certainty. That is, accrual basis accounting aids in predicting future cash flows by reporting transactions and events with cash consequences at the time the transactions and events occur, rather than when the cash is received and paid.

*This material is covered in an Appendix in the text.

TIPS ON CHAPTER TOPICS

TIP: This chapter is an extremely important one. A good understanding of this chapter and an ability to think and work quickly with the concepts incorporated herein are necessary for comprehending subsequent chapters. Although adjusting entries were introduced in your principles course, you are likely to discover new dimensions to this subject in your intermediate accounting course. Pay close attention when studying this chapter!

TIP: When you encounter a transaction, always analyse it in terms of its effects on the elements of the basic accounting equation (or **balance sheet equation**). For your analysis to be complete, it must maintain balance in the basic accounting equation. The **basic accounting equation** is as follows:

$$\text{ASSETS} = \text{LIABILITIES} + \text{OWNERS' EQUITY}$$
or
$$A = L + OE$$

Assets are economic resources. Liabilities and owners' equity are sources of resources; liabilities are creditor sources, and owners' equity represents owner sources (owner investments and undistributed profits). The basic accounting equation simply states that the total assets (resources) at a point in time equal the total liabilities plus total owners' equity (sources of resources) at the same point in time.

TIP: **An understanding of the following terms is important.** (1) **Event:** a happening of consequence. An event generally is the source or cause of changes in assets, liabilities, and equity. Events may be external or internal. (2) **Transaction:** an external event involving a transfer or exchange between two or more entities. (3) **Account:** a systematic arrangement that shows the effect of transactions and other events on a specific asset or equity. A separate account is kept for each type of asset, liability, revenue, and expense, and for capital (owners' equity). (4) **Permanent and Temporary accounts:** Permanent (real) accounts are asset, liability, and equity accounts; they appear on the balance sheet. Temporary (nominal) accounts are revenue, expense, and dividend accounts; except for dividends, they appear on the income statement. Temporary accounts are periodically closed; permanent accounts are left open. (5) **Ledger:** the book (or computer printouts) containing the accounts. Each account usually has a separate page. A general ledger is a collection of all the asset, liability, owners' equity, revenue and expense accounts. A subsidiary ledger contains the details related to a given general ledger account. (6) **Journal:** the book of original entry where transactions and selected other events are initially recorded. (7) **Posting:** the process of transferring the essential facts and figures from the book of original entry to the ledger accounts. (8) **Trial balance:** a list of all open accounts in the ledger and their balances. A trial balance may be prepared at any time. (9) **Adjusting entries:** entries made at the end of an accounting period to bring all accounts up to date on an accrual accounting basis so that correct financial statements can be prepared. (10) **Financial statements:** statements that reflect the accounting data's collection, tabulation, and final summarization. Financial statements consist of the balance sheet, the income statement, the statement of cash flows and the statement of retained earnings. (11) **Closing entries:** the formal process by which all temporary accounts are reduced to zero, and the net income or net loss is determined and transferred to the appropriate owners' equity account.

TIP: **Transactions** are the economic events of an entity recorded by accountants. Some events (happenings of consequence to an entity) are not measurable in terms of money and do not get recorded in the accounting records. Hiring employees, placing an order for supplies, greeting a customer and quoting prices for products are examples of activities that do not by themselves constitute transactions.

TIP: In accordance with the **revenue recognition principle**, revenue is to be recognized (reported) in the period in which it is realized (or realizable) and earned. In accordance with the **matching principle**, the expenses incurred in generating revenues should be recognized in the same period as the revenues they helped to generate. First, the revenue recognition principle is applied to determine in what period(s) to recognize revenue. Then, the matching principle is applied to determine in what period(s) to recognize expense.

TIP: Adjusting entries are often required so that revenues and expenses are reflected on an accrual basis of accounting (revenues recognized when earned and expenses recognized when incurred) rather than on a cash basis of accounting. Therefore, adjusting entries reflect the accruals and prepayments of revenues and expenses and also estimated expenses. Adjusting entries are simply entries required to bring account balances up to date before financial statements can be prepared. The failure to record proper adjustments will cause errors in both the income statement and the balance sheet.

TIP: **Prepayments** result from **cash** flows that occur **before** expense or revenue recognition. That is, cash is paid for expenses that apply to more than one accounting period or cash is received for revenue that applies to more than one accounting period. The portion of the expense that applies to future periods is deferred by reporting a prepaid expense (asset) or the portion of the revenue that applies to future periods is deferred by reporting unearned revenue (liability) on the balance sheet.

Accruals result from **cash** flows that occur **after** expense or revenue recognition. That is, cash is to be paid or received in a future accounting period for an expense incurred or a revenue earned in the current period.

TIP: Notice that **none** of the adjusting entries discussed in Chapter 3 involves the **Cash** account. Therefore, if you are instructed to record **adjusting entries**, double check your work when it is completed. If you have used the Cash account in any adjusting entry, it is very likely in error. (The only time Cash belongs in an adjusting entry is when a bank reconciliation discloses a need to adjust the Cash account—this will be explained in Chapter 7—or when an error has been made that involves the Cash account, in which case a correcting entry is required.)

TIP: Notice that each adjusting entry discussed in this chapter involves a balance sheet account **and** an income statement account.

TIP: When preparing homework assignments, working through *The Problem Solving Survival Guide,* and answering exam questions, pay careful attention to whether a prepayment situation relates to a **cash inflow** or **cash outflow** for the entity in question. Be sure you then use the proper related account for recording the cash receipt or disbursement and correct terminology in explaining the scenario. If cash is **received** in a rental situation, the amount will be recorded (by a credit) in either an earned rent revenue account or an unearned rent revenue account, **not** in an expense or a prepaid expense account. If cash is **paid** in a rental situation, the amount will be recorded (by a debit) in either an expense or a prepaid expense account.

TIP: In an adjusting entry for an accrual (accrued revenue or accrued expense), the word "accrued" is **not** needed in either account title. If you choose to use the word "accrued" in an account title, it is appropriate to do so **only** in the balance sheet account title. For example, the entry to record accrued salaries of $1,000 is as follows:

Salaries Expense	1,000	
Salaries Payable		1,000

The word "accrued" is not needed in either account title, but it could be used in the liability account title if desired (the account title would then be Accrued Salaries Payable). It would be wrong to insert the word "accrued" in the expense account title. Some people simply call the credit account "Accrued Salaries" (rather than "Salaries Payable") but we advise that you include the key word "Payable" and omit the unnecessary word "Accrued."

TIP: An unadjusted trial balance is referred to as either "unadjusted trial balance" or simply "trial balance." An adjusted trial balance is referred to as either "adjusted trial balance" or the "adjusted trial."

TIP: Closing entries are necessary at the end of an accounting period to prepare the temporary accounts (revenues, expenses, gains, and losses) for the recording of transactions for the next accounting period. Closing entries are prepared after the temporary account balances have been used to prepare the income statement. Only temporary accounts are closed. Permanent accounts are never closed; their balances continue into the next accounting period. **Temporary** accounts are often called **nominal** accounts; **permanent** accounts are often called **real** accounts.

TIP: A temporary account with a credit balance is closed by a debit to that account and a credit to Income Summary. A temporary account with a debit balance is closed by a credit to that account and a debit to Income Summary. The Income Summary account is closed to an owners' equity account (Retained Earnings for a corporation) and is often called the Revenue and Expense Summary.

TIP: If a separate account is used to record owner withdrawals or owner distributions (such as Dividends Declared for a corporation or Owner's Drawings for a proprietorship or partnership), this account is also closed at the end of the accounting period, but it is **not** closed to the Income Summary account because it is not a component of the net income calculation. Rather, it is closed directly to Retained Earnings (for a corporation) or to Owner's Capital (for a proprietorship or partnership).

TIP: A **post-closing trial balance** contains only permanent accounts because the temporary accounts all have a zero balance after the closing process. A post-closing trial balance is prepared to check on the equality of debits and credits after the closing process.

TIP: In preparing a 10-column work sheet, the debit and credit columns for every column pair must be equal before you can proceed to the next column pair. (This pertains to the first three column pairs). All five pairs of columns must balance for a work sheet to be complete.

TIP: You should be able to define the following four terms and describe the related adjusting entry for each; they are:

   1.   A **prepaid expense** is an expense that has been paid but has not been incurred. An adjusting entry for a deferred expense involves an EXPENSE account and an ASSET (prepaid expense) account. Ex. Prepaid rent, rent expense.

   2.   An **unearned revenue** is a revenue that has been collected but has not been earned. An adjusting entry for an unearned revenue involves a LIABILITY (unearned revenue) account and a REVENUE account. Ex. Cash collected for a magazine subscription. When the magazine is mailed to the customer, the unearned revenue would be earned.

   3.   An **accrued expense** is an expense that has been incurred but has not been paid. An adjusting entry for an accrued expense involves an EXPENSE account and a LIABILITY (payable account). Ex. Wages payable, wages expense.

4.   An **accrued revenue** is a revenue that has been earned but has not been received. An adjusting entry for accrued revenue involves an ASSET (receivable) account and a REVENUE account. Ex. A painter that has painted a house, but has not received payment yet.

TIP: A **prepaid expense** may be called a **deferred expense**. A deferred expense is so named because the recognition of expense is being deferred (put-off) to a future period; thus, a debit is carried on the balance sheet now and will be released to the income statement in a future period when the related benefits are consumed (expense is incurred).

TIP: An **unearned revenue** may be called a **deferred revenue** because the recognition of revenue is being deferred to a future period; thus, a credit is carried on the balance sheet now and will be released to the income statement in a future period when the related revenue is earned.

TIP: An adjusting entry for prepaid insurance expense (expense paid but not incurred) involves an expense account and an asset account. The expense account is often called Insurance Expense or Expired Insurance. Possible titles for the asset account include Prepaid Insurance, Deferred Insurance Expense, Prepaid Insurance Expense, Deferred Insurance, and Unexpired Insurance.

TIP: An adjusting entry for unearned rent revenue (revenue collected but not earned) involves a liability account and a revenue account. Possible titles for the liability account include Unearned Rent Revenue, Unearned Rent, Deferred Rent Revenue, Rent Revenue Received in Advance, and Rental Income Collected in Advance. The use of Prepaid Rent Revenue as an account title is **not** appropriate because the term prepaid usually refers to the payment of cash in advance, not the receipt of cash in advance. The revenue account is often called Rent Revenue or Rental Income or Rent Earned.

TIP: In an adjusting entry to record accrued interest revenue (revenue earned but not received), the debit is to an asset account and the credit is to a revenue account. Possible names for that asset account are Interest Receivable and Accrued Interest Receivable. Possible names for the revenue account include Interest Revenue, Interest Income, and Interest Earned.

TIP: In an adjusting entry to record accrued salaries expenses (expense incurred, but not paid) the debit is to an expense account and the credit is to a liability account. The expense account is usually titled Salaries Expense. Possible names for the liability account include Salaries Payable and Accrued Salaries Payable.

ILLUSTRATION 3-1
DOUBLE-ENTRY (DEBIT AND CREDIT)
ACCOUNTING SYSTEM (L.O. 2)

The debit and credit rules are summarized below:

Asset Accounts				Liability Accounts	
Debit	Credit			Debit	Credit
Increase	Decrease			Decrease	Increase
+	-			-	+

Dividends Account				Shareholders' Equity Accounts	
Debit	Credit			Debit	Credit
Increase	Decrease			Decrease	Increase
+	-			-	+

Expense Accounts				Revenue Accounts	
Debit	Credit			Debit	Credit
Increase	Decrease			Decrease	Increase
+	-			-	+
↑				↑	
Normal Balance				**Normal Balance**	

Notice that the accounts above are arranged in such a way that all of the increases ("+" signs) are on the outside and all of the decreases ("-" signs) are on the inside of this diagram.

TIP: An **account** is an individual accounting record of increases and decreases in a specific asset, liability, or stockholders' equity item. In its simplest form, an account consists of three parts: (1) the title of the account, (2) a left or debit side, and (3) a right or credit side. Because the alignment of these parts an account resembles the letter T, it is often referred to as a **T-account.**

TIP: "Credit" does **not** always mean favourable or unfavourable. In accounting, "debit and "credit" simply mean left and right, respectively. "Debit" is a term that refers to the left side of any account. Thus, the debit side of an account is always the left side. "Credit" is a word that simply refers to the right side of an account. Thus, the credit side of an account is always the right side of the account. The phrase "to debit an account" means to enter an amount on the debit (left) side of an account. Debit can be abbreviated as "Dr." and credit is abbreviated as "Cr."

TIP: A "+" indicates an increase and a "-" indicates a decrease. Therefore, a transaction, which causes an increase in an asset, is recorded by a debit to the related asset account; a transaction, which causes a decrease in the same asset, is recorded by a credit to the same account.

ILLUSTRATION 3-1 (Continued)

TIP: The **normal balance** of an account is the side where increases are recorded. Therefore, the normal balance of an asset account is a debit balance; the normal balance of a liability account is a credit balance.

TIP: A separate account should exist in the general ledger for each item that will appear on the financial statements.

TIP: At this stage of your study of accounting, you should be able to quickly and correctly identify the debit and credit rules for any given account. If you are slow at this process, drill on the rules until you improve. If you memorize the rules for an asset account, you can figure out the rules for all other types of accounts by knowing which rules are the opposite of the rules for assets and which are the same. Increases in assets are recorded by debits. Because liabilities and owners' equity are on the other side of the equals sign in the basic accounting equation, they must have debit and credit rules opposite of the rules for assets. Therefore, a liability or an owners' equity account is increased by a credit entry. Revenues earned increase owners' equity (retained earnings for a corporate form of organization) so the rules to record increases in revenue are the same as the rules to record increases in an owners' equity account (increases are recorded by credits). Because expenses and owners' withdrawals reduce owners' equity, they have debit/credit rules which are opposite of the rules for an owners' equity account.

TIP: In the double-entry system of accounting, for every debit there must be a credit(s) of equal amount, and vice versa.

EXERCISE 3-1

Purpose: (L.O. 2) This exercise will test your understanding of the debit and credit rules.

Instructions

For each account listed below, put a check mark (√) in the appropriate column to indicate if it is increased by an entry in the debit (left) side of the account or by an entry in the credit (right) side of the account. The first one is done for you.

		Debit	Credit
1.	Cash	√	
2.	Sales Revenue		
3.	Commissions Expense		
4.	Advertising Expense		
5.	Salaries Payable		
6.	Prepaid Insurance		
7.	Property Taxes Payable		
8.	Property Tax Expense		
9.	Dividends Declared		
10.	Interest Revenue		
11.	Salaries Expense		
12.	Commissions Revenue		
13.	Unearned Rent Revenue		
14.	Equipment		
15.	Note Payable		
16.	Building		
17.	Accounts Payable		
18.	Supplies on Hand		
19.	Accounts Receivable		
20.	Common Shares		
21.	Retained Earnings		
22.	Mortgage Payable		
23.	Loan Receivable		
24.	Bank Loan Payable		
25.	Audit Fees Incurred		
26.	Dividend Income		
27.	Fees Incurred		
28.	Fees Earned		
29.	Utilities Expense		
30.	Utilities Payable		

TIP: In essence, you are being asked to identify the normal balance of each of the accounts listed. The **normal balance** of an account is the side where increases are recorded.

Solution to Exercise 3-1

Approach: Determine the classification of the account (asset, liability, owners' equity, revenue or expense). Think about the debit and credit rules for that classification. Refer to **Illustration 3-1** and the related **TIPS** for those rules. In determining the classification of an account, look for the key words, if any, in each individual item. For example: (1) the words Revenue, Earned, or Income are often associated with a revenue account, (2) the words Expense, Incurred, or Expired are often associated with an expense account, (3) the words Receivable or Prepaid Expense refer to types of asset accounts, and (4) the words Payable or Unearned Revenue refer to types of liabilities.

		Debit	Credit	Classification
1.	Cash	√		Asset
2.	Sales Revenue		√	Revenue
3.	Commissions Expense	√		Expense
4.	Advertising Expense	√		Expense
5.	Salaries Payable		√	Liability
6.	Prepaid Insurance	√		Asset
7.	Property Taxes Payable		√	Liability
8.	Property Tax Expense	√		Expense
9.	Dividends Declared	√		Owners' Equity (Owners' Withdrawals)
10.	Interest Revenue		√	Revenue
11.	Salaries Expense	√		Expense
12.	Commissions Revenue		√	Revenue
13.	Unearned Rent Revenue		√	Liability
14.	Equipment	√		Asset
15.	Note Payable		√	Liability
16.	Building	√		Asset
17.	Accounts Payable		√	Liability
18.	Supplies on Hand	√		Asset
19.	Accounts Receivable	√		Asset
20.	Common Stock		√	Owners' Equity (Owners' Investments)
21.	Retained Earnings		√	Owners' Equity (Earned Capital)
22.	Mortgage Payable		√	Liability
23.	Loan Receivable	√		Asset
24.	Bank Loan Payable		√	Liability
25.	Audit Fees Incurred	√		Expense
26.	Dividend Income		√	Revenue
27.	Fees Incurred	√		Expense
28.	Fees Earned		√	Revenue
29.	Utilities Expense	√		Expense
30.	Utilities Payable		√	Liability

EXERCISE 3-2

Purpose: (L.O. 4) This exercise will review how to record transactions in the general journal.

Transactions for the Motorboat Repair Shop, Inc. for August 2001 are listed below.

1. August   1   Joan and Phillip began the business by each depositing $2,500 of personal funds in the business bank account in exchange for common shares of the newly formed corporation.
2. August   2   Joan rented space for the shop behind a strip mall and paid August rent of $800 out of the business bank account.
3. August   3   The shop purchased supplies for cash, $3,000.
4. August   4   The shop paid *Cupboard News*, a local newspaper, $300 for an ad appearing in the Sunday edition.
5. August   5   The shop repaired a boat for a customer. The customer paid cash of $1,300 for services rendered.
6. August   13   The shop purchased supplies for $900 by paying cash of $200 and charging the rest on account.
7. August   14   The shop repaired a boat for Zonie Kinkennon, a champion skier, for $3,600. Phillip collected $1,000 in cash and put the rest on Zonie's account.
8. August   24   The shop collected cash of $400 from Cheris Vasallo.
9. August   28   The shop paid $200 to Mini Maid for cleaning services for the month of August.
10. August   31   The board of directors of the corporation declared and paid a dividend of $400 in cash to its shareholders.

Instructions
(a) Explain the impact of each transaction on the elements of the basic accounting equation and translate that into debit and credit terms.
(b) Journalize the transactions listed above. Include a brief explanation with each journal entry.

SOLUTION TO EXERCISE 3-2

(a) 1.   Increase in Cash.   Debit Cash
           Increase in Common Shares.   Credit Common Shares

     2.   Increase in Rent Expense.   Debit Rent Expense
           Decrease in Cash.   Credit Cash

     3.   Increase in Supplies on Hand.   Debit Supplies on Hand
           Decrease in Cash.   Credit Cash

     4.   Increase in Advertising Expense.   Debit Advertising Expense
           Decrease in Cash.   Credit Cash

5. Increase in Cash.   Debit Cash
   Increase in Service Revenue.   Credit Service Revenue

6. Increase in Supplies on Hand.   Debit Supplies on Hand
   Decrease in Cash.   Credit Cash
   Increase in Accounts Payable.   Credit Accounts Payable

7. Increase in Cash.   Debit Cash
   Increase in Accounts Receivable.   Debit Accounts Receivable
   Increase in Service Revenue   Credit Service Revenue

8. Increase in Cash.   Debit Cash
   Decrease in Accounts Receivable.   Credit Accounts Receivable

9. Increase in Cleaning Expense.   Debit Cleaning Expense
   Decrease in Cash.   Credit Cash

10. Decrease in Retained Earnings.   Debit Retained Earnings
    Increase in Dividends Payable.   Credit Dividends Payable

Approach: Write down the effects of each transaction on the basic accounting equation. Think about the individual asset, liability, or shareholders' equity accounts involved. Apply the debit and credit rules to translate the effects into a journal entry. Refer to **Illustration 3-1** for the debit and credit rules for each type of account.

GENERAL JOURNAL   J1

	Date		Account Titles and Explanations	Ref.	Debit	Credit
(b)						
	2001					
1.	Aug.	1	Cash		5,000	
			Common Shares			5,000
			(Issued shares of stock for cash)			
2.		2	Rent Expense		800	
			Cash			800
			(Paid August rent)			
3.		3	Supplies on Hand		3,000	
			Cash			3,000
			(Purchased supplies for cash)			
4.		4	Advertising Expense		300	
			Cash			300
			(Paid *Cupboard News* for advertising)			
5.		5	Cash		1,300	
			Service Revenue			1,300
			(Received cash for service fees earned)			
6.		13	Supplies on Hand		900	
			Cash			200
			Accounts Payable			700
			(Purchased supplies for cash and on credit)			
7.		14	Cash		1,000	
			Accounts Receivable		2,600	
			Service Revenue			3,600
			(Performed services for customer for cash and on credit)			
8.		24	Cash		400	
			Accounts Receivable			400
			(Received cash from Cheris Vasallo on account)			
9.		28	Cleaning Expense		200	
			Cash			200
10.		31	Retained Earnings (or Dividends Declared)		400	
			Dividends Payable			400

EXERCISE 3-3

Purpose: (L.O. 5) This exercise will provide you with examples of adjusting entries for the accrual of expenses and revenues.

The following information relates to the Yuppy Clothing Sales Company at the end of 2002. The accounting period is the calendar year. This is the company's first year of operations.

1. Employees are paid every Friday for the five-day work week ending on that day. Salaries amount to $2,400 per week. The accounting period ends on a Thursday.
2. On October 1, 2002, Yuppy borrowed $8,000 cash by signing a note payable due in one year at 8% interest. Interest is due when the principal is paid.
3. A note for $2,000 was received from a customer in a sales transaction on May 1, 2002. The note matures in one year and bears 12% interest per annum. Interest is due when the principal is due.
4. A portion of Yuppy's parking lot is used by executives of a neighboring company. A person pays $6 per day for each day's use, and the parking fees are due by the fifth business day following the month of use. The fees for December 31, 2002 amount to $1,260.

Instructions

Using the information given above, prepare the necessary adjusting entries at December 31, 2002.

Solution to Exercise 3-3

1. Salaries Expense 1,920

   Salaries Payable 1,920

   ($2,400 ÷ 5 = $480); ($480 x 4 = $1,920 accrued salaries)

2. Interest Expense 160

   Interest Payable 160

   ($8,000 x 8% x 3/12 = $160 accrued interest)

3. Interest Receivable 160

   Interest Revenue 160

   ($2,000 x 12% x 8/12 = $160 accrued interest)

4. Parking Fees Receivable 1,260

   Parking Fees Revenue 1,260

Approach and Explanation: Write down the definitions for accrued expense and accrued revenue. Think about what is to be accomplished by each of the adjustments required in this exercise. An **accrued expense** is an expense that has been incurred but not paid. The "incurred" part results in an increase in Expense (debit) and the "not paid" part results in an increase in Payable (credit). An **accrued revenue** is a revenue that has been earned but not received. The "earned" part results in an increase in Revenue (credit) and the "not received" part results in an increase in Receivable (debit).

EXERCISE 3-4

Purpose: (L.O. 5) This exercise will provide you with examples of adjusting entries for prepaid expenses and unearned revenues (that is, for the deferral of expenses and revenues).

The following information relates to the "I AM" Magazine Company at the end of 2002. The accounting period is the calendar year.

1.   An insurance premium of $8,000 was paid on April 1, 2002, and was charged to Prepaid Insurance. The premium covers a 24-month period beginning April 1, 2002.

2.   The Office Supplies on Hand account showed a balance of $3,500 at the beginning of 2002. Supplies costing $12,000 were purchased during 2002 and debited to the asset account. Supplies of $2,200 were on hand at December 31, 2002.

3.   On July 1, 2002, cash of $48,000 was received from subscribers (customers) for a 36-month subscription period beginning on that date. The receipt was recorded by a debit to Cash and a credit to Unearned Subscription Revenue.

4.   At the beginning of 2002, the Unearned Advertising Revenue account had a balance of $75,000. During 2002, collections from advertisers of $800,000 were recorded by credits to Advertising Revenue. At the end of 2002, revenues received but not earned are computed to be $51,000.

Instructions

Using the information given above, prepare the necessary adjusting entries at December 31, 2002.

SOLUTION TO EXERCISE 3-4

1.	Insurance Expense	3,000	
	Prepaid Insurance		3,000
	($8,000 × 9/24 = $3,000 expired cost)		
2.	Supplies Expense	13,300	
	Office Supplies on Hand		13,300
	($3,500 + $12,000 - $2,200 = $13,300 supplies consumed)		
3.	Unearned Subscription Revenue	8,000	
	Subscription Revenue		8,000
	($48,000 × 6/36 = $8,000 earned revenue)		
4.	Unearned Advertising Revenue	824,000	
	Advertising Revenue		824,000
	($75,000 + $800,000 - $51,000 = $824,000 earned revenue)		

Approach and Explanation: Write down the definitions for prepaid expense and unearned revenue. Think about what is to be accomplished by each of the adjustments required in this exercise. A **prepaid expense** is an expense that has been paid but not incurred. In a case where the prepayment was recorded as an increase in an asset account (such as Prepaid Expense or Supplies on Hand), the adjusting entry will record the increase in Expense (debit) and a decrease in the recorded Asset (credit) due to the consumption of the benefits yielded by the earlier prepayment. An **unearned revenue** is a revenue that has been received but not earned. In a case where the cash receipt was recorded as an increase in a liability account (such as Unearned Revenue), the adjusting entry will record a decrease in the recorded liability Unearned Revenue (debit) and an increase in Earned Revenue (credit) due to the earning of all or a portion of the revenue represented by the earlier cash receipt.

It is helpful to sketch a T-account for the related asset or liability account. Enter the amounts reflected in that account before adjustment, enter the desired ending balance, and notice how the required adjustment is then obvious from facts reflected in your T-account. The T-accounts would appear as follows:

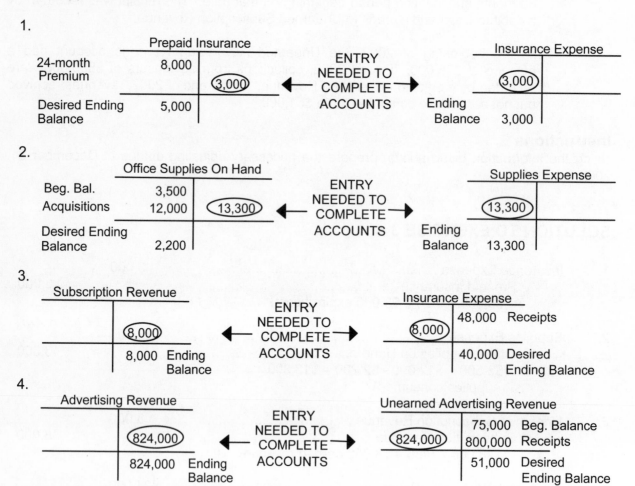

ILLUSTRATION 3-2
SUMMARY OF ADJUSTMENT RELATIONSHIPS
AND EXPLANATIONS (L.O. 5)

Type of Adjustment	Account Relationship	Reason for Adjustment	Account Balances Before Adjustment	Adjusting Entry
1. Prepaid Expense	Asset and Expense	(a) Prepaid expense initially recorded in asset account has been consumed; or,	Asset overstated Expense understated	Dr. Expense Cr. Asset
		*(b) Prepaid expense initially recorded in expense account has not been consumed.	Asset understated Expense overstated	Dr. Asset Cr. Expense
2. Unearned Revenue	Liability and Revenue	(a) Unearned revenue initially recorded in liability account has been earned; or,	Liability overstated Revenue understated	Dr. Liability Cr. Revenue
		*(b) Unearned revenue initially recorded in revenue account has not been earned.	Liability understated Revenue overstated	Dr. Revenue Cr. Liability
3. Accrued Expense	Expense and Liability	Expense incurred has not been billed nor paid nor recorded.	Expense understated Liability understated	Dr. Expense Cr. Liability
4. Accrued Revenues	Asset and Revenue	Revenue earned has not been billed nor collected nor recorded.	Asset understated Revenue understated	Dr. Asset Cr. Revenue
5. Estimated Item	Asset and Expense	(a) A previously recorded long-lived asset has now been partially consumed; or,	Asset overstated Expense understated	Dr. Expense Cr. Contra Asset
		(b) An existing asset is not fully realizable.	Asset overstated Expense understated	Dr. Expense Cr. Contra Asset

Explanation:

1. When expenses are paid for before they are incurred, the payment may either be recorded by a debit to an asset account (prepaid expense) or by a debit to an expense account. At the end of the accounting period, the accounts are adjusted as needed. If the prepayment was initially recorded by use of a prepaid (asset) account, the consumed portion is transferred to an expense account in the adjusting entry. Whereas, if the prepayment was initially recorded by use of an expense account, an adjusting entry is required only if a portion of the expense remains prepaid at the end of the accounting period (in which case the unconsumed portion is transferred to an asset account). (See **Illustration 3-3** for an example.)

2. When revenues are received before they are earned, the receipt may either be recorded by a credit to a liability account (unearned revenue) or by a credit to a revenue account. At the end of the accounting period, the accounts are adjusted as needed. If the collection was initially recorded by a credit to a liability account (unearned revenue), the earned portion is transferred to a revenue account in the adjusting entry. Whereas, if the collection was initially recorded by use of a revenue account, an adjusting entry is required only if a portion of the revenue remains unearned at the end of the accounting period (in which case the unearned portion is transferred to a liability account). (See **Illustration 3-3** for an example.)

ILLUSTRATION 3-2 (Continued)

3.   Expenses are often incurred before they are paid. An expense incurred but not yet paid is called an **accrued expense**. If at the end of an accounting period this accrued expense has not been recorded (which is often the case because it usually has not been billed yet by the vendor), it must be recorded by way of an adjusting entry. Expense that accrues with the passage of time (such as interest expense) is a good example of a reason to need an accrued expense (or accrued liability) type adjusting entry.

4.   Revenues are often earned before they are collected. Revenue earned but not received is called an **accrued revenue**. If at the end of an accounting period this accrued revenue has not been recorded (which is often the case because it usually has not been billed yet), it must be recorded by way of an adjusting entry. Revenue that accrues with the passage of time (such as interest revenue) is a good example of a reason to need an accrued revenue (or accrued asset) type adjusting entry.

TIP: Examine each type of adjustment explained above and notice the logic of the resulting entry. For example, an adjustment to recognize supplies used (when the supplies were recorded in an asset account when purchased) should reduce assets and increase expenses.

TIP: Keep in mind that for accrued items (accrued revenues and accrued expenses), the related cash flow **follows** the period in which the relevant revenue or expense is recognized; whereas, with prepayment type items (unearned revenues and prepaid expenses), the related cash flow **precedes** the period in which the relevant revenue or expense is recognized.

   For example, assume the accounting period is the calendar year. Consider an accrued expense such as accrued salaries at the end of 2002. An adjusting entry will be recorded at the end of 2002 so the expense will get reported on the 2002 income statement. The related cash payment to employees will take place in the following accounting period (2003, in this case). For another example, consider a prepaid expense such as the prepayment of rent in December 2002 for January 2003 occupancy. The cash payment occurs in December 2002. The expense is incurred and recognized in the following accounting period (January 2003).

5.   The cost of most long-lived tangible assets is allocated to expense in a systematic and rational manner. The entry to record the expiration of cost due to the consumption of benefits yielded by the asset is a debit to Amortization Expense and a credit to Accumulated Amortization. The amortization of intangibles is treated in a similar manner. A reduction in the net realizable value of accounts receivable or inventories is recorded in an adjusting entry by a charge to expense and a credit to a contra asset account.

ILLUSTRATION 3-3
ALTERNATIVE TREATMENTS OF PREPAID EXPENSES
AND UNEARNED REVENUES (L.O.5)

When a company writes a cheque to pay for an item that affects expense in at least two different time periods (such as for an insurance premium or a licence or dues), the bookkeeper may record the payment in one of two ways. Either as a prepaid expense (asset) or as an expense. The first way is used most often in introductory accounting textbooks; the second is used most often in the real world. Regardless of the way the payment is recorded, an appropriate adjusting entry will be made at the end of the accounting period so that correct balances appear on the income statement and the balance sheet. For example, a $1,200 payment is made on April 1, 2002, for a twelve-month insurance premium covering the time between April 1, 2002 and March 31, 2003. (Assume a calendar year reporting period.) A comparison of the two possible approaches appears below.

Prepayment (Cash Paid) Initially Debited to Asset Account			OR	Prepayment (Cash Paid) Initially Debited to Expense Account		
4/1	Prepaid Insurance	1,200		4/1	Insurance Expense	1,200
	Cash		1,200		Cash		1,200
12/31	Insurance Expense	900		12/31	Prepaid Insurance	300
	Prepaid Insurance		900		Insurance Expense		300

After posting the entries, the accounts appear as follows:

Prepaid Insurance					Prepaid Insurance		
4/1	1,200	12/31 Adj.	900		12/31 Adj.	300	
12/31 Bal.	300						

Insurance Expense					Insurance Expense		
12/31 Adj.	900				4/1	1,200	12/31 Adj. 300
					12/31 Bal.	900	

Notice that regardless of the path, you end up at the same place—with a balance of $300 in Prepaid Insurance and a balance of $900 in Insurance Expense. That was your objective—to report balances in accordance with the accrual basis of accounting.

TIP: Reversing entries are never required. But if it is company policy to use reversing entries where appropriate, would either or both of the above adjusting entries get reversed? The adjusting entry illustrated in the left column would **not** get reversed since to do so would result in reestablishing an asset amount that the adjusting entry indicated had expired. The adjusting entry illustrated in the right column **can be** reversed since a reversing entry will record $300 of insurance expense in the new accounting period (2003) which is the period we expect the remaining $300 of premium to pertain.

Illustration 3-3 (Continued)

When a company receives cash from a customer in advance of earning the related revenue, the bookkeeper may record the receipt in one of two ways. Either as an unearned revenue (liability) or as an earned revenue. The first way is used most often in introductory accounting textbooks; the second is used most often in the real world. Regardless of the way the receipt is recorded, an appropriate adjusting entry will be made at the end of the accounting period so that correct balances appear on the income statement and the balance sheet. For example, $1,200 is received on May 1, 2002, for a twelve-month magazine subscription covering the time between May 1, 2002 and April 30, 2003. (Assume a calendar year reporting period.) A comparison of the two possible approaches appears below:

Unearned Revenue (Cash Received) Initially Credited to Liability Account				OR		Unearned Revenue (Cash Received) Initially Credited to Revenue Account		
5/1	Cash	1,200			5/1	Cash	1,200	
	Unearned Sub. Rev.		1,200			Subscription Revenue		1,200
12/31	Unearned Sub. Rev.	800			12/31	Subscription Revenue	400	
	Subscription Revenue		800			Unearned Sub Rev.		400

After posting the entries, the accounts appear as follows:

Unearned Subscription Revenue					Unearned Subscription Revenue			
12/31 Adj.	800	5/1	1,200				12/31 Adj.	400
		12/31 Bal.	400					

Subscription Revenue					Subscription Revenue			
		12/31 Adj.	800		12/31 Adj.	400	5/1	1,200
							12/31 Bal.	800

Notice that the balances in the accounts are the same regardless of the approach used; that is, Unearned Subscription Revenue is $400, and Subscription Revenue is $800 at December 31, 2002.

TIP: The adjusting entry illustrated in the left column would not be subject to reversal; a reversing entry can be used with the approach illustrated in the right column.

EXERCISE 3-5

Purpose: (L.O. 5) This exercise will provide you with examples of adjusting entries for:
   (1)   Prepaid expenses when cash payments are recorded in an asset (permanent) account.
   (2)   Prepaid expenses when cash payments are recorded in an expense (temporary) account.
   (3)   Unearned revenues when cash receipts are recorded in a liability (permanent) account.
   (4)   Unearned revenues when cash receipts are recorded in a revenue (temporary) account.
   Thus, this exercise will review the alternative treatments of prepaid expenses and unearned revenues discussed in **Illustration 3-3**.

Each situation described below is **independent** of the others.

(1)   Office supplies are recorded in an asset account when acquired. There were $400 of supplies on hand at the beginning of the period. Cash purchases of office supplies during the period amount to $900. A count of supplies at the end of the period shows $320 worth to be on hand.

(2)   Office supplies are recorded in an expense account when acquired. There were $400 of supplies on hand at the beginning of the period. Cash purchases of office supplies during the period amount to $900. A count of supplies at the end of the period shows $320 worth to be on hand. No reversing entries are used.

(3)   Receipts from customers for magazine subscriptions are recorded as a liability when cash is collected in advance of delivery. The beginning balance in the liability account was $6,700. During the period, $54,000 was received for subscriptions. At the end of the period, it was determined that the balance of the Unearned Subscription Revenue account should be $8,000.

(4)   Receipts from customers for magazine subscriptions are recorded as revenue when cash is collected in advance of delivery. The beginning balance in the liability account was $6,700. During the period, $54,000 was received for subscriptions. At the end of the period, it was determined that the balance of the Unearned Subscription Revenue account should be $8,000. No reversing entries are used.

Instructions
For each of the **independent** situations above:
(a)   Prepare the appropriate adjusting entry in general journal form.
(b)   Indicate the amount of revenue or expense that will appear on the income statement for the period.
(c)   Indicate the balance of the applicable asset or liability account at the end of the period.
(d)   Indicate the amount of cash received or paid during the period.
(e)   Indicate the change in the applicable asset or liability account from the beginning of the period to the end of the period.

> **TIP:** It would be helpful to draw T-accounts for each situation. Enter the information given as it would be, or needs to be, reflected in the accounts. Solve for the adjusting entry that would be necessary to "reconcile" the facts given.

Solution to Exercise 3-5

(1)   a.   Office Supplies Expense   980
                  Office Supplies on Hand   980
        b.   Office Supplies Expense $980
        c.   Office Supplies on Hand $320
        d.   Cash paid $900
        e.   Decrease in Office Supplies on Hand $ 80

Approach:

(2)   a.   Office Supplies Expense   80
                  Office Supplies on Hand   80
        b.   Office Supplies Expense $980
        c.   Office Supplies on Hand $320
        d.   Cash paid $900
        e.   Decrease in Office Supplies on Hand $ 80

Approach:

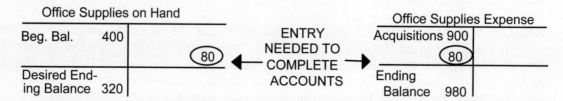

> **TIP:** Compare situation (1) with situation (2). Notice the facts are the same **except** for the account debited for acquisitions of office supplies. The solution is then the same **except** for the adjusting entry required.

(3)   a.   Unearned Subscription Revenue   52,700
                  Subscription Revenue....................................   52,700
        b.   Subscription Revenue $52,700
        c.   Unearned Subscription Revenue $ 8,000
        d.   Cash received $54,000
        e.   Increase in Unearned Subscription Revenue $ 1,300

Approach:

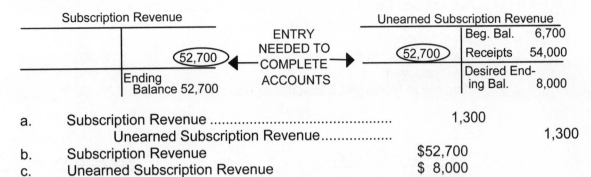

(4) a. Subscription Revenue 1,300
             Unearned Subscription Revenue.................. 1,300
   b. Subscription Revenue $52,700
   c. Unearned Subscription Revenue $ 8,000
   d. Cash received $54,000
   e. Increase in Unearned Subscription Revenue $ 1,300

Approach:

TIP: Compare situation (3) with situation (4). Notice the facts are the same **except** for the account credited for receipt of revenue in advance of the period in which the revenue is earned. The solution is the same **except** for the adjusting entry required.

TIP: You should be able to handle what for most students can be the most challenging situations. Refer back to the descriptions of situations (2) and (4). Redo them, assuming that reversing entries **are** used. Reversing entries are described in Appendix 3-A in the text. Those new solutions should appear as follows.

(2) Assuming reversing entries **are** used.
   a. Office Supplies on Hand... 320
          Office Supplies Expense.............................. 320
   b. Office Supplies Expense $980
   c. Office Supplies on Hand $320
   d. Cash paid $900
   e. Decrease in Office Supplies on Hand $ 80

Approach:

(4)   Assuming reversing entries **are** used.

			Dr.	Cr.
a.	Subscription Revenue		8,000	
	Unearned Subscription Revenue.................			8,000
b.	Subscription Revenue		$52,700	
c.	Unearned Subscription Revenue		$ 8,000	
d.	Cash received		$54,000	
e.	Increase in Unearned Subscription Revenue		$ 1,300	

Approach:

Unearned Subscription Revenue					Subscription Revenue	
	Beg. Bal. 6,700	ENTRY			Reversing 6,700	
Reversing 6,700	8,000	NEEDED TO		8,000	Receipts 54,000	
	Desired End-ing Bal. 8,000	COMPLETE ACCOUNTS			Ending Balance 52,700	

EXERCISE 3-6

Purpose: (L.O. 5) This exercise will illustrate the preparation of adjusting entries from an unadjusted trial balance and additional data.

The following list of accounts and their balances represents the unadjusted trial balance of Tami Corp. at December 31, 2002.

	Dr.	Cr.
Cash	$ 15,000	
Accounts Receivable	122,500	
Allowance for Doubtful Accounts		$ 1,875
Inventory	162,500	
Prepaid Insurance	7,350	
Prepaid Rent	33,000	
Investment in Lamb Corp. Bonds	45,000	
Land	25,000	
Plant and Equipment	260,000	
Accumulated Amortization		45,000
Accounts Payable		23,275
Bonds Payable		125,000
Discount on Bonds Payable	3,750	
Common Shares		250,000
Retained Earnings (January 1, 2002)		201,650
Sales		533,275
Rent Revenue		25,500
Cost of Goods Sold	410,250	
Transportation-out	22,500	
Salaries and Wages	87,500	
Interest Expense	9,000	
Miscellaneous Expense	2,225	
	$1,205,575	$1,205,575

Additional Information:

1. On March 31, 2002, Tami rented a warehouse for $2,750 per month, paid $33,000 in advance, and debited Prepaid Rent to record the payment.
2. On September 1, 2002, Tami received $25,500 rent from its lessee for a 12-month lease on a parking lot, beginning on that date. The receipt was recorded by a credit to Rent Revenue.
3. Tami estimates that 1% of the credit sales made during 2002 will result in accounts receivable that will ultimately become uncollectible. All sales are made on credit (on account).
4. Prepaid Insurance contains the $7,350 premium cost of a policy that is for a 2-year term and was taken out on May 1, 2002.
5. On April 1, 2002, Tami issued 125, $1,000, 8% bonds, maturing on April 1, 2012, at 97% of par value. Interest payment dates are April 1 and October 1. The straight-line method is used to amortize any bond premium or discount. Amortization is recorded only at year-end.
6. The regular rate of amortization is 10% of acquisition cost per year. Acquisitions and retirements during a year are depreciated at half this rate. Assets costing $16,000 were retired during the year. On December 31, 2001, the balance of Plant and Equipment was $230,000.
7. On September 1, 2002, Tami purchased 45, $1,000, 10% Lamb Corp. bonds, at par. The bonds mature on August 31, 2004. Interest is to be received every August 31 and February 28.

Instructions

Prepare the year-end adjusting entries in general journal form using the information above. (Round amounts to the nearest dollar.)

Solution to Exercise 3-6

1. Rent Expense.. 24,750
       Prepaid Rent.. 24,750
          ($33,000 x 9/12 = $24,750 expired rent)

2. Rent Revenue 17,000
       Unearned Rent Revenue 17,000
          ($25,500 x 8/12 = $17,000 unearned revenue)

3. Bad Debt Expense 5,333
       Allowance for Doubtful Accounts 5,333
          ($533,275 x 1% = $5,333 bad debt expense)

> **TIP:** If the estimate for uncollectible accounts receivable is to be based on a percentage of net sales, the expense figure is a percentage of net sales and any existing balance in the Allowance account will **not** affect the amount of the adjusting entry. If the estimate for uncollectible accounts receivable is to be based on an ageing of accounts receivable or a percentage of accounts receivable existing at the balance sheet date, the desired ending balance for the Allowance account is determined and any existing balance in the Allowance account **will** affect the amount of the adjusting entry. (This subject will be more thoroughly reviewed in Chapter 7.)

4.		Insurance Expense	2,450	
		Prepaid Insurance...		2,450
		($7,350 x 8/24 = $2,450 expired insurance)		

5.	a.	Interest Expense..	2,500	
		Interest Payable..		2,500
		($125,000 x 8% x 3/12 = $2,500		
		accrued interest)		
	b.	Interest Expense..	281	
		Discount on Bonds Payable		281
		(125 x $1,000 x 97% = $121,250)		
		[(125 x $1,000) - $121,250 = $3,750]		
		($3,750 x 9/120 = $281 discount amortization)		

6.		Amortization Expense	24,500	
		Accumulated Amortization......................................		24,500
		($230,000 - $16,000 assets retired =		
		$214,000 assets used for full year)		
		($214,000 x 10% = $21,400 amortization		
		on assets held for full year)		
		($16,000 x 10% x 1/2 = $800 amortization		
		on assets disposed of during the year)		
		($260,000 - $214,000 = $46,000		
		assets acquired during the year)		
		($46,000 x 10% x 1/2 = $2,300 amortization		
		on assets acquired during the year)		
		($21,400 + $800 + $2,300 = $24,500		
		total amortization for the year)		

7.		Interest Receivable	1,500	
		Interest Revenue		1,500
		($45,000 x 10% x 4/12 = $1,500 accrued interest)		

TIP: An interest rate is an annual rate unless otherwise indicated. For preparing an adjusting entry involving interest, calculate interest assuming the rate given is for a whole year, unless it is evident that this is not the case. Also, assume a 360 day year, unless otherwise indicated.

Approach and Explanation: Identify each item as involving: (1) a prepaid expense, (2) an accrued expense, (3) an unearned revenue, (4) an accrued revenue, or (5) an estimated item. From the facts, determine the existing account balances. Read the facts carefully to determine the desired account balances for financial statements in accordance with generally accepted accounting principles (historical cost principle, revenue recognition principle, matching principle, etc.). Determine the adjusting entries necessary to bring existing account balances to the appropriate account balances.

1.   This situation involves a prepaid expense. The advance payment was for twelve months and was recorded in an asset account. At December 31, 2002, nine months have passed for which the rent was paid, so the expired portion of the

rent must be removed from the Prepaid Rent (asset) account and put into the Rent Expense account.

2. This situation involves unearned revenue. On September 1, 2002, cash was received and recorded as follows:

Cash	25,500	
Rent Revenue...		25,500

At December 31, 2002, before adjustment, there is no Unearned Rent Revenue account on the trial balance. We need a balance of $17,000 ($25,500 x 8/12) in Unearned Rent Revenue at the balance sheet date. Therefore, in an adjusting entry, Unearned Rent Revenue is credited for $17,000. The other half of an adjusting entry dealing with Unearned Rent Revenue always has to be Rent Revenue. The debit to Rent Revenue in this exercise will reduce the balance in the earned revenue account to the amount actually earned during 2002 ($8,500).

3. This situation involves an estimated expense. The bad debt expense for the year is estimated to be 1% of credit sales and all sales are on account. Thus, an expense of $5,333 (1% of $533,275 sales) is recorded and a valuation account to Accounts Receivable is credited. The $1,875 balance in that valuation account (Allowance for Doubtful Accounts) before adjustment does **not** affect the amount required in the adjusting entry in this case.

4. This item involves a prepaid expense. Before adjustment, the total cost of the insurance premium is in the Prepaid Insurance account. The expired portion must be taken out of Prepaid Insurance (credit) and put into Insurance Expense (debit).

5. This situation involves an accrued expense and amortization of a related discount. Interest must be accrued since the last interest payment date (October 1) so three months of interest belong in the accrual entry. The discount (3% of the par value) is to be amortized on a straight-line basis from the date of issuance (April 1, 2002) to the date of maturity (April 1, 2012), which is a ten-year period.

6. Of the $260,000 ending balance in Plant and Equipment, $230,000 represents items held during the whole year. There were retirements of $16,000 during the year so we can compute the $46,000 amount of acquisitions. (Acquisitions and retirements are to be amortized for only one-half of a year—that is, at a 5% rate). A 10% rate of amortization per year is equivalent to amortizing assets over a 10-year period using the straight-line method.

7. This situation involves an accrued revenue. Interest must be accrued since the last interest payment date, which is four months. The 10% interest rate stated is expressed on an annual basis.

EXERCISE 3-7

Purpose: (L.O. 6) This exercise will review the preparation of closing entries.

The adjusted trial balance for the Motorboat Repair Corporation at December 31, 2001 appears as follows:

Motorboat Repair Corporation
ADJUSTED TRIAL BALANCE
December 31, 2001

	Debit	Credit
Cash	$ 2,600	
Accounts Receivable	2,200	
Supplies on Hand	2,100	
Accounts Payable		$ 700
Common Shares		3,000
Retained Earnings (January 1, 2001)		1,300
Service Revenue		4,900
Rent Expense	800	
Advertising Expense	300	
Cleaning Expense	200	
Utilities Expense	80	
Utilities Payable		80
Supplies Expense	1,700	
	$ 9,980	$ 9,980

Instructions

(a)   Prepare the appropriate closing entries at December 31, 2001.
(b)   Explain why closing entries are necessary.

Solution to Exercise 3-7

(a)   Service Revenue 4,900
           Income Summary 4,900
               (To close the revenue account
                 to Income Summary)

       Income Summary 3,080
           Rent Expense 800
           Advertising Expense 300
           Cleaning Expense 200
           Utilities Expense 80
           Supplies Expense 1,700
               (To close expense accounts to Income Summary)

       Income Summary 1,820
           Retained Earnings 1,820
               (To close Income Summary to Retained Earnings)
               ($4,900 total revenues - $3,080 total expenses =
                 $1,820 credit balance in Income Summary before closing)
(b)   The major reason closing entries are needed is that they prepare the temporary
       (nominal) accounts for the recording of transactions of the next accounting period.

Closing entries produce a zero balance in each of the temporary accounts so that they can be used to accumulate data pertaining to the next accounting period. Because of closing entries, the revenues of 2002 are not commingled with the revenues of the prior period (2001). A second reason closing entries are needed is that the Retained Earnings account will reflect a true balance only after closing entries have been completed. Closing entries formally recognize in the ledger the transfer of net income (or loss) and dividends declared to retained earnings as indicated in the statement of retained earnings.

> **TIP:**   The Income Summary account is used only in the closing process. Before it is closed, the balance in this account must equal the net income or net loss figure for the period.
>
> **TIP:**   Where do you look for the accounts (and their amounts) to be closed? If a work sheet is used, you can use the amounts listed in the Income Statement column pair and the balance of the Dividends Declared (or Owner's Drawing) account. If a work sheet is not used, you must refer to the temporary accounts (after adjustment) in the ledger to determine the balances to be closed.

EXERCISE 3-8

Purpose: (L.O. 8) This exercise will allow you to quickly check your knowledge of how items are extended on a 10-column work sheet.

Instructions

The last six columns of an incomplete 10-column work sheet are illustrated below. Place an "X" in the appropriate columns to indicate the proper work sheet treatment of the balance in each of the accounts listed. (The accounts are **not** listed in their usual order, the work sheet is **only partially** illustrated, and the Trial Balance and Adjustments columns have been **omitted**.)

Handy Dandy Hardware
WORK SHEET
For the Year Ended December 31, 2002

Account	Adjusted Trial Balance		Income Statement		Balance Sheet	
	Debit	Credit	Debit	Credit	Debit	Credit
Advertising Expense						
Amortization Expense						
Land						
Store Equipment						
Wages and Salaries Expense						
Mortgage Payable						
Cash						
Salaries Payable						
Prepaid Insurance						
Delivery Equipment						
Accumulated Amortization						
Revenue Received in Advance						
Rent Expense						
Sales Revenue						
Prepaid Rent						
Dividends Declared						
Repairs Expense						
Wages Payable						
Interest Receivable						
Accounts Receivable						
Net Income						
Retained Earnings						

Solution to Exercise 3-8

Handy Dandy Hardware
WORK SHEET
For the Year Ended December 31, 2002

Account	Adjusted Trial Balance		Income Statement		Balance Sheet	
	Debit	Credit	Debit	Credit	Debit	Credit
Advertising Expense	X		X			
Amortization Expense	X		X			
Land	X				X	
Store Equipment	X				X	
Wages and Salaries Expense	X		X			
Mortgage Payable		X				X
Cash	X				X	
Salaries Payable		X				X
Prepaid Insurance	X				X	
Delivery Equipment	X				X	
Accumulated Amortization		X				X
Revenue Received in Advance		X				X
Rent Expense	X		X			
Sales Revenue		X		X		
Prepaid Rent	X				X	
Dividends Declared	X				X	
Repairs Expense	X		X			
Wages Payable		X				X
Interest Receivable	X				X	
Accounts Receivable	X				X	
Net Income			X			X
Retained Earnings		X				X

TIP: The amount shown for Retained Earnings on the work sheet above is the balance of that account **before** considering dividends declared during the period (determined by the fact that a separate Dividends Declared account appears on the same work sheet) and **before** considering net income for the period.

TIP: Every amount appearing in the Adjusted Trial Balance column pair must be extended to one of the four statement (income statement or balance sheet) columns. Debit amounts go to a debit column further to the right and credit amounts go to a credit column further to the right of the adjusted trial balance column pair.

TIP: When a dollar amount is added to balance the income statement column pair of columns, the same amount must be added in an opposite debit or credit column in the balance sheet column pair. This amount in a balance sheet column indicates the impact of net income (or net loss) on owners' equity.

EXERCISE 3-9

Purpose: (L.O. 3, 8, 9A) This exercise reviews the procedures involved in the accounting cycle when two optional steps, a work sheet and reversing entries, are employed.

Instructions
Ten steps in the accounting cycle for a company, which uses a work sheet and reversing entries, are listed below in random order. Arrange the 10 procedures carried out in the accounting cycle in the order in which they should be performed by numbering them "1," "2," and so forth in the spaces provided.

_____   a.   Journalize and post closing entries.

_____   b.   Prepare financial statements from the work sheet.

_____   c.   Prepare a post-closing trial balance.

_____   d.   Balance the ledger accounts and prepare a trial balance on the work sheet.

_____   e.   Journalize and post adjustments made on the work sheet.

_____   f.   Record transactions in the journals.

_____   g.   Journalize and post reversing entries.

_____   h.   Post from journals to the ledgers.

_____   i.   Complete the work sheet (adjusting entries, adjusted trial balance, and extend amounts to the appropriate financial statement columns).

_____   j.   Identify and analyse business transactions and events.

Solution to Exercise 3-9

a.	8	c.	9	e.	7 (or 6)	g.	10	i.	5
b.	6 (or 7)	d.	4	f.	2	h.	3	j.	1

Approach: As you work through this exercise, concentrate on the logical progression and the flow of information in the data gathering process. Think about the purpose served by each step involved in the process of identifying, recording, classifying, summarizing, reporting, and interpreting transactions and other events relating to enterprises. This process is summarized below, first assuming no work sheet is used. Then differences introduced by use of a work sheet are discussed.

Explanation:
(1)   Transactions and other events that are to be recognized (recorded) are first **identified** and **analysed**. Many happenings (such as interviews of prospective employees and the order for placement of an advertisement in a local newspaper) are not recorded. However, the payment or accrual for salaries to employees and amounts owed to vendors of services are recordable events.

(2)   Transactions and other events are **recorded** chronologically in the journal(s). A transaction can be viewed in its entirety in a journal.

(3)   Transactions and events are **classified** by posting from the journal(s) to the ledger(s).

(4)   All transactions and events affecting individual accounts are **summarized** by balancing the accounts (determining the balances of all accounts).

(5)   Adjusting entries are recorded in the general journal and posted to the general ledger to update the accounts for accruals, deferrals, and estimated items. An adjusted trial balance is prepared to prove the maintenance of the equality of total debits and total credits after the adjustments.

(6)   The **income statement** is prepared using the balances of accounts for revenues, expenses, gains, and losses (temporary or nominal accounts).

(7)   **Closing entries** are recorded in the general journal and posted to the general ledger. Closing entries are necessary to prepare the temporary (nominal) accounts for recordings of the subsequent period. Closing entries also update the balance of the Retained Earnings account for the balance sheet.

(8)   The statement of retained earnings is prepared to report the changes in retained earnings during the period. It uses the net income figure as one reason for change.

(9)   The **balance sheet** is prepared. It reports the balances of assets, liabilities, and owners' equity.

(10)   A **post-closing** trial balance is prepared.

(11)   **Reversing entries** may be recorded and posted to facilitate certain recordings in the subsequent period.

(12)   Financial statements are **interpreted** by users after careful analysis of all items reported.

TIP: A **work sheet** is usually prepared to facilitate the process of adjusting the accounts and accumulating the balances needed for the financial statements. When a work sheet is employed, the adjusting entries and the adjusted trial balance are entered directly on the work sheet. The adjusted account balances are then sorted on the work sheet and all balances needed for the financial statements are accumulated in one handy place (on the work sheet). The actual journalizing and posting of adjusting entries and closing entries are then normally done after the financial statements are completed.

EXERCISE 3-10

Purpose: (L.O. 9A) This exercise will provide practice in determining which adjusting entries may be reversed.

Instructions

The following represent adjusting entries prepared for the Bent Tree Company at December 31, 2002 (end of the accounting period). The company has the policy of using reversing entries when appropriate. For each adjusting entry below, indicate if it would be appropriate to reverse it at the beginning of 2003. Indicate your answer by circling "yes" or "no."

Yes	No	1.	Deferred Advertising Expense......................	4,500	
			Advertising Expense		4,500
Yes	No	2.	Interest Expense...	800	
			Discount on Bonds Payable.................		800
Yes	No	3.	Interest Receivable......................................	690	
			Interest Revenue		690
Yes	No	4.	Unearned Rental Income..............................	900	
			Rental Income......................................		900
Yes	No	5.	Insurance Expense.......................................	1,600	
			Prepaid Insurance...............................		1,600
Yes	No	6.	Salaries Expense..	1,100	
			Salaries Payable..................................		1,100

Solution to Exercise 3-10

1.	Yes	3.	Yes	5.	No
2.	No	4.	No	6.	Yes

TIP: A **reversing entry** is an entry made at the very beginning of an accounting period that is the exact opposite of an adjusting entry made at the end of the previous period. The recording of reversing entries is an **optional** step in the accounting cycle. The **purpose** of a reversing entry is to simplify the recording of transactions in the new accounting period. The use of reversing entries does not change the amounts reported in financial statements.

Approach: Write down what the related reversing entry would look like and then (1) think about the effects that the reversing entry would have on the account balances in the accounting period that follows the one for which the adjustment was made, and (2) think about whether those effects are appropriate or not. It is appropriate to reverse an adjusting entry involving a prepaid expense or unearned revenue **only if** the adjustment increases (rather than decreases) a balance sheet account. It is **always** appropriate to reverse an adjusting entry involving an accrual. It is **never** appropriate to reverse an adjusting entry for depreciation or amortization or bad debts.

Explanation:
1.   An adjustment for a deferred expense can be reversed if the adjustment increases an asset or liability account. This adjustment increases a prepaid expense (asset) account.
2.   Never reverse an adjustment for amortization of a discount or premium.
3.   An accrual type adjustment can always be reversed.
4.   A reversal of this entry would put back into the Unearned Rental Revenue account the amount that the adjustment indicated has been earned.
5.   An adjustment for a deferral can be reversed only if it increases a balance sheet account. This adjustment decreases an asset account.
6.   An accrual type adjustment can always be reversed. You can tell the adjusting entry is for an accrued expense because the debit is to an expense account and the credit is to a payable account.

EXERCISE 3-11

Purpose: (L.O. 9A) This exercise will give you practice in identifying adjusting entries that may be reversed.

Instructions
Refer to **Exercise 3-6** and the **Solution to Exercise 3-6**. Indicate the adjusting entries that can be reversed.

Solution to Exercise 3-11

Approach and Explanation: Think of the types of adjustments and whether they can be reversed. Accrual type adjusting entries can always be reversed. Therefore, items 5a and 7 can be reversed. Estimated items such as amortization of plant assets, the recognition of bad debts, and amortization of intangibles and discounts and premiums on receivables and payables should never be reversed. Therefore, items 3, 6, and 5b should **not** be reversed. Adjustments involving deferrals can be reversed **if** the original cash entry involved a temporary account (revenue or expense account) rather than a prepaid or unearned account (a permanent account) and the adjustment **increases** a prepaid expense or unearned revenue account. Therefore, item 2 **can be** reversed but items 1 and 4 should **not** be reversed.

ILLUSTRATION 3-4
REVERSING ENTRIES FOR ACCRUED EXPENSES
ILLUSTRATED AND COMPARISON OF
SYSTEM USING REVERSING ENTRIES WITH
SYSTEMS WHERE NO REVERSALS ARE USED (L.O. 5, 9A)

An entity can choose to use or not use reversing entries. The advantage of using reversing entries is that the reversal of an adjustment for accrued expense (or accrued revenue) facilitates the recording of the subsequent payment (or receipt) of cash. The subsequent payment (or receipt) can then be recorded to a temporary account rather than a permanent account.

When an entity chooses **not** to use a reversing entry for an adjustment for accrued expense (or accrued revenue) at the end of Year 1 and the entity wishes to record the subsequent payment (or receipt) of cash in Year 2 to a temporary account rather than a permanent account, the adjustment process at the end of Year 2 can accommodate the situation.

Assume the following data applies to GuardDog Corp.:
1. The company began operations in 2001.
2. During 2001, interest of $80,000 was paid.
3. At the end of 2001, accrued interest on a note payable amounted to $5,500.
4. During 2002, interest of $50,000 was paid.
5. At the end of 2002, accrued interest amounted to $8,200.
6. During 2003, interest of $65,000 was paid.
7. At the end of 2003, accrued interest amounted to $3,000.

There are three paths the information could take through the accounting records. Regardless of the path taken, the true amount of expense incurred should be reported on the income statement each year, and the amount incurred but not paid should be reported on the balance sheet at the end of each period.

Examine each path below.

	Reversing entries	Payment entries recorded to
PATH A	Yes	temporary account
PATH B	No	permanent and temporary account
PATH C	No	temporary account

The individual effects that the above events have on the accounts, depending on the path chosen, are illustrated on the following pages. The description of the flow of data through the accounting records is organized into the following sections:

I. The journal entries required to reflect the transactions in the accounts in 2001 and 2002.
II. The postings of journal entries to T-accounts in 2001 and 2002.
III. The resulting account balances at the end of 2001 and 2002.

I. The journal entries required to reflect the transactions in the accounts in 2001 and 2002.

Date	EVENT	PATH A — Reversing entries are made. Payment entries are charged to temporary account (Interest Expense).	PATH B — Reversing entries are not made. Payment entries are allocated to a permanent account (Interest Payable) and to a temporary account (Interest Expense).	PATH C — Reversing entries are not made. Payment entries are charged to a permanent account (Interest Expense).
During 2001	(1) Paid $80,000 interest	Interest Expense 80,000 / Cash 80,000	Interest Expense 80,000 / Cash 80,000	Interest Expense 80,000 / Cash 80,000
12/31/02	(2) Adjusting entry—$5,500 accrued interest	Interest Expense 5,500 / Interest Payable 5,500	Interest Expense 5,500 / Interest Payable 5,500	Interest Expense 5,500 / Interest Payable (5,500)
12/31/02	(3) Closing entry	Income Summary 85,000 (85,500) / Interest Expense 85,000	Income Summary 85,000 (85,500) / Interest Expense 85,000	Income Summary 85,000 (85,500) / Interest Expense 85,000 (85,500)
1/1/02	(4) Reversing entry	Interest Payable 5,500 / Interest Expense 5,500	NONE	NONE
During 2002	(5) Paid $50,000 interest	Interest Expense 50,000 / Cash 50,000	Interest Payable 5,000 (5,500 ✓) / Interest Expense 44,500 / Cash 50,000	Interest Expense 50,000 / Cash 50,000
12/31/02	(6) Adjusting entry — $8,200 accrued interest	Interest Expense 8,200 / Interest Payable 8,200	Interest Expense 8,200 / Interest Payable 8,200	Interest Expense 2,700 / Interest Payable (2,700)
12/31/02	(7) Closing entry	Income Summary 52,700 / Interest Expense 52,700	Income Summary 52,700 (58,200) / Interest Expense 52,700 (58,200)	Income Summary 52,700 / Interest Expense 52,700
1/1/03	(8) Reversing entry	Interest Expense 8,200 / Interest Payable 8,200	NONE	NONE
During 2003	(9) Paid $65,000 interest	Interest Expense 65,000 / Cash 65,000	Interest Payable 8,200 / Interest Expense 56,800 / Cash 65,000	Interest Expense 65,000 / Cash 65,000
12/31/03	(10) Adjusting entry — $3,000 accrued interest	Interest Expense 3,000 / Interest Payable 3,000	Interest Expense 3,000 / Interest Payable 3,000	Interest Expense 5,200 / Interest Payable 5,200
12/31/03	(11) Closing entry	Income Summary 59,800 / Interest Expense 59,800	Income Summary 59,800 / Interest Expense 59,800	Income Summary 59,800 / Interest Expense 59,800

(handwritten notes: "temporary account"; "correcting permanent account to correct balance – common method")

II. The postings of journal entries to T-accounts in 2001 and 2002.

	PATH A		PATH B		PATH C	
	Reversing entries are made.		Reversing entries are **not** made.		Reversing entries are **not** made.	
	Payment entries are charged to **temporary** account (Interest Expense).		Payment entries are allocated to a **permanent** account (Interest Payable) **and** to a **temporary** account (Interest Expense).		Payment entries are charged to a **temporary** account (Interest Expense).	
The T-accounts would appear as follows:	Interest Expense	Interest Payable	Interest Expense	Interest Payable	Interest Expense	Interest Payable
(1) During 2001	80,000		80,000		80,000	
(2) 12/31/01 Adj.	5,500	5,500	5,500	5,500	5,500	5,500
Balances 12/31/01	85,500	5,500	85,500	5,500	85,500	5,500
(3) 12/31/01 Closing	85,500		85,000		85,000	
(4) 1/1/02 Reversing	5,500	5,500				
(5) During 2002	50,000		44,500	5,500	50,000	
(6) 12/31/02 Adj.	8,200	8,200	8,200	8,200	2,700	2,700
Balances 12/31/02	52,700	8,200	52,700	8,200	52,700	8,200
(7) 12/31/02 Closing	52,700		52,700		52,700	
(8) 1/1/03 Reversing	8,200	8,200				
(9) During 2003	65,000		56,800	8,200	65,000	
(10) 12/31/03 Adj.	3,000	3,000	3,000	3,000	5,200	5,200
Balances 12/31/03	59,800	3,000		59,800		
(11) 12/31/03 Closing	59,800		59,800		5,200	

III. The account balances resulting at the end of 2001 and 2002.

AMOUNT OF ITEM	PATH A	PATH B	PATH C
Interest Expense on Income Statement for year ending Dec. 31, 2001	$85,500	$85,500	$85,500
Interest Payable on Balance Sheet at December 31, 2001	$ 5,500	$ 5,500	$ 5,500
Interest paid on Statement of Cash Flows for year ending Dec. 31, 2001	$80,000	$80,000	$80,000
Interest Expense on Income Statement for year ending Dec. 31, 2002	$52,700	$52,700	$52,700
Interest Payable on Balance Sheet at Dec. 31, 2002	$ 8,200	$ 8,200	$ 8,200
Interest paid on Statement of Cash Flows for year ending Dec. 31, 2002	$50,000	$50,000	$50,000
Interest Expense on Income Statement for year ending Dec. 31, 2003	$59,800	$59,800	$59,800
Interest Payable on Balance Sheet at Dec. 31, 2003	$ 3,000	$ 3,000	$ 3,000
Interest paid on Statement of Cash Flows for year ending Dec. 31, 2003	$65,000	$65,000	$65,000

ILLUSTRATION 3-5
REVERSING ENTRIES (COMPARISON OF SYSTEM USING REVERSING ENTRIES WITH SYSTEMS WHERE NO REVERSALS ARE USED) (L.0.8)

JOURNAL ENTRIES	Accounting System Where Reversing Entries ARE Used	Accounting System Where Reversing Entries are NOT Used

(1) During 2001	(1) Interest Expense 80,000
	      Cash 80,000
		(1) Interest Expense
		      Cash

(2) 12/31/01 Adjusting	(2) Interest Expense 5,500
	      Interest Payable 5,500
		(2) Interest Expense
		      Interest Payable

(3) 12/31/01 Closing	(3) Income Summary 85,500
	      Interest Expense 85,500
		(3) Income Summary
		      Interest Expense

(4) 1/1/02 Reversing	(4) Interest Payable 5,500 Interest Expense 5,500	(4) No entry

(5) 1/1/02 Payment	(5) Interest Expense 6,000
	      Cash 6,000
		(5) Interest Expense
		      Interest Payable
		      Cash

LEDGER ACCOUNT POSTINGS	Interest Expense		Interest Payable	Interest Expense	
(1) During 2001	80,000			80,000	
(2) 12/31/01 Adjusting	5,500		5,500	5,500	
(3) 12/31/01 Closing		85,000			85,500
(4) 1/1/02 Reversing		5,500	5,500		
(5) 1/1/02 Payment	6,000			500	

FINANCIAL STATEMENTS

Interest Expense for the year 2001	$85,500
Interest Paid in 2001	$80,000
Balance of Interest Payable at close of business on 12/31/01	$5,500
Interest Expense for the day 1/1/02	$ 500
Balance of Interest Payable at close of business on 1/1/02	$ 0

ANALYSIS OF MULTIPLE-CHOICE TYPE QUESTIONS

QUESTION

1.   (L.O. 1) Which of the following is a temporary account?
      a.   Prepaid Insurance
      b.   Unearned Revenue
      c.   Insurance Expense
      d.   Interest Receivable

Approach and Explanation: Read the question. Before looking at the answer selections, write down the meaning of the term "temporary account." Then answer "true" or "false" as you ask whether each answer selection is a temporary account. A temporary account is an account whose balance is closed at the end of an accounting period. Revenue and expense accounts are closed; permanent accounts (including asset and liability accounts) are never closed. Prepaid Insurance and Interest Receivable are asset accounts. Unearned Revenue is a liability account. Insurance Expense is a temporary account. (Solution = c.)

QUESTION

2.   (L.O. 4) Which of the following errors will cause an imbalance in the trial balance?
      a.   Omission of a transaction in the journal.
      b.   Posting an entire journal entry twice to the ledger.
      c.   Posting a credit of $720 to Accounts Payable as a credit of $720 to Accounts Receivable.
      d.   Listing the balance of an account with a debit balance in the credit column of the trial balance.

Approach and Explanation: Analyse each error (answer selection) and write down whether or not the error will cause the trial balance to be out of balance. Look for the selection that will cause an imbalance (selection "d"). Selections "a," "b," and "c" do not cause an imbalance in the trial balance. (Solution = d.)

QUESTION

3.   (L.O. 5) Which of the following statements is associated with the accrual basis of accounting?
      a.   The timing of cash receipts and disbursements is emphasized.
      b.   A minimum amount of record keeping is required.
      c.   This method is used less frequently by businesses than the cash method of accounting.
      d.   Revenues are recognized in the period they are earned, regardless of the time period the cash is received.

Approach and Explanation: Mentally define the accrual basis of accounting. Write down the key words and phrases of your definition. Compare each answer selection with your definition and choose the one that best matches. Using the **accrual basis of accounting**, events that change a company's financial statements are recorded in the periods in which the events occur. Thus, revenues are recognized in the period in which they are earned, and expenses are recognized in the period in which they are incurred, regardless of when the related cash is received or paid. Answer selections "a" and "b" refer to the cash basis of accounting that is not GAAP. (Solution = d.)

QUESTION

4.   (L.O. 5) An accrued expense is an expense that:
a.   has been incurred but has not been paid.
b.   has been paid but has not been incurred.
c.   has been incurred for which payment is to be made in installments.
d.   will never be paid.

Approach and Explanation: Write down a definition for accrued expense. Compare each answer selection with your definition and choose the best match. Expenses may be paid for in the same period in which they are incurred or they may be paid for in the period before or in the period after the one in which they are incurred. An **accrued expense** refers to an expense that has been incurred but has not yet been paid. It will be paid for in a period subsequent to the period in which it was incurred. (Solution = a.)

QUESTION

5.   (L.O. 5) In reviewing some adjusting entries, you observe an entry which contains a debit to Prepaid Insurance and a credit to Insurance Expense. The purpose of this journal entry is to record a(n):
a.   accrued expense.
b.   deferred expense.
c.   expired cost.
d.   prepaid revenue.

Approach and Explanation: Write down the entry so you can see what the entry does. Notice the entry records a prepaid expense (an asset). Then examine each answer selection one at a time. A debit to Prepaid Insurance records an increase in a prepaid expense. A prepaid expense is an expense that has been paid but has not been incurred. Another name for a prepaid expense is deferred expense. A deferred expense is an expense whose recognition is being deferred (put off) until a future period. An accrued expense is an expense incurred, but not paid. An expired cost is an expense or a loss. Prepaid revenue is a bad term for unearned revenue (or deferred revenue). (Solution = b.)

QUESTION

6.   (L.O. 5) An adjusting entry to record an accrued expense involves a debit to a(an):
a.   expense account and a credit to a prepaid account.
b.   expense account and a credit to Cash.
c.   expense account and a credit to a liability account.
d.   liability account and a credit to an expense account.

Approach and Explanation: Write down a definition for accrued expense and the types of accounts involved in an adjusting entry to accrue an expense. Find the answer selection that describes your entry.

Dr.   Expenses
    Cr.   Liabilities

Notice the logic of the entry. An **accrued expense** is an expense incurred but not yet paid. Thus, you record the incurrence by increasing an expense account and you record the "not paid" aspect by increasing a liability account. (Solution = c.)

QUESTION

7.   (L.O. 5) The failure to properly record an adjusting entry to accrue an expense will result in an:

    a.   understatement of expenses and an understatement of liabilities.
    b.   understatement of expenses and an overstatement of liabilities.
    c.   understatement of expenses and an overstatement of assets.
    d.   overstatement of expenses and an understatement of assets.

Approach and Explanation: Write down the adjusting entry to record an accrued expense. Analyse the effects of the entry. This will help you to determine the effects of the failure to properly make that entry. (Solution = a.)

Dr.	Expenses	xx	
Cr.	Liabilities		xx

This entry increases expenses and liabilities. Therefore, the failure to make this entry would result in an understatement of expenses and an understatement of liabilities.

QUESTION

8.   (L.O. 5) Which of the following properly describes a prepayment for which an adjusting entry will typically have to be made at a future date?

    a.   Cash is received after revenue is earned.
    b.   Cash is received before revenue is earned.
    c.   Cash is paid after expense is incurred.
    d.   Cash is paid in the same time period that an expense is incurred.

Approach and Explanation: Think about the nature of a prepayments and the relative timing of revenue or expense recognition and the related cash flow. **Prepayments** result from cash flows that occur **before** expense or revenue recognition. That is, cash is paid for expenses that apply to more than one accounting period or cash is received for revenue that applies to more than one accounting period. The portion of the expense that applies to future periods is deferred by reporting a prepaid expense (asset) or the portion of the revenue that applies to future periods is deferred by reporting unearned revenue (liability) on the balance sheet.

Accruals result from cash flows that occur **after** expense or revenue recognition. That is, cash is to be paid or received in a future accounting period for an expense incurred or a revenue earned in the current period. Items a. and c. above are accrual situations. Item d. is neither an accrual or deferral situation. (Solution = b.)

QUESTION

9.   (L.O. 5) An adjusting entry to allocate a previously recorded asset to expense involves a debit to an:

    a.   asset account and a credit to Cash.
    b.   expense account and a credit to Cash.
    c.   expense account and a credit to an asset account.
    d.   asset account and a credit to an expense account.

Approach and Explanation: Write down the sketch of an adjusting entry to transfer an asset to expense. Compare each answer selection with your entry and choose the one that matches.

        Dr.   Expenses

             Cr.   Assets

(Solution = c.)

QUESTION

10.   (L.O. 5) Which of the following adjusting entries will cause an increase in revenues and a decrease in liabilities?
    a.   Entry to record an accrued expense.
    b.   Entry to record an accrued revenue.
    c.   Entry to record the consumed portion of an expense paid in advance and initially recorded as an asset.
    d.   Entry to record the earned portion of revenue received in advance and initially recorded as unearned revenue.

Approach and Explanation: For each answer selection, write down the sketch of the adjusting entry described and the effects of each half of the entry. Compare the stem of the question with your analyses to determine the correct answer. (Solution = d.)

The entry to record an accrued expense:
        Dr.   Expenses
            Cr.   Liabilities
The effects of the entry are to increase expenses and to increase liabilities.

The entry to record an accrued revenue:
        Dr.   Assets
            Cr.   Revenues
The effects of the entry are to increase assets and to increase revenues.

The entry to record the consumed portion of a prepaid expense initially recorded as an asset is:
        Dr.   Expenses
            Cr.   Assets
The effects of the entry are to increase expenses and to decrease assets.

The entry to record the earned portion of unearned revenue initially recorded as a liability is:
        Dr.   Liabilities
            Cr.   Revenues
The effects of the entry are to decrease liabilities and to increase revenues.

QUESTION

11.   (L.O. 5) The Office Supplies on Hand account had a balance at the beginning of year 3 of $1,600. Payments for acquisitions of office supplies during year 3 amounted to $10,000 and were recorded by a debit to the asset account. A physical count at the end of year 3 revealed supplies costing $1,900 were on hand. The required adjusting entry at the end of year 3 will include a debit to:

a.   Office Supplies Expense for $300.
b.   Office Supplies on Hand for $300.
c.   Office Supplies Expense for $9,700.
d.   Office Supplies on Hand for $1,900.

Approach and Explanation: Draw T-accounts. Enter the data given and solve for the adjusting entry. Compare each alternative answer to the adjusting entry you have sketched in the accounts. (Solution = c.)

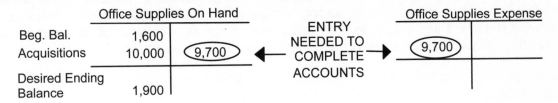

QUESTION

12.   (L.O. 5) The book value of a piece of equipment is the:

a.   original cost of the equipment.
b.   current replacement cost of the used equipment.
c.   current market value of the used equipment.
d.   difference between the original cost of the equipment and its related accumulated amortization.

Explanation: Equipment benefits the operations of several accounting periods; thus, in compliance with the matching principle, a portion of the cost of a long-lived asset should be reported as an expense during each period of the asset's useful life. Amortization is the process of allocating the cost of an asset to expense over its useful life in a rational and systematic manner. The annual charge for amortization is recorded by a debit to Amortization Expense and a credit to Accumulated Amortization. The Accumulated Amortization—Office Equipment is a contra asset account and reflects the total amortization to date. The difference between the balance in the Equipment account (the original cost of the asset) and balance in the related Accumulated Amortization account at any given point in time represents the book value (often called carrying value or carrying amount) of the equipment. This amount will rarely equal the asset's current market value. (Solution = d.)

QUESTION

13.   (L.O. 6) The purpose of recording closing entries is to:
   a.   reduce the number of temporary accounts.
   b.   enable the accountant to prepare financial statements at the end of a accounting period.
   c.   prepare revenue and expense accounts for the recording of the next period' revenues and expenses.
   d.   establish new balances in some asset and liability accounts.

Approach and Explanation: Cover up the answer selections while you read the question. Attempt to complete the statement started by the stem of the question. Think about when closing entries are made and what they do. Then go through the selections using a process of elimination approach Closing entries clear out the balances of revenue and expense accounts so that the accounts are ready to accumulate data for a new accounting period. Selection "c" is correct. Selection "a" is incorrect; closing entries do not change the number of accounts. Selection "b" is incorrect; financial statements are prepared before closing entries are done. If closing entries were posted first, the income statement would include nothing but zero amounts. Selection "d" is incorrect, closing entries will affect only temporary accounts and owners' equity. (Solution = c.)

QUESTION

14.   (L.O. 9A) The Office Supplies on Hand account had a balance at the beginning of year 3 of $1,600. Payments for acquisitions of office supplies during year 3 amounted to $10,000 and were recorded as expense. A physical count at the end of year 3 revealed supplies costing $1,900 were on hand. Reversing entries are used by this company. The required adjusting entry at the end of year 3 will include a debit to:
   a.   Office Supplies Expense for $300.
   b.   Office Supplies on Hand for $300.
   c.   Office Supplies Expense for $9,700.
   d.   Office Supplies on Hand for $1,900.

Approach and Explanation: Draw T-accounts. Enter the data given and solve for the adjusting entry. Compare each alternative answer to the adjusting entry you have sketched in the accounts (Solution = d.)

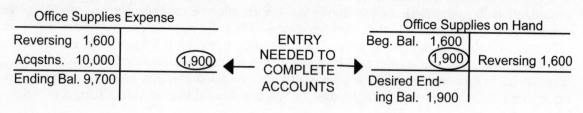

QUESTION

15.   (L.O. 9A) The Office Supplies on Hand account had a balance at the beginning of year 3 of $1,600. Payments for purchases of office supplies during year 3 amounted to $10,000 and were recorded by a debit to an expense account. A physical count at the end of year 3 revealed supplies costing $1,900 were on hand. Reversing entries are **not** used by this company. The required adjusting entry at the end of year 3 will include a debit to:

   a.   Office Supplies Expense for $300.
   b.   Office Supplies on Hand for $300.
   c.   Office Supplies Expense for $9,700.
   d.   Office Supplies on Hand for $1,900.
   e.   None of the above.

Approach and Explanation: Draw T-accounts. Enter the data given and solve for the adjusting entry. Compare each alternative answer to the adjusting entry you have sketched in the accounts. (Solution = b.)

CHAPTER 4

Reporting Financial Performance

OVERVIEW

An income statement reports on the results of operations of an entity for a period of time. It is important to classify revenues, expenses, gains, and losses properly on the income statement. In this chapter, we discuss the income statement classifications and the content of the statement of retained earnings along with related disclosure issues such as irregular items and earnings per share. It is imperative that charges and credits that represent elements of income determination be properly reflected in the financial statements. Errors in the determination of income cause errors on the income statement, statement of retained earnings, and balance sheet.

SUMMARY OF LEARNING OBJECTIVES

1.   **Identify the uses and limitations of an income statement.** The income statement provides investors and creditors with information that helps them predict the amount, timing and uncertainty of future cash flows. Also, the income statement helps users determine the risk (level of uncertainty) of not achieving particular cash flows. The limitations of an income statement are: (1) the income statement does not include many items that contribute to general growth and well-being of an enterprise; and (2) income numbers are often affected by the accounting methods used; and (3) income measures are subject to estimates.

     The **transaction approach** focuses on the activities that have occurred during a given period; instead of presenting only a net change, it discloses the components of the change. The transaction approach to income measurement requires the use of revenue, expense, loss, and gain accounts.

2.   **Prepare a single-step income statement.** In a **single-step income statement**, just two groupings exist: revenues and expenses. Expenses are deducted from revenues to arrive at net income or net loss—a single subtraction. Frequently, income tax is reported separately as the last item before net income to indicate its relationship to income before income tax.

3.   **Prepare a multiple-step income statement.** A **multiple-step income statement** shows two further classifications: (1) a separation of operating results from those obtained through the subordinate or nonoperating activities of the company; and (2) a classification of expenses by functions, such as merchandising or manufacturing, selling, and administration.

4.   **Explain how irregular items are reported.** Irregular gains or losses or nonrecurring items are generally closed to Income Summary and are included in the income statement. These are treated in the income statement as follows: (1) Discontinued operations of a segment of a business is classified as a separate item, after continuing operations; (2) The unusual, material, nonrecurring items that are significantly different from the typical or customary business activities are shown in a separate section for "extraordinary items," below discontinued operations; (3) Other items of a material amount that are of an unusual or nonrecurring nature and are not considered extraordinary are separately disclosed and are included as part of continuing operations.

5.   **Measure and report gains and losses from discontinued operations.** The gain or loss on disposal of a segment involves the sum of: (1) income or loss from operations to the measurement date, and (2) the gain or loss on disposal of the business segment (operating incomes or losses during the phase-out period and the gain or loss on the sale of the net assets). These two items are reported separately net of tax among the irregular items in the income statement.

6.   **Explain intraperiod tax allocation.** The tax expense for the year should be related, where possible, to specific items on the income statement to provide a more informative disclosure to statement users. This procedure is called **intraperiod tax allocation**, that is, allocation within a period. Its main purpose is to relate the income tax expense for the fiscal period to the following items that affect the amount of the tax provisions: (1) income from continuing operations, (2) discontinued operations, and (3) extraordinary items.

7.   **Explain where earnings per share information is reported.** Because of the inherent dangers of focusing attention solely on earnings per share, the profession concluded that earnings per share must be disclosed on the face of the income statement. A company that reports a discontinued operation, an extraordinary item, or the cumulative effect of a change in accounting principle, must report per share amounts for these line items either on the face of the income statement or in the notes to financial statements.

8.   **Prepare a retained earnings statement.** The retained earnings statement should disclose net income (loss), dividends, prior period adjustments, and transfers to and from retained earnings (appropriations).

TIPS ON CHAPTER TOPICS

TIP: The **income statement** or **statement of income** is often referred to as the statement of operations or the operating statement because it reports on the results of operations for a period of time. Other names include the "earnings statement," "statement of earnings," and "profit and loss statement" (or "P&L statement").

TIP: The income statement is often referred to as a link between balance sheets because it explains one major reason why the balance of owners' equity changed during the period. Owners' equity (net assets) at the beginning of the period can be reconciled with ending owners' equity as follows:

$$
\begin{array}{ll}
& \text{Owners' equity at the beginning of the period} \\
+ & \text{Additional owner investments during the period} \\
- & \text{Owner withdrawals during the period} \\
\underline{+/-} & \underline{\text{Results of operations for the period (net income or net loss)}} \\
= & \text{Owners' equity at the end of the period}
\end{array}
$$

TIP: The income statement is used by investors and creditors to (1) evaluate the enterprise's past performance; (2) provide a basis for predicting future performance; and (3) help assess the risk or uncertainty of achieving future cash flows.

TIP: The income statement is limited in its usefulness by the accounting policy choices, estimations and assumptions, which are reflected in the numbers.

TIP: The higher the quality of information, the more useful the income statement is to users. High quality earnings are reflected in choice of accounting policies and estimations that require less judgement, and reduce bias. Cash flows that are more closely correlated with the event in the same time period and which have more predictive and feedback value and represent economic reality all increase the quality of earnings.

TIP: A **contra revenue** item has the same effect on net income as that of an expense; it decreases net income. Contra revenue accounts include Sales Discounts and Sales Returns and Allowances.

TIP: It is often helpful to form an acronym when attempting to remember a list of items. In looking at the order of the things that can appear after the "Income from Continuing Operations" line on an income statement, you might come up with **DEC** to help you to remember the exact order of these items:
    Discontinued operations
    Extraordinary items
    Cumulative effect of changes in accounting principles

TIP: The income tax consequences of all items appearing above the line "Income from continuing operations before income taxes" are summarized in the line "Income taxes." Revenues cause an increase in income taxes and expenses cause a decrease in income taxes. The income tax consequences of items appearing below the "income from continuing operations" line are reported right along with the items (hence, these items are reported "net of tax"). This procedure of allocating income taxes within a period is referred to as **intraperiod tax allocation**.

TIP: An extraordinary item is reported "net of tax" by deducting the tax effect from the related gain or loss. For example, if the tax rate is 30%, an extraordinary gain of $400,000 will be reported at $280,000 net of tax. Likewise, an extraordinary loss of $400,000 will be reported at $280,000 net of tax. The gain situation increases net income, whereas the loss reduces it.

TIP: Corrections for errors in the reporting of revenues and expenses in prior periods are accounted for as prior period adjustments. A **prior period adjustment** is reported as an adjustment (debit or credit, whichever is applicable) to the opening balance of Retained Earnings on the retained earnings statement for the current period (period in which the adjustment is made) and is shown net of any related income tax effect.

TIP: Net income minus preferred stock dividend requirements (i.e., income applicable to common shareholders) is divided by the weighted average of common stock shares outstanding to arrive at **earnings per share (EPS)**. This is a key ratio in financial analysis and must be disclosed on the face of the income statement. A per share amount must **always** be disclosed for "net income." Also, the following holds true:
(1)   A company that reports discontinued operations must report a per share amount for that item.
(2)   A company that reports an extraordinary item must report a per share amount for the extraordinary item.
(3)   A company that reports a change in accounting principle must report a per share amount for the cumulative effect of a change in accounting principle.

TIP: In the EPS calculation, preferred dividends are deducted from net income if they were declared; however, if the preferred share is cumulative, the preferred dividend preference for the current period is deducted whether or not the dividends were declared. Dividends declared on common share have no effect on the EPS calculation.

EXERCISE 4-1

Purpose: (L.O. 1) This exercise reviews the basic accounting formula (Assets = Liabilities + Owners' Equity) and the connection between the income statement and the balance sheet (which is a change in owners' equity due to the net income or net loss for the period).

The following data were extracted from the records of Dora Loesing's Cookies, a sole proprietorship:

Total assets, beginning of the period	$100,000	
Total liabilities, beginning of the period		36,000
Owner withdrawals during the period	30,000	
Total assets, end of the period		108,000
Total liabilities, end of the period		38,000
Owner's contributions during the period		10,000

Instructions
Calculate the amount of net income (or loss) for the period. Show calculations.

Solution to Exercise 4-1

Beginning owner's equity	$ 64,000[a]
Additional owner contributions	10,000
Owner withdrawals during the period	(30,000)
Subtotal	44,000
Net income (loss) for the period	+ x
Ending owner's equity	$ 70,000[b]

Solving for X, net income	=	$ 26,000

[a]$A = L + OE$
$\$100,000 = \$36,000 + ?$
Beginning owner's equity = $64,000

[b]$A = L + OE$
$\$108,000 = \$38,000 + ?$
Ending owner's equity = $70,000

Approach: The question asks you to solve for net income; however, no information is given regarding revenues and expenses for the period. Only balance sheet data and transactions affecting owner's equity are given. Net income (or net loss) for a period is one reason for a change in the balance of owner's equity. Write down the items that reconcile the beginning owner's equity balance with the ending owner's equity balance, enter the amounts known, calculate beginning and ending owner's equity balances by use of the basic accounting equation, and then solve for the amount of net income. Recall that assets - liabilities = net assets; that is, assets - liabilities = owner's equity at a point in time.

TIP: The basic accounting equation $(A = L + OE)$ is applied at a specific point in time. When you have the facts for the equation components at two different points in time for the same entity (such as amounts as of the beginning of a year and amounts as of the end of a year), you can modify the basic accounting equation to reflect that total changes in assets equals total changes in liabilities + total changes in owners' equity. Using the symbol Δ to designate change, the following equation also holds true:
$$\Delta A = \Delta L + \Delta OE$$
        Reasons for changes in owners' equity include:
           (1)   additional owner investments,
           (2)   owner withdrawals, and
           (3)   results of operations (net income or net loss).

TIP: When using the **capital maintenance** (or **change in equity**) approach, the amount of owners' equity is determined at the beginning and at the end of the period (using the same valuation method). The difference between these two amounts, adjusted for owner withdrawals and additional owner investments during the same period, is the measure of net income for the period.

TIP: Net income (or net loss) is the change in owners' equity for a period of time, other than from capital transactions. Capital transactions are those that involve owners acting in their capacity of being owners of the entity.

ILLUSTRATION 4-1
ELEMENTS OF THE INCOME STATEMENT (L.O. 1)

REVENUES. Increases in economic resources either by way of inflows or enhancements of an entity's assets of an entity or settlement of liabilities resulting from its ordinary activities.

EXPENSES. Decreases in economic resources, either by outflows or reductions of assets or incurrence of liabilities, resulting from a entity's ordinary revenue-generating activities.

GAINS. Increases in equity (net assets) from peripheral or incidental transactions of an entity from all other transactions or events and circumstances affecting the entity during a period except those that result from revenues or investments by owners.

LOSSES. Decreases in equity (net assets) from peripheral or incidental transactions of an entity and from all other transactions and other events and circumstances affecting the entity during a period except those that result from expenses or distributions to owners. (*CICA Handbook*, Section 1000, pars. .37-.40.)

Revenues take many forms, such as sales revenue, fees earned, dividend income, and rents earned. Expenses also take many forms, such as cost of goods sold, rent, salaries, depreciation, interest, and taxes.

Revenues and gains are similar (they both increase net income), and expenses and losses are similar (they both decrease net income). However, these terms are dissimilar in the fact that they convey significantly different information about an enterprise's performance. Revenues and expenses result from an entity's ongoing major or central operations and activities—that is, from activities such as producing or delivering goods, rendering services, lending, insuring, investing, and financing. In contrast, gains and losses result from incidental or peripheral transactions of an enterprise with other entities and from other events and circumstances affecting it. Gains and losses often arise from the sale of investments; disposal of plant assets; settlement of liabilities for an amount other than their book value; and write-offs of assets due to obsolescence, casualty, or theft.

Revenues and expenses are commonly displayed as **gross** inflows or outflows of net assets; while gains and losses are usually displayed as **net** inflows or outflows. For example, assume a company buys an inventory item for $6,000, sells it for $10,000, and pays a sales representative a $1,000 commission. Further, the same company sells for $20,000 a plant asset with a book value (carrying value) of $15,000 and pays an outside agency $2,100 for finding the buyer. The various flows associated with the first transaction (the company's major activity or regular operations) will be reported gross on its income statement, and the various elements of the second transaction (a peripheral transaction) will be reported net. Assuming these were the only two transactions completed during the period and ignoring income taxes, the income statement would reflect the following:

Sales revenue	$ 10,000
Cost of goods sold expense	6,000
Gross profit	4,000
Selling expense (sales commission)	1,000
Income from operations	3,000
Gain on sale of plant asset	2,900[a]
Net income	$ 5,900

[a]$20,000 proceeds - $15,000 book value - $2,100 finders fee = $2,900 gain on sale.

TIP: Net income results from revenue, expense, gain, and loss transactions. These transactions are summarized in the income statement. This method of income measurement is called the **transaction approach** because it focuses on the income-related activities (broken down into completed transactions) that have occurred during the period.

TIP: Single-step income statement has only two groupings (Revenues and Expenses). It eliminates classification problems and is often used for simplicity.

EXERCISE 4-2

Purpose: (L.O.4) This exercise will help you to determine which type of business activities should be classified as regular (normal operations) and which are irregular (unusual or extraordinary)

From the following list of activities, determine whether this would be classified as regular business activities, unusual or extraordinary. Mark an **(x)** in the appropriate column:

	Continuing Operations	**Extraordinary**
1. Losses due to expropriation of assets in a foreign country		
2. Revenues from Vancouver Grizzlies selling pop and hot dogs		
3. Loss due to Hurricane at Jamaican subsidiary		
4. Loss due to Hurricane at Calgary subsidiary		
5. Loss of inventory at a warehouse due to flood in Halifax		
6. Toronto Maple Leafs selling hockey jerseys		
7. Loss due to power outage caused by severe ice-storm in Ottawa		
8. Gain from winning a lawsuit against a major competitor		
9. Loss due to a strike at a subsidiary		
10. Gain of $2,000,000 from winning the Lotto 6-49 jackpot from a ticket purchased with company funds		

Approach: Define each of the terms "continuing operations" and "extraordinary item". A continuing operation results from activities in the normal course of operations for an enterprise. This will differ from one enterprise to another in different industries. An extraordinary item must meet all three criteria (infrequent in nature, atypical of normal business activities and do not depend on decisions of management or owners).

1. Expropriation of assets does meet all three of the requirements of an extraordinary item.
2. Even though the Grizzlies are a basketball team, vending sales would be part of the normal operations of the organization.
3. Losses due to a Hurricane in Jamaica would be a fairly normal occurrence for the Caribbean and thus would be considered continuing operations. If the losses were severe, they may be classified as unusual in nature, but management was fully aware of the regular occurrence of Hurricanes in the Caribbean when they established the business there.
4. A Hurricane in Calgary however is not a regular occurrence and thus would be classified as an extraordinary event as this would not be anticipated by management as a regular occurrence.
5. The loss due to a flood would be determined as an extraordinary item depending on the regularity of flooding. If this were built on the flood plains of the Mississippi, it would be a normal occurrence and hence, continuing operations, but since this is not a regular occurrence in Halifax, it would be considered extraordinary.
6. The Toronto Maple Leafs are a hockey team, but it is management intention to make revenues selling Hockey Jerseys, thus this is considered regular income.

7. Again, the ice-storm is a situation which does occur in Ottawa. The severity of the storm and materiality of the losses would determine whether this is classified as unusual or extraordinary.

8. A gain from a lawsuit would be considered to be an unusual item. It is a result of normal business operations, but investors would want to know that this is not considered a normal earnings stream for the company and, thus it would be separated out on the income statement as unusual (depending on materiality).

9. A strike, unpleasant as it may be, is a normal occurrence in a business setting and thus would be considered to be continuing operations. The severity and materiality of losses occurring from the strike would need to be identified as to whether it is classified as unusual.

10. This, extraordinary as it may seem, would not be considered an extraordinary item. The definition of extraordinary requires the event not to be primarily on decisions made by management. Management, in this case purchased the ticket with the hope of winning, thus it is a result of a management action. It would be classified as unusual so as to not let investors think this will be a normal revenue stream for the company.

ILLUSTRATION 4-2
SECTIONS OF A MULTIPLE-STEP INCOME STATEMENT (L.O. 3)

1. **OPERATING SECTION.** A report of the revenues and expenses of the company's principal operations. (This section may or may not be presented on a departmental basis.)
   (a) **SALES OR REVENUE SECTION.** A subsection presenting sales, discounts, allowances, returns, and other related information. Its purpose is to arrive at the net amount of sales revenue.
   (b) **COST OF GOODS SOLD SECTION.** A subsection that shows the cost of goods that were sold to produce the sales.
   (c) **SELLING EXPENSES.** A subsection that lists expenses resulting from the company's efforts to make sales.
   (d) **ADMINISTRATIVE OR GENERAL EXPENSES.** A subsection reporting expenses of general administration.

2. **NONOPERATING SECTION.** A report of revenues and expenses resulting from secondary or auxiliary activities of the company. In addition, special gains and losses that are infrequent or unusual, but not both, are normally reported in this section. Generally these items break down into two main subsections:
   (a) **OTHER REVENUES AND GAINS.** A list of the revenues earned or gains incurred, generally net of related expenses, from nonoperating transactions.
   (b) **OTHER EXPENSES AND LOSSES.** A list of the expenses or losses incurred, generally net of any related incomes, from nonoperating transactions.

3. **INCOME TAXES.** A short section reporting federal and provincial taxes levied on income from continuing operations.

4. **DISCONTINUED OPERATIONS.** Material gains or losses resulting from the disposal of a segment of the business (net of tax).

5. **EXTRAORDINARY ITEMS.** Unusual and infrequent material gains and losses (net of tax).

6. **CUMULATIVE EFFECT OF A CHANGE IN ACCOUNTING PRINCIPLE (net of tax).**

7. **EARNINGS PER SHARE.**

EXERCISE 4-2

Purpose: (L.O. 2, 3, 7) This exercise will allow you to contrast the multiple-step format and the single-step format for the income statement.

The accountant for Bubble Bath Products, Inc. has compiled the following information from the company's records as a basis for an income statement for the year ended December 31, 2002. (There was no change during the year in the 12,000 shares of common shares outstanding.)

Net sales	$ 970,000
Amortization on plant assets (60% selling, 40% administrative)	70,000
Dividends declared	14,400
Rent revenue	30,000
Interest on notes payable	17,000
Market appreciation on land held as an investment	44,000
Merchandise purchases	421,000
Transportation-in—merchandise	37,000
Merchandise inventory, January 1, 2002	82,000
Merchandise inventory, December 31, 2002	81,000
Purchase returns and allowances	11,000
Wages and salaries—sales	95,000
Materials and supplies—sales	11,400
Income taxes	45,000
Wages and salaries—administrative	135,900
Other administrative expenses	46,700
Advertising expense	20,000
Express mail	6,000

Instructions
(a)   Prepare a multiple-step income statement.
(b)   Prepare a single-step income statement.

Solution to Exercise 4-2

(a)

Bubble Bath Products, Inc.
INCOME STATEMENT
For the Year Ending December 31, 2002

Sales Revenue
  Net sales revenue $970,000

Cost of Goods Sold
  Merchandise inventory, Jan. 1 $ 82,000
  Purchases $ 421,000
  Less purchase returns & allowances   11,000
  Net purchases   410,000
  Transportation-in   37,000   447,000
  Total merchandise available for sale   529,000
  Less merchandise inventory, Dec. 31   81,000
      Cost of goods sold   448,000

Gross profit   522,000

Operating Expenses
  Selling expenses
    Wages and salaries   95,000
    Advertising   20,000
    Materials and supplies   11,400
    Amortization (60% x $70,000)   42,000
    Express mail   6,000   174,400
  Administrative expenses
    Wages and salaries   135,900
    Amortization (40% x $70,000)   28,000
    Other administrative expenses   46,700   210,600   385,000

Income from operations   137,000

Other Revenues and Gains
  Rent revenue   30,000
                                                                               167,000

Other Expenses and Losses
  Interest expense   17,000

Income before taxes   150,000
    Income taxes   45,000
Net income $105,000

Earnings per share ($105,000 ÷ 12,000) $8.75

TIP:	Dividends declared do not appear on the income statement. They are a distribution of corporate income—**not** a determinant of net income. Increases in the market value of assets held (such as plant assets, inventory, and most investments) are not recognized in the accounts until they are realized through the sale of the assets. Hence, the market appreciation on the land held as an investment does **not** appear on the income statement.

(b)

Bubble Bath Products, Inc.
INCOME STATEMENT
For the Year Ending December 31, 2002

Revenues

Net sales	$ 970,000
Rent revenue	30,000
Total revenue	1,000,000

Expenses

Cost of goods sold	448,000
Selling expenses	174,400
Administrative expenses	210,600
Interest expense	17,000
Total expenses	850,000

Income before taxes	150,000
Income taxes	45,000
Net income	$ 105,000

Earnings per share	$8.75

TIP:	In the single-step income statement, just two groupings exist: revenues and expenses. Expenses are deducted from revenues to arrive at net income or loss. The expression "single-step" is derived from the single subtraction necessary to arrive at net income. Frequently, however, income taxes are reported separately to indicate their direct relationship to income before income taxes.
TIP:	In the multiple-step income statement, there are three major subtotals presented before arriving at net income. They are: net sales revenue, gross profit, and income from operations. These subtotals emphasize (1) a classification of expenses by function, such as merchandising or manufacturing (cost of goods sold), selling, and administration, and (2) a separation of operating and subordinate or nonoperating activities of the company. The "other revenues and gains" and "other expenses and losses" sections include (1) investing and financing revenues and expenses such as interest revenue, dividend revenue (from dividends received), and interest expense, and (2) the results of nonoperating items such as the sale of plant assets and investments.

TIP:	The nature of an entity's typical operations is critical in determining whether the results of a transaction should be classified as an operating or a nonoperating revenue, gain, expense, or loss. For example, consider rental activities. A business specializing in equipment rentals will classify rent revenue as an operating revenue. Whereas, a retail establishment that occasionally rents its temporarily idle assets to others will classify rent revenue as a nonoperating (other) revenue. For a second example, consider the sale of an investment. An investment dealer will report the revenue from a sale as an operating revenue. Whereas, a retail entity that occasionally sells an investment will report the difference between the proceeds from the sale and the investment's carrying value as a nonoperating gain or loss.
TIP:	There is no specific order in which the individual selling expenses and administrative expenses are to be listed in the multiple-step income statement. Very often, they appear in order of decreasing magnitude.
TIP:	Some accountants prefer to use a multiple-step income statement format because it discloses the amount of income from operations. Thus, by this disclosure, the difference between regular and irregular or incidental activities is highlighted. Irregular activities encompass transactions and other events that are derived from developments outside the normal operations of the business. Thus, they may not be expected to continue at the same level in future periods.
TIP:	Some investors prefer a multi-step income statement as it helps to identify specific types of revenues and expenses, which are primary or ancillary to normal business activities, as well as year over year comparisons. This helps determine repetitiveness and importance of earnings

EXERCISE 4-3

Purpose: (L.O. 2, 8) This exercise will give you practice in identifying components of net income and the order of items appearing on a single-step income statement and on a retained earnings statement.

Presented on the next page is the adjusted trial balance of the Tragically Hip Corporation at December 31, 2002. The account titles and balances are **not** in the customary order.

Tragically Hip Corporation
ADJUSTED TRIAL BALANCE
December 31, 2002

	Debits	Credits
Sales		$ 958,500
Notes Receivable	$ 80,000	
Investments	88,500	
Accounts Payable		51,000
Accumulated Amortization—Equipment		31,000
Sales Discounts	10,500	
Sales Returns	17,500	
Purchase Discounts		8,000
Cash	190,000	
Accounts Receivable	95,000	
Rent Revenue		14,000
Retained Earnings		240,000
Salaries Payable		22,000
Notes Payable		75,000
Common Shares, $15 par		300,000
Income Tax Expense	68,000	
Cash Dividends Declared	70,000	
Allowance for Doubtful Accounts		6,500
Supplies on Hand	11,000	
Freight-In	16,000	
Selling Expenses	212,000	
Administrative Expenses	114,000	
Land	65,000	
Equipment	130,000	
Merchandise Inventory	79,000	
Building	104,000	
Purchases	500,000	
Dividend Income		10,000
Loss on Sale of Investment	13,000	
Interest Revenue		9,000
Interest Expense	12,500	
Bonds Payable		100,000
Gain on Sale of Land		24,500
Accumulated Amortization—Building		26,500
Totals	$ 1,876,000	$ 1,876,000

The company uses the periodic inventory system. A physical count of inventory on December 31 resulted in an inventory amount of $100,000.

Instructions

(a) Prepare an income statement for the year ending December 31, 2002 using the single-step form. Assume that twenty thousand shares of common stock were outstanding the entire year.

(b) Prepare a retained earnings statement for the year ending December 31, 2002. Assume that the only changes in retained earnings during the current year were from net income and dividends.

Solution to Exercise 4-3

(a)

Tragically Hip Corporation
INCOME STATEMENT
For the Year Ended December 31, 2002

Revenues	
Net sales *	$ 930,500
Gain on sale of land	24,500
Rent revenue	14,000
Dividend income	10,000
Interest revenue	9,000
Total revenues	988,000
Expenses	
Cost of goods sold**	487,000
Selling expenses	212,000
Administrative expenses	114,000
Loss on sale of investment	13,000
Interest expense	12,500
Total expenses	838,500
Income before taxes	149,500
Income taxes	68,000
Net income	$ 81,500
Earnings per common share ($81,500 ÷ 20,000)	$ 4.08

*Net sales:				
Sales			$ 958,500	
Less:	Sales discounts	$ 10,500		
	Sales returns	17,500	28,000	
	Net sales		$ 930,500	

**Cost of goods sold:			
Merchandise inventory, Jan. 1		$ 79,000	
Purchases	$ 500,000		
Less purchase discounts	8,000		
Net purchases		492,000	
Add freight-in		16,000	
Merchandise available for sale		587,000	
Less merchandise inventory, Dec. 31		100,000	
Cost of merchandise sold		$ 487,000	

TIP: The solution presented here reports income taxes separately as the last item before net income to indicate their relationship to income before taxes. It is acceptable to list the income taxes in the expenses classification and omit the subtotal "income before taxes."

(b)

Tragically Hip Corporation
RETAINED EARNINGS STATEMENT
For the Year Ended December 31, 2002

Balance, January 1	$240,000
Add: Net income	81,500
	321,500
Less: Cash dividends declared	70,000
Balance, December 31	$251,500

Approach:

(1)   Go through the adjusted trial balance and lightly cross through any account title that does **not** pertain to the calculation of net income. With the exception of the balance of Merchandise Inventory (which is used to calculate cost of goods sold when a periodic inventory system is in use), balance sheet account balances are not used in determining net income.

(2)   Calculate intermediate subtotals for items such as (a) net sales, (b) cost of goods sold, (c) selling expenses, and (d) administrative expenses. Show your calculations for these subtotals. (In this particular exercise, selling expenses and administrative expenses are already summarized.)

(3)   Identify revenue and gain items.

(4)   Identify expense and loss items.

(5)   Identify income taxes for the period.

(6)   Identify any discontinued operations, extraordinary items, and cumulative effect on prior periods of a change in accounting principle (none of these appear in this exercise).

(7)   Calculate net income.

(8)   Calculate earnings per share.

(9)   Identify the retained earnings balance at the beginning of the period.

(10)   Include any prior period adjustments on the statement of retained earnings (none are identified in this exercise).

(11)   Add net income for the period.

(12)   Deduct dividends declared.

(13)   Arrive at the retained earnings balance at the end of the period.

> **TIP:**   The account balances in the adjusted trial balance that are **not** used for the solution requested are as follows: Notes Receivable, Investments, Accounts Payable, Accumulated Amortization—Equipment, Cash, Accounts Receivable, Salaries Payable, Notes Payable, Common Shares, Allowance for Doubtful Accounts, Supplies on Hand, Land, Equipment, Building, Bonds Payable, and Accumulated Amortization—Building.

EXERCISE 4-4

Purpose:　(L.O. 3, 4, 6, 7, 8) This exercise is designed to give you practice in preparing a condensed multiple-step income statement and a retained earnings statement when an extraordinary item and a change in accounting principle are to be reported.

Presented below is information related to Smith Corp., for the year 2002.

Net sales	$ 650,000
Cost of goods sold	400,000
Selling expenses	32,000
Administrative expenses	24,000
Dividend revenue	10,000
Interest revenue	7,000
Interest expense	15,000
Write-off of goodwill due to impairment	25,000
Amortization expense omitted in 2000	35,000
Uninsured loss due to flood (unusual and infrequent)	60,000
Dividends declared	42,000
Retained earnings at December 31, 2001	1,800,000
Cumulative effect on prior years of change in accounting principle (credit)	75,000
Tax rate of 30% on all items	

Instructions

(a)　Prepare a multiple-step income statement for 2002. Assume that 50,000 common shares were outstanding during 2002.

(b)　Prepare a retained earnings statement for 2002.

Solution to Exercise 4-4

(a)

Smith Corp.
INCOME STATEMENT
For the Year Ended December 31, 2002

Net sales		$ 650,000
Cost of goods sold		400,000
Gross profit		250,000
Operating expenses		
Selling expenses	$ 32,000	
Administrative expenses	24,000	56,000
Income from operations		194,000
Other revenues and gains		
Dividend revenue	10,000	
Interest revenue	7,000	17,000
		211,000
Other expenses and losses		
Interest expense	15,000	
Loss due to write-off of goodwill	25,000	40,000
Income before taxes and extraordinary item and		
cumulative effect of change in accounting principle		171,000
Income taxes		51,300
Income before extraordinary item and cumulative		
effect of change in accounting principle		119,700
Extraordinary item—loss from flood	60,000	
Less applicable income tax effect	18,000	42,000
Cumulative effect on prior years of change in		
accounting principle	75,000	
Less applicable income tax effect	22,500	52,500
Net income		$ 130,200

Per common share:	
Income before extraordinary item and cumulative effect	
of change in accounting principle ($119,700 ÷ 50,000)	$2.39
Extraordinary item (net of tax) ($42,000 ÷ 50,000)	(.84)
Cumulative effect of accounting change (net of tax)	
($52,500 ÷ 50,000)	1.05
Net income ($130,200 ÷ 50,000)	$2.60

> **TIP:** The total income taxes pertaining to 2002 for this company was $33,300. This amount resulted from a tax bill of $51,300 that relates to the tax consequences of all items reportable on the 2002 tax return **before** considering the casualty loss of $60,000. This casualty loss caused a tax savings of $18,000. Because the casualty loss is reported as an extraordinary item on the income statement, the requirement for a net-of-tax presentation calls for the $18,000 tax reduction to be reported along with the extraordinary loss, leaving income taxes of $51,300 to be matched with income before extraordinary items. The income tax effect of the accounting change involves deferred income taxes, which are discussed in Chapter 20.
>
> **TIP:** In this case, the change in accounting principle caused an increase in the reported amount of net income for 2002 (because it was a credit). Sometimes the cumulative effect of a change in accounting principle is a charge (debit) to the current income statement which reduces net income.

(b)

Smith Corp.
RETAINED EARNINGS STATEMENT
For the Year Ended December 31, 2002

Retained earnings, Jan. 1, 2002, as previously reported		$ 1,800,000
Correction of an error in amortization in prior period		
(net of $10,500 income tax effect)*	(24,500)	
Adjusted balance of retained earnings at Jan. 1, 2002		1,775,500
Net income		130,200
		1,905,700
Dividends declared		42,000
Retained earnings, December 31, 2002		$ 1,863,700

* Omitted Amortization	(35,000)
less: tax savings (30%)	10,500
net correction to retained earnings	(24,500)

ILLUSTRATION 4-3
TREATMENT OF IRREGULAR ITEMS (L.O. 4)

1. **DISCONTINUED OPERATIONS.** The (1) results of operations (income or loss) of a segment of business that has been or will be disposed of, and (2) gain or loss on disposal of the discontinued segment are reported in a separate income statement category called "Discontinued operations." This category appears **after** continuing operations but **before** extraordinary items. Each of the possible two components of this category is reported net of the related income tax effect.

2. **EXTRAORDINARY ITEMS.** Extraordinary items are reported individually in a separate category (immediately after discontinued operations, if any) net of any related income tax effect. Extraordinary items are defined as nonrecurring (infrequent) material items that differ significantly from the entity's typical business activities. In addition to being material in amount, a transaction or event must meet **all three** of the following criteria to be classified as extraordinary:
   (a) **INFREQUENCY OF OCCURRENCE.** The underlying event or transaction should be of a type that would not reasonably be expected to recur in the foreseeable future, taking into account the environment in which the entity operates.
   (b) **UNUSUAL NATURE.** The underlying event or transaction should possess a high degree of abnormality and be of a type clearly unrelated to, or only incidentally related to, the ordinary and typical activities of the entity, taking into account the environment in which the entity operates.
   (c) **DETERMINATION BY MANAGEMENT.** The underlying event or transaction are **not** the result of actions or decisions taken by management or owners.

   Examples of items that are **not** classified as extraordinary:
   (a) Write down or write off of receivables, inventories, equipment leased to others, deferred research and development costs, or other intangible assets.
   (b) Gains or losses from exchange or translation of foreign currencies, including those relating to major devaluations and revaluations.
   (c) Gains or losses on disposal of a segment of a business.
   (d) Other gains or losses from sale or abandonment of property, plant, or equipment used in the business.
   (e) Effects of a strike, including those against competitors and major suppliers.
   (f) Adjustment of accruals on long-term contracts.

   Examples of items that **are** classified as extraordinary:
   An event or transaction that clearly meets all criteria (unusual in nature and infrequent in occurrence and not the result of management or owner intervention) and gives rise to a gain or loss from the write down or write off of assets or to a gain or loss from disposal of assets and is a **direct result** of one of the following:
   (a) A **major casualty** (such as an earthquake, tornado, hurricane, flood, or hail storm).
   (b) An **expropriation** (such as the confiscation of assets by a government or the exercise of eminent domain or condemnation).
   (c) A **prohibition** under a newly enacted law or regulation.

ILLUSTRATION 4-3 (Continued)

> **TIP:** Material gains and losses from extinguishment of debt should be reported as extraordinary items even though these gains or losses often do not meet the normal two criteria.

3. **UNUSUAL GAINS AND LOSSES.** A gain or loss that arises from a transaction that is unusual or infrequent, but not both, should be reported in the income statement as part of "income from continuing operations" (or "income before extraordinary items"). If the amount is material, it should be separately disclosed; if the amount is immaterial, it may be combined with other items on the income statement. In a multiple-step income statement, unusual gains and losses normally are classified in the "other revenues and gains" or "other expenses and losses" section, although a separate unusual items section may be displayed. Unusual gains and losses are **not** to be reported net of tax; rather, the tax consequences of these items are combined with the tax effects of all other components of income from continuing operations in the line called "income taxes."

4. **CHANGES IN ACCOUNTING PRINCIPLE.** A change in accounting principle occurs when a company changes from one generally accepted method to another generally accepted method. Because such a change violates consistency and, therefore, reduces or destroys comparability of successive financial statements, a change in principle should only be made when the newly adopted principle is preferable (e.g., for better matching of revenues and expenses). A change in accounting principle is generally recognized by including the cumulative effect of the change (net of the related income tax effect) as a separate item following extraordinary items in the income statement. This cumulative effect is based on a retroactive computation. That is, the effect on prior periods of using the old method is compared to the effect that would have occurred if the new method had been used for all prior periods; the difference is the cumulative effect of the change on all prior periods. (This subject is more thoroughly discussed in Chapter 22.)

5. **CHANGES IN ACCOUNTING ESTIMATE (Normal Recurring Corrections and Adjustments).** A change from one good faith estimate to another good faith estimate because of new information or experience constitutes a change in accounting estimate. A change in an estimate will affect the amount of related revenue or expense reported in the period of change if the change affects only that period, or in the period of change (called the current period) and future periods if the change affects both. Examples are   a change in the estimate of uncollectible accounts receivable (bad debts expense) and a change in the estimated service life of a plant (fixed) asset (amortization expense). A change in estimate is **not** considered a correction of an error (prior period adjustment); therefore, it is **not** handled retroactively.

EXERCISE 4-5

Purpose: (L.O. 4) This exercise will test your knowledge of the elements and arrangement of the major sections of the income statement.

Instructions

The following list represents captions that would appear on an income statement (single-step format) for a company reporting an extraordinary gain, losses from discontinued operations, and a change in amortization method, as well as the results of continuing operations for the period. You are to "unscramble" the list and prepare a skeleton income statement using the captions given. (If you do not wish to write out each caption above, you may still test your knowledge by listing the appropriate letters in the correct order.)

(a)   Income before extraordinary item and cumulative effect of a change in accounting principle
(b)   Revenues
(c)   Cumulative effect on prior years of a change in amortization method (net of tax)
(d)   Income taxes
(e)   Discontinued operations:
(f)   Extraordinary gain (net of tax)
(g)   Expenses
(h)   Loss from disposal of discontinued segment of business (net of tax)
(i)   Net income
(j)   Income from continuing operations before income taxes
(k)   Loss from operations of discontinued segment of business (net of tax)
(l)   Income from continuing operations

Solution to Exercise 4-5

Company Name
INCOME STATEMENT
For the Year Ended December 31, 20XX

(b)   Revenues
(g)   <u>Expenses</u>
(j)   Income from continuing operations before income taxes
(d)   <u>Income taxes</u>
(l)   Income from continuing operations
(e)   Discontinued operations:
(k)   Loss from operations of discontinued segment of business (net of tax)
(h)   <u>Loss from disposal of discontinued segment of business (net of tax)</u>
(a)   Income before extraordinary item and cumulative effect of a change in accounting principle
(f)   Extraordinary gain (net of tax)
(c)   <u>Cumulative effect on prior years of a change in amortization method (net of tax)</u>
(i)   Net income

> **TIP:** The **current operating performance concept** would call for all irregular gains and losses and corrections of revenues and expenses of prior periods to be taken directly into the Retained Earnings account, rather than reported in the current period's income statement. Whereas, the **all-inclusive concept** would call for these items to all be reported in the current period's income statement. Generally accepted accounting principles currently requires a **modified all-inclusive concept**. This means the corrections of revenues and expenses of prior periods go directly to Retained Earnings and, with minor exceptions, all other items (such as unusual gains and losses, discontinued operations, extraordinary items, and the effects of accounting changes) are reported on the income statement.

EXERCISE 4-6

Purpose: (L.O. 3, 4, 6, 7, 8) This exercise will enable you to practice identifying the proper classification for items on an income statement. It will also give you an example of how the tax effects of various items are reflected in the income statement.

Margaret Moylan had the following selected transactions and events occur during 2002. The corporation is subject to a 30% tax rate on all items. All amounts are material. The corporation is engaged in the sale of energy products.

1.   The corporation experienced an uninsured flood loss in the amount of $60,000 during the year. A flood is unusual and infrequent in the region where the corporation resides.

2.   At the beginning of 2000, the corporation purchased an office machine for $108,000 (salvage value of $18,000) that has a useful life of six years. The bookkeeper used straight-line amortization for 2000 and 2001, but failed to deduct the salvage value in computing the amortizable base. The same amortization calculations were used for tax purposes.

3.   Sale of securities held as a part of Moylan's portfolio resulted in a loss of $62,200 (pretax).

4.   When its president died, the corporation realized $100,000 from an insurance policy. The cash surrender value of this policy had been carried on the books as an investment in the amount of $34,000 (the gain is nontaxable).

5.   The corporation disposed of a segment of business at a loss of $140,000 before taxes. Assume that this transaction meets the criteria for being classified as discontinued operations. There were no results of operations for this division during 2002.

6.   The corporation decided to change its method of inventory pricing from average cost to the FIFO method. The effect of this change on prior years would be to increase 2000 income by $64,000 and decrease 2001 income by $20,000 before taxes. The FIFO method has been used for 2002.

Instructions:

Describe how each of the items above will be reported in a multiple-step income statement for 2002. Indicate the amount that will be reported and the section of the income statement in which the amount will appear.

Solution to Exercise 4-6:

1.   A loss of $42,000 ($60,000 minus 30% of $60,000) will be reported in the extraordinary items section of the income statement.

2.   Amortization expense of $15,000 [($108,000 - $18,000) ÷ 6 years] will appear in the administrative expense (an operating expense) section of the 2002 income statement. The correction of prior periods' amortization (a prior period adjustment) will **not** appear on the income statement. Rather, a credit of $4,200 will appear on the statement of retained earnings for 2002 as an adjustment to the beginning balance of retained earnings. The prior period adjustment is reported net of tax.
       Calculations:
             $108,000 ÷ 6 = $18,000 amortization taken in 2000.
             $108,000 ÷ 6 = $18,000 amortization taken in 2001.
             ($108,000 - $18,000) ÷ 6 = $15,000 correct annual depreciation.
             $15,000 x 2 = $30,000 correct amortization for 2000 and 2001.
             ($18,000 + $18,000) - $30,000 = $6,000 overstated expense in prior years.
             $6,000 - 30%($6,000) = $4,200 addition to retained earnings.

3.   A loss of $62,200 will be reported in the other expenses and losses section of the income statement. It is **not** reported net of tax.

4.   A gain of $66,000 ($100,000 - $34,000) will appear in the other revenues and gains section of the income statement. It is **not** reported net of tax (in this case, it had no tax effect anyway). A good caption for this item is "Gain from proceeds of life insurance policy."

5.   A loss of $98,000 ($140,000 minus 30% of $140,000) will appear as a "loss on disposal of assets of discontinued segment" in the discontinued operations section of the income statement.

6.   A cumulative effect on prior periods of a change in accounting principle will appear as a $30,800 credit on the 2002 income statement. This is the last item shown on the statement before arriving at net income.
       Calculations:

             $64,000 credit (increase in prior period income)
              20,000 debit (decrease in prior period income)
              44,000 credit (net catch-up adjustment needed)
                70% net of tax rate
             $30,800 credit (cumulative effect, net of tax)

EXERCISE 4-7

Purpose: (L.O. 5) This exercise will give you examples of the various situations possible [realized gains (losses) and expected gains (losses)] when you have an extended phase-out period for discontinued operations.

Bass Company has discontinued operations. The basic facts are as follows:
  Measurement date: October 1, 2002.
  Disposal is expected to be completed by May 1, 2003.
  Accounting period ends December 31, 2002.

Instructions

For each of the following independent cases, indicate the amount of "gain (loss) on disposal of segment" to be reported on the 2002 and 2003 income statements by filling in the blanks provided. Assume all amounts are net of tax.

Case	Realized Income (Loss) from Operations Oct. 1, 2002- Dec. 31, 2002	Realized Gain (Loss) on Sale of Assets Oct. 1, 2002- Dec. 31, 2002	Expected Income (Loss) from Operations Jan. 1, 2003- May 1, 2003	Expected Gain (Loss) on Sale of Assets Jan. 1, 2003- May 1, 2003	Gain (Loss) on Disposal of Segment
1	(144,000)	(52,500)	(117,600)	(88,200)	2002 _(402.3)_ 2003 _0_
2	300,000	(52,500)	(117,600)	(88,200)	2002 _(41.7)_ 2003 _0_
3	(144,000)	(52,500)	324,000	(88,200)	2002 _0.7_ 2003 _39.3_
4	(144,000)	(52,500)	(117,600)	360,000	2002 _0_ 2003 _45.9_
5	300,000	(52,500)	324,000	(88,200)	2002 _247.5_ 2003 _235.8_

Solution to Exercise 4-7

	2002	2003
Case 1	(402,300)	-0-
Case 2	41,700	-0-
Case 3	-0-	39,300
Case 4	-0-	45,900
Case 5	247,500	235,800

Approach and Explanation: To calculate the amount to report as the gain or loss on disposal of a segment:
(1)   Calculate the net realized items.
(2)   Calculate the net estimated items.

(3) Follow the rules for handling the income (loss) on operations and the gains and losses on disposal of assets estimated in the phase-out of discontinued operations, which are as follows:

    (a) If the estimated items net to a loss, accrue the net estimated losses in total to the period of the date of measurement.

    (b) If the estimated items net to a gain and the realized items net to a gain, defer recognition of all of the estimated items to the period these gains are realized (period of date of disposal).

    (c) If the estimated items net to a gain and the realized items net to a loss, use the net estimated gain (or portion thereof) to offset the net realized loss in the period of the date of measurement. Defer the recognition of any excess of net estimated gains over net realized losses.

Case	Net Realized Items	Net Estimated Items	Treatment
1	($196,500)	$(205,800)	Accrue net estimated losses to 2002 (See "a" above).
2	$247,500	$(205,800)	Accrue net estimated losses to 2002 (see "a" above).
3	$(196,500)	$235,800	Use some estimated gains to offset net realized losses in 2002; defer the rest to 2003 (see "c" above).
4	$(196,500)	$242,400	Use some estimated gains to offset net realized losses in 2002; defer the rest to 2003 (see "c" above).
5	$247,500	$235,800	Do not reflect any estimated gains in 2002; there are no realized losses to offset. Defer all estimated gains to period realized (2003) (see "b" above).

TIP: To qualify for treatment as discontinued operations, the assets, results of operations, and activities of a segment of business must be clearly distinguishable, physically and operationally, from the other assets, results of operations, and activities of the entity. The **measurement date** is the date that management commits itself to a formal plan to dispose of a segment of business. The **disposal date** is the date of closing the sale if the disposal is by sale or the date that operations cease if the disposal is by abandonment. The period of time between the measurement date and the disposal date is called the **phase-out period**.

TIP: Discontinued operations are reported in a separate section of the income statement, net of tax. There are two components to this section of the income statement: (1) income or loss from operations of the discontinued segment, and (2) gain or loss on disposal of the discontinued segment. The first component reflects the results of operations (revenues and expenses) of the discontinued segment from the beginning of the year (period) **up to the measurement date**. Included in the second component are the results of operations of the discontinued segment **after the measurement date** (the phase-out period) and the gain or loss on disposal of the assets of the discontinued segment.

TIP: An extended phase-out period for discontinued operations refers to a situation where the disposal of the discontinued segment of business occurs in the reporting period following the reporting period in which the date of measurement occurs. Thus, at the date financial statements are to be prepared, estimates must be made for the (1) income (loss) from operations of the discontinued segment during the phase-out period, and (2) ultimate gain or loss on disposal of the assets of the discontinued segment.

ANALYSIS OF MULTIPLE-CHOICE TYPE QUESTIONS

QUESTION

1.   (L.O. 3) In a multiple-step income statement, the excess of gross profit over operating expenses is called:
   a.   net margin.
   b.   income from operations.
   c.   net profit.
   d.   earnings.

Approach and Explanation: Visualize a multiple-step income statement. Net sales less cost of goods sold yields gross profit (sometimes called gross margin). Gross profit less operating expenses equals income from operations. From there, other revenues and gains are added, other expenses and losses are deducted, and income tax expense is deducted to arrive at net income. Another popular name for net income is earnings. Net profit would likely refer to net income. Net margin is not a term applied to the income statement. (Solution = b.)

QUESTION

2.   (L.O. 3) The following expenses and loss were among those incurred by Mitzer Company during 2002:

Rent for office space	$ 660,000
Loss on sale of office furniture	55,000
Interest	132,000
Accounting and legal fees	352,000
Freight-out	70,000

One-half of the rented premises is occupied by the sales department. How much of the items listed above should be classified as general and administrative expenses in Mitzer's income statement for 2002?
   a. $682,000
   b. $869,000
   c. $884,000
   d. $939,000

Approach and Explanation: For each item listed, identify where it is reported. Then collect together the ones that you identify as general and administrative (G&A) expenses.

Rent for office space:	One-half selling; one-half G&A
Loss on sale of equipment:	Other expenses and losses
Interest:	Other expenses and losses
Accounting and legal fees:	G&A expenses
Freight-out:	Selling expenses

One-half of office space (0.5 x $660,000)	$330,000
Accounting and legal fees	352,000
General and administrative expenses	$682,000

(Solution = a.)

QUESTION

3.   (L.O. 3) Which of the following is **not** a selling expense?
   a.   Advertising expense
   b.   Office salaries expense
   c.   Freight-out
   d.   Store supplies consumed

Approach and Explanation: Take each account and determine its classification. Items "a," "c," and "d" are selling expenses because they are associated with the sales function. Office salaries are related to normal operations, but they are not related to the sales function of the business. Therefore, they are not classified as a selling expense. (Solution = b.)

QUESTION

4.   (L.O. 3) The accountant for the Orion Sales Company is preparing the income statement for 2002 and the balance sheet at December 31, 2002. The January 1, 2002 merchandise inventory balance will appear:
   a.   only as an asset on the balance sheet.
   b.   only in the cost of goods sold section of the income statement.
   c.   as a deduction in the cost of goods sold section of the income statement and as a current asset on the balance sheet.
   d.   as an addition in the cost of goods sold section of the income statement and as a current asset on the balance sheet.

Explanation: The January 1, 2002 inventory amount is the beginning inventory figure. Beginning inventory is a component of the cost of goods available for sale for the period which is a component of cost of goods sold. (Solution = b.)

TIP: If the question asked about the December 31, 2002 merchandise inventory balance (ending inventory) rather than the beginning inventory balance, the correct answer would have been "c" (as a deduction in calculating cost of sales and as a current asset).

QUESTION

5.   (L.O. 2, 3) The following amounts relate to the current year for the Ira Company:

Beginning inventory	$ 20,000
Ending inventory	28,000
Purchases	166,000
Purchase returns	4,800
Transportation-out	6,000

The amount of cost of goods sold for the period is:
   a. $169,200.
   b. $162,800.
   c. $153,200.
   d. $147,200.

Approach and Explanation: Write down the calculation model for cost of goods sold. Enter the amounts given and solve for the unknown.

$ 20,000		**B**eginning **I**nventory
+ 166,000	+	**P**urchases
- 4,800	-	**P**urchase **R**eturns and **A**llowances
	-	**P**urchase **D**iscounts
	+	**F**reight-in
181,200	=	**C**ost of **G**oods **A**vailable for **S**ale
- 28,000	-	**E**nding **I**nventory
$ 153,200	=	**C**ost of **G**oods **S**old

(Solution = c.)

> **TIP:** Transportation-out is classified as a selling expense, not a component of cost of goods sold. "Transportation-out" is often called "freight-out; "transportation-in" is another name for "freight-in."

QUESTION

6.   (L.O. 4) A loss from the disposal of a segment of business should be reported in the income statement:

a.   after extraordinary items and before cumulative effect of an accounting change.

b.   before extraordinary items and after cumulative effect of an accounting change.

c.   after extraordinary items and cumulative effect of an accounting change.

d.   before extraordinary items and cumulative effect of an accounting change.

Approach and Explanation: Keep in mind the acronym **DEC**. Write the items down in the proper order. Read each answer response to see if it properly describes the order in which you have listed the items.

The correct order of the items involved in the question is as follows:

(1)   **D**iscontinued operations

(2)   **E**xtraordinary items

(3)   **C**umulative effect of a change in accounting principle (Solution = d.)

QUESTION

7.   (L.O. 4) A material loss should be presented separately as a component of income from continuing operations when it is:

a.   unusual in nature and infrequent in occurrence.

b.   unusual in nature but not infrequent in occurrence.

c.   an extraordinary loss.

d.   a cumulative effect of a change in accounting principle.

Approach and Explanation: Visualize an income statement and mentally identify the section that reports income from continuing operations. Read one answer at a time and determine if it correctly describes how the statement in the question stem can be completed. A material loss that is (1) unusual in nature **and** (2) infrequent in occurrence should be reported as an extraordinary item. A loss that meets one of the criteria for being classified as extraordinary, but not both, should be separately disclosed as a component of income from continuing operations.

An extraordinary item and a cumulative effect of a change in accounting principle are to be reported **after** (and not part of) income from continuing operations. (Solution = b.)

QUESTION

8.   (L.O. 4) During the year ended December 31, 2002, Schmelya Corporation incurred the following infrequent losses:

   1.   A factory was shut down during a major strike by employees; costs were $120,000.
   2.   A loss of $50,000 was incurred on the abandonment of computer equipment used in the business.
   3.   A loss of $82,000 was incurred as a result of flood damage to a warehouse.

How much total loss should Schmelya report in the extraordinary item section of its 2002 income statement?
   a. $82,000
   b. $120,000
   c. $202,000
   d. $252,000

Approach and Explanation: It is wise to review the list of items that are classified as extraordinary items and the list of items that are not extraordinary items (see **Illustration 4-3**) until you can readily recognize items that appear in the list. In the question at hand, the first two items are on the list of items that are **not** extraordinary. Therefore, the only possible one being extraordinary is the loss from flood damage. A flood would be considered infrequent in some locations but not others. The stem of the question indicates it is deemed infrequent for Schmelya. To be classified as extraordinary, an item needs to be unusual in nature and infrequent in occurrence. However, there are certain items that do **not** constitute extraordinary items. (Solution = a.)

QUESTION

9.   (L.O. 4) Which of the following should be classified as an extraordinary item?
   a.   Loss from extinguishment of debt.
   b.   Loss from exchange of foreign currencies.
   c.   Loss from abandonment of plant assets.
   d.   Loss from write down of goodwill.

Explanation: Answer selections "b.", "c.", and "d." involve transactions that appear on the list of items that are **not** to be classified as extraordinary items on the income statement. A gain or loss from extinguishment of debt is to be classified as an extraordinary item even though the extinguishment of debt does not meet the three criteria for classifying an item as an extraordinary item (unusual in nature, infrequent in occurrence and not the result of management or owner actions or decisions). (Solution = a.)

QUESTION

10.   (L.O. 4) When a piece of office equipment is sold at a gain of $70,000 less related taxes of $28,000, and the gain is not considered unusual or infrequent, the income statement for the period would show these effects as:

a.   an extraordinary item net of applicable income taxes, $420,000.
b.   a prior period adjustment net of applicable income taxes, $420,000.
c.   an other gain net of applicable income taxes, $420,000.
d.   an other gain of $700,000 and an increase in income tax expense of $280,000.

Explanation: A gain or loss on the disposal of property, plant and equipment that is **not** unusual and infrequent is **not** to be classified as an extraordinary item. Therefore, a gain from such a disposal goes in the "other revenues and gains" classification. The related tax effect is reflected in the "income tax expense" figure.   The only items reported net of tax are extraordinary items, discontinued operations, changes in accounting principle, and prior period adjustments. The tax effects of all other transactions are summarized in the amount captioned "income tax expense." (Solution = d.)

QUESTION

11.   (L.O. 8) A correction of an error in prior periods' income will be reported:

	In the income statement	Net of tax
a.	Yes	Yes
b.	No	No
c.	Yes	No
d.	No	Yes

Approach and Explanation: Write down what you know about the accounting for a correction of an error in calculating income in a prior period. Then answer "yes" or "no" to each question posed at the top of the appropriate column. Find the combination that matches yours. A correction of an error is a prior period adjustment; it is reported net of tax as an adjustment to the beginning retained earnings balance on the statement of retained earnings in the period the error is corrected. (Solution = d.)

QUESTION

12.   (L.O. 8) The OVA Company had the following errors occur in its financial statements:

	2001	2002
Ending inventory	$12,000 Understated	$18,000 Overstated
Amortization expense	$24,000 Overstated	$14,000 Overstated

Assuming that none of the errors were detected or corrected, by what amount will retained earnings at December 31, 2002 be misstated?

a. $18,000 overstated.
b. $20,000 understated.
c. $32,000 understated.
d. $14,000 understated.
e.   None of the above.

Approach and Explanation: Explain the effects of each error separately and then combine your results. The $12,000 understatement of ending inventory for 2001 causes a $12,000 understatement of net income for 2001 and a $12,000 overstatement of net income for 2002 (because the ending inventory for 2001 is the beginning inventory for 2002); this nets to be a zero impact on the retained earnings balance at December 31, 2002. The $24,000 over-statement of amortization expense in 2001 causes an understatement of net income for 2001 and a corresponding $24,000 understatement of retained earnings at December 31, 2001 and at December 31, 2002. The $18,000 overstatement of ending inventory for 2002 causes an overstatement of net income for 2002 and an $18,000 overstatement of retained earnings at December 31, 2002. A $14,000 overstatement of amortization expense for 2002 causes a $14,000 understatement of net income for 2002 and a $14,000 understatement of retained earnings at December 31, 2002. The net effect on retained earnings at December 31, 2002 is therefore a $24,000 understatement + an $18,000 overstatement + a $14,000 understatement which equals a $20,000 understatement. (Solution = b.)

QUESTION

13.   (L.O. 5) When a segment of a business has been discontinued during the year, that segment's operating losses of the current year after the measurement date should be included in the:

a.   income statement as part of the income (loss) from operations of the discontinued segment.

b.   income statement as part of the gain (loss) on disposal of the discontinued segment.

c.   income statement as part of the income (loss) from continuing operations.

d.   statement of retained earnings as a direct decrease in retained earnings.

Approach and Explanation: Read the question and write down the two captions used to report discontinued operations and also write down a brief description of what goes in each category. Read each answer selection and answer **True** or **False** as to whether or not it correctly completes the statement in the stem. There are two lines in the "discontinued operations" section of the income statement: (1) income (loss) from operations of discontinued segment, and (2) gain or loss on disposal of discontinued segment. The results of operations of the discontinued segment from the beginning of the year up to the measurement date are to be reported in the first line. The results of operations of the discontinued segment after the measurement date go in the second line, along with the gain or loss in disposal of the assets of the discontinued segment. (Solution = b.)

CHAPTER 5

FINANCIAL POSITION AND CASH FLOWS

OVERVIEW

A balance sheet reports on the financial position of an entity at a point in time. A statement of cash flows reports reasons for cash receipts and cash payments during the period. In this chapter, we discuss the classifications of a balance sheet and a statement of cash flows along with related disclosure issues. It is extremely important that items are properly classified. Errors in classification will result in incorrect ratio analyses, which can lead to misinterpretations of the meaning of the information conveyed. This can affect the decisions that are being made based on that information.

SUMMARY OF LEARNING OBJECTIVES

1. **Identify the uses and limitations of a balance sheet.** The balance sheet provides information about the nature and amounts of investments in enterprise resources, obligations to creditors, and the owners' equity in net resources. The balance sheet contributes to financial reporting by providing a basis for: (1) calculating rates of return, (2) evaluating the enterprise's capital structure, and (3) assessing the enterprise's liquidity, solvency, and financial flexibility. The limitations of a balance sheet are: (1) the balance sheet does not reflect current value because accountants have adopted a historical cost basis in valuing and reporting assets and liabilities; (2) judgements and estimates must be used in preparing a balance sheet. The collectibility of receivables, the saleability of inventory, and the useful life of long-term tangible and intangible assets are difficult to determine. (3) the balance sheet necessarily omits many items that are of financial value to the business but cannot be recorded objectively, for example, human resources, customer base, and reputation.

2. **Identify the major classifications of the balance sheet.** The general elements of the balance sheet are assets, liabilities, and equity. The major classifications within the balance sheet on the asset side are current assets; long-term investments; property, plant, and equipment; intangible assets; and other assets. The major classifications of liabilities are current liabilities and long-term liabilities. In a corporation, owners' equity is generally classified as capital shares, contributed surplus, and retained earnings.

3. **Prepare a classified balance sheet.** The most common format lists liabilities and shareholders' equity directly below assets on the same page.

4. **Identify balance sheet information requiring supplemental disclosure.** Five types of information normally are supplemental to account titles and amounts presented in the balance sheet: (1) **Contingencies:** material events that have an uncertain outcome; (2) **Accounting policies:** explanations of the valuation methods used or the basic assumptions made concerning inventory valuation, amortization methods, investments in subsidiaries, etc.; (3) **Contractual situations:** explanations of certain restrictions or covenants attached to specific assets or, more

likely, to liabilities; (4) *Detailed information*: clarifies in more detail the composition of balance sheet items; and (5) *Subsequent events*: events that happen after the balance sheet date.

5.   **Identify major disclosure techniques for the balance sheet.** There are four methods of disclosing pertinent information in the balance sheet: (1) **Parenthetical explanations:** additional information or description is often provided by parenthetical explanation following the item; (2) **Notes:** notes are used if additional explanations or descriptions cannot be shown conveniently as parenthetical explanations; (3) **Cross reference and contra items:** a direct relationship between an asset and a liability is "cross referenced" on the balance sheet; (4) **Supporting schedules:** often a separate schedule is needed to present more detailed information about certain assets or liabilities, because the balance sheet provides just a single summary item.

6.   **Indicate the purpose of the statement of cash flows.** The primary purpose of a statement of cash flows is to provide relevant information about an enterprise's cash receipts and cash payments of an enterprise during a period. Reporting the sources, uses, and net increase or decrease in cash enables investors, creditors, and others who want to know what is happening to a company's most liquid resource.

7.   **Identify the content of the statement of cash flows.** Cash receipts and cash payments during a period are classified in the statement of cash flows in three different activities: (1) **Operating activities** involve the cash effects of transactions that enter into the determination of net income. (2) **Investing activities** include making and collecting loans and acquiring and disposing of investments (both debt and equity) and property, plant, and equipment. (3) **Financing activities** include (a) obtaining capital from owners and providing them with a return on their investment, (b) borrowing money from creditors and repaying the amounts borrowed.

8.   **Prepare a statement of cash flows.** The information to prepare a statement of cash flows usually comes from (1) comparative balance sheets, (2) the current income statement, and (3) selected transaction data. Preparing the statement of cash flows from these sources involves the following steps: (1) determine the net cash provided by operations; (2) determine the net cash provided by or used in investing and financing activities; (3) determine the net change (increase or decrease) in cash during the period; and (4) reconcile the net change in cash with the beginning and the ending cash balances. An alternative method is to analyse in detail the "cash and cash equivalents" general ledger account, grouping cash flows into operating, investing, and financing activities.

9.   **Understand the usefulness of the statement of cash flows.** Creditors examine the cash flow statement carefully because they are concerned about being paid. The amount and trend of net cash flow provided by operating activities in relation to the company's liabilities is helpful in making this assessment. In addition, measures such as a free cash flow analysis provide creditors and shareholders with a better picture of the company's financial flexibility.

*10.   **Identify the major types of financial ratios and what they measure.** Ratios express the mathematical relationship between one quantity and another, in terms of a percentage, a rate, or a proportion. Liquidity ratios measure the short-run ability to pay maturing obligations. Activity ratios measure the effectiveness of asset usage. Profitability ratios measure the success or failure of an enterprise. Coverage ratios measure the degree of protection for long-term creditors and investors.

        *This material is covered in Appendix 5-A in the text.

TIPS ON CHAPTER TOPICS

TIP: Financial statements are classified based on similar grouping characteristics and reported based on differing characteristics. Assets that differ in type or expected function should be reported separately. Assets and liabilities with different implications for the enterprise's financial flexibility should be reported separately, and assets and liabilities that differ in liquidity characteristics should be reported as separate items.

TIP: Memorize the definition of current assets. **Current assets** are cash and other assets that are expected to be converted into cash, sold, or consumed within the year or operating cycle that immediately follows the balance sheet date, whichever is longer. Think about how various examples of current assets meet this definition. Accounts receivable are current assets because they will be converted to cash shortly after the balance sheet date; inventory is a current asset because it will be sold within the year that follows the balance sheet date; prepaid insurance is a current asset because it will be consumed (used up) within the next year.

TIP: A normal **operating cycle** is the length of time required to go from release of cash back to receipt of cash. That is, for an entity, which sells products, the operating cycle is the time required to take cash out to buy (or to manufacture) inventory then sell the inventory and receive cash (either from a cash sale or the collection of an account receivable stemming from a credit sale). Thus, the length of an entity's operating cycle depends on the nature of its business. Unless otherwise indicated, always assume the operating cycle for an entity is less than a year so that the one-year test is used as the cutoff between current and noncurrent.

TIP: Memorize the definition of current liabilities. **Current liabilities** are obligations, which are expected to require the use of current assets or the incurrence of other current liabilities. A liability may be due within a year of the balance sheet and **not** be a current liability. An example is a debt due in six months that will be liquidated by use of a noncurrent asset.

TIP: In a classified balance sheet, any asset that is not classified as a current asset is a noncurrent asset. There are four noncurrent asset classifications: long-term investments; property, plant and equipment; intangible assets; and other assets.

TIP: In a classified balance sheet, liabilities are classified either as current or noncurrent liabilities. The noncurrent liabilities are usually titled "long-term liabilities" or "long-term debt."

TIP: It is extremely important that items are properly classified on a balance sheet. Errors in classification can result in incorrect ratio analyses (to be discussed in Chapter 22), which, may lead to misrepresentations of the meaning of the information conveyed and can effect decisions that are based on those analyses.

TIP: Current assets are listed in the order of their liquidity, with the most liquid ones being listed first. Property, plant and equipment items are listed in order of length of life, with the longest life first. Current liabilities are not listed in any prescribed order; however, notes payable (short-term) is usually listed first followed by accounts payable (and the remainder of the current liabilities are often listed in descending order of amount).

TIP: "**Short-term**" is synonymous with "**current**," and "**long-term**" is synonymous with "**noncurrent**." Therefore, "short-term debt" can be used to refer to "current liabilities." Asset classifications are typically titled current and noncurrent; whereas, liability classifications are typically titled current and long-term.

TIP: All noncurrent assets (assets in classifications other than "current assets") are resources that are **not** expected to be converted into cash or fully consumed in operations within one year or the operating cycle, whichever is longer.

TIP: An investment may be classified as a current asset (if it is a short-term investment) or as a noncurrent asset (if it is a long-term investment). For an investment to be classified as current: (1) it should be readily marketable, and (2) there should be a lack of management intent to hold it for a long-term purpose.

TIP: If an account title starts with "Allowance for...," then it generally is a contra balance sheet account.

TIP: If an account title starts with "Provision for...," it is generally an income statement account.

TIP: The balance of liabilities and the balance of owners' equity at a point in time simply serve as scorecards of the total amounts of unspecified assets, which have come about from creditor sources (liabilities) and owner sources (owners' equity). Thus, you can **not** determine the amount of cash (or any other specific asset) held by an entity by looking at the balance of owners' equity or liabilities. You must look at the listing of individual assets on the balance sheet to determine the amount of cash owned.

TIP: A **reserve** is an appropriation of retained earnings. An appropriation of retained earnings refers to a portion of retained earnings, which for one reason or another is restricted, which simply means it cannot be used as a basis for the declaration of dividends.

TIP: A **valuation account** is an account whose balance is needed to properly value the item to which the valuation account relates. A **contra account** is a valuation account whose normal balance (debit versus credit) is opposite of the normal balance of the account to which the valuation account relates. An **adjunct account** is a valuation account whose normal balance is the same as the normal balance of the account to which it relates.

TIP: Interest on debt is due annually or more frequently (semi-annually or monthly, for example). Therefore, interest accrued on long-term debt is generally classified as a current liability. Likewise, interest receivable stemming from the accrual of interest on long-term receivables is generally classified as a current asset.

TIP: A fund can consist of restricted cash or noncash assets such as shares and bonds of other companies. Funds are reported in the long-term investment classification. Other long-term investment classifications include investments in nonconsolidated subsidiaries or affiliated companies, investments in securities, (such as bonds, common shares, or long-term notes), and investments in tangible fixed assets such as land held for speculation.

TIP:	In answering questions regarding the classification of items on a balance sheet, always assume an individual item is material unless it is apparent otherwise.

ILLUSTRATION 5-1
BALANCE SHEET CLASSIFICATIONS (L.O. 2)

CURRENT ASSETS: includes cash and other assets, which are expected to be realizable within the next year or operating cycle, whichever is longer.

LONG-TERM INVESTMENTS: includes long-term receivables, restricted funds, investments in shares and bonds of others, and land held for future plant site or for speculation.

PROPERTY, PLANT AND EQUIPMENT: includes long-lived tangible assets (land, building, equipment, and machinery) that are currently being used in operations to generate income. Assets in this category are often referred to as plant assets or fixed assets. They are not held for resale.

INTANGIBLE ASSETS: includes assets that lack physical substance, such as a patent, copyright, franchise, trademark, or trade names that give the holder exclusive right of use for a specified period of time. Their value to a company is generally derived from the rights or privileges granted by governmental or other authority.

OTHER ASSETS: includes assets that by common practice are not classified elsewhere.

CURRENT LIABILITIES: obligations that are due within a year and are expected to require the use of current assets or the incurrence of other current liabilities to liquidate them.

LONG-TERM LIABILITIES: obligations that do not meet the criteria to be classified as current liabilities.

CAPITAL SHARES: the exchange value of shares issued.

CONTRIBUTED SURPLUS: Includes premiums on shares issued, capital donations, and other.

RETAINED EARNINGS: Excess of net incomes over net losses and dividend distributions since inception of the business. An appropriation of retained earnings is a restricted portion of the total retained earnings figure. Sometimes referred to as earned surplus.

EXERCISE 5-1

Purpose: (L.O. 2) This exercise lists examples of balance sheet accounts and enables you to practise determining where they are classified.

Instructions

Indicate which balance sheet classification is the most appropriate for reporting each account listed below by selecting the abbreviation of the corresponding section.

CA	Current Assets		CL	Current Liabilities
INV	Long-term Investments		LTL	Long-term Liabilities
PPE	Property, Plant, and Equipment		CS	Capital Shares
ITG	Intangible Assets		CON	Contributed Surplus
OA	Other Assets		RE	Retained Earnings

If the account is a contra account, indicate that fact by putting the abbreviation in parenthesis. If the exact classification depends on facts which are not given, indicate your answer of "depends on" by the abbreviation **DEP** and the possible classifications. If the account is reported on the income statement rather than the balance sheet, indicate that fact with an **IS**. Assume all items are material.

Classifi-cation	Account	Classifi-cation	Account
_____	1. Accounts Payable.	_____	11. Advances to Vendors.
_____	2. Accounts Receivable.	_____	12. Advertising Expense.
_____	3. Accrued Interest Receivable on Long-term Investments.	_____	13. Allowance for Bad Debts.
		_____	14. Allowance for Amortization.
_____	4. Accrued Interest Payable.	_____	15. Allowance for Doubtful Accounts.
_____	5. Accrued Taxes Payable.	_____	16. Allowance for Excess of Cost Over Market Value of Inventory.
_____	6. Accumulated Amortization—Building.	_____	17. Allowance for Inventory Price Declines.
_____	7. Accumulated Amortization—Machinery.	_____	18. Allowance for Purchase Discounts.
_____	8. Mineral Reserves.	_____	19. Allowance for Sales Discounts.
_____	9. Advances by Customers.	_____	20. Allowance for Uncollectible Accts.
_____	10. Advances to Affiliates.		

Classifi-cation	**Account**	**Classifi-cation**	**Account**
_____	21. Appropriation for Bond Sinking Fund.	_____	39. Current Portion of Mortgage Payable.
_____	22. Appropriation for Contingencies.	_____	40. Current Portion of Long-term Debt.
_____	23. Appropriation for Future Plant Expansion.	_____	41. Customers' accounts with credit balances.
_____	24. Work in Process.	_____	42. Customers' Deposits.
_____	25. Bank Overdraft.	_____	43. Vouchers Payable.
_____	26. Bond Interest Payable.	_____	44. Unexpired Insurance.
_____	27. Bond Interest Receivable.	_____	45. Deferred Property Tax Expense.
_____	28. Bond Sinking Fund.	_____	46. Deferred Office Supplies.
_____	29. Building.	_____	47. Deferred Rental Income.
_____	30. Cash.	_____	48. Deferred Subscription Revenue.
_____	31. Cash in Preferred Share Redemption Fund.	_____	49. Deferred Service Contract Revenue.
_____	32. Cash Surrender Value of Life Insurance.	_____	50. Deposits on Equipment Purchases.
_____	33. Certificate of Deposit.	_____	51. Amortization of Equipment.
_____	34. Common Shares.	_____	52. Discount on Bonds Payable.
_____	35. Construction in Process (entity's new plant under construction).	_____	53. Unearned Subscription Income.
_____	36. Creditor's accounts with debit balances.	_____	54. Discount on Notes Payable.
_____	37. Current Maturities of Bonds Payable (to be paid from Bond Sinking Fund).	_____	55. Discount on Notes Receivable.
_____	38. Current Maturities of Bonds Payable (to be paid from general cash account).	_____	56. Dishonoured Notes Receivable.
		_____	57. Dividend Payable in Cash.
		_____	58. Dividend Payable in Common Share.
		_____	59. Earned Rental Revenue.
		_____	60. Accrued Pension Liability.

Classifi-cation	Account		Classifi-cation	Account
_____	61. Estimated Liability for Income Taxes.		_____	81. Land Used for Parking Lot.
_____	62. Estimated Liability for Warranties.		_____	82. Leasehold Improvements.
			_____	83. Leasehold Costs.
_____	63. Estimated Premium Claims Outstanding.		_____	84. Loss on Sale of Marketable Securities.
_____	64. Factory Supplies.		_____	85. Machinery and Equipment.
_____	65. Finished Goods Inventory.		_____	86. Machinery and Equip. Sitting Idle.
_____	66. Furniture and Fixtures.		_____	87. Marketable Securities.
_____	67. Gain on Sale of Equipment.		_____	88. Merchandise Inventory.
_____	68. General and Administrative Expenses.		_____	89. Mortgage Payable.
_____	69. Goodwill.		_____	90. Notes Payable.
_____	70. Income Tax Payable.		_____	91. Notes Payable to Banks.
_____	71. Income Tax Refund Receivable.		_____	92. Notes Receivable.
			_____	93. Notes Receivable from Officers.
_____	72. Income Tax Withheld (from employees).		_____	94. Office Supplies on Hand.
_____	73. Interest Payable.		_____	95. Office Supplies Prepaid.
_____	74. Interest Receivable.		_____	96. Office Supplies Expense.
_____	75. Interest Revenue.		_____	97. Office Supplies Used.
_____	76. Investment in Nortel Shares.		_____	98. Patents.
			_____	99. Petty Cash Fund.
_____	77. Investment in Canada Savings. Bonds.		_____	100. Plant and Equipment.
_____	78. Investment in Unconsolidated Subsidiary.		_____	101. Preferred Share Redemption Fund.
_____	79. Land.		_____	102. Premium on Bonds Payable.
_____	80. Land Held for Future Plant Site.		_____	103. Premium on Common Shares.

Classifi-cation	Account	Classifi-cation	Account
_____	104. Prepaid Advertising.	_____	118. Store Supplies.
_____	105. Prepaid Insurance.	_____	119. Store Supplies Used.
_____	106. Prepaid Insurance Expense.	_____	120. Tools and Dies (5-year life).
_____	107. Prepaid Office Supplies.	_____	121. Tools and Dies (6-mos. life).
_____	108. Prepaid Royalty Payments.	_____	122. Unearned Royalties.
_____	109. Prepaid Property Taxes.	_____	123. Unamortized Bond Issue Costs.
_____	110. Provision for Bad Debts.	_____	124. Unamortized Discount on Bonds Payable.
_____	111. Provision for Income Taxes.		
_____	112. Rent Revenue.	_____	125. Unearned Rental Income.
_____	113. Salaries Payable.		
_____	114. Sales Discounts and Allowances.		
_____	115. Selling Expense Control.		
_____	116. Share Dividends Distributable.		
_____	117. Share Dividends Payable.		

Solution to Exercise 5-1

Solution	Explanation and/or Comment
CL	1. These are trade payables usually due within 30 or 60 days.
CA	2. These are trade receivables usually due within 30 or 60 days.
CA	3. Interest is usually due annually or more frequently.
CL	4. A better title is simply Interest Payable (item 73).
CL	5. A better title is simply Taxes Payable.
(PPE)	6. This is a contra account. It is another title for item 14 (item 6 is used more frequently).
(PPE)	7. This is a contra account and an alternative title for item 14.
PPE	8. Tracks of natural resources are classified in PPE.
DEP: CL or LTL	9. These advances refer to revenue amounts received in advance from customers.
DEP: CA or INV or OA	10. These advances are loans.
DEP: CA or INV or OA	11. These advances can be prepayments or loans.

Solution		**Explanation and/or Comment**
IS	12.	This is a selling expense.
(CA)	13.	This is another title for Allowance for Doubtful Accounts.
(PPE)	14.	This is another title for Accumulated Amortization (items 6 & 7).
(CA)	15.	This is contra to Accounts Receivable.
(CA)	16.	This account arises because of the use of the lower of cost or market rule. It is contra to Inventory.
(CA)	17.	This is contra to Inventory; it is another title for item 16.
(CL)	18.	This account reflects amounts included in Accounts Payable that will not be paid because of purchase discounts to be taken.
(CA)	19.	This account reflects amounts included in Accounts Receivable that will not be collected because of sales discounts allowed.
(CA)	20.	This is another title for Allowance for Doubtful Accounts.
RE	21.	This is a restriction on retained earnings (portion of total retained earnings).
RE	22.	This is a restriction on retained earnings (portion of total retained earnings).
RE	23.	This is a restriction on retained earnings (portion of total retained earnings).
CA	24.	This is an inventory account for a manufacturer.
CL	25.	When the item exists, it is usually listed as the first item under current liabilities.
CL	26.	
CA	27.	
INV	28.	A fund can be comprised of restricted cash or securities.
PPE	29.	
CA	30.	This is unrestricted cash.
INV	31.	This cash is restricted for a long-term purpose.
INV or OA	32.	The assumption is that the entity will continue the insurance coverage rather than take the cash surrender value.
DEP: CA or INV	33.	Some CDs are for 90 days, 180 days, 30 months, or 60 months.
CS	34.	This reflects the par or stated value of issued shares.
PPE	35.	This is one of two exceptions to the general guidelines for items to be included in the PPE classification.
CA	36.	A creditor has been overpaid or items purchased on account have been returned for credit after payment of account has been made.
LTL	37.	This answer assumes that the Bond Sinking Fund is classified under long-term investments.
CL	38.	This item will require current assets to settle the debt.
CL	39.	"Current portion" refers to the portion that is coming due within a year of the balance sheet date.
CL	40.	Some accountants list this item first in the list of current liabilities, others list it last.
CL	41.	This arises when customers overpay or return goods after full payment is made.
DEP: CL or LTL	42.	A deposit may be an advance payment for goods and services or a security deposit.
CL	43.	This is another title for Accounts Payable when a voucher system is in use.
CA	44.	This is another title for prepaid insurance.

Solution		**Explanation and/or Comment**
CA	45.	This is another title for item 109, Prepaid Property Taxes.
CA	46.	This is another title for items 94, 95, and 107.
DEP: CL or LTL	47.	This is another title for item 125, Unearned Rental Income.
DEP: CL or LTL	48.	Some subscriptions are for one year, others are for two or more years. This is another title for item 127, Unearned Subscription Revenue.
DEP: CL or LTL	49.	A service contract often covers two or more years; revenue has been collected but not earned.
PPE	50.	This is the second of two exceptions to the general guidelines for items to be included in the PPE classification.
IS	51.	This refers to the depreciation charges for the current period.
(LTL)	52.	In the rare instance where the bonds payable are classified as current, the discount would be current also.
DEP: (CL) or (LTL)	53.	This is another title for item 48.
DEP: (CL) or (LTL)	54.	A discount occurs when the effective rate exceeds the stated rate.
DEP: (CA) or (INV)	55.	A discount results when the note is issued below par.
CA	56.	A dishonoured note receivable is one that has reached its maturity date and remains uncollected.
CL	57.	A dividend is usually paid approximately three to four weeks after it is declared.
CS	58.	This is a bad title for Share Dividend Distributable. This is the same as items 116 and 117.
IS	59.	This is another title for Rent Revenue.
LTL	60.	
CL	61.	This is another title for Income Tax Payable.
DEP: CL or LTL	62.	Some warranties are for more than one year.
DEP: CL or LTL	63.	Premiums in this context are similar to prizes.
CA	64.	This item is similar to a prepaid expense; these supplies will be part of factory overhead (hence, work in process inventory) when used.
CA	65.	This is one of three inventory accounts for a manufacturer.
PPE	66.	
IS	67.	
IS	68.	
ITG	69.	This is referred to as an unidentifiable intangible asset with an indefinite life.
CL	70.	
CA	71.	
CL	72.	
CL	73.	This is another title for item 4 (item 73 is the preferable title).
CA	74.	
IS	75.	
CA	76.	This answer assumes there is no reason to hold the share for a long-term purpose.
DEP: CA or INV	77.	
INV	78.	The fact that the investee is a subsidiary means there is an intention to hold the investee's share for a long-term purpose.
PPE	79.	
INV	80.	
PPE	81.	

Solution		Explanation and/or Comment
PPE	82.	Some textbooks suggest classifying Leasehold Improvements as intangible assets. Most real life companies report them as PPE.
ITG	83.	These are costs incurred in obtaining a lease.
IS	84.	
PPE	85.	
OA	86.	
CA or INV	87.	This is a title often used to refer to short-term investments; it can also refer to securities (shares and/or bonds of other entities) held for long-term purposes.
CA	88.	This is another title for Inventory for a retailer.
LTL	89.	The portion of this balance due within the next year will be reclassified and reported as a current liability.
DEP: CL or LTL	90.	
DEP: CL or LTL	91.	
DEP: CA or INV	92.	
DEP: CA or INV	93.	Separate disclosure must be made of related party transactions.
CA	94.	This is another title for items 46, 95, and 107.
CA	95.	This is another title for items 46, 94, and 107.
IS	96.	
IS	97.	This is another title for Office Supplies Expense.
ITG	98.	
CA	99.	
PPE	100.	
INV	101.	
LTL	102.	This is an adjunct type valuation account. If the related bonds payable are classified as a current liability, this valuation account will also be in current liabilities.
APC	103.	This is an adjunct type valuation account.
CA	104.	This is a prepaid expense.
CA	105.	This is another title for items 44 and 106.
CA	106.	This is another title for items 44 and 105.
CA	107.	This is another title for items 46, 94, and 95.
CA	108.	This is a prepaid expense.
CA	109.	This is another title for item 45.
IS	110.	This is another title for Uncollectible Accounts Expense or Bad Debt Expense.
IS	111.	This is another title for Income Tax expense.
IS	112.	
CL	113.	This is another title for Accrued Salaries or Accrued Salaries Payable. Salaries Payable is the preferred title.
IS	114.	This is a contra sales revenue item.
IS	115.	A control account is an account in the general ledger for which the details appear in a subsidiary ledger.
CS	116.	This is another title for items 58 and 117. The title in item 116 is the preferred title.
CS	117.	This is another title for items 58 and 116. This is a misleading title because the word "payable" suggests a liability, which a share dividend is not.

__Solution__		__Explanation and/or Comment__
CA	118.	This answer assumes the supplies are on hand rather than used.
IS	119.	This item refers to Store Supplies Expense.
PPE	120.	
IS	121.	The service life is so short that the benefits yielded do not extend beyond one year. Therefore, the expenditure is not capitalized.
DEP: (CL) or (LTL)	122.	Revenue has been received, but not earned; hence, an obligation exists to provide a service or good or a refund in the future.
OA	123.	This is usually called Bond Issue Costs.
(LTL)	124.	This is another title for item 52. In the rare instance where the bonds payable are classified as a current liability, the discount would be contra current liability.
DEP: CL or LTL	125.	This is another title for item 47.

Approach: For each balance sheet classification, write down a definition or description of what is to be reported in that classification. Refer to those notes as you go down the list of items to be classified. Your notes should contain the guidelines summarized in **Illustration 5-1**.

EXERCISE 5-2

Purpose: (L.O. 3) This exercise will enable you to practise identifying errors and other deficiencies in a balance sheet.

Lee Ward Company has decided to expand its operations. The bookkeeper recently completed the balance sheet presented below to submit to the bank in order to obtain additional funds for expansion.

Lee Ward Company
BALANCE SHEET
For the Year Ended 2002

Current assets

Cash (net of bank overdraft of $15,000)	$ 180,000
Accounts receivable (net)	380,000
Inventories, at lower of FIFO cost or market	435,000
Marketable securities—at cost (fair value $110,000)	90,000

Property, plant, and equipment

Building (net)	590,000
Office equipment (net)	180,000
Land held for future use	75,000

Intangible assets

Franchise	90,000
Cash surrender value of life insurance	80,000
Prepaid insurance	6,000

Current liabilities

Salaries payable	18,000
Accounts payable	85,000
Note payable, due June 30, 2004	100,000
Pension obligation	92,000
Taxes payable	40,000
Note payable, due October 1, 2003	25,000
Discount on bonds payable	50,000

Long-term liabilities

Bonds payable, 8%, due May 1, 2006	400,000

Shareholders' equity

Common shares, authorized 500,000 shares, issued 310,000 shares	310,000
Contributed Surplus	279,000
Retained earnings	?

Instructions

Prepare a revised balance sheet in good form. Correct any errors and weaknesses you find in the presentation above. Assume that the accumulated amortization balance for the building is $150,000 and for the office equipment, $105,000. Marketable securities are classified as trading securities. The allowance for doubtful accounts has a balance of $20,000. The pension obligation is considered to be a long-term liability.

Solution to Exercise 5-2

Lee Ward Company
BALANCE SHEET
December 31, 2002

Assets

Current Assets
Cash			$ 195,000
Trading securities, at fair value (cost is $90,000)			90,000
Accounts receivable		$ 400,000	
Less allowance for doubtful accounts		20,000	380,000
Inventories, at lower of FIFO cost or market			435,000
Prepaid insurance			6,000
Total current assets			1,106,000

Long-term Investments
Land held for future use		75,000	
Cash surrender value of life insurance		80,000	
Total long-term investments			155,000

Property, Plant, and Equipment
Building	$ 740,000		
Less accumulated amortization—building	150,000	590,000	
Office equipment	285,000		
Less accumulated amortization—office equipment	105,000	180,000	
Total property, plant, and equipment			770,000

Intangible Assets
Franchise			90,000
Total assets			$ 2,121,000

Liabilities and Shareholders' Equity

Current Liabilities
Bank overdraft			$ 15,000
Note payable, due October 1, 2003			25,000
Accounts payable			85,000
Taxes payable			40,000
Salaries payable			18,000
Total current liabilities			183,000

Long-term Liabilities
Note payable, due June 30, 2004		$ 100,000	
8% Bonds payable, due May 1, 2006	$ 400,000		
Less discount on bonds payable	50,000	350,000	
Pension obligation		92,000	
Total long-term liabilities			542,000
Total liabilities			725,000

Shareholders' equity
Paid-in capital			
Common shares, authorized 500,000			
shares, issued and outstanding 310,000 shares	310,000		
Contributed Surplus	279,000	589,000	
Retained earnings		807,000	
Total shareholders' equity			1,396,000
Total liabilities and shareholders' equity			$ 2,121,000

Explanation:

1. A bank overdraft in one bank account should not be reflected as an offset to positive cash items (such as a positive balance in another account). A bank overdraft must be reported as a current liability. (The one exception to this rule is as follows: if an account with a positive balance exists in the same bank as the overdraft, the overdraft can be reflected as an offset to the extent of that positive balance.)

2. Marketable securities in a trading portfolio are to be reported on the balance sheet at the lower of cost or market. (This topic will be more fully explained in Chapter 10.)

3. Land held for future use is not to be classified in the property, plant, and equipment section because the land is not currently being used in operations.

4. Cash surrender value of life insurance is an intangible item in a legal sense (because it lacks physical substance), but it is classified as a long-term investment for accounting purposes.

5. Prepaid expenses such as prepaid insurance represent prepayments that relate to benefits that are expected to be consumed within the year that follows the balance sheet date. Hence, they are current assets.

6. A pension obligation is generally not expected to become due in the near future and, therefore, is not expected to require the use of current assets within a year of the balance sheet date. Hence, it is a long-term liability.

7. Discount on Bonds Payable is a contra type valuation account. A valuation account should always be reported with the account to which it relates.

8. Bonds payable are always assumed to be a long-term liability unless the facts make them appear to meet the definition for a current liability.

9. The balance of retained earnings for this exercise can be derived by determining the amount needed to cause total liabilities and shareholders' equity to equal total assets.

EXERCISE 5-3

Purpose: (L.O. 3) This exercise will enable you to practise identifying errors and other deficiencies in a balance sheet.

Presented on the next page is a balance sheet for the Gabby Corporation.

Gabby Corporation
BALANCE SHEET
December 31, 2002

Current assets	$ 520,000	Current liabilities	$ 365,000
Investments	700,000	Long-term liabilities	920,000
Property, plant, & equip.	2,185,000	Shareholders' equity	2,690,000
Intangible assets	570,000		
	$ 3,975,000		$ 3,975,000

The following information is available:

1.   The current asset section includes: cash $120,000, accounts receivable $190,000 less $10,000 for allowance for doubtful accounts, inventories $230,000, and unearned revenue $10,000 (credit balance). Inventories are stated at their replacement cost; original cost on a FIFO basis is $200,000.

2.   The investments section includes the cash surrender value of a life insurance contract $60,000; investments in common shares, short-term $70,000 and long-term $160,000; bond sinking fund $220,000; organizational costs $70,000; and land upon which a new plant is being constructed $120,000. Investments are all classified as available for sale and have fair values equal to their cost.

3.   Property, plant, and equipment includes buildings $1,600,000 less accumulated amortization $375,000; equipment $400,000 less accumulated amortization $240,000; land $500,000; and land held for future use $300,000. The building is stated at a recent appraisal value of $1,600,000; original cost was $1,250,000.

4.   Intangible assets include a franchise $140,000, goodwill $80,000, discount on bonds payable $30,000, and construction in process $320,000 (a new plant is under construction and will be ready for operations within nine months).

5.   Current liabilities include accounts payable $80,000, notes payable—short-term $110,000, notes payable—long-term $150,000, and salaries payable $25,000. It does not include any amount for loss contingencies. The company's attorney states that it is probable the company will have to pay $60,000 in 2003 due to litigation pending at the balance sheet date.

6.   Long-term liabilities are composed of 10% bonds payable (due June 1, 2010) $800,000 and pension obligation $120,000.

7.   Shareholders' equity includes preferred stock, 200,000 shares authorized with 70,000 shares issued for $450,000; and common shares, $2 par value, 300,000 shares authorized with 100,000 shares issued at an average price of $10. In addition, the corporation has retained earnings of $1,240,000.

Instructions
Prepare a corrected balance sheet in good form.

Solution to Exercise 5-3

Gabby Corporation
BALANCE SHEET
December 31, 2002

Assets

Current Assets

Cash			$ 120,000
Available-for-sale securities—at fair value			70,000
Accounts receivable		$ 190,000	
Less allowance for doubtful accounts		10,000	180,000
Inventories, at lower of FIFO cost or market			200,000
Total current assets			570,000

Investments

Available-for-sale securities—at fair value		160,000	
Bond sinking fund		220,000	
Cash surrender value of life insurance		60,000	
Land held for future use		300,000	
Total long-term investments			740,000

Property, Plant, and Equipment

Land		620,000	
Buildings	$ 1,250,000		
Less accumulated amortization—building	375,000	875,000	
Construction in process		320,000	
Equipment	400,000		
Less accumulated amortization—equip.	240,000	160,000	
Total property, plant, and equipment			1,975,000

Intangible Assets

Organization costs		70,000	
Franchise		140,000	
Goodwill		80,000	
Total intangible assets			290,000
Total assets			$ 3,575,000

Gabby Corporation
BALANCE SHEET
December 31, 2002
(Continued)

Liabilities and Shareholders' Equity

Current Liabilities			
Notes payable			$ 110,000
Accounts payable			80,000
Estimated litigation obligation			60,000
Salaries payable			25,000
Unearned revenue			10,000
Total current liabilities			285,000
Long-term Liabilities			
Notes payable		$ 150,000	
10% bonds payable, due June 1, 2010	$ 800,000		
Less discount on bonds payable	30,000	770,000	
Pension obligation		120,000	
Total long-term liabilities			1,040,000
Total liabilities			1,325,000
Shareholders' Equity			
Paid-in capital			
Preferred shares; 200,000 shares authorized, 70,000 issued and outstanding	450,000		
Common shares, $2 par value; 300,000 shares authorized, 100,000 issued and outstanding	200,000		
Contributed Surplus	800,000*	1,450,000	
Retained earnings		800,000**	
Total shareholders' equity			2,250,000
Total Liabilities and Shareholders' Equity			$ 3,575,000

*100,000 shares x ($10 - $2) = $800,000.

**The corrected balance for the Retained Earnings account can be reconciled
     with the before corrected amount as follows:

Retained Earnings, before corrections	$1,240,000
Overstatement of inventory	(30,000)
Overstatement of buildings	(350,000)
Understatement of litigation liability	(60,000)
Corrected Retained Earnings balance	$ 800,000

The errors that Gabby had on the balance sheet affected some income
statement accounts (which were closed to Retained Earnings) or directly
affected the Retained Earnings account.

TIP: The $620,000 reported amount for land is comprised of land $500,000 plus land upon which a new plant is being constructed $120,000.

ILLUSTRATION 5-2
OPERATING, INVESTING, AND FINANCING ACTIVITIES (L.O. 7)

DEFINITIONS:

Operating Activities: Operating activities represent the enterprise's principle revenue-producing activities and all other activities not related to investing and financing. Cash flows from operating activities are generally the cash effects of transactions and other events that enter into the determination of net income.

Investing Activities: Investing activities represent the acquisitions and disposal of long-term assets and other investments not included in cash equivalents, include (a) making and collecting loans; (b) acquiring and disposing of debt and equity instruments of other entities; and (c) acquiring and disposing of property, plant, and equipment and other productive assets.

Financing Activities: Financing activities represent activities that result in changes in the size and composition of the enterprise's equity capital and borrowings, including (a) obtaining resources from owners and providing them with a return on and a return of their investment; (b) borrowing money and repaying the amounts borrowed, or otherwise settling the obligation; and (c) obtaining and paying for other resources obtained from creditors.
(*CICA Handbook*, Section 1540, par. .06.)

EXAMPLES:
Operating Activities:
   Cash inflows:
      From sales of goods or services (includes cash sales and collections on account).
      From returns on loans (interest received) and on equity securities (dividends received).
      From other transactions, such as: Amounts received to settle lawsuits, and refunds
         from suppliers.
   Cash outflows:
      To suppliers for inventory and other goods and services (includes cash purchases
         and payments on account).
      To employees for services.
      To government for taxes.
      To lenders for interest.
      To others for items such as: Payments to settle lawsuits, refunds to customers, and
         contributions to charities.
Investing Activities:
   Cash inflows:
      From sale of property, plant, and equipment.
      From sale of debt or equity securities of other entities.
      From collection of principal on loans to other entities.
   Cash outflows:
      To purchase property, plant, and equipment.[a]
      To purchase debt or equity securities of other entities.
      To make loans to other entities.
Financing Activities:
   Cash inflows:
      From sale of equity securities (company's own shares).
      From issuance of debt instruments (bonds and notes).

ILLUSTRATION 5-2 (Continued)

Cash outflows:
  To pay dividends to shareholders.
  To reacquire capital shares.
  To pay debt (both short-term and long-term) other than accounts payable.

[a]The cash outflows included in this category are payments at the time of purchase or soon before or after purchase to acquire property, plant, and equipment and other productive assets. Generally, only advance payments, the down payment, or other amounts paid at the time of purchase or soon before or after purchase of property, plant, and equipment and other productive assets are investing cash outflows. **Incurring directly related debt to the seller is a financing transaction and subsequent payments of principal on that debt thus are financing cash outflows.**

TIP:	The statement of cash flows summarizes all of the transactions occurring during a period that have an impact on the cash balance. The activity format is used whereby cash inflows and cash outflows are summarized by the three categories: operating, investing and financing.
TIP:	The difference between net income and net cash provided by operating activities can be substantial.
TIP:	The statement of cash flows can provide significant insight into the strategy of the management team by determining the efficient and effective use of company resources.

EXERCISE 5-4

Purpose: (L.O. 7) The exercise enables you to practise identifying investing and financing activities.

Instructions
Place the appropriate code in the blanks to identify each of the following transactions as giving rise to an:

Code	
II	inflow of cash due to an investing activity, or
IO	outflow of cash due to an investing activity, or
FI	inflow of cash due to a financing activity, or
FO	outflow of cash due to a financing activity.

_____   1. Sell common shares to new shareholders.

_____   2. Purchase treasury shares.

_____   3. Borrow money from bank by issuance of short-term note.

_____   4. Repay money borrowed from bank.

_____   5. Purchase bonds as an investment.

_____   6. Sell investment in real estate.

_____   7. Loan money to an affiliate.

_____   8. Collect on loan to affiliate.

_____   9. Buy equipment.

_____   10. Sell a plant asset.

_____   11. Pay cash dividends to shareholders.

Solution to Exercise 5-4

1.	FI	4.	FO	7.	IO	10.	II		
2.	FO	5.	IO	8.	II	11.	FO		
3.	FI	6.	II	9.	IO				

Approach:

1. Reconstruct journal entries for the transactions. Examine each entry to identify if there is an inflow of cash (debit to Cash) or an outflow of cash (credit to Cash).

2. Write down the definitions for investing activities and financing activities (see below). Analyse each transaction to see if it fits one of these definitions.

   a) **Investing activities**—include (1) making and collecting loans, (2) acquiring and disposing of investments in debt and equity instruments, and (3) acquiring and disposing of property, plant, and equipment and other productive assets.

   b) **Financing activities**—include (1) obtaining capital from owners and providing them with a return on and a return of their investment, and (2) borrowing money from creditors and repaying the amounts borrowed, and (3) obtaining and paying for other resources obtained from creditors.

3. Assume purchases and sales of items are for cash, unless otherwise indicated.

TIP: The journal entry to record a transaction that is an investing activity which results in a cash flow will involve: (1) Cash and (2) an asset account other than Cash, such as Investments (short-term or long-term), Land, Building, Equipment, Patent, Franchise, etc.

TIP: The journal entry to record a transaction that is a financing activity which results in a cash flow will involve: (1) Cash and (2) a liability account or an owners' equity account, such as Bonds Payable, Note Payable, Dividends Payable, Common Shares, Contributed Surplus, Treasury Shares, etc.

EXERCISE 5-5

Purpose: (L.O. 8) This exercise will enable you to practise reconciling net income with net cash provided by operating activities.

The following data relate to the L. Heckenmueller Co. for 2002.

Net income	$ 75,000
Increase in accounts receivable	7,000
Decrease in prepaid expenses	3,200
Increase in accounts payable	5,000
Decrease in taxes payable	900
Gain on sale of investment	1,700
Amortization	3,500
Loss on sale of equipment	600

Instructions
Calculate the net cash provided by operating activities for 2002.

Solution to Exercise 5-5

Net income	$ 75,000
Increase in accounts receivable	(7,000)
Decrease in prepaid expenses	3,200
Increase in accounts payable	5,000
Decrease in taxes payable	(900)
Gain on sale of investment	(1,700)
Amortization	3,500
Loss on sale of equipment	600
Net cash provided by operating activities	$ 77,700

Explanation:
1.   Net income is a summary of all revenues earned, all expenses incurred, and all gains and losses recognized for a period. Most revenues earned during the year result in a cash inflow during the same period but there may be some cash and/or revenue flows that do not correspond. Most expenses incurred during the year result in a cash outflow during the same period but there may be some cash and/or expense flows that do not correspond.

2.   An increase in accounts receivable indicates that revenues earned exceed cash collected from customers and, therefore, net income exceeds net cash provided by operating activities.

3.   A decrease in prepaid expenses indicates that expenses incurred exceed cash paid and, therefore, net income is less than net cash provided by operating activities.

4.   An increase in accounts payable indicates that expenses incurred exceed cash paid and, therefore, net income is less than net cash provided by operating activities.

5.   A decrease in taxes payable indicates expenses incurred are less than the cash paid, and, therefore, net income is greater than net cash provided by operating activities.

6.   When an investment is sold, the entire proceeds are to be displayed as an investing activity on the statement of cash flows. The gain included in net income must, therefore, be deducted from net income to arrive at the net cash provided by operating activities. If this adjustment was not made, there would be double counting for the gain amount. For example: An investment with a carrying value of $4,000 is sold for $7,000. The entire $7,000 proceeds is an investing inflow; the $7,000 includes the gain of $3,000 and a recovery of the investment's $4,000 carrying value; the $3,000 gain will be deducted from net income to arrive at the net cash from operating activities figure.

7.   Amortization is a noncash charge (debit) against income. It must be added to net income to arrive at the amount of net cash provided by operating activities.

8.   A loss on the sale of equipment does not cause a cash outlay so it is added back to net income to arrive at the amount of net cash provided by operating activities. The cash proceeds from the sale of equipment are shown as a cash inflow from an investing activity.

EXERCISE 5-6

Purpose: (L.O. 8) This exercise will give you practise in preparing a statement of cash flows.

The comparative balance sheets of Spencer Corporation at the beginning and end of year 2002 appear below.

Spencer Corporation
Balance Sheets

	Dec. 31 2002	Dec. 31 2001	Inc./Dec.	
ASSETS				
Cash	$10,500	$7,100	Inc.	3,400
Accounts receivable	18,000	9,400	Inc.	8,600
Prepaid expenses	2,700	3,200	Dec.	500
Investments	-0-	11,300	Dec.	11,300
Equipment	56,000	42,000	Inc.	14,000
Less: Accumulated amortization	(10,000)	(5,000)	Dec.	5,000
Total	$77,200	$68,000	Inc.	9,200

LIABILITIES AND
SHAREHOLDERS' EQUITY

Accounts payable	$ 4,900	$ 4,500	Inc.	400
Unearned revenue	1,700	6,000	Dec.	4,300
Common shares	14,000	10,000	Inc.	4,000
Retained earnings	56,600	47,500	Inc.	9,100
Total	$77,200	$68,000	Inc.	9,200

During the year 2002, Spencer purchased equipment for $14,000 cash, declared and paid cash dividends of $2,500, sold investments for an amount equal to their cost, and reported net income of $11,600.

Instructions

Prepare a statement of cash flows for Spencer Corporation for the year ending December 31, 2002.

Solution to Exercise 5-6

Spencer Corporation
Statement of Cash Flows
For the Year Ending December 31, 2002

Cash flows from operating activities:		
Net income		$11,600
Adjustments to reconcile net income		
to net cash provided by operating activities:		
Increase in accounts receivable	($8,600)	
Decrease in prepaid expenses	500	
Increase in accounts payable	400	
Decrease in unearned revenue	(4,300)	
Amortization expense	5,000	(7,000)
Net cash provided by operating activities		4,600
Cash flows from investing activities:		
Sale of investments	$11,300	
Purchase of equipment	(14,000)	
Net cash used by investing activities		(2,700)
Cash flows from financing activities:		
Issuance of common shares	$4,000	
Payment of cash dividends	(2,500)	
Net cash provided by financing activities		1,500
Net increase in cash		3,400
Cash at beginning of the year		7,100
Cash at end of the year		$10,500

Approach and Explanation: The net change in cash for the year can easily be determined by taking the difference between the cash balance at the end of the year ($10,500) and the cash balance at the beginning of the year ($7,100), which yields a net increase of $3,400. The reasons for that net increase of $3,400 can be found by analysing all of the transactions that caused changes in all of the balance sheet accounts other than Cash.

The changes in Accounts Receivable, Prepaid Expenses, Accounts Payable and Unearned Revenues are all due to accruals and prepaids, which help to reconcile the net income figure with the amount of net cash provided (used) by operating activities. The changes in Investments and Equipment are due to transactions, which constitute investing activities. The changes in Accumulated Amortization are usually due to the recording of depreciation expense for the current period and disposals of plant assets. The changes in nontrade liability accounts (such as Mortgage Payable, Bonds Payable, Bank Note Payable) and most changes in shareholders' equity accounts are due to transactions, which constitute financing activities.

An increase of $8,600 in Accounts Receivable indicates that sales revenue (on an accrual basis) exceeded cash collections from customers by $8,600. That in turn causes net income to exceed net cash provided by operating activities, so $8,600 is deducted from net income in reconciling net income to a cash basis figure. A decrease of $500 in Prepaid Expenses indicates that expenses incurred on an accrual basis exceeded the cash payments for expenses by $500 which in turn caused net income to be less than net cash provided by operating activities. (Remember that expenses are a negative component of net income so as expenses go up, net income goes down.) An increase in Accounts Payable of $400 results from an excess of expenses incurred over cash payments for expenses, which causes net income to be less than net cash from operations.

Thus, both a decrease in Prepaid Expenses of $500 and an increase in Accounts Payable of $400 are added to net income to calculate a cash basis income amount. A decrease in Unearned Revenue of $4,300 reflects an excess of revenue earned over cash collections from customers this period; this means net income exceeds net cash provided by operations. Thus, the $4,300 decrease in Unearned Revenue is deducted from net income in reconciling net income to net cash provided by operating activities.

It is helpful to reconstruct the journal entry for each transaction that caused a change in the remaining balance sheet accounts. You will be able to see the impact on Cash. Assume the most common transaction caused a change in a particular account. The entries and analyses are as follows:

Cash	11,300	
Investments		11,300
(Sale of investments at book value)		

There was an inflow of cash due to an investing activity—sale of investments.

Equipment..	14,000	
Cash		14,000
(Purchase of equipment)		

There was an outflow of cash due to an investing activity—purchase of property, plant, and equipment.

Amortization Expense...	5,000	
Accumulated Amortization		5,000
(Recording of amortization for current period)		

There was no impact on cash. There was an expense recorded but there was no cash outflow. Therefore, the amount of amortization expense is added to net income in order to reconcile net income to net cash provided by operating activities.

Cash	4,000	
Common Shares		4,000
(Sale of common shares)		

There was an inflow of cash due to a financing activity—issuance of common shares (obtaining resources from owners).

Retained Earnings	2,500	
Cash		2,500
(Declaration and payment of cash dividends)		

There was an outflow of cash due a financing activity—payment of dividends (giving owners a return on their investment).

Income Summary..	11,600	
Retained Earnings		11,600
(Net income amount is closed to Retained Earnings)		

The balance of the Income Summary account before closing is a summarized figure reflecting all revenues and all expenses; it is a summary of all transactions dealing with operations for the period. Most revenues increase cash and most expenses decrease cash so we use net income (a summary of all revenues and all expenses) as our starting point in calculating cash provided by operating activities. The net income figure is then "adjusted" for the following items:
1. revenue transactions that did not bring in cash this period.
2. expense transactions that did not require a cash outlay this period.
3. revenue items of another period that produced a cash inflow this period.
4. expense items of another period that produced a cash outflow this period.

The result is the amount of net cash provided (used) by operating activities (a cash basis income figure).

ILLUSTRATION 5-3
A SUMMARY OF FINANCIAL RATIOS (L.O. 10)

Ratio	Formula for Calculation	Purpose or Use
I. Liquidity		
1. Current ratio	Current assets / Current liabilities	Measures short-term debt-paying ability.
2. Quick or acid-test ratio	Cash, marketable securities, and receivables (net) / Current liabilities	Measures immediate short-term liquidity.
3. Current cash debt ratio	Net cash provided by operating activities / Average current liabilities	Measures the company's ability to pay off its current liabilities out of its operations for a given year.
II. Activity		
4. Receivable turnover	Net sales / Average trade receivables (net)	Measures liquidity of receivables
5. Inventory turnover	Cost of goods sold / Average inventory	Measures liquidity of inventory.
6. Asset turnover	Net sales / Average total assets	Measures how efficiently assets are used to generate sales.
III. Profitability		
7. Profit margin on sales	Net income / Net sales	Measures net income generated by each dollar of sales.
8. Rate of return on assets	Net income / Average total assets	Measures overall profitability of assets.
9. Rate of return on common share equity	Net income minus preferred dividends / Average common shareholders' equity	Measures profitability of owners' investment.

ILLUSTRATION 5-3 (Continued)

Ratio	Formula for Calculation	Purpose or Use
10. Earnings per share	Net income minus <u>preferred dividends</u> Weighted shares outstanding	Measures net income earned on each common share.
11. Price earnings ratio	<u>Market price of shares</u> Earnings per share	Measures the ratio of the market price per share to earnings per share.
12. Payout ratio	<u>Cash dividends</u> Net income	Measures percentage of earnings distributed in the form of cash dividends.
IV. Coverage 13. Debt to total assets	<u>Total debt</u> Total assets or equities	Measures the percentage of total assets provided by creditors.
14. Times interest earned	Income before interest <u>charges and taxes</u> Interest charges	Measures ability to meet interest payments as they come due.
15. Cash debt coverage ratio	Net cash provided by <u>operating activities</u> Average total liabilities	Measures a company's ability to repay its total liabilities in a given year out of its operations.
16. Book value per share	Common share- <u>holders' equity</u> Outstanding shares	Measures the amount each common share would receive if the company were liquidated at the amounts reported on the balance sheet.

TIP: Throughout the remainder of the textbook, ratios are provided to help understand and interpret the information provided. In the Financial Statement Analysis Primer on the Digital Tool, an extensive discussion of financial statement analysis, of which ratio analysis is only a part, is presented. Above, we provide you with the ratios that will be used throughout the text. You should find the chart helpful as you examine these ratios in more detail in the following chapters.

ANALYSIS OF MULTIPLE-CHOICE TYPE QUESTIONS

QUESTION

1.   (L.O. 1) The amount of time that is expected to elapse until an asset is realized or otherwise converted into cash is referred to as:
a.   solvency.
b.   financial flexibility.
c.   liquidity.
d.   exchangeability.

Explanation: Liquidity describes the amount of time that is expected to elapse until an asset is realized or otherwise converted into cash or until a liability has to be paid; liquidity refers to the "nearness to cash" of assets and liabilities. Current assets are listed in the order of liquidity (with the most liquid items first) on a balance sheet. Solvency refers to the ability of an enterprise to pay its debts as they mature. Liquidity and solvency affect an entity's financial flexibility which measures the ability of an enterprise to take effective actions to alter the amounts and timing of cash flows so it can respond and adapt to financial adversity and unexpected needs and opportunities. (Solution = c.)

QUESTION

2.   (L.O.2) The Heather Miller Company has the following obligations at December 31, 2002:

I.	Accounts payable	$ 72,000
II.	Taxes payable	60,000
III.	Notes payable issued November 1, 2002, due October 31, 2003	80,000
IV.	Bonds payable issued December 1, 1993, due November 30, 2003 (to be paid by use of a sinking fund)	100,000

The amount that should be reported for total current liabilities at December 31, 2002 is:
a. $312,000.
b. $212,000.
c. $132,000.
d. $72,000.

Approach and Explanation: Write down the definition (or key phrases therein) for a current liability. (A **current liability** is an obligation which is coming due within a year of the balance sheet date and is expected to require the use of current assets or the incurrence of another current liability to liquidate it.) Analyse each of the obligations listed to see if it meets the criteria for being classified as current.

Accounts payable and taxes payable will both be due shortly after the balance sheet date and will require cash to liquidate the debts. The notes payable are due within a year of the balance sheet date and there is no evidence to indicate that assets other than current assets will be used for settlement; thus, the notes payable are a current liability. The bonds payable are coming due within a year, but they will **not** require the use of current assets to liquidate the debt because a sinking fund (restricted cash or securities classified as a long-term investment) is to be used to extinguish that debt: $72,000 + $60,000 + $80,000 = $212,000. (Solution = b.)

QUESTION

3.　　(L.O. 2) Land held for a future plant site should be classified in the section for:
- a.　　current assets.
- b.　　long-term investments.
- c.　　property, plant, and equipment.
- d.　　intangible assets.

Approach and Explanation: Review the descriptions of what goes in each of the asset classifications. Then read each answer selection and respond **True** or **False** if the selection answers the question. The land is not being used in operations, so it doesn't belong in property, plant, and equipment. It is not lacking physical existence, so it can't be an intangible asset. The land is not expected to be converted to cash or sold or consumed within the next year, so it is not a current asset. The land properly belongs in long-term investments. (Solution = b.)

QUESTION

4.　　(L.O. 2) Working capital is:
- a.　　current assets less current liabilities.
- b.　　total assets less total liabilities.
- c.　　the same as retained earnings.
- d.　　capital which has been reinvested in the business.

Explanation: The excess of total current assets over total current liabilities is referred to as working capital. Working capital represents the net amount of a company's relatively liquid resources. That is, it is the liquid buffer available to meet the financial demands of the operating cycle. (Solution = a.)

QUESTION

5.　　(L.O. 2) Treasury shares is classified as a(n):
- a.　　current asset.
- b.　　long-term investment.
- c.　　other asset.
- d.　　contra shareholders' equity item.

Explanation: Treasury shares are a company's redemption of their own shares that have been previously issued, but not cancelled. The acquisition of treasury shares represents a contraction of owners' equity; thus it is reported as a reduction of shareholders' equity. (Solution = d.)

QUESTION

6.　　(L.O. 2) Which of the following is classified as an intangible asset on a balance sheet?
- a.　　Long-term receivable.
- b.　　Long-term investment in shares of another enterprise.
- c.　　Licences.
- d.　　Accounts Receivable.

Explanation: Intangible assets lack physical substance and usually have a high degree of uncertainty concerning their future benefits. Although receivables and investments in shares lack physical existence, they are properly classifiable elsewhere so they are **not** classified for accounting purposes as intangible assets. Accounts receivable are classified as current assets, long-term receivables and long-term investments in shares are classified as long-term investments, and licences are classified as intangible assets. (Solution = c.)

QUESTION

7.   (L.O.2) Which of the following should not be found in the long-term investment section of the balance sheet?
    a.   Land held for speculation.
    b.   Bond sinking fund.
    c.   Cash surrender value of life insurance.
    d.   Patent.

Explanation: A patent is classified as an intangible asset. Long-term investments, often referred to simply as investments, normally consist of one of four types:
    1. Investments in securities, such as bonds, common shares, or long-term notes receivable.
    2. Investments in tangible fixed assets not currently used in operations, such as land held for speculation or future plant site.
    3. Investments set aside in special funds such as a sinking fund, pension fund, or plant expansion fund. The cash surrender value of life insurance is included here.
    4. Investments in nonconsolidated subsidiaries or affiliated companies.
(Solution = d.)

QUESTION

8.   (L.O. 4) A loss contingency that has a level of likelihood rated as reasonably possible and an amount that can be reasonably estimated should be:

	Accrued	Disclosed
a.	Yes	Yes
b.	Yes	No
c.	No	Yes
d.	No	No

Approach and Explanation: Read the stem and write down how you would complete the statement in the stem. Then look at the answer selections one at a time to find the one that corresponds with your anticipated response. A loss contingency that is probable and estimable should be accrued. A loss contingency that is reasonably possible should be disclosed only in the notes (and not be accrued). A loss contingency that is only remotely possible can usually be ignored and not accrued or disclosed. (Solution = c.)

QUESTION

9.   (L.O.3) Which of the following is a contra account?
    a.   Premium on bonds payable
    b.   Unearned revenue
    c.   Patents
    d.   Accumulated amortization

Approach and Explanation: After reading the stem and before reading the answer selections, write down the description of the term "contra account." (A **contra account** is a valuation account whose normal balance is opposite of the balance of the account to which it relates.) Then take each answer selection and answer **True** or **False** whether it meets that description. Premium on bonds payable is a valuation account, but it is an adjunct type (its normal balance is the same as the normal balance of the account to which it relates). Unearned Revenue and Patents are not valuation accounts. Accumulated Amortization is a valuation account for property, plant, and equipment. The normal balance of the Accumulated Amortization account is a credit and the normal balance of a property, plant, and equipment account is a debit. Hence, Accumulated Amortization is a contra account. (Solution = d.)

QUESTION
10.   (L.O.7) Which of the following should be classified as an inflow of cash in the investing section of a statement of cash flows?
       a.   Cash sale of merchandise inventory
       b.   Sale of delivery equipment at book value
       c.   Sale of common shares
       d.   Issuance of a note payable to a bank

Approach and Explanation: Read the stem and, before reading the answer selections, write down the items that appear in the definition of investing activities. (**Investing activities** include making and collecting loans to others, acquiring and disposing of stocks and bonds of other entities, acquiring and disposing of property, plant, and equipment and other productive assets.) Think of the items included in that definition that would produce a cash inflow (collecting loans, disposing of investments and property, plant, and equipment). Look for the answer selection that fits that analysis. As you analyse each answer selection, indicate what kind of activity it represents. A cash sale of merchandise inventory is an operating activity. The sale of common shares is a financing activity. The issuance of a note payable is a financing activity. A sale of equipment is an investing activity. (Solution = b.)

QUESTION
11.   (L.O.7) An example of a cash flow from an operating activity is:
       a.   payment to employees for services.
       b.   payment of dividends to shareholders.
       c.   receipt of proceeds from the sale of an investment.
       d.   receipt of proceeds from the sale of common shares to shareholders.

Explanation: Operating activities include the cash effects of transactions that ultimately create revenues and expenses and thus enter into the determination of net income. Operating activities include collections from customers, collections of interest and dividends, payments for merchandise and other goods and services, and payments for interest and taxes. The payment of dividends is a financing activity. The sale of an investment is an investing activity. The sale of common shares is a financing activity. (Solution = a.)

QUESTION

12.   (L.O. 7) In preparing a statement of cash flows, the sale of property, plant and equipment at an amount greater than its carrying value will be classified as a(n):

a.   operating activity.
b.   investing activity.
c.   financing activity.
d.   extraordinary activity.

Approach and Explanation: Think about the nature of each of the three categories on a statement of cash flows and select the one involving disposal of plant assets:

1) Operating Activities: Operating activities represent the enterprise's principle revenue-producing activities and all other activities not related to investing and financing. Cash flows from operating activities are generally the cash effects of transactions and other events that enter into the determination of net income.

2) Investing Activities: Investing activities represent the acquisitions and disposal of long-term assets and other investments not included in "cash equivalents", include (a) making and collecting loans; (b) acquiring and disposing of debt and equity instruments of other entities; and (c) acquiring and disposing of property, plant, and equipment and other productive assets.

3) Financing Activities: Financing activities represent activities that result in changes in the size and composition of the enterprise's equity capital and borrowings, including (a) obtaining resources from owners and providing them with a return on and a return of their investment; (b) borrowing money and repaying the amounts borrowed, or otherwise settling the obligation; and (c) obtaining and paying for other resources obtained from creditors.
(*CICA Handbook*, Section 1540, par. .06)

There is **no** category called "extraordinary activity" on a statement of cash flows. The fact that the asset was sold for a price exceeding the carrying value does not impact the answer because the entire proceeds from the sale are to be reported in the financing activity section. In the operating activity section, the amount of gain reflected in the net income figure is deducted from net income to arrive at "net cash provided by operating activities". (Solution = b.)

QUESTION

13.   (L.O. 7) In a statement of cash flows, proceeds from the issuance of common shares should be classified as a cash inflow from:

a.   operating activities.
b.   investing activities.
c.   financing activities.
d.   lending activities.

Explanation: The issuance of common shares by a corporation is the company's way of obtaining resources from an owner (i.e., owner investment into the business). Financing activities include obtaining resources from owners. There is no category called "lending activities." (Solution = c.)

QUESTION

14.   (L.O. 7) Which of the following would be classified as an investing activity on a statement of cash flows:

        a.   Issuance of bonds payable at a premium.
        b.   Purchase of land to be used in operations.
        c.   Issuance of common shares at the current market price of $5.
        d.   Payment of dividends to shareholders.

Approach and Explanation: Think about the types of items to be included in investing activities. Investing activities include making and collecting loans, acquiring and disposing of investments (both debt and equity) and acquiring and disposing of property, plant, and equipment. Take each of the answer choices and identify where it should go on a statement of cash flows. The issuance of bonds and the issuance of shares (regardless of price) are both financing activities that usually bring an inflow of cash. The payment of dividends is a financing outflow. The purchase of land (regardless of use) is an investing outflow. (Solution = b.)

QUESTION

15.   (L.O. 7) In preparing a statement of cash flows, the payment of interest to a creditor should be classified as a cash outflow due to:

        a.   operating activities.
        b.   investing activities.
        c.   financing activities.
        d.   borrowing activities.

Explanation: Borrowing money is a financing activity. Repaying amounts (the principal borrowed) is a financing activity. Paying interest on amounts borrowed is an operating activity because it is **not** included in the definition of financing activities and because the interest paid will be related to the interest incurred (interest expense) which is a transaction that enters into the determination of net income. (Solution = a.)

QUESTION

16.   (L.O. 8) Alley Cat Corporation had net income for 2002 of $5,000,000. Additional information is as follows:

Amortization of plant assets		$2,000,000
Amortization of intangibles		$400,000
Increase in accounts receivable		$700,000
Increase in accounts payable	$900,000	

        Alley Cat's net cash provided by operating activities for 2002 was:
        a. $2,800,000.
        b. $7,200,000.
        c. $7,400,000.
        d. $7,600,000.

Explanation: The amortization amounts are items that reduce net income but do not cause a decrease in cash during the current period. The increase in accounts receivable indicates that sales revenue earned for the period exceeded the cash collections from customers, and therefore net income exceeded the net cash provided by operating activities. The increase in accounts payable indicates that expenses incurred exceeded cash payments for expense type items which caused net income to be less than net cash provided by operating activities. The solution is as follows:

Net income	$5,000,000
Amortization of plant assets	2,000,000
Amortization of intangibles	400,000
Increase in accounts receivable	(700,000)
Increase in accounts payable	900,000
Net cash provided by operating activities	$7,600,000

(Solution = d.)

QUESTION

17.   (L.O. 8) Net cash flow from operating activities for 2002 for Graham Corporation was $75,000. The following items are reported on the financial statements for 2002:

Amortization	$5,000
Cash dividends paid on common shares	3,000
Increase in accrued receivables	6,000

Based only on the information above, Graham's net income for 2002 was:
a. $64,000.
b. $66,000.
c. $74,000.
d. $76,000.
e.   None of the above.

Approach and Explanation: Write down the format for the reconciliation of net income to net cash flow from operating activities. Fill in the information given. Solve for the unknown.

Net income	$ X
Amortization	5,000
Increase in accrued receivables	(6,000)
Net cash flow from operating activities	$ 75,000

Solving for X, net income = $76,000. Cash dividends paid on common shares have no effect on this calculation because cash dividends paid is not a component of net income and not an operating activity. Cash dividends paid is classified as a financing activity. (Solution = d.)

QUESTION

18.   (L.O. 9) Free cash flow is:
a.   net cash provided by operating activities minus capital expenditures and dividends.
b.   net cash provided by operating activities minus retirement of debt and purchases of treasury stock.
c.   the amount of cash obtained from donations.
d.   the amount of net cash increase during the period.

Explanation: One method of examining a company's financial flexibility is to develop a free cash flow analysis. This analysis starts with net cash provided by operating activities and ends with free cash flow which is calculated as net cash provided by operating activities less capital expenditures and dividends. Free cash flow is the amount of discretionary cash flow a company has for purchasing additional investments, retiring its debt, purchasing treasury stock, or simply adding to its liquidity. This measure indicates a company's level of financial flexibility. (Solution = a.)

QUESTION
19.   (L.O. 9) Net cash provided by operating activities divided by average total liabilities equals the:
a.   Current cash debt coverage ratio.
b.   Cash debt coverage ratio.
c.   Free cash flow.
d.   Current ratio.

Approach and Explanation: Visualize the calculation of each ratio or calculation referenced in the answer selections. The current cash debt coverage ratio equals net cash provided by operating activities provided by average current liabilities. The cash debt coverage ratio is calculate d by taking the net cash provided by operating activities divided by average total liabilities. Free cash flow is calculated as net cash provided by operating activities less capital expenditures and dividends. The current ratio is current assets divided by current liabilities. (Solution = b.)

QUESTION
20.   (L.O. 10) Activity ratios measure the effectiveness of asset usage. One of the activity ratios is the:
a.   inventory turnover ratio.
b.   current ratio.
c.   quick ratio.
d.   rate of return on assets.

Explanation: The activity ratios include the (1) receivable turnover ratio, (2) inventory turnover ratio, and (3) asset turnover ratio. The current ratio and the quick (or acid-test) ratio are both liquidity ratios. The rate of return on assets ratio is a profitability ratio. (Solution = a.)

QUESTION
21.   (L.O. 10) The current ratio is 3:1 for the Hamstock Company at December 31, 2002. What is the impact on that ratio of a collection of accounts receivable?
a.   Current ratio is increased.
b.   Current ratio is decreased.
c.   Current ratio is unaffected.

Approach and Explanation: Reconstruct the journal entry for the transaction. Analyse the effect of the debit portion of the entry on each element of the ratio and then analyse the effect of the credit portion of the entry on each element of the ratio. The entry to record the collection of accounts receivable involves a debit to Cash and a credit to Accounts Receivable. There is no change in the total amount of current assets. There is no change in the total amount of current liabilities. Thus, there is no change in the current ratio which is current assets divided by current liabilities. (Solution = c.)

CHAPTER 6

REVENUE RECOGNITION

OVERVIEW

The revenue recognition principle provides that revenue is to be recognized when (1) the earnings process is substantially complete, (2) the revenue can be reasonably measurable, and (3) collectibility is reasonably assured. This rule sounds simple enough, but the many methods of marketing products and services make it extremely difficult to apply in certain situations. Although a large percentage of entities find it appropriate to recognize revenue at the point of sale (delivery) of a good or service, other entities find it appropriate to use some other basis of revenue recognition, which may result in recognizing revenue prior to delivery or at a point in time after delivery. In this chapter, we discuss accounting guidelines for the recognition of revenue.

SUMMARY OF LEARNING OBJECTIVES

1. **Apply the revenue recognition principle.** The revenue recognition principle provides that revenue is recognized when (1) it is earned (including measurability) and (2) collection is reasonably assured. Revenues are **earned** when the entity has substantially accomplished what it must do to be entitled to the benefits represented by the revenues, that is, when the earning process is complete or virtually complete.

2. **Describe accounting issues involved with revenue recognition for sale of goods.** The two conditions for recognizing revenue are usually met by the time a product or merchandise is delivered or services are rendered to customers (risks and rewards of ownership passed) Consider earlier or later points.

3. **Explain accounting for consignment sales.** The risks and rewards remain with the seller in this case and therefore a real sale does not occur until the goods are sold to a third party. Special accounts separate inventory on consignment.

4. **Describe accounting issues involved with revenue recognition for services and long-term contracts.** The earnings process is more likely a continuous one involving many significant events. Often, the customer is found upfront. Therefore, revenue is recognized throughout the earnings process.

5. **Apply the percentage-of-completion method for long-term contracts.** To apply the percentage-of-completion method to long-term contracts, one must have some basis for measuring the progress toward completion at particular interim dates. One of the most popular input measures used to determine the progress toward completion is the cost-to-cost basis. Using this basis, the percentage of completion is measured by comparing costs incurred to date with the most recent

estimate of the total costs to complete the contract. The percentage that costs incurred bear to total estimated costs is applied to the total revenue or the estimated total gross profit on the contract in arriving at the revenue or the gross profit amount to be recognized to date.

6.   **Apply the completed-contract method for long-term contracts.** Under this method, revenue and gross profit are recognized only at point of sale, that is, when the contract is completed. Costs of long-term contracts in process and current billings are accumulated, but there are no interim charges or credits to income statement accounts for revenues, costs, and gross profit. The annual entries to record costs of construction, progress billings, and collections from customers would be identical to those for the percentage-of-completion method with the significant exclusion of the recognition of revenue and gross profit.

7.   **Account for losses on long-term contracts.** Two types of losses can become evident under long-term contracts: (1) **Loss in current period on a profitable contract:** Under the percentage-of-completion method only, the estimated cost increase requires a current period adjustment of excess gross profit recognized on the project in prior periods. This adjustment is recorded as a loss in the current period because it is a change in accounting estimate. (2) **Loss on an unprofitable contract:** Under both the percentage-of-completion and the completed-contract methods, the entire expected contract loss must be recognized in the current period.

8.   **Discuss how to deal with measurement uncertainty.** Transactions that involve buy-back or rights of return may require measurement. Existence of the practice of trade loading and channel stuffing may also require remeasuring of the transaction.

9.   **Discuss how to deal with collection uncertainty.** Normally, if estimable, a provision for uncollectible amounts is accrued. In certain types of sales arrangements, payment is extended over the longer term. In these cases, the instalments or cost recovery methods may be used. These methods allow revenue recognition upfront but gross profits are deferred.

10.   **Explain and apply the instalment sales method of accounting.** The instalment sales method recognizes income in the periods of collection rather than in the period of sale. The instalment method of accounting is justified on the basis that when there is no reasonable approach for estimating the degree of collectibility, revenue should not be recognized until cash is collected.

11.   **Explain and apply the cost recovery method of accounting.** Under the cost recovery method, no profit is recognized until cash payments by the buyer exceed the seller's cost of the merchandise sold. After all costs have been recovered, any additional cash collections are included in income. The income statement for the period of sale reports sales revenue, the cost of goods sold, and the gross profit—both the amount that is recognized during the period and the amount that is deferred. The deferred gross profit is offset against the related receivable on the balance sheet. Subsequent income statements report the gross profit as a separate item of revenue when it is recognized as earned.

12.*   **Explain revenue recognition for franchises.** In a franchise arrangement, the initial franchise fee is recorded as revenue only when and as the franchisor makes substantial performance of the services it is obligated to perform and collection of the fee is reasonably assured. Continuing franchise fees are recognized as revenue when they are earned and receivable from the franchisee.

          *This material is covered in Appendix 6-A in the text.

TIPS ON CHAPTER TOPICS

TIP: All revenues cause an increase in net assets (owners' equity); thus, a revenue item also results in either an increase in assets or a decrease in liabilities. **Revenues** are defined in *CICA Handbook,* Section 1000, par. .37 as: "Revenues are increases in economic resources, either by way of inflows or enhancements of assets or reductions of liabilities, resulting from the ordinary activities of an entity. Revenues of entities normally arise from the sale of goods, the rendering of services or the use by others of entity resources yielding rent, interest, royalties or dividends."

TIP: The amount of revenue for a period is generally determined independently of expenses. The **revenue recognition principle** is applied to determine in what period(s) revenue transactions are to be reported. Then the **matching principle** is applied to determine in what period(s) expense transactions are to be reported; expenses are to be recognized in the same period as the revenues to which the expenses contributed.

TIP: To **recognize** means to give expression in the accounts. To recognize a revenue means to record an item as revenue in the accounts; thus, the item will get reported as revenue in the financial statements. Likewise, to recognize an asset means to record an increase in an asset account. **Recognition** is "the process of including an item in the financial statements of an entity" (*CICA Handbook,* Section 1000). For an asset or liability, recognition involves recording not only acquisition or incurrence of the item but also later changes in it, including removal from the financial statements.

TIP: Recognition is **not** the same as realization, although the two are sometimes used interchangeably in accounting literature and practice. **Realization** is "the process of converting noncash resources and rights into money and is most precisely used in accounting and financial reporting to refer to sales of assets for cash or claims to cash" (*SFAC No. 3*, par. 83).

TIP: In accordance with the revenue recognition principle: (a) revenue from selling products is recognized at the date of sale, usually interpreted to mean the date of delivery to customers; (b) revenue from services rendered is recognized when services have been performed and are billable; (c) revenue from permitting others to use enterprise assets such as interest, rent, and royalties, is recognized as time passes or as the assets are used; and, (d) revenue from disposing of assets other than products is recognized at the date of sale.

TIP: **Revenue** is a **gross** amount (an amount before costs are deducted); whereas, **gain** is a **net** amount (an amount after costs are subtracted). Gains (as contrasted to revenues) commonly result from transactions and other events that do not involve an earning process. For gain recognition, being earned is generally less significant than being realized or realizable. Gains are commonly recognized at the time of sale of an asset, disposition of a liability, or when prices of certain assets change. The following example illustrates how revenue is a gross concept, and gain is a net concept.

A company sells two assets for $1,000 each. The first asset is an inventory item which cost $600. The second asset is a piece of equipment which cost $900 and has been amortized $300 thus far. The first item would cause the following to be reflected in the income statement:

Sales revenue	$1,000
Cost of goods sold	600
Gross profit	$ 400

The second item would cause the following to be reflected in the "other income" section of a multiple-step income statement:

Gain on sale of equipment $400*
     *$900 cost - $300 accumulated amortization = $600 carrying value
     $1,000 selling price - $600 carrying value = $400 gain

In the case of the second item, it is not an item held for sale in the main course of business. The proceeds ($1,000) and the related cost (carrying value of $600) are netted off the statement, and only the net amount ($400 gain) appears on the face of the income statement.

TIP: In determining who has the risks and rewards of ownership and hence whether a sale has occurred at the point of delivery, it is important to look at who has the possession of the goods and who has the legal title (e.g. Terms of sale, FOB shipping point means title transfers to the buyer when the goods leave the shipping dock, while FOB destination indicates title does not transfer until the goods arrive at the buyers location).

TIP: Goods shipped on consignment are **not** considered to be a sale as the revenue recognition criteria are not fully met as full performance by the seller is not complete since ownership (legal title) of the goods are maintained by the seller.

TIP: The revenue recognition bases or methods, the criteria for their use, and the reasons for departing from the sale basis when accounting for the sale of a product are summarized in **Illustration 6-2**. Review those methods and be able to explain when and why they are used.

TIP: The term **income** is sometimes used to refer to a gross amount (such as dividend income, rent income, interest income), which makes its usage synonymous with revenue. The term income is also used to refer to a net amount, such as net income for a period. Thus, if an exam question asks for the calculation of income to be recognized for the current period for a long-term construction contract using the percentage-of-completion method, it may be unclear whether the question is using "income" to mean "revenue" or if "income" means "gross profit" (revenue net of related costs). If it is a multiple choice question, a calculation for both revenue and gross profit may quickly solve the mystery.

TIP: The percentage of completion method is used for long-term construction contracts where revenue is appropriately recognized during production (prior to completion and delivery). Justification for recognition of revenue during the construction period is based on the fact that the ultimate sale and the selling price are assured by the contract. The percentage-of-completion method recognizes revenue, costs, and gross profit as progress is made toward completion on a long-term contract. The progress made during a period may be supplied by engineering estimates or determined by the cost-to-cost method (the latter method is used in most textbook situations). Using the cost-to-cost

$$\left[\frac{\text{Costs incurred to date}}{\text{Estimate of total costs}} \times \begin{array}{c}\text{Estimated total}\\\text{revenue (or}\\\text{gross profit)}\end{array} \right] - \begin{array}{c}\text{Total revenue (or gross}\\\text{profit) recognized}\\\text{in prior periods}\end{array} = \begin{array}{c}\text{Current period}\\\text{revenue (or}\\\text{gross profit)}\end{array}$$

In this formula, estimated total revenue is determined by the contract price, and estimated total gross profit is determined by the contract price reduced by an estimate of total costs. The estimate of total costs includes costs incurred to date **plus** an estimate of remaining costs to be incurred to complete the contract. Costs incurred to date include costs incurred in prior periods **plus** costs incurred in the current period.

TIP: Regardless of whether the percentage-of-completion method or the completed-contract method is used, the difference between the balance of the Construction in Process account and the balance of the Billings on Construction in Process account is reported as a current liability (if Billings on Construction in Process has the larger balance) or as a current asset (if Construction in Process has the larger balance). The balance of the Billings on Construction in Process account is offset against the balance of the inventory account (Construction in Process) because the inventory amount should not be double counted (i.e., the inventory account was not removed when the Accounts Receivable account was increased at the date of a billing to a customer).

TIP: The **instalment sales method of revenue recognition** emphasizes collection of the selling price rather than the sale. It recognizes income in the periods of collection rather than in the period of sale. The instalment sales method is **not** a generally accepted method; it is to be used only for situations where uncollectible accounts cannot be reasonably estimated at the time of sale.

TIP: When using the **instalment sales method of accounting**, the amount of gross profit to be recognized for a particular period is determined by multiplying the amount of cash collected during the period on instalment receivables by the appropriate gross profit percentage(s). A rather difficult exam question may give the amount of gross profit recognized along with the gross profit percentage and require the examinee to solve for the amount of cash collected. For example, if gross profit recognized for 2002 is $90,000 and the gross profit percentage is 30%, cash collections during the period amount to $300,000 ($90,000 ÷ 30% = $300,000).

TIP: In a sale and buyback arrangement, professional judgement as to whether a sale has indeed taken place must be used. Legal title has transferred, but the economic substance of the transaction indicates the seller retains the risks of ownership.

TIP: Goods on consignment should be reported as inventory by the consignor, not the consignee.

ILLUSTRATION 6-1
JOURNAL ENTRIES FOR LONG-TERM CONSTRUCTION CONTRACTS (L.O. 3, 4)

ENTRY	PERCENTAGE-OF-COMPLETION METHOD	COMPLETED-CONTRACT METHOD

To record costs of construction	Construction in Process
	    Materials, Cash, Payables, etc.
		Construction in Progress
		    Materials, Cash, Payables, etc.

To record progress billings	Accounts Receivable
	    Billings on Construction in Process
		Accounts Receivable
		    Billings on Construction in Process

To record collections	Cash
	    Accounts Receivable
		Cash
		    Accounts Receivable

To recognize revenue and gross profit	Construction in Process GP**
	Construction Expenses COSTS
	    Revenue from Long-
	    Term Contracts REV
		No Entry*

To record final approval of the contract	Billings on Construction in Process
	    Construction in Process
		Billings on Const. In Process REV
		    Revenue from Long-
		    Term Contracts REV
		
		Construction Expenses*** COSTS
		    Construction in Process COSTS

GP = Gross Profit   COSTS = Costs Incurred   REV = Revenue

*A loss on an unprofitable contract is recognized, in full, immediately under either method. A loss would be recorded under the completed-contract method by a debit to Loss from Long-Term Contracts and a credit to Construction in Process for the estimated amount of loss.

**When a loss is estimated, this account (Construction in Process) gets credited for the estimated amount of loss. The rest of the entry is the same as what is shown for a profitable situation.

***The account Construction Expenses can be titled Construction Costs or Costs of Construction

> **TIP:** An estimated loss on a long-term construction contract is to be recognized in the period it is determined there will ultimately be a loss on completion of the contract, regardless of the method being used to account for the contract. The justification for recognizing the loss before completion even under the completed-contract method lies with the conservatism constraint and the axiom—anticipate no profits but provide for all losses.

ILLUSTRATION 6-2
REVENUE RECOGNITION BASES OTHER THAN
THE SALE BASIS FOR PRODUCTS (L.O. 3, 4, 6, 7)

Recognition Basis (or Method of Applying a Basis)	Criteria for Use of Basis	Reason(s) for Departing from Sale Basis
Percentage-of-completion method	Long-term construction of property; dependable estimates of extent of progress and cost to complete; reasonable assurance of collectibility of contract price; expectation that both contractor and buyer can meet obligations; and absence of inherent hazards that make estimates doubtful.	Availability of evidence of ultimate proceeds; better measure of periodic income; avoidance of fluctuations in revenues, expenses, and income; performance is a "continuous sale" and therefore not a departure from the sale basis.
Completed-contract method	Use on short-term contracts, and whenever percentage-of-completion criteria are not met for long-term contracts.	Existence of inherent hazards in the contract beyond the normal, recurring business risks; conditions for using the percentage-of-completion method are absent.
Completion-of-production basis	Immediate marketability at quoted prices; unit interchangeability; difficulty of determining costs; and no significant distribution costs.	Known or determinable revenues; inability to determine costs and thereby defer expense recognition until sale.
Instalment sales method	Absence of a reasonable basis for estimating degree of collectibility and costs of collection.	Collectibility of the receivable is so uncertain that gross profit is not recognized until cash is actually received.
Cost recovery method	Absence of a reasonable basis for estimating degree of collectibility and cost of collection.	Collectibility of the receivable is so doubtful that no income is recognized until the amount of cash received exceeds the cost of the good sold.
Deposit method	Cash received before the sales transaction is completed.	No recognition of revenue and income because there is not sufficient transfer of the risks and rewards of ownership.

Source: Adapted from *Survey of Present Practices in Recognizing Revenues, Expenses, Gains, and Losses*, FASB, 1981, pp. 12 and 13.

EXERCISE 6-1

Purpose: (L.O. 5, 6) This exercise will allow you to compare the results of using the percentage-of-completion method versus the results of applying the completed-contract method to calculate the amount of gross profit to be recognized in each year of a three-year contract.

At the beginning of 2002, Build-a-lot Construction Company signed a fixed-price contract to construct a sports arena at a price of $26,000,000. Information relating to the costs and billings for this contract is as follows:

	2002	**2003**	**2004**
Costs incurred during the period	$ 8,320,000	$11,360,000	$ 3,520,000
Estimated costs to complete, as of December 31	12,480,000	4,320,000	-0-
Billings during the year	3,900,000	15,900,000	6,200,000
Collections during the year	3,120,000	12,000,000	10,880,000

Instructions
(a) Assuming the completed-contract method is used, calculate the gross profit to be recognized in (1) 2002, (2) 2003, and (3) 2004.
(b) Assuming the percentage-of-completion method is used, calculate the gross profit to be recognized in (1) 2002, (2) 2003, and (3) 2004.
(c) Assuming the percentage-of-completion method is used, show how the details related to this construction contract would be disclosed on the balance sheet at December 31, 2003.

Solution to Exercise 6-1

(a) (1) 2002   -0-
    (2) 2003   -0-
    (3) 2004 $2,800,000*

        *Calculations:

Total revenue	$26,000,000
Total costs incurred	23,200,000**
Total gross profit	$ 2,800,000

**Costs incurred in 2002	$ 8,320,000
Costs incurred in 2003	11,360,000
Costs incurred in 2004	3,520,000
Total costs incurred	$23,200,000

Explanation: When the completed-contract method is used, the recognition of all revenue and related costs (and, therefore, resulting gross profit) is deferred until the period of completion (2004 in this case). The only exception to this guideline is in the case where a loss is expected. A loss should be recognized immediately in the period in which it is determined that a loss will result.

(b) (1) 2002 $2,080,000
    (2) 2003 $ (440,000)
    (3) 2004 $1,160,000

Calculations:

2002: Costs incurred to date (12/31/02) $ 8,320,000
        Estimated costs to complete as of 12/31/02   12,480,000
        Estimate of total costs as of 12/31/02 $ 20,800,000

        Total revenue (contract price) $ 26,000,000
        Estimate of total costs   20,800,000
        Estimated total gross profit $ 5,200,000

$$\frac{\$8,320,000}{\$20,800,000} \times \$5,200,000 = \underline{\$2,080,000}$$ Gross profit to be recognized in 2002

2003: Costs incurred to date (12/31/03)($8,320,000 + $11,360,000) $ 19,680,000
        Estimated costs to complete as of 12/31/03   4,320,000
        Estimate of total costs as of 12/31/03 $ 24,000,000

        Total revenue (contract price) $26,000,000
        Estimate of total costs   24,000,000
        Estimated total gross profit $ 2,000,000

$$\frac{\$19,680,000}{\$24,000,000} \times \$2,000,000 - \$2,080,000 = \underline{\$(440,000)}$$ Loss to be recognized in 2003

2004: Costs incurred in 2002 $ 8,320,000
        Costs incurred in 2003   11,360,000
        Costs incurred in 2004   3,520,000
        Total costs incurred   23,200,000

        Total revenue (contract price) $26,000,000
        Total costs incurred   23,200,000
        Total gross profit earned on contract   2,800,000
        Gross profit recognized in 2002   (2,080,000)
        Loss recognized in 2003   440,000
        Gross profit to be recognized in 2004 $ 1,160,000

Approach and Explanation: Gross profit to be recognized in a particular year can be determined by applying the following formula:

$$\left[\begin{array}{c} \text{Costs incurred} \\ \text{to date} \\ \hline \text{Estimate of} \\ \text{total costs} \end{array} \times \begin{array}{c} \text{Estimated total} \\ \text{gross profit} \end{array} \right] - \begin{array}{c} \text{Total gross} \\ \text{profit recognized} \\ \text{in prior periods} \end{array} = \begin{array}{c} \text{Current period} \\ \text{gross profit} \end{array}$$

In the calculation for estimated total gross profit, the current (most up-to-date) estimate of total costs is deducted from total revenue (the contract price). The estimate of total costs is likely to change every year, which will cause the estimated total gross profit to change each year. Such is the case in this exercise.

In the second year of the contract, Build-a-lot's cost estimates increased dramatically, which caused the gross profit recognized to date (2002's gross profit of $2,080,000) to exceed the $1,640,000 total gross profit earned to date ($19,680,000 ÷ $24,000,000 x $2,000,000 = $1,640,000). This excess is recognized as a loss of $440,000 in 2003 to bring the total gross profit recognized by the end of 2003 to $1,640,000.

In the last year of the contract, total costs incurred on the contract are deducted from total revenue on the contract to arrive at total gross profit earned on the contract. The amounts reported on prior income statements as gross profit (loss) are deducted from (added to) this amount to arrive at the gross profit to recognize in the last period.

In the situation at hand, the costs incurred in 2004 are less than what was expected, according to the cost estimates at the end of 2003, which results in more total gross profit than was predicted at the end of 2003.

TIP: Notice that **neither** the amount of billings **nor** the amount of cash collections during the year has an impact on the amount of gross profit to be recognized.

TIP: Notice that a loss was recognized in the second year using the percentage-of-completion method but no loss was recognized using the completed-contract method. The reasons for this are that the loss was an interim loss, not an overall loss on the contract. An interim loss refers to the loss that results when the total gross profit to date (at the end of 2003) is less than the amount of gross profit recognized in prior periods (2002). It is a loss in the current period (2003) on a profitable contract. It results from an increase in estimated costs which requires a current period adjustment of excess gross profit recognized on the contract in prior periods. This adjustment is recorded in the current period because it is a change in accounting estimate. If an overall loss is expected on a contract, it must also be recognized immediately even under the completed-contract method.

(c)   Current assets:

Accounts receivable		$4,680,000
Inventories		
Construction in process	$21,320,000	
Less: Billings on construction in process	19,800,000	
Costs and recognized profit in excess of billings		$1,520,000

Approach and Explanation: Draw T-accounts. Mentally think through the journal entries that would be recorded for the facts given. Post these amounts to the T-accounts on paper.

Accounts Receivable						Construction in Process				
2002	3,900,000		2002	3,120,000		2002	8,320,000		2003	440,000
2003	15,900,000		2003	12,000,000		2002	2,080,000			
						2003	11,360,000			
12/31/03						12/31/03				
Bal.	4,680,000					Bal.	21,320,000			

Billings on Construction in Process			
		2002	3,900,000
		2003	15,900,000
		12/31/03	
		Bal.	19,800,000

TIP: Notice that the amounts reflected in the balance sheet for accounts receivable ($4,680,000) and inventories ($1,520,000) when combined with the increase in cash from collections of billings ($15,120,000 collections to date) equals $21,320,000 (the balance in the Construction in Process account), which also equals the percentage of the total contract revenue earned to date ($19,680,000/ $24,000,000 x $26,000,000 = $21,320,000). The balance of the Billings on Construction in Process account is deducted from the balance in the Construction in Process account so as not to double count assets related to accounting for construction contracts. The total amount billed thus far ($19,800,000) is either collected ($15,120,000 has been collected so the Cash account has increased which is not shown here) or uncollected ($4,680,000 balance in Accounts Receivable).

EXERCISE 6-2

Purpose: (L.O. 5, 6) This exercise will illustrate the calculations, journal entries, and balance sheet presentations involved in the use of the completed-contract and percentage-of-completion methods of accounting for long-term construction contracts.

The Nifty Construction Company entered into a long-term contract in 2000. The contract price was $1,600,000, and the company initially estimated the total costs of the project to be $1,150,000. The following data pertains to the three years that the contract was in process:

Year	Costs Incurred During the Year	Estimated Costs at End of the Year to Complete Contract	Billings During the Year	Collections During the Year	Operating Expenses
2000	$224,000	$896,000	$ 200,000	$170,000	$80,000
2001	712,000	264,000	1,000,000	900,000	82,000
2002	344,000	-0-	400,000	430,000	74,000

Instructions

(a) Calculate the gross profit to be reported in each of the three years using the completed-contract method.

(b) Calculate the gross profit to be reported in each of the three years using the percentage-of-completion method based on the costs incurred to date and the estimated costs to complete the contract. (Also calculate the amount of revenue and cost of sales reflected in each gross profit figure.)

(c) Prepare the related journal entries for all three years using the completed-contract method.

(d) Prepare the related journal entries for all three years using the percentage-of-completion method.

(e) Prepare a partial balance sheet at the end of each of the three years assuming (1) the completed-contract method is used and (2) the percentage-of-completion method is used.

TIP: The use of T-accounts is helpful here to determine the balances of accounts at the balance sheet date.

Solution to Exercise 6-2

(a) 2000   -0-
     2001   -0-
     2002 $1,600,000 - ($224,000 + $712,000 + $344,000) = $320,000

(b) **2000**   Estimate of total costs = $224,000 + $896,000 = $1,120,000
           Estimate of total gross profit = $1,600,000 - $1,120,000 = $480,000

           Gross profit to be recognized in 2000 = $\dfrac{\$224,000}{\$1,120,000}$ x $480,000 = $96,000

     2001   Costs incurred to date = $224,000 + $712,000 = $936,000
           Estimate of total costs = $936,000 + $264,000 = $1,200,000
           Estimate of total gross profit = $1,600,000 - $1,200,000 = $400,000
           Gross profit to be recognized in 2001 =

$$\left(\frac{\$936,000}{\$1,200,000} x \$400,000 \right) - \$96,000 = \underline{\$216,000}$$

     2002   Total costs incurred for project = $224,000 + $712,000 + $344,000
             = $1,280,000
           Contract price of $1,600,000 minus total costs incurred of $1,280,000
             equals total gross profit on project of $320,000
           Gross profit to be recognized in 2002 = $320,000 - ($96,000 + $216,000)
             = $8,000

2000   Revenue for 2000 $= \dfrac{\$224,000}{\$1,120,000}$ x $1,600,000 = $320,000

Costs to match with revenue for 2000 = $224,000

Gross profit for 2000 = $320,000 - $224,000 = $96,000

2001   Revenue for 2001 $= \left(\dfrac{\$936,000}{\$1,200,000} \times \$1,600,000 \right)$ - $320,000 = $928,000

Costs to match with revenue for 2001 = $712,000

Gross profit for 2001 = $928,000 - $712,000 = $216,000

2002   Revenue for 2002 = $1,600,000 - ($320,000 + $928,000) = $352,000

Costs to match with revenue for 2002 = $344,000

Gross profit for 2002 = $352,000 - $344,000 = $8,000

(c)   **Journal Entries—Completed Contract Method**

	2000		2001		2002	
Accounts	**Dr.**	**Cr.**	**Dr.**	**Cr.**	**Dr.**	**Cr.**
Const. in Process	224,000		712,000		344,000	
Operating Expenses	80,000		82,000		74,000	
Materials, Cash,						
Payables, Etc.		304,000		794,000		418,000
Accounts Receivable	200,000		1,000,000		400,000	
Billings on Const.						
in Process		200,000		1,000,000		400,000
Cash	170,000		900,000		430,000	
Accounts Rec.		170,000		900,000		430,000
Billings on Const. in						
Process					1,600,000	
Revenue from						
Long-term						
Contracts						1,600,000
Construction Exp.					1,280,000	1,280,000
Const. in Process						

(d) **Journal Entries—Percentage-of-Completion Method**

Accounts	2000 Dr.	2000 Cr.	2001 Dr.	2001 Cr.	2002 Dr.	2002 Cr.
Const. in Process	224,000		712,000		344,000	
Operating Expenses	80,000		82,000		74,000	
Materials, Cash, Payables, Etc.		304,000		794,000		418,000
Accounts Receivable	200,000		1,000,000		400,000	
Billings on Const. in Process		200,000		1,000,000		400,000
Cash	170,000		900,000		430,000	
Accounts Rec.		170,000		900,000		430,000
Const. Expenses	224,000		712,000		344,000	
Const. in Process	96,000		216,000		8,000	
Revenue from Long-Term Contracts		320,000		928,000		352,000
Billings on Const. in Process					1,600,000	
Const. in Process						1,600,000

(e)   1.   **Partial Balance Sheet—Completed-Contract Method**

	End of 2000	End of 2001	End of 2002
Current assets:			
Accounts receivable	$30,000	$130,000	$100,000
Inventories			
Construction in process	$224,000		
Less: Billings on const. in process	200,000		
Unbilled contract costs	$24,000		
Current liabilities:			
Billings on const. in process		$1,200,000	
Less: Construction in process		936,000	
Billings in excess of costs and recognized profit		$264,000	

Approach: Draw T-accounts and post journal entries to determine account balances.

2.   **Partial Balance Sheet—Percentage-of-Completion Method**

	End of 2000	End of 2001	End of 2002
Current assets:			
Accounts receivable	$30,000	$130,000	$100,000
Inventories			
Construction in process	$320,000	$1,248,000	
Less: Billings on const. in			
process	200,000	1,200,000	
Costs and recognized profit			
in excess of billings	$120,000	$48,000	

Approach: Draw T-accounts and post journal entries to determine account balances.

EXERCISE 6-3

Purpose: (L.O. 10, 11) This exercise will (1) illustrate the calculations involved with the instalment method of accounting, (2) examine the classification of the Deferred Gross Profit account and (3) apply the cost recovery method.

Arnie Sagar Company has appropriately used the instalment method of accounting since it began business in 2001. The following data were obtained for the years 2001 and 2002:

	2001	2002
Instalment sales	$800,000	$900,000
Cost of instalment sales	592,000	684,000
Cash collections on sales of 2001	280,000	320,000
Cash collections on sales of 2002	-0-	400,000

Instructions
(a)   Calculate the amount of realized gross profit to report for (1) 2001, and (2) 2002.
(b)   Calculate the balance in the deferred gross profit accounts on (1) December 31, 2001, and (2) December 31, 2002.
(c)   Explain the classification of the total deferred gross profit on the balance sheet at December 31, 2002.
(d)   Prepare the journal entry to record the repossession of merchandise because of a defaulting customer. Assume that at the date of default in 2002, the balance on the related instalment receivable (which originated in 2001) was $14,000 and the fair value of the merchandise was $8,500.
(e)   Assume the cost recovery method is used rather than the instalment method. Calculate the amount of realized gross profit that would be recognized (1) on the 2001 income statement, and (2) on the 2002 income statement.

Solution to Exercise 6-3

(a) (1) Gross Profit Ratio—2001:

Instalment sales for 2001	$ 800,000
Cost of instalment sales for 2001	(592,000)
Gross profit on instalment sales for 2001	$ 208,000

$$\frac{\$208,000 \text{ Gross Profit}}{\$800,000 \text{ Sales}} = \underline{26\%} \text{ Gross profit ratio on 2001 sales}$$

Cash collections in 2001 on sales of 2001	$ 280,000
Gross profit ratio for 2001 sales	26%
Gross profit realized in 2001 on 2001 sales	$ 72,800

(2) Gross Profit Ratio—2002:

Instalment sales for 2002	$ 900,000
Cost of instalment sales for 2002	(684,000)
Gross profit on instalment sales for 2002	$ 216,000

$$\frac{\$216,000 \text{ Gross profit}}{\$900,000 \text{ Sales}} = \underline{24\%} \text{ Gross profit ratio on 2002 sales}$$

Cash collections in 2002 on sales of 2002	$ 400,000
Gross profit ratio for 2002 sales	24%
Gross profit realized in 2002 on 2002 sales	$ 96,000

Cash collections in 2002 on sales of 2001	$ 320,000
Gross profit ratio for 2001 sales	26%
Gross profit realized in 2002 on 2001 sales	$ 83,200

Gross profit realized in 2002 on 2002 sales	$ 96,000
Gross profit realized in 2002 on 2001 sales	83,200
Total gross profit realized in 2002	$ 179,200

TIP: Always calculate a separate gross profit ratio for each year in which there are instalment sales. Clearly label each ratio so it is ready for use in subsequent calculations. For any given year, the cash collections during the year on Year 1 instalment sales multiplied by the gross profit ratio on Year 1 instalment sales will yield the gross profit realized during that given year on Year 1 instalment sales. The balance of Instalment Accounts Receivable, Year 1, at a balance sheet date, multiplied by the gross profit ratio for Year 1 instalment sales will yield the appropriate adjusted balance for the related Deferred Gross Profit, Year 1 account at the same date.

(b)   (1)

Deferred Gross Profit, 2001

2001	72,800[b]	2001	208,000[a]
		12/31/01 Bal.	<u>135,200</u>

(2)

Deferred Gross Profit, 2001				Deferred Gross Profit, 2002		
2002	83,200[c]	12/31/01 Bal.	135,200	2002	96,000[e]	2002 216,000[d]
		12/31/02 Bal.	<u>52,000</u>			12/31/02 Bal. <u>120,000</u>

[a] Gross profit on 2001 instalment sales = $800,000 - $592,000 = $208,000.
[b] Gross profit realized in 2001 on 2001 sales = $280,000 collections x 26% = $72,800.
[c] Gross profit realized in 2002 on 2001 sales = $320,000 collections x 26% = $83,200.
[d] Gross profit on 2002 instalment sales = $900,000 - $684,000 = $216,000.
[e] Gross profit realized in 2002 on 2002 sales = $400,000 collections x 24% = $96,000.

> **TIP:** The $52,000 balance in the Deferred Gross Profit, 2001 account at December 31, 2002 can be independently verified by multiplying the balance of Instalment Accounts Receivable, 2001 at December 31, 2002 [$800,000 - ($280,000 + $320,000) = $200,000] by the gross profit ratio for 2001 instalment sales (26%).

(c)   Per the answers to part (b) (2) above, the total deferred gross profit at December 31, 2002 amounts to $172,000 [$52,000 + $120,000 = $172,000]. In *SFAC No. 3*, par. 156-158, the deferred gross profit on instalment sales may be treated as either an unearned revenue (current liability) or a contra asset account (as a valuation of instalment accounts receivable).

(d)   **Approach:**

Do Second	Deferred Gross Profit (26% x $14,000)	3,640
Do Third	Repossessed Merchandise	8,500
Plug	Loss on Repossession	1,860
Do First	Instalment Accounts Receivable	14,000

Explanation: The amount of the loss is determined by (1) subtracting the deferred gross profit from the amount of the account receivable to determine the unrecovered cost (or book value) of the merchandise repossessed ($14,000 - $3,640 = $10,360), and (2) subtracting the estimated fair value of the merchandise repossessed from the unrecovered cost to get the amount of the loss on repossession ($10,360 - $8,500 = $1,860). As an alternative, the loss on repossession can be charged to the Allowance for Doubtful Accounts account.

(e)   (1)   Using the cost recovery method, no gross profit would be recognized on the 2001 income statement because the $280,000 cash collections did not exceed the $592,000 cost of the merchandise sold.

        (2)   Using the cost recovery method of revenue recognition, gross profit of $8,000 would be reported in 2002 due to instalment sales made in 2001. No gross profit

(2)   Using the cost recovery method of revenue recognition, gross profit of $8,000 would be reported in 2002 due to instalment sales made in 2001. No gross profit would be recognized on 2002 sales because cash collections did not exceed the cost of the merchandise sold.

Calculations:

Cumulative cash collections on 2001 sales	$ 600,000*
Cost of 2001 instalment sales	(592,000)
Gross profit to be recognized in 2002 using cost recovery method	$ 8,000

*$280,000 + $320,000 = $600,000

Explanation: The cost recovery method provides for gross profit to be recognized **only** after all costs of related sales have been recovered. All subsequent cash collections are recognized as profit.

EXERCISE 6-4

Purpose: (L.O. 12) This exercise will examine the treatment for an initial franchise fee under three scenarios.

Ma's Best Cookies Inc. charges an initial franchise fee of $110,000. Upon the signing of the agreement, a payment of $50,000 is due; thereafter, three annual payments of $20,000 are required. The credit rating of the franchisee is such that it would have to pay interest at 10% to borrow money.

Instructions

Prepare the entries to record the initial franchise fee on the books of the franchisor under the following assumptions:

(a)   The down payment is not refundable, no future services are required by the franchisor, and collection of the note is reasonably assured.

(b)   The franchisor has substantial services to perform, and the collection of the note is very uncertain.

(c)   The down payment is not refundable, collection of the note is reasonably certain, the franchisor has yet to perform a substantial amount of services, and the down payment represents a fair measure of the services already performed.

Solution to Exercise 6-4

(a)	Cash..	50,000	
	Notes Receivable	60,000	
	Discount on Notes Receivable............................		10,263
	[$60,000 - ($20,000 x 2.48685*)]		
	Revenue from Franchise Fees		99,737
	($50,000 + $60,000 - $10,263)		
(b)	Cash..	50,000	
	Unearned Franchise Fees		50,000
(c)	Cash..	50,000	
	Notes Receivable	60,000	
	Discount on Notes Receivable............................		10,263
	Revenue from Franchise Fees		50,000
	Unearned Franchise Fees ($20,000 x 2.48685*).........		49,737

*The factor for the present value of an ordinary annuity of 1 for $n = 3$,
$i = 10\%$ is 2.48685.

TIP: The amount of revenue recognized and the carrying value of the note receivable recorded by the franchisor upon the receipt of the franchise agreement and the initial franchise fee depend upon several factors, including: (1) whether or not the fee may be refundable, (2) an estimate of the collectibility of the note, (3) a measure of the future services to be performed by the franchisor, and (4) the incremental borrowing rate of the franchisee.

EXERCISE 6-5

Purpose: (L.O. 3) This exercise will review calculations involved with consignment sales.

On April 15, 2002, Stayfit Company consigned 70 treadmills, costing $600 each, to Higley Company. The cost of shipping the treadmills amounts to $800 and was paid by Stayfit Company. On December 30, 2002, an account sales was received from the consignee, reporting that 35 treadmills had been sold for $700 each. Remittance was made by the consignee for the amount due, after deducting a commission of 6%, advertising of $200, and total delivery costs of $300 on the treadmills sold.

Instructions
(a) Calculate the inventory value of the units unsold in the hands of the consignee.
(b) Calculate the profit for the consignor for the units sold.
(c) Calculate the amount of cash that will be remitted by the consignee.

Solution to Exercise 6-5

(a)   Inventoriable Costs:

70 units shipped at cost of $600 each	$ 42,000
Freight to consignee	800
Total inventoriable cost	$ 42,800
35 units on hand (1/2 x $42,800)	$ 21,400

(b)   Calculation of Consignment Profit:

Consignment sales (35 x $700)	$ 24,500
Cost of units sold (1/2 x $42,800)	(21,400)
Commission charged by consignee (6% x $24,500)	(1,470)
Advertising costs	(200)
Delivery costs to customers	(300)
Profit on consignment sales	$ 1,130

(c)   Remittance of Consignee:

Consignment sales		$ 24,500
Less: Commissions	$ 1,470	
Advertising	200	
Delivery	300	1,970
Remittance from consignee		$ 22,530

ANALYSIS OF MULTIPLE-CHOICE TYPE QUESTIONS

QUESTION

1.   (L.O. 1) The process of formally including an item in the financial statements of an entity is:
    a.   allocation.
    b.   articulation.
    c.   realization.
    d.   recognition.

Approach and Explanation: Write down a brief definition of each term listed. Select the one that matches the description in the stem of the question. **Allocation** is the accounting process of assigning or distributing an amount according to a plan or formula. Allocation is a broad term and includes amortization, which is the accounting process of reducing an amount by periodic payments or writedowns. **Articulation** refers to the interrelation of elements of the financial statements. **Realization** means the process of converting noncash resources and rights into money (such as the sale of assets for cash or claims to cash). **Recognition** is defined in *CICA Handbook, Section 1000* as the process of including an item in the financial statements of an entity. (Solution = d.)

QUESTION

2.   (L.O. 1,10) Dot Point, Inc. is a retailer of washers and dryers and offers a three-year service contract on each appliance sold. Although Dot Point sells the appliances on an instalment basis, all service contracts are cash sales at the time of purchase by the buyer. Collections received for service contracts should be recorded as:

a.   service revenue.
b.   unearned service revenue.
c.   a reduction in instalment accounts receivable.
d.   a direct addition to retained earnings.

Approach and Explanation: Recall the revenue recognition principle and think about how it would apply to this situation. Revenue is to be recognized when performance is substantially complete and when collection is reasonably assured, (*CICA Handbook,* Section 3400, par. .06.). The service contract revenue is realized at the date the cash is received; however, it is earned over the three-year period to which the contract pertains. Therefore, at the point of collection, the cash should be recorded by a credit to an Unearned (Deferred) Service Revenue account. The revenue will be earned over the three-year period as the company performs the services it promises by the contract. (Solution = b.)

QUESTION

3.   (L.O. 8) On December 31, 2001, Mahoney sold a piece of equipment to C. Bailey for $30,000 with the following terms: 2% cash discount if paid within 30 days, 1% discount if paid between 31 and 60 days of purchase, or payable in full within 90 days if not paid within a discount period. Bailey had the right to return this equipment to Mahoney if Bailey could not resell it before the end of the 90-day payment period, in which case Bailey would no longer be obligated to Mahoney. How much should be included in Mahoney's net sales for 2001 because of the sale of this machine?

a. $30,000
b. $29,700
c. $29,400
d. $0

Explanation: Per the terms of the sale/purchase, Bailey has the right to return the equipment to the seller if Bailey is not able to resell the equipment before expiration of the 90-day payment period. If the right to return the product exists, there are three alternatives available: (1) not recording the sale until all return privileges have expired; (2) recording the sale, but reducing the sales by an estimate of future returns; and (3) recording the sale and accounting for the returns as they occur. Due to the uncertainty of sales, it would be best to withhold recognizing revenue until Bailey sells the equipment. (Solution = d.)

QUESTION

4.   (L.O. 5) Bella Construction Co. uses the percentage-of-completion method. In 2001, Bella began work on a contract for $2,200,000; it was completed in 2002. The following cost data pertain to this contract:

	Year Ended December 31	
	2001	2002
Costs incurred during the year	$780,000	$560,000
Estimated costs to complete at end of year	520,000	--

The amount of gross profit to be recognized on the income statement for the year ended December 31, 2001 is:
a. $0.
b. $516,000.
c. $540,000.
d. $900,000.

Approach and Explanation: Write down the formula used to calculate the gross profit recognized to date at the end of 2001. Use the data given to calculate the gross profit.

$$\left[\frac{\text{Costs incurred to date}}{\text{Estimate of total costs}} \times \text{Estimated total gross profit} \right] - \text{Total gross profit recognized in prior periods} = \text{Current period gross profit}$$

$$\left[\frac{\$780,000}{\$780,000 + \$520,000} \times [\$2,200,000 - (\$780,000 + \$520,000)] \right] - \$0 =$$

$$\left[\frac{\$780,000}{\$1,300,000} \times (\$2,200,000 - \$1,300,000) \right] - \$0 =$$

$$[.60 \times \$900,000] - \$0 = \underline{\$540,000} \qquad \text{(Solution = c.)}$$

QUESTION

5.   (L.O. 5) Refer to the facts for **Question 4** above. The amount of gross profit to be recognized on the income statement for the year ended December 31, 2002 is:
a. $860,000.
b. $360,000.
c. $344,000.
d. $320,000.

Explanation: Use the formula shown for **Question 4** and plug in the data for 2002.

$$\left[\frac{\$780,000 + \$560,000}{\$780,000 + \$560,000 + \$0} \times [\$2,200,000 - (\$780,000 + \$560,000)] \right] - \$540,000 =$$

$$\left[\frac{\$1,340,000}{\$1,340,000} \times (\$2,200,000 - \$1,340,000) \right] - \$540,000 =$$

$$\$860,000 - \$540,000 = \underline{\$320,000}$$

(Solution = d.)

QUESTION

6.   (L.O. 6) Refer to the data for **Question 4** above. If the completed-contract method of accounting were used, the amount of gross profit to be reported for years 2001 and 2002 would be:

	2001	**2002**
a.	$0	$860,000
b.	$0	$900,000
c.	$900,000	$(40,000)
d.	$860,000	$0

Explanation: The completed-contract method calls for deferral of all revenue and costs related to a contract (project) until the period of completion. Thus, the entire gross profit ($2,200,000 total revenue - $1,340,000 total costs = $860,000 total gross profit) is recognized in the period the contract is completed. (Solution = a.)

QUESTION

7.   (L.O. 5) Designer Homes Construction Company uses the percentage-of-completion method. The costs incurred to date as a proportion of the estimated total costs to be incurred on a project are used as a measure of the extent of progress made toward completion of the project. During 2001, the company entered into a fixed-price contract to construct a mansion for Donald Thrumper for $24,000,000. The following details pertain to that contract:

	At Dec. 31, 2001	**At Dec. 31, 2002**
Percentage of completion	25%	60%
Estimated total costs of contract	$18,000,000	$20,000,000
Gross profit recognized to date	1,500,000	2,400,000

The amount of construction costs incurred during 2002 was:
a. $2,000,000.
b. $4,500,000.
c. $7,500,000.
d. $12,000,000.

Approach and Explanation: Write down the formula used to calculate the gross profit recognized to date at the end of 2002. Look at the components of the fraction.

$$\frac{\text{Costs incurred to date}}{\text{Estimate of total costs}} \times \begin{array}{c}\text{Estimated total}\\\text{gross profit}\end{array} = \begin{array}{c}\text{Total gross profit}\\\text{earned to date}\end{array}$$

According to the facts given, the fraction at December 31, 2002 is equal to 60%. Therefore, the costs incurred by the end of 2002 = 60% x $20,000,000 = $12,000,000. According to the facts given, the fraction for the same formula at the end of 2001 is equal to 25%. Therefore, the costs incurred by the end of 2001 = 25% x $18,000,000 = $4,500,000. The difference between the cumulative costs at the end of 2002 ($12,000,000) and the cumulative costs at the end of 2001 ($4,500,000) equals the costs incurred during 2002 of $7,500,000. (Solution = c.)

QUESTION

8.   (L.O. 1, 9, 10, 11) A manufacturer of large equipment sells on an instalment basis to customers with questionable credit ratings. Which of the following methods of revenue recognition is **least** likely to overstate the amount of gross profit reported?

a.   at the time of completion of the equipment (completion of production method)

b.   at the date of delivery (sale method)

c.   the instalment sales method

d.   the cost recovery method

Explanation: Recognition of income at the time the equipment is completed would be the method **most** likely to overstate gross profit. The recognition of gross profit at the time the equipment is completed or at the date the equipment is delivered would provide for the recognition of profits before any or much of the cash has been received; thus, these methods are not appropriate for situations where there is doubt about the collectibility of the selling price. The use of the instalment sales method would allow for the recognition of profits in proportion to the amount of the revenue collected in cash. The cost recovery method defers the recognition of all gross profit until cash collections of revenue are equal to the cost of the item sold; all remaining cash collections are reported as profit. Therefore, the cost recovery method is **least** likely to overstate the amount of gross profit reported. (Solution = d.)

QUESTION

9.   (L.O. 10) Eazy-Pay Sales Company has appropriately used the instalment method of accounting since it began operations at the beginning of 2002. The following information pertains to its operations for 2002:

Instalment sales	$ 600,000
Cost of instalment sales	420,000
Collections on instalment sales	240,000
General and administrative expenses	60,000

The amount to be reported on the December 31, 2002 balance sheet as Deferred Gross Profit should be:

a. $360,000.
b. $144,000.
c. $108,000.
d. $72,000.

Explanation: The $360,000 balance of Instalment Accounts Receivable, 2002 ($600,000 - $240,000 = $360,000) is multiplied by the 2002 gross profit ratio of 30% ($600,000 - $420,000 = $180,000; $180,000 ÷ $600,000 = 30%) to arrive at deferred gross profit of $108,000 ($360,000 x 30% = $108,000) at the balance sheet date. (Solution = c.)

TIP:	General and administrative expenses have no effect on the calculations of realized gross profit or deferred gross profit. They are to be classified as operating expenses on the income statement of the period in which they are incurred.

QUESTION

10.   (L.O. 10) Kayla Inc. appropriately uses the instalment method of accounting to recognize income in its financial statements. Some pertinent data relating to this method of accounting include:

	2001	**2002**
Instalment sales	$ 300,000	$ 360,000
Cost of sales	180,000	252,000
Gross profit	$ 120,000	$ 108,000
Collections during year:		
On 2001 sales	100,000	100,000
On 2002 sales		120,000

What amount of realized gross profit should be reported on Kayla's income statement for 2002?

a. $108,000
b. $88,000
c. $76,000
d. $66,000
e.   None of the above

Approach and Explanation: (1) Calculate the gross profit percentages for 2001 and 2002. (2) Apply the appropriate gross profit percentage to the amount of collections of instalment receivables during 2002.

Calculations:

(1) $120,000 ÷ $300,000 = 40% gross profit percentage for 2001 instalment sales

$108,000 ÷ $360,000 = 30% gross profit percentage for 2002 instalment sales

(2)

Collections in 2002 on 2001 instalment sales	$ 100,000
Gross profit percentage for 2001 instalment sales	40%
Gross profit realized in 2002 on 2001 instalment sales	$ 40,000
Collections in 2002 on 2002 instalment sales	$ 120,000
Gross profit percentage for 2002 instalments sales	30%
Gross profit realized in 2002 on 2002 instalment sales	$ 36,000
Gross profit realized in 2002 on 2001 instalment sales	$ 40,000
Gross profit realized in 2002 on 2002 instalment sales	36,000
Total gross profit realized in 2002	$ 76,000

(Solution = c.)

QUESTION

11.   (L.O. 10) Marvel Mart sells large-screen televisions on an instalment basis and appropriately uses the instalment sales method of accounting. A customer with an account balance of $4,000 refuses to make any more payments and the merchandise is repossessed. The gross profit rate on the original sale is 40%. Marvel estimates that the television can be sold as is for $1,250, or for $1,500 if $100 is spent to refurbish the cabinet. The loss on repossession is:
   a. $1,000.
   b. $1,150.
   c. $1,600.
   d. $2,750.

Approach and Explanation: Prepare the journal entry to record the repossession; it is as follows:

Deferred Gross Profit ($4,000 x 40%).................................	1,600	
Repossessed Merchandise ($1,500 - $100)	1,400	
Loss on Repossession	1,000	
[($4,000 - $1,600) - ($1,500 - $100)]		
Instalment Accounts Receivable		4,000

The book value of the receivable is removed from the accounts ($4,000 - $1,600), the repossessed merchandise is recorded at its fair value (or net realizable value of $1,400 in this case), and a loss ($1,000) is recorded for the excess of the receivable's book value ($4,000 - $1,600 = $2,400) over its net realizable value ($1,400) (a measure of fair value). (Solution = a.)

CHAPTER 7

FINANCIAL ASSETS: CASH AND RECEIVABLES

OVERVIEW

In previous chapters, you learned the basic formats for general purpose financial statements. In this chapter you begin your in-depth study of accounting for items appearing on the balance sheet: (1) what is to be included in an item classification, (2) related internal control procedures, (3) rules for determining the dollar amount to be reported, (4) disclosure requirements, and (5) special accounting procedures which may be required. In this chapter, you will learn what is to be included under the cash caption on the balance sheet and some key internal controls which should be employed for business activities involving cash. Also discussed are the methods of accounting for accounts receivable and notes receivable.

Many businesses grant credit to customers. They know that, when making sales "on account," a risk exists because some accounts will never be collected. However, the cost of these bad debts is more than offset by the profit from the extra sales made due to the attraction of granting credit. The collections department may make many attempts to collect an account before "writing-off" a bad debtor. Frequently, an account is deemed to be uncollectible a year or more after the date of the credit sale. In this chapter, we will discuss the allowance method of accounting for bad debts. The allowance method permits the accountant to estimate the amount of bad debt expense that should be matched with current revenues rather than waiting to book expense at the time of an actual write-off.

SUMMARY OF LEARNING OBJECTIVES

1. **Identify items considered cash.** To be reported as "cash," an asset must be readily available for the payment of current obligations and free from contractual restrictions that limit its use in satisfying debts. Cash consists of coin, currency, and available funds on deposit at the bank. Negotiable instruments such as money orders, certified cheques, cashier's cheques, personal cheques, and bank drafts are also viewed as cash. Savings accounts are usually classified as cash.

2. **Indicate how cash and related items are reported.** Cash is reported as a current asset in the balance sheet. The reporting of other related items are: (1) **Restricted cash:** legally restricted deposits held as compensating balances against short-term borrowing be stated separately among the "cash and cash equivalent items" in Current Assets. Restricted deposits held against long-term borrowing arrangements should be separately classified as noncurrent assets in either the Investments or Other Assets sections. (2) **Bank overdrafts:** They should be reported separately in the current liabilities section and are usually added to the amount reported as accounts payable. If material, these items should be separately disclosed either on the face of the balance sheet or in the related notes. (3) **Cash equivalents:** This item is often reported together with cash as "cash and cash equivalents."

3. **Define receivables and identify the different types of receivables.** Receivables are claims held against customers and others for money, goods, or services. The receivables are classified

into three types: (1) current or noncurrent, (2) trade or nontrade, and (3) accounts receivable or notes receivable.

4. **Explain accounting issues related to the recognition of accounts receivable.** Two issues that may complicate the measurement of accounts receivable are: (1) the availability of discounts (trade and cash discounts) and (2) the length of time between the sale and the payment due dates (the interest element).

    Ideally, receivables should be measured in terms of their present value—that is, the discounted value of the cash to be received in the future. Receivables arising from normal business transactions that are due in customary trade terms within approximately one year are excluded from present value considerations.

5. **Explain accounting issues related to the valuation of accounts receivable.** Short-term receivables are valued and reported at net realizable value—the net amount expected to be received in cash, which is not necessarily the amount legally receivable. Determining net realizable value requires an estimation of both uncollectible receivables and any returns or allowances.

6. **Explain accounting issues related to the recognition of notes receivable.** Short-term notes are recorded at face value. Long-term notes receivable are recorded at the present value of the cash expected to be collected. When the interest stated on an interest-bearing note is equal to the effective (market) rate of interest, the note sells at face value. When the stated rate is different from the effective rate, either a discount or premium is recorded.

7. **Explain accounting issues related to the valuation of notes receivable.** Like accounts receivable, short-term notes receivable are recorded and reported at their net realizable value. The same is true of long-term receivables. Special issues relate to impairments and notes receivable past due.

8. **Explain accounting issues related to disposition of accounts and notes receivable.** To accelerate the receipt of cash from receivables, the owner may transfer the receivables to another company for cash. The transfer of receivables to a third party for cash may be accomplished in one of two ways: (1) **Secured borrowing:** A creditor often requires that the debtor designate or pledge receivables as security for a loan. (2) **Sales (factoring) of receivables:** Factors are finance companies or banks that buy receivables from businesses and then collect the remittances directly from the customers. In many cases, transferors may have some continuing involvement with the receivables sold. A financial components approach is used to record this type of transaction.

9. **Explain how receivables are reported and analysed.** Disclosure of receivables requires valuation accounts be appropriately offset against receivables, receivables be appropriately classifed as current or noncurrent, pledged or designated receivables be identified, and concentrations of risks arising from receivables be identified. Receivables may be analysed relative to turnover and the days outstanding.

*10. **Explain common techniques employed to control cash.** The common techniques employed to control cash are: (1) **Using bank accounts:** a company can vary the number and location of banks and the types of accounts to obtain desired control objectives. (2) **The imprest petty cash system:** It may be impractical to require small amounts of various expenses to be paid by cheque, yet some control over them is important. (3) **Physical protection of cash balances:** Adequate control of receipts and disbursements is a part of the protection of cash balances. Every effort should be made to minimize the cash on hand in the office. (4) **Reconciliation of bank balances:** Cash on deposit is not available for count and is proved by preparing a bank reconciliation.

*This material is covered in Appendix 7-A in the text.

TIPS ON CHAPTER TOPICS

TIP: Cash is the most liquid of assets, and is the standard medium of exchange and the basis for measuring and accounting for most items. It is also the most susceptible to theft and improper use. Internal controls are imperative to safeguard and ensure accuracy of accounting records.

TIP: Restricted cash is classified as either current or long-term assets, depending upon the date of availability or disbursement.

TIP: Cash and Cash Equivalents are short-term, highly liquid investments that are both readily convertible to known amounts of cash, and so near to their maturity that they present insignificant risk of change in interest rates. Generally, only investments with maturities of three months or less qualify as cash and cash equivalents.

TIP: Bank overdrafts occur when cheques are written for more than the balance in the cash account. These are recorded as current liabilities and normally included with account's payable.

TIP: Trade accounts receivable result from the sale of products or services to customers. Nontrade accounts receivable (amounts that are due from nontrade customers who do not buy goods or services in the normal course of the company's main business activity) should be listed separately on the balance sheet from the trade accounts receivable balance.

TIP: In the event that a customer's account has a credit balance on the balance sheet date, it should be classified as a current liability and not offset against other accounts receivable with debit balances.

TIP: The net realizable value of accounts receivable is the amount of the receivables expected to be ultimately converted to cash.

TIP: Whenever you want to analyse the effect of (1) recording bad debt expense, (2) writing off an individual customer's account receivable, and/or (3) the collection of an account receivable that was previously written off, write down the related journal entry(ies) and analyse each debit and credit separately. (See **Illustration 7-1** for examples.)

TIP: There are two methods of accounting for bad debts; they are:
1.   **Direct Write-Off Method:** No entry is made until a specific account has definitely been established as uncollectible. Then the loss is recorded by crediting Accounts Receivable and debiting Bad Debt Expense.
2.   **Allowance Method:** An estimate is made of the expected uncollectible accounts from all sales made on account or from the total of outstanding receivables. This estimate is entered as an expense and an indirect reduction in accounts receivable (via an increase in the allowance account) in the period in which the sale is recorded.

The direct write-off method is not a generally accepted method for an entity having a material amount of bad debts because it fails to properly match bad debt expense with the related revenue (in the period the credit sale was recognized) and it overstates Accounts Receivable as to their net realizable value.

TIP: Short-term notes receivables are generally recorded at face value (less allowances) because the interest implicit in the maturity value is immaterial, while long-term notes receivables should be recorded at the present value of the cash expected to be collected.

TIP: A note receivable is considered to be **impaired** when it is probable that the creditor will be unable to collect all amounts due (both principal and interest) according to the contractual terms of the loan. In that case, the present value of the expected future cash flows is determined by discounting those flows at the historical effective rate. This present value amount is deducted from the carrying amount of the receivable to measure the loss.

TIP: The objective of a bank reconciliation is to explain all reasons why the bank balance differs from the book balance and to identify errors and omissions in the bank's records and in the book records. In the context of a bank reconciliation, "per bank" refers to the records of the bank pertaining to the depositor's account and "per books" refers to the depositor's records of the same bank account.

TIP: Total receipts per bank for a month include all deposits made by the depositor during the month plus any bank credit memos (such as for interest credited by the bank or a customer's note receivable collected by the bank).

TIP: Total disbursements per bank for a month include all the depositor's cheques which cleared the banking system during the month plus any bank debit memos originating during the month (such as for bank service charges or a customer's NSF cheque).

TIP: Beginning cash balance per bank plus total receipts for the month per bank minus total disbursements for the month per bank equals ending cash balance per bank.

TIP: Beginning cash balance per books plus total receipts for the month per books minus total disbursements for the month per books equals ending cash balance per books.

EXERCISE 7-1

Purpose: (L.O.1) This exercise will review the items which are included in the "Cash" caption on a balance sheet.

In auditing the balance sheet at December 31, 2002 for the Show-me-the-Money Company, you find the following:

(a) Coins and currency for change funds.
(b) Coins and currency which are from the current day's receipts which have not yet been deposited in the bank.
(c) Petty cash.
(d) General chequing account at First Union Bank.
(e) General chequing account at Sun Trust Bank.
(f) Unused stamps.
(g) Deposit in transit.
(h) Customer's NSF cheque (returned with bank statement).
(i) Postdated cheques from customers.
(j) Certificate of deposit—60 day CD purchased on December 1, 2002.
(k) Certificate of deposit—5 year CD purchased 2 years ago.
(l) 100 Labatt's shares (intention is to sell in one year or less).
(m) Cash to be used to retire long-term debt.
(n) Travel advances made to executives for business purposes.

Instructions
Select the items from the list above that should be included in the "Cash" caption on the balance sheet as of December 31, 2002. For any item not included in "Cash", indicate the proper classification.

Solution to Exercise 7-1

Items to be **included** as "Cash" on the balance sheet include:

(a) Coins and currency for change funds.
(b) Coins and currency which are from the current day's receipts which have not yet been deposited in the bank—this is said to be "cash on hand" or could be considered a "deposit in transit."
(c) Petty cash.
(d) General chequing account at First Union Bank—the amount included should be the "adjusted cash balance" per a bank reconciliation.
(e) General chequing account at Sun Trust Bank—the amount included should be the "adjusted cash balance" per a bank reconciliation.
(g) Deposit in transit—this amount is already reflected in the "balance per books" and will be reflected in the "adjusted cash balance" per the bank reconciliation.

Items to be **excluded** from "Cash" include:

(f)   Unused stamps—report as prepaid expense.

(h)   Customer's NSF cheque—classify as a receivable.

(i)   Postdated cheques from customers—accounts receivable.

(j)   Certificate of deposit—60 day—original maturity date was 3 months or less—cash equivalent. Some entities include cash equivalents with cash; others report them as short-term (temporary) investments.

(k)   Certificate of deposit—original maturity date not 3 months or less—short-term investment.

(l)   100 Labatt's Shares—short-term investment because there is a lack of intent to hold for a long-term purpose and is readily marketable.

(m)   Cash to be used to retire long-term debt—long-term investment (assuming the related debt is classified as long-term).

(n)   Travel advances made to executives for business purposes—prepaid expense.

ILLUSTRATION 7-1
ENTRIES FOR THE ALLOWANCE METHOD (L.O.5)

Journal Entry			Effect on Net Income	Effect on Working Capital	Effect on Allowance Account	Effect on Net Receivables
Entry to record bad debt expense, $1,000						
Bad Debt Expense	1,000		Decrease $1,000	No effect	No effect	No effect
Allowance for Doubtful Accounts		1,000	No effect	Decrease $1,000	Increase $1,000	Decrease $1,000
Net effect of entry			Decrease $1,000	Decrease $1,000	Increase $1,000	Decrease $1,000
Entry to write-off a customer's account, $200						
Allowance for Doubtful Accounts	200		No effect	Increase $200	Decrease $200	Increase $200
Accounts Receivable		200	No effect	Decrease $200	No effect	Decrease $200
Net effect of entry			No effect	No effect	Decrease $200	No effect
Entries to record collection of account receivable previously written off, $120						
Accounts Receivable	120		No effect	Increase $120	No effect	Increase $120
Allowance for Doubtful Accounts		120	No effect	Decrease $120	Increase $120	Decrease $120
Cash	120		No effect	Increase $120	No effect	No effect
Accounts Receivable		120	No effect	Decrease $120	No effect	Decrease $120
Net effect of entries			No effect	No effect	Increase $120	Decrease $120

TIP: Be careful to distinguish the entry to write-off a customer account from the entry to record the bad debt expense. The journal entry to record the estimated bad debt expense for a period and to adjust the corresponding allowance for doubtful accounts involves a debit to Bad Debt Expense and a credit to Allowance for Doubtful Accounts. The entry to write off an individual customer's account (an actual bad debt) involves a debit to Allowance for Doubtful Accounts and a credit to Accounts Receivable.

TIP: Two entries are necessary to record the recovery of an account that was previously written off:
1. An entry to record the reinstatement of the account receivable (debit Accounts Receivable and credit Allowance for Doubtful Accounts). This is simply a reverse of the write-off entry.
2. An entry to record the collection of the receivable (debit Cash and credit Accounts Receivable).

TIP: Allowance for Doubtful Accounts is often called Allowance for Uncollectible Accounts. Bad Debt Expense is often called Uncollectible Accounts Expense **or** Doubtful Accounts Expense. Provision for Bad Debts is another name for the Bad Debt Expense account; Reserve for Bad Debts is a frequently used but objectionable title for the allowance account.

ILLUSTRATION 7-1 (Continued)

TIP: Notice that the entry to record bad debts reduces current assets and reduces net income. The entry to record the write-off of an individual account has **no** net effect on the amount of current assets nor does it affect income. It merely reduces Accounts Receivable and the Allowance for Doubtful Accounts account (which is a contra item) so the entry has no **net** effect on the net realizable value of accounts receivable. Thus, it is the entry to record the bad debt expense that impacts **both** the income statement and the balance sheet.

TIP: The normal balance of the Allowance for Doubtful Accounts is a credit. Therefore, a debit balance in this account indicates an abnormal balance. It is not uncommon to have a debit balance in the allowance account before adjusting entries are prepared because individual accounts may be written off at various times during a period and the entry to adjust the allowance account is prepared at the end of the period before financial statements are prepared. After adjustment, the allowance account should have a credit balance.

TIP: When using the allowance method of accounting for bad debts, there are two methods available for determining the amount of the adjusting entry to record bad debts expense and to adjust the allowance account. Each method has adaptations.

1.   Percentage-of-Sales (Income Statement) approach:
   a.   The average percentage relationship between actual bad debt losses and net credit sales is ascertained from prior experience. This percentage, adjusted for current conditions, is then applied to the actual net credit sales of the period to determine the amount of expense for the period.
   b.   Use of the same procedure as in "a" above, except the percentage of bad debts to total sales is used. This method is not as logical as "a" because cash sales will not result in bad debts, and, if the relationship between cash sales and credit sales shifts, that change will necessitate revision of the percentage being used to estimate bad debts.

2.   Percentage-of-Receivables (Balance Sheet) approach:
   a.   From experience, the average percentage relationship between uncollectible accounts receivable and outstanding accounts receivable is determined. This percentage, adjusted for current conditions, is applied each period to the ending balance in accounts receivable to determine the desired balance of the allowance account.
   b.   Total uncollectible accounts at the end of an accounting period is determined by an ageing analysis. The balance in the allowance account is then adjusted so that it equals the total amount of the estimated uncollectible accounts. This ageing method is preferable to "2a" because it takes into consideration the age of a receivable. (The older the age, the lower the probability of collection.)

Both methods (and their variations) listed above are acceptable. The first method discussed, estimation of bad debt expense based on credit sales, focuses on matching current bad debt expense with revenues of the current period and thus emphasizes the income statement. The second method, estimation of the net realizable value of existing receivables, focuses on an evaluation of the net realizable value of all accounts receivable and thus emphasizes the balance sheet. It only incidentally measures bad debt expense; the expense reported may not be directly related to the credit sales of the current period, thus violating the matching principle. If this method is to be used, the ageing technique is preferable to the use of a simple percentage times total accounts receivable.

TIP: Very often, an entity may use the percentage-of-sales method to account for bad debts for interim periods and then use the ageing method to adjust the allowance account at year-end for annual reporting purposes.

ILLUSTRATION 7-1 (Continued)

TIP: When it is time to prepare the adjusting entry for bad debts (at the end of an accounting period), the existing balance in the Allowance for Doubtful Accounts account (that is, the balance before adjustment) is **NOT** considered in determining the amount of the adjusting entry **IF** the percentage-of-sales approach is used. However, the balance in the allowance account before adjustment **IS** used in determining the amount of the adjusting entry when the ageing analysis approach (one method of estimating the net realizable value of existing receivables) is used to implement the allowance method of accounting for bad debts. The application of these two guidelines is illustrated by the **Solution to Exercise 7-2** (entries 1 and 2).

TIP: When using the allowance method and estimating bad debt expense as a percentage of credit sales for the period, the amount of bad debt expense is simply calculated and recorded; a by-product of this approach is the increasing of the allowance account. When using the allowance method and estimating the net realizable value of accounts receivable (such as by an ageing analysis), the amount of uncollectible accounts calculated represents the new ending balance of the allowance account. The adjusting entry records the amount necessary to increase (or decrease) the current allowance account balance to equal the newly calculated one. A by-product of this approach is the increasing of bad debt expense for the period.

EXERCISE 7-2

Purpose: (L.O. 5, 8) This exercise will require you to record: (1) the adjusting entry to recognize bad debt expense and adjust the Allowance for Doubtful Accounts account, and (2) the transfer of accounts receivable without recourse.

The trial balance before adjustment at December 31, 2002 for the Liz Company shows the following balances:

	Dr.	Cr.
Accounts Receivable	$ 90,000	
Allowance for Doubtful Accounts	2,120	
Sales (all on credit)		$ 500,000
Sales Returns and Allowances	7,600	

Instructions

Using the data above, give the journal entries required to record each of the following cases (each situation is **independent**):

1. The company estimates bad debts to be 1.5% of net credit sales.
2. Liz performs an ageing analysis at December 31, 2002, which indicates an estimate of $6,000 of uncollectible accounts.
3. The company wants to maintain the Allowance for Doubtful Accounts at 4% of gross accounts receivable.
4. To obtain additional cash, Liz factors, without recourse, $20,000 of accounts receivable with Fleetwood Finance. The finance charge is 10% of the amount factored.

Solution to Exercise 7-2

1. Bad Debt Expense [($500,000 - $7,600) x 1.5%]...................... 7,386
        Allowance for Doubtful Accounts.................................... 7,386

    Explanation: The percentage of net credit sales approach to applying the allowance method of accounting for bad debts focuses on determining an appropriate expense figure. The existing balance in the allowance account is **not** relevant in the calculation.

2. Bad Debt Expense 8,120
        Allowance for Doubtful Accounts
        ($6,000 + $2,120)... 8,120

    Explanation: An ageing analysis provides the best estimate of the net realizable value of accounts receivable. By using the results of the ageing to adjust the allowance account, the amount reported for net receivables on the balance sheet is the net realizable value of accounts receivable. It is important to notice that the balance of the allowance account before adjustment is a determinant in the adjustment required. The following T-account reflects the facts used to determine the necessary adjustment:

    Allowance for Doubtful Accounts

Unadjusted balance	2,120	Adjustment needed	8,120
		Desired balance at 12/31/02	6,000

3. Bad Debt Expense 5,720
        Allowance for Doubtful Accounts
        [($90,000 x 4%) + $2,120].. 5,720

    Explanation: This entry is to adjust the allowance account. A by-product of the entry is the recognition of uncollectible accounts expense. Because an appropriate balance for the valuation account is determined to be a percentage of the receivable balance at the balance sheet date, the existing balance ($2,120 debit) in the allowance account **must** be considered in calculating the necessary adjustment.

4. Cash 18,000
    Loss on Sale of Receivables ($20,000 x 10%) 2,000
        Accounts Receivable... 20,000

    Explanation: The factoring of accounts receivable without recourse is accounted for as a sale of accounts receivable; hence, the receivables are removed from the accounts, cash is recorded, and a loss is recognized for the excess of the face value of the receivables over the proceeds received.

EXERCISE 7-3

Purpose: (L.O. 6) This exercise will illustrate the accounting for two situations involving the exchange of a noncash asset or service for a promissory note: (1) the exchange of land for a promissory note where the fair value of the land is known, and (2) the exchange of services for a note where the fair value of the services are not known.

General Host's annual accounting period ends on December 31. Reversing entries are used when appropriate. On July 1, 2002, General Host Company made two sales:

1. It sold land having a fair market value of $700,000 in exchange for a four-year noninterest-bearing promissory note with a face amount of $1,101,460. The land is carried on General Host Company's books at a cost of $620,000.
2. It rendered services in exchange for a 3%, 8-year promissory note having a face value of $300,000 with interest payable annually. General Host recently had to pay 8% interest for money that it borrowed from Alberta National Bank. The customer in this transaction has a credit rating that requires them to borrow money at 12% interest.

Instructions

(a) Prepare the two journal entries that should be recorded by General Host for the sales transactions above.

(b) Prepare the amortization schedule for the note receivable accepted in the first transaction [Note (1)].

(c) Prepare the amortization schedule for the note receivable accepted in the second transaction [Note (2)].

(d) Prepare the necessary journal entries at December 31, 2002 and December 31, 2003 that relate to the first transaction.

(e) Prepare the necessary journal entries at December 31, 2002, January 1, 2003 (reversing entry), June 30, 2003, and December 31, 2003 that relate to the second transaction. Assume the customer makes the scheduled interest payments on time. Also, assume amortization is recorded only at year-end.

Solution to Exercise 7-3

(a) (1)   Timeline:

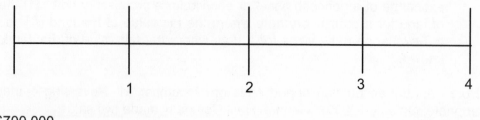

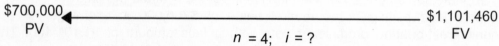

7/1/02	Notes Receivable [Note (1)]	1,101,460.00	
	Discount on Notes Receivable		401,460.00
	Land		620,000.00
	Gain on Sale of Land		
	($700,000 - $620,000)		80,000.00

The exchange price is equal to the fair market value of the property (which is $700,000). The interest rate implicit in this price is therefore calculated by:

$700,000 = $1,101,460 x PV Factor
$700,000 ÷ $1,101,460 = .63552

By reference to Table 6-2 (Present Value of 1 Table), .63552 is the PV factor for $n = 4$, $i = 12\%$.

(2)   Timeline:

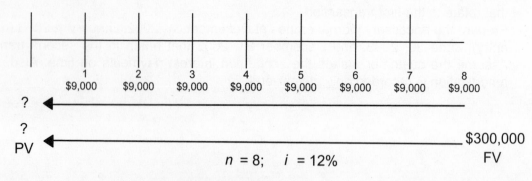

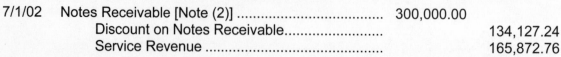

7/1/02	Notes Receivable [Note (2)]	300,000.00	
	Discount on Notes Receivable		134,127.24
	Service Revenue		165,872.76

Use the market rate of interest to calculate the present value of the note, which is then used to establish the exchange price in the transaction. The market rate of interest should be the rate the borrower normally would have to pay to borrow money for similar activities.

Calculation of the present value of the note:

Maturity value	$300,000.00
Present value of $300,000 due in 8 years at 12% ($300,000 x .40388)	$121,164.00
Present value of $9,000 payable annually for 8 years at 12% ($9,000 x 4.96764)	44,708.76
Present value of the note and interest	165,872.76
Discount on note receivable	$134,127.24

(b)   **Amortization Schedule for Note (1)**

Date	0% Stated Interest	12% Effective Interest	Amortization of Discount	PV Balance
7/01/02				$ 700,000.00
6/30/03	$0	$ 84,000.00a	$ 84,000.00	784,000.00
6/30/04	0	94,080.00	94,080.00	878,080.00
6/30/05	0	105,369.60	105,369.60	983,449.60
6/30/06	0	18,010.40[1]	118,010.40	1,101,460.00
Totals	$0	$401,460.00	$ 401,460.00	

a$700,000.00 x 12% = $84,000.00.
[1]Includes rounding error of $3.55.

(c)   **Amortization Schedule for Note (2)**

Date	3% Stated Interest	12% Effective Interest	Amortization of Discount	PV Balance
7/01/02				$ 165,872.76
6/30/03	$9,000.00a	$ 19,904.73b	$ 10,904.73c	176,777.49d
6/30/04	9,000.00	21,213.30	12,213.30	188,990.79
6/30/05	9,000.00	22,678.89	13,678.89	202,669.68
6/30/06	9,000.00	24,320.36	15,320.36	217,990.04
6/30/07	9,000.00	26,158.80	17,158.80	235,148.84
6/30/08	9,000.00	28,217.86	19,217.86	254,366.70
6/30/09	9,000.00	30,524.00	21,524.00	275,890.70
6/30/10	9,000.00	33,109.30[1]	24,109.30	300,000.00
Totals	$72,000.00	$206,127.24	$ 134,127.24	

a$300,000.00 face value x 3% stated interest rate = $9,000.00 stated interest.
b$165,872.76 present value x 12% effective interest rate = $19,904.73 effective interest.
c$19,904.73 effective interest - $9,000.00 stated interest = $10,904.73 discount amortization.
d$165,872.76 PV balance 7/01/02 + $10,904.73 discount amortization for 12 months = $176,777.49 PV balance 6/30/03.
[1]Includes rounding error of $2.42.

(d)   12/31/02   Discount on Notes Receivable 42,000.00
                    Interest Revenue 42,000.00
                         (1/2 x $84,000 = $42,000)

      12/31/03   Discount on Notes Receivable 89,040.00
                    Interest Revenue 89,040.00
                         (1/2 x $84,000 = $42,000;
                         1/2 x $94,080 = $47,040;
                         $42,000 + $47,040 = $89,040)

(e)   12/31/02   Interest Receivable...   4,500.00
                    Discount on Notes Receivable 5,452.37
                    Interest Revenue 9,952.37
                         (1/2 x $9,000 = $4,500;
                         1/2 x $19,904.73 = $9,952.37)

      1/1/03   Interest Revenue 4,500.00
                    Interest Receivable...   4,500.00
                         (To reverse last period's accrual)

      6/30/03   Cash 9,000.00
                    Interest Revenue 9,000.00

      12/31/03   Interest Receivable...   4,500.00[a]
                    Discount on Notes Receivable ....   11,559.01[b]
                    Interest Revenue ....   16,059.01[c]

[a]1/2 x $9,000.00 = $4,500.00 interest receivable at 12/31/03.
[b]1/2 x $19,904.73 = $9,952.36 interest earned 1/1/03 thru 6/30/03;
   1/2 x $21,213.30 = $10,606.65 interest earned 7/1/03 thru 12/31/03;
   $9,952.36 + $10,606.65 = $20,559.01 total interest earned in 2003;
   $20,559.01 effective interest for 2003 - $9,000.00 stated interest for
   2003 = $11,559.01 discount amortization for 2003.
[c]$20,559.01 total interest for 2003 - $4,500.00 balance in Interest
   Revenue account before adjustment = $16,059.01 interest to record
   at 12/31/03.

Explanation: When a note is received in exchange for property, goods, or services in a bargained transaction entered into at arms length, the stated interest rate is assumed to be fair and is thus used to calculate interest revenue unless:

1.   No interest rate is stated, or
2.   The stated interest rate is unreasonable, or
3.   The face amount of the note is materially different from the current cash sales price for the same or similar items or from the current market value of the debt instrument.

In these circumstances, the present value of the note is measured by the fair value of the property, goods, or services. (General Host received a note in exchange for land, and the fair value of the land was known to be $700,000; thus, the fair value of the land was used to establish the present value of the note.) If the fair value of the property, goods, or services is not readily determinable, the market value of the note is used to establish the present value of the note. If the note has no ready market, the present value of the note is approximated by discounting all of the related future cash receipts (for interest and principal) on the note at the market rate of interest. This rate is referred to as an imputed rate and should be equal to the borrower's incremental borrowing rate (that is, the rate of interest the maker of the note would currently have to pay if it borrowed money from another source for this same purpose). General Host received a second note in exchange for services. No information was given about the fair value of the services or the market value of the note. Thus, 12% was used to impute interest and determine the note's present value.

ILLUSTRATION 7-2
ACCOUNTING FOR TRANSFERS OF RECEIVABLES (L.O. 8)

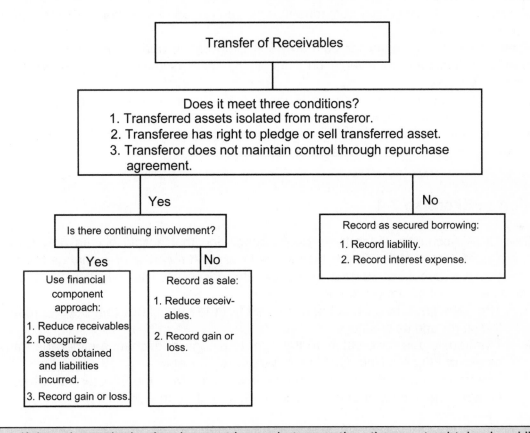

TIP: If there is continuing involvement in a sale transaction, the assets obtained and liabilities incurred must be recorded at fair value.

EXERCISE 7-4

Purpose: (L.O.8) This exercise will help you to compare two possible ways of structuring a sale of accounts receivable (1) without recourse, or (2) with recourse.

Raytech Corporation factors $90,000 of accounts receivable with NL Financing, Inc. NL Financing will collect the receivables. The receivable records are transferred to NL Financing on August 15, 2002. NL Financing assesses a finance charge of 4% of the amount of accounts receivable and also retains an amount equal to 6% of accounts receivable to cover probable adjustments.

Instructions

(a)   Explain the conditions that must be met for a transfer of receivables with recourse to be accounted for as a sale.

(b)   Explain when the financial components approach is used in accounting for a transfer of accounts receivable.

(c)   Prepare the journal entry for both Raytech Corporation and NL Financing to record the transfer of accounts receivable on August 15, 2002 assuming the receivables are sold without recourse.

(d)   Prepare the journal entry for both Raytech Corporation and NL Financing to record the transfer of accounts receivable on August 15, 2002 assuming the receivables are sold with recourse and the conditions required for sale accounting are met. Further, assume the recourse obligation has a fair value of $2,000.

Solution to Exercise 7-4

(a)   The CICA Accounting Standards Board concluded that a sale occurs only if the seller surrenders control of the receivables to the buyer and receives in exchange consideration other than a beneficial interest in the transferred asset. The following three conditions must be met before a sale can be recorded:
1.   The transferred asset has been isolated from the transferor (put beyond reach of the transferor and its creditors).
2.   The transferees have obtained the right to pledge or exchange either the transferred assets or beneficial interests in the transferred assets.
3.   The transferor does not maintain effective control over the transferred assets through an agreement to repurchase or redeem them before their maturity.

If the three conditions are met, a sale occurs. Otherwise, the transferor should record the transfer as a secured borrowing. If sale accounting is appropriate, it is still necessary to consider assets obtained and liabilities incurred in the transaction. If there is continuing involvement in a sale transaction, the assets obtained and liabilities incurred must be recorded at fair value.

(b)   A **financial components approach** is used to account for a transfer of accounts receivable with recourse whenever the transfer arrangement meets the conditions necessary for the transfer to be accounted for as a sale (see answer (a) above). If receivables are sold (factored) with recourse, the seller guarantees payment to the purchaser in the event the debtor fails to pay. Under the financial components approach, each party to the sale recognizes the assets and liabilities that it controls after the sale and no longer recognizes the assets and liabilities that were sold or extinguished.

(c)   Sale of receivables without recourse:

Raytech Corp.			**NL Financing**		
Cash	81,000		Accounts Receivable	90,000	
Due from Factor	5,400*		Due to Raytech		5,400
Loss on Sale of Re-			Financing Revenue		3,600
ceivables	3,600**		Cash		81,000
Accounts Receivable		90,000			

*$90,000 x 6% = $5,400
**$90,000 x 4% = $3,600

> **TIP:**   The factor's profit will be the difference between the financing revenue of $3,600 and the amount of any uncollectible receivables.

(d)   Sale of receivables with recourse:

Raytech Corp.			**NL Financing**		
Cash	81,000		Accounts Receivable	90,000	
Due from Factor	5,400		Due to Raytech		5,400
Loss on Sale of Re-			Financing Revenue		3,600
ceivables	5,600*		Cash		81,000
Accounts Receivable		90,000			
Recourse Liability		2,000			

*Cash received	$81,000
Due from factor	5,400
Subtotal	86,400
Resource obligation	(2,000)
Net proceeds expected	$84,400
Carrying (book) value	$90,000
Net proceeds	(84,400)
Loss on sale of receivables	$ 5,600

> **TIP:**   In this case, a liability of $2,000 is recorded by Raytech to indicate the probable payment to NL Financing for uncollectible receivables. If all the receivables are collected, Raytech would eliminate its recourse liability and increase net income. NL Financing's profit is the financing revenue of $3,600 because it will have no bad debts related to these receivables.

EXERCISE 7-5

Purpose: (L.O. 8) This exercise will illustrate the calculations and entries involved in accounting for the transfer of receivables that is treated as a secured borrowing transaction.

Banff Winery transfers $350,000 of its accounts receivable to Calgary International Financial (CIF) as collateral for a $250,000 note on September 1, 2002. Ashton will continue to collect the accounts receivable; the account debtors are not notified of the arrangement. CIF assesses a finance charge of 1% of the accounts receivable and interest on the note of 12%. Settlement by Banff Winery to CIF is made monthly for all cash collected on the receivables.

Instructions

Prepare the journal entries for both Banff Winery and Calgary International Financial to record the following:
(a)   Transfer of accounts receivable and issuance of the note on September 1, 2002.
(b)   Collection in September of $220,000 of the transferred accounts receivable less cash discounts of $3,000. In addition, sales returns of $7,000 were processed.
(c)   Remittance by Banff of September collections plus accrued interest to the bank on October 1.
(d)   Collection in October of the balance of the transferred accounts receivable less $1,000 written off as uncollectible.
(e)   Remittance by Banff of the balance due of $33,000 ($250,000 - $217,000) on the note plus interest on November 1.

Solution to Exercise 7-5

(a)

Banff Winery			**Calgary International Financial**		
Cash	246,500		Notes Receivable	250,000	
Finance Charge	3,500*		Finance Revenue		3,500*
Notes Payable		250,000	Cash		246,500

*1% x $350,000 = $3,500

(b)

(No Entry)

Cash	217,000	
Sales Discounts	3,000	
Sales Returns	7,000	
Accounts Receivable		227,000*

*$220,000 + $7,000 = $227,000

(c)

Banff Winery			Calgary International Financial		
Interest Expense	2,500*		Cash	219,500	
Notes Payable	217,000		Interest Revenue		2,500*
Cash		219,500	Notes Receivable		217,000

*$250,000 x .12 x 1/12 = $2,500

(d)

Cash	122,000		(No Entry)	
Allowance for Doubtful				
Accounts	1,000			
Accounts Receivable		123,000*		

*$350,000 - $227,000 = $123,000

(e)

Interest Expense	330*		Cash	33,330	
Notes Payable	33,000		Interest Revenue		330*
Cash		33,330	Notes Receivable		33,000

*$33,000 x .12 x 1/12

TIP: Receivables are often used as collateral in a borrowing transaction. A creditor often requires that the debtor designate or pledge receivables as security for the loan. If the loan is not paid when due, the creditor has the right to convert the collateral to cash—that is, to collect the receivables. (If the receivables are transferred to the transferee for custodial purposes, the custodial arrangement is often referred to as a **pledge**.) **Factors** are finance companies or banks that buy receivables from businesses for a fee and then collect remittances directly from the customers. This exercise **(Exercise 7-5)** illustrates a borrowing transaction whereas **Exercise 7-4** illustrates a sales transaction.

ILLUSTRATION 7-3
TWO FORMATS FOR BANK RECONCILIATIONS (L.O. 10)

First One:

Balance per bank
- Add positive items per books not on bank's records.
- Deduct negative items per books not on bank's records.
- Add or deduct, whichever is applicable, bank error in recording receipts or disbursements.

Correct cash balance

Balance per books
- Add positive items per bank not on books.
- Deduct negative items per bank not on books.
- Add or deduct, whichever is applicable, depositor error in recording receipts or disbursements.

Correct cash balance

Second One:

Balance per bank
- Add positive items per books not on bank's records.
- Deduct negative items per books not on bank's records.
- Add or deduct, whichever is applicable, bank error in recording receipts or disbursements.
- Deduct positive items per bank not on books.
- Add negative items per bank not on books.
- Add or deduct, whichever is applicable, depositor error in recording receipts or disbursements.

Balance per books

Examples of reconciling items:

Positive item per books not on bank's records:
  Deposit in transit
Negative item per books not on bank's records:
  Outstanding cheque
Positive item per bank not on books:
  Note collected by bank
  Interest paid by bank to depositor on account balance
Negative item per bank not on books:
  Bank service charge
  Customer's NSF cheque returned by bank
  Note paid by bank
Error by bank:
  In recording receipt
  In recording disbursement
Error by depositor:
  In recording receipt
  In recording disbursement

ILLUSTRATION 7-3 (Continued)

TIP: If you have a chequing account, look at the back of your bank statement. A bank often includes a form to assist you in reconciling your bank account. Very often that form reconciles the cash balance per bank to the cash balance per books rather than reconciling both the bank cash balance and the book cash balance to the correct (adjusted) cash balance.

TIP: The "Balance per bank" caption on a bank reconciliation is often replaced with "Balance per bank statement," and "Balance per books" is often titled "Balance per ledger."

TIP: The "Correct cash balance" caption on a bank reconciliation is often replaced with "Adjusted cash balance." The adjusted cash balance as determined by the bank reconciliation will be the amount used to report for cash on the balance sheet. (The Cash account in the general ledger often includes cash on hand and cash in the bank, although separate ledger accounts such as Cash in Bank and Cash on Hand may be used. The balance of this account and any other unrestricted cash accounts, such as the Petty Cash account, are added together to report cash on the balance sheet.)

TIP: Some items in a bank reconciliation will require adjustments either on the depositor's books or in the bank's records, while the others will not. When the balance per bank to correct cash balance format is used in preparing a single-column bank reconciliation, all of the reconciling items appearing in the lower half of the reconciliation (balance per books to correct cash balance) require adjustment on the depositor's books. All of the reconciling items appearing in the upper half of the reconciliation **except** for deposits in transit and outstanding cheques require adjustment on the bank's books.

TIP: Unless otherwise indicated, an NSF cheque is assumed to be a customer's NSF cheque; that is, an NSF cheque is considered to be from a customer of the depositor, rather than a depositor's NSF cheque.

TIP: A depositor's chequing account is a liability on the bank's books, so a bank debit memo decreases the depositor's cash balance and a bank credit memo increases the depositor's cash balance. On the bank statement, debits appear as a result of cheques that have cleared during the month or bank debit memos for items such as bank service charges (BSC). Credits on the bank statement represent deposits or bank credit memos.

EXERCISE 7-6

Purpose: (L.O. 10) This exercise will help you review situations that give rise to reconciling items on a bank reconciliation and identify those which require adjusting entries on the depositor's books.

A sketch of the bank reconciliation at July 31, 2002 for the Ace Electric Company and a list of possible reconciling items appear on the next page.

Ace Electric Co.
BANK RECONCILIATION
July 31, 2002

Balance per bank statement, July 31		$X,XXX
A. Add:	$XXX	
	XXX	X,XXX
		X,XXX
B. Deduct:		X,XXX
Correct cash balance, July 31		$X,XXX
Balance per books, July 31		$ X,XXX
C. Add:	$XXX	
	XXX	X,XXX
		X,XXX
D. Deduct:	XXX	
	XXX	
	XXX	
	XXX	X,XXX
Correct cash balance, July 31		$X,XXX

_____   1.   Deposits of July 30 amounting to $1,482 have not reached the bank as of July 31.

_____   2.   A customer's cheque for $40 that was deposited on July 20 was returned NSF by the bank; return has not been recorded by Ace.

_____   3.   Bank service charge for July amounts to $3.

_____   4.   Included with the bank statement was cheque No. 422 for $702 as payment of an account payable. In comparing the cheque with the cash disbursement records, it was discovered that the cheque was incorrectly entered in the cash disbursements journal for $720.

_____   5.   Outstanding cheques at July 31 amount to $1,927.

_____   6.   The bank improperly charged a cheque of the Ace Plumbing Co. for $25 to Ace Electric Co.'s account.

_____   7.   The bank charged $8 during July for printing cheques.

_____   8.   During July, the bank collected a customer's note receivable for the Ace Electric Co.; face amount $1,000, interest $20, and the bank charged a $2 collection fee. This transaction has not been recorded by Ace.

_____   9.   A cheque written by Ace in June for $180 cleared the bank during July.

_____   10. Deposits of June 30 for $1,200 were recorded by the company on June 30 but were not recorded by the bank until July 2.

Instructions

(a)   Indicate how each of the 10 items listed above would be handled on the bank reconciliation by placing the proper code letter in the space provided. The applicable code letters appear in the sketch of the bank reconciliation. Use the code "NR" for any item which is not a reconciling item on July 31.

(b)   Assume that the July 31 balance per bank statement was $4,332. Complete the bank reconciliation using the items given and answer the questions that follow:

1.   What is the adjusted (correct) cash balance at July 31? $_____

2.   What is the balance per books **before** adjustment at July 31? $_____

3.   What reconciling items require an adjusting entry on Ace Electric Company's books? (Identify by item numbers.) _____

4.   What item(s) requires a special entry on the bank's records to correct an error(s)? _____

Solution to Exercise 7-6

(a)   1.   A   6.   A
        2.   D   7.   D
        3.   D   8.   C, D
        4.   C   9.   NR
        5.   B   10.   NR

TIP: Items 9 and 10 would have been reconciling items of cash balances on the June 30 bank reconciliation (the prior month).

(b)   1. $3,912* ($4,332 + $1,482 + $25 - $1,927 = $3,912)
        2. $2,927* [X + $18 + $1,020 - $40 - $3 - $8 - $2 = $3,912 (answer to question 1)]
                X = $2,927
        3.   2; 3; 4; 7; 8
        4.   6
                *See the completed bank reconciliation on the following page.

Approach to part (b) 2: You can calculate the correct cash balance by completing the top half of the bank reconciliation (balance per bank to correct cash balance). The correct cash balance can then be entered on the last line of the bottom half of the reconciliation and used along with certain reconciling items to "work backwards" to calculate the $2,927 cash balance per books before adjustment.

Ace Electric Co.
BANK RECONCILIATION
July 31, 2002

Balance per bank statement, July 31		$ 4,332
Add: Deposits in transit on July 31	$1,482	
Cheque improperly charged by bank	25	1,507
		5,839
Deduct: Cheques outstanding as of July 31		1,927
Correct cash balance at July 31		$3,912
Balance per books, July 31		$2,927
Add: Error in recording cheque No. 422	$ 18	
Collection of customer's note receivable and interest by bank	1,020	1,038
		3,965
Deduct: Customer's NSF cheque	40	
Bank service charge for July	3	
Cost of printing cheques	8	
Bank collection fee	2	53
Correct cash balance at July 31		$3,912

TIP: The required adjusting entries on the depositor's books would be:

Cash..	18	
Accounts Payable		18
(To correct error in recording cheque No. 422)		
Cash..	1,020	
Note Receivable...		1,000
Interest Revenue...		20
(To record collection of note receivable by bank)		
Accounts Receivable	40	
Cash		40
(To record customer's NSF cheque)		
Miscellaneous Expense	13	
Cash		13
(To record bank service charges: [$3 + $8 + $2 = $13])		

TIP: The above entries can be combined into one compound entry.

EXERCISE 7-7

Purpose: (L.O. 10) This exercise will illustrate how to determine deposits in transit and outstanding cheques.

Shown below for Molly's Folly are the:
  (1)   bank reconciliation at September 30, 2002.
  (2)   listing of deposits for October per the bank statement.
  (3)   listing of deposits for October per the books.
  (4)   listing of cheques paid by the bank during October.
  (5)   listing of cheques written by the depositor during October.

Molly's Folly
BANK RECONCILIATION
September 30, 2002

Balance per bank statement		$ 15,000
Add: Deposits in transit		
September 29	$ 2,000	
September 30	1,600	3,600
		18,600
Deduct: Outstanding cheques		
No. 514	650	
No. 516	410	
No. 520	560	
No. 521	740	
No. 522	1,000	3,360
Correct cash balance		$ 15,240
Balance per books		$ 15,690
Deduct: Customer's NSF cheque	$ 400	
Bank service charge	50	450
Correct cash balance		$ 15,240

Bank Statement for October—Deposits

Date	Amount	Date	Amount	Date	Amount
10/1	$ 2,000	10/11	$ 1,200	10/25	$ 100
10/2	1,600	10/15	200	10/27	600
10/3	500	10/18	400	10/28	800
10/5	300	10/21	700	10/29	1,300
10/11	1,100	10/22	900	Total	$ 11,700

Cash Receipts Journal

Date	Amount		Date	Amount		Date	Amount
10/1	$ 500		10/20	$ 700		10/29	$ 1,400
10/4	300		10/21	900		10/30	1,500
10/8	1,100		10/23	100		10/31	550
10/10	1,200		10/25	600		Total	$ 11,550
10/13	200		10/27	800			
10/16	400		10/28	1,300			

Bank Statement for October—Cheques Paid and Debit Memos

Date	Cheque #	Amount		Date	Cheque #	Amount
10/1	514	$ 650		10/13	534	$ 220
10/1	520	560		10/14	535	240
10/4	521	740		10/18	538	380
10/4	522	1,000		10/18	536	250
10/5	525	120		10/18	537	320
10/5	526	140		10/18	539	430
10/6	528	230		10/19	540	510
10/8	529	310		10/23	541	330
10/8	527	210		10/25	542	340
10/8	530	420		10/29	545	540
10/11	532	160		10/29	546	470
10/11	531	130		10/31	DM	30
10/12	533	190		Total		$ 8,920

Cash Payments Journal—Cheques Issued

Date	Cheque #	Amount		Date	Cheque #	Amount
10/1	525	$ 120		10/14	538	$ 380
10/1	526	140		10/15	539	430
10/3	527	210		10/17	540	510
10/4	528	230		10/20	541	330
10/5	529	310		10/23	542	340
10/5	530	420		10/25	543	110
10/7	531	130		10/26	544	160
10/7	532	106		10/27	545	540
10/7	533	190		10/28	546	470
10/11	534	220		10/31	547	590
10/11	535	240		10/31	548	640
10/12	536	250		Total		$ 7,386
10/14	537	320				

Instructions

(a)   Prepare a list of deposits in transit at October 31, 2002.
(b)   Prepare a list of outstanding cheques at October 31, 2002.
(c)   Locate any errors per books, assuming that the information recorded in the bank's records is correct.
(d)   Locate any bank memoranda that will need to be recorded on the books.

Solution to Exercise 7-7

(a)   Deposits in transit at October 31, 2002:

October 29	$ 1,400
October 30	1,500
October 31	550
Total	$ 3,450

(b)   Outstanding cheques at October 31, 2002:

No.	Amount
516	$ 410
543	110
544	160
547	590
548	640
	$ 1,910

(c)   Cheque No. 532 was recorded on the depositor's books for $106 when it should have been recorded for the correct amount of $160.

(d)   The DM for $30 on October 31 will need to be recorded on the depositor's books. (The DM is likely for bank service charges for October.)

Approach and Explanation:

(a)   To identify the deposits in transit at October 31:

(1)   Compare the deposits in transit at September 30 (per the company's bank reconciliation at that date) with the October bank statement. If the deposit did not get recorded by the bank during October it is to be considered a deposit in transit at October 31. (It would be extremely rare for a particular deposit to be listed as a deposit in transit on **two** successive bank reconciliations because it would indicate the deposit was lost in the mail or lost in the bank's facilities or a victim of some strange fate.)

For Molly's Folly, the $2,000 and $1,600 items deposited at the end of September (deposits in transit at September 30, 2002) both were recorded by the bank in early October as expected.

(2) Compare the deposits made during October per company records with the October deposits per the bank's records. Deposits not recorded by the bank represent **deposits in transit**. As can be expected, the receipts recorded on the books at the very end of October have not had enough time to be processed by the bank by the end of the day on October 31. These include the deposits made by Molly's Folly on October 29 ($1,400), October 30 ($1,500), and October 31 ($550).

(b) To identify the outstanding cheques at October 31, 2002:

(1) Compare the cheques outstanding at September 30, 2002 (per the September 30th bank reconciliation) with the cheques clearing the bank as shown on the October bank statement. If a September cheque remains unpaid at the end of October, it is an outstanding cheque at October 31. For Molly's Folly, cheque numbers 514, 520, 521, and 522 all cleared the bank during October, but cheque number 516 ($410) remains unpaid at October 31, 2002. (The cheque could be lost in the mail or lost in the banking system. More likely, the cheque is still in the hands of the payee, who for some reason has not yet deposited it to his account.)

(2) Compare the cheques written by Molly's Folly during October with the cheques paid by the bank. Issued cheques, which have not been paid by the bank represent **outstanding cheques**.

For Molly's Folly, October cheque numbers 543 ($110), 544 ($160), 547 ($590), and 548 ($640) were written during October and are outstanding at October 31.

(c) To identify errors on either the bank's records or the depositor's books, compare all of the figures on the October bank statement with their source on the depositor's records. If there are any discrepancies, determine which is in error. For Molly's Folly, cheque number 532 correctly cleared the bank for $160 but was entered in the cash payments journal as $106. (The facts of the problem state that the bank's records are correct.) This transposition-type error caused the depositor's bank balance per ledger to be overstated by $54 ($160 - $106 = $54).

TIP: Note that a transposition error (reversing the order of numbers) will cause a difference that is divisible by 9.

EXERCISE 7-8

Purpose: (L.O. 10) This exercise will allow you to practise preparing a bank reconciliation.

A bank reconciliation should be prepared by a depositor every month.

The cash balance per bank at October 31 is $17,780, and the cash balance per Molly's Folly's books at October 31 is $19,404.

Instructions

(a) Using the data in **Exercise 7-7** and the solution to that exercise, prepare a bank reconciliation for Molly's Folly at October 31, 2002.

(b) Prepare the adjusting entries at October 31 for the depositor's books. Assume cheque No. 532 was issued to the power company for utilities.

Solution to Exercise 7-8

(a)

Molly's Folly
BANK RECONCILIATION
October 31, 2002

Balance per bank statement		$ 17,780*
Add: Deposits in transit [Answer (a) Exercise 7-7]		3,450
		21,230
Deduct: Outstanding cheques [Answer (b) Exercise 7-7]		1,910
Correct cash balance		$ 19,320
Balance per books		$ 19,404**
Deduct: Bank service charge	$ 30	
Error in recording cheque No. 532	54	84
Correct cash balance		$ 19,320

*To add to the complexity of this exercise, you could be asked to solve for the $17,780 cash balance per bank statement. The calculation would be as follows:

Balance per bank statement at September 30, 2002	$ 15,000
Add: Deposits recorded during October and credit memoranda	11,700
Deduct: Cheques paid during October and debit memoranda	8,920
Balance per bank statement at October 30, 2002	$ 17,780

**To add to the complexity of this exercise, you could be asked to solve for the $19,404 cash balance per books at October 31, 2002. The calculation would be as follows:

Balance per books at September 30, 2002 before adjustment	$ 15,690
Deduct: NSF cheque recorded by an adjusting entry	
Deduct: Bank service charge for September recorded by	
an adjusting entry	50
Correct cash balance at September 30	15,240
Add: Deposits made during October	11,550
Deduct: Cheques written (issued) during October	7,386
Balance per books at October 31, 2002	$ 19,404

An alternate approach to solving for the balance per books before adjustment is illustrated in the **Solution to Exercise 7-6** part (b) 2.

> **TIP:** Keep in mind that deposits in transit and outstanding cheques are reconciling items but do **not** require adjusting entries on either the bank's books or the depositor's books.

(b)   Oct. 31   Miscellaneous Expense..   30
                        Cash   30
                            (To record the bank service charges for Oct.)

        Oct. 31   Utilities Expense..   54
                        Cash   54
                            (To correct error in recording cheque no. 532)

EXERCISE 7-9

Purpose: (L.O. 10) This exercise reviews the journal entries involved with establishing and maintaining a petty cash fund.

The Montreal Smoked Meat Corporation makes most expenditures by cheque. The following transactions relate to an imprest fund established by the Montreal Smoked Meat Corporation to handle small expenditures on an expedient basis.

Transactions

May	4	Wrote a $100 cheque to establish the petty cash fund.
	6	Paid taxi $2 to deliver papers to a branch office.
	6	Purchased stamps, $13.
	8	Paid $15 for advertising posters.
	12	Paid $6 for mail received with "postage due."
	12	Paid $8 for coffee supplies.
	13	Paid $17 for office supplies.
	14	Paid bus charges of $18 to ship goods to a customer.
	15	Counted the remaining coins and currency in the fund, $20. Wrote a cheque to replenish the fund.

Instructions
(a)   Record the transactions in general journal form.
(b)   Answer the questions that follow:

1.   How much coin and currency should have been in the petty cash box at the end of the day on May 12? $_____

2.   How much coin and currency should have been in the petty cash box on May 15 before replenishment? $_____

3.   What was the balance in the Petty Cash ledger account on May 12? $_____

4.   What was the balance in the Petty Cash ledger account at the end of the day, May 15? $_____

TIP: In order to answer the last two questions, it would be helpful to post the journal entries to a T-account for Petty Cash.

Solution to Exercise 7-9

(a)   May 4   Petty Cash..   100

         Cash   100

              (To establish a petty cash fund)

        May 15   Miscellaneous Expense ($2 + $8)   10

              Postage Expense ($13 + $6)......................................   19

              Advertising Expense...   15

              Office Supplies   17

              Transportation-out   18

              Cash Over and Short..   1

              Cash   80

              (To replenish the petty cash fund)

(b)   1. There should have been $56 in coin and currency in the fund at the end of the day on May 12. ($100 - $2 - $13 - $15 - $6 - $8 = $56)

       2. There should have been $21 in coin and currency in the fund on May 15 before replenishment. ($100 - $2 - $13 - $15 - $6 - $8 - $17 - $18 = $21)

TIP: Because only $20 was found in the fund at that date, there was a shortage of $1 which must be recorded by a debit to the Cash Over and Short account.

---

       3. $100
       4. $100

TIP: The balance of the Petty Cash account changes **only** when the fund is established or the size of the fund is increased or decreased. The Petty Cash account balance is **not** affected by expenditures from the fund nor replenishments. (No journal entry is made at the time the expenditure is made. Expenditures from the fund are accounted for at the date of replenishment.)

TIP: Petty Cash is not normally reported separately on the balance sheet. The balance of the Petty Cash account is generally lumped together with all other cash items when a balance sheet is prepared.

EXERCISE 7-10

Purpose: (L.O. 10) This exercise will allow you to practise preparing a proof of cash.

The following data pertain to the Burghard Company for 2002:

1.   Per the bank statement for February: January 31 balance, $20,000; February receipts, $22,000; February disbursements, $24,000; February 28 balance, $18,000.

2.   Per the books: January 31 unadjusted balance, $16,020; February receipts, $19,410; February disbursements, $21,505, February 28 balance, $13,925.

3.   Bank service charge of $20 for January is included in book disbursements for February.

4.   Bank service charge of $35 for February is included on the bank statement for February.

5.   The first deposit shown on the February bank statement was $5,000 and was included in January's cash receipts per books.

6. $7,000 of cheques written in February have not cleared the bank by February 28.

7.   A cheque written for office supplies in February for $970 was incorrectly recorded in the cash disbursements journal and in the cheque register as $790. This cheque cleared the bank in February for $970. Office supplies are charged to Office Supplies Expense when purchased.

8.   The bank credited the firm's account in error for $500 in February for another firm's deposit.

9.   The bank collected a $1,000 note receivable for the company in February plus $90 interest. The company has not yet recorded this transaction.

10.   Cash receipts for February 28 of $4,000 did not reach the bank until March 2.

11.   All $9,000 of cheques outstanding at January 31 cleared the banking system during February.

12.   A customer's NSF cheque in the amount of $300 was returned with the February bank statement. This cheque was redeposited in March. As of the end of February, Burghard has not yet made an entry for the return of this cheque by the bank.

Instructions
(a)   Prepare a bank reconciliation for the Burghard Co. for February.
(b)   Prepare any adjusting entry(ies) required for the books.

Solution to Exercise 7-10

(a)

Burghard Company
BANK RECONCILIATION
For February , 2002

Balance per bank statement		$ 18,000*
Add: Outstanding deposit (February 28)		4,000
		22,000
Deduct: Outstanding cheques	$7,000	
Bank error	500	7,500
Correct cash balance		$ 14,500
Balance per books		$ 13,925*
Add: Cash Collection on Note (including $90 interest)**	$1,090	1,090
		15,015
Deduct: Bank service charge	35	
Error in recording cheque (office supplies)	180	
N.S.F. Cheque	300	515
Correct cash balance		$14,500

* The starting point is the ending balances for both the bank and company books.
  The only reconciliation, which needs to be performed are for items that the other party does not know about, (ex. Bank service charge recorded in February is already included in the opening balance of the company's books and does not need to be reconciled).

**The note collected by the bank and associated interest can be recorded individually or lumped together, however, the associated journal entry (see below) must record the two types of revenues individually.

(b)

Office Expenses—Bank Charges	35	
Cash		35
Office Supplies Expense	180	
Cash		180
Cash	1,090	
Note Receivable		1,000
Interest Revenue		90
Accounts Receivable...	300	
Cash		300

ANALYSIS OF MULTIPLE-CHOICE TYPE QUESTIONS

QUESTION
1.   (L.O. 1) Which of the following items should **not** be included in the Cash caption on the balance sheet?
a.   Coins and currency in the cash register
b.   Cheques from other parties presently in the cash register
c.   Amounts on deposit in chequing account at the bank
d.   Postage stamps on hand

Explanation: Cash on hand, cash in banks, and petty cash are often combined and reported simply as Cash. Undeposited cheques from other parties is a component of cash on hand. Postage stamps on hand are classified as a prepaid expense. (Solution = d.)

QUESTION
2.   (L.O. 2) Legally restricted deposits held at a bank as compensating balances against long-term borrowing arrangements should be:
a.   used to reduce the amount reported as long-term debt on the balance sheet.
b.   reported separately among the "cash and cash equivalent items" in Current Assets on the balance sheet.
c.   separately classified as noncurrent assets in either the Investments or Other Assets sections of the balance sheet.
d.   used to reduce the amount reported as short-term debt on the balance sheet.

Explanation: The SEC recommends that legally restricted deposits held as compensating balances against short-term borrowing arrangements be stated separately among the "cash and cash equivalent items" in Current Assets. Restricted deposits held as compensating balances against long-term borrowing arrangements should be separately classified as noncurrent assets in either the Investments or Other Assets sections, using a caption such as "Cash on Deposit Maintained as Compensating Balance." To use the asset balance to directly reduce a debt (answer selections "a" and "d" would be "offsetting assets against liabilities" which violates a rule against offsetting or setoff. Only in rare circumstances is it permissable to offset assets and liabilities.) (Solution = c.)

QUESTION
3.   (L.O. 5) Gatorland recorded uncollectible accounts expense of $30,000 and wrote off accounts receivable of $25,000 during the year. The net effect of these two transactions on working capital was a decrease of:
a. $55,000
b. $30,000
c. $25,000
d. $5,000

Approach and Explanation: Reconstruct both entries referred to in the question. Then analyse each debit and each credit separately as to its effect on working capital (total current assets minus total current liabilities). (Refer to **Illustration 7-1**.)

			Effect on Working Capital
Uncollectible Accounts Expense	30,000		None
Allow. for Uncollectible Accounts		30,000	Decrease 30,000
Allowance for Uncollectible Accounts	25,000		Increase 25,000
Accounts Receivable		25,000	Decrease 25,000
Net Effect			Decrease 30,000
			(Solution = b.)

QUESTION

4.   (L.O. 5) Chelser Corporation performed an analysis and an ageing of its accounts receivable at December 31, 2002, which disclosed the following:

Accounts receivable balance	$ 100,000
Allowance for uncollectible accounts balance	5,000
Accounts deemed uncollectible	7,400

The net realizable value of the accounts receivable at December 31 is:
a. $87,600
b. $92,600
c. $95,000
d. $97,600

Approach and Explanation: Read the last sentence of the question: "The net realizable value of the accounts receivable at December 31 is..." Underline "net realizable value of accounts receivable." Write down the definition of net realizable value of accounts receivable—amount of accounts receivable ultimately expected to be converted into cash. Read the details of the question. If an ageing shows $7,400 of the $100,000 accounts are deemed uncollectible, then the remaining $92,600 are expected to be converted into cash. (Because the balance of the allowance account does not agree with the amount of uncollectibles per the ageing, the allowance for uncollectible accounts balance must be the unadjusted balance or the percentage of sales method is being used to determine the amount to record as bad debt expense.) (Solution = b.)

QUESTION

5.   (L.O. 5) The following data are available for 2002:

Sales, cash	$ 200,000
Sales, credit	500,000
Accounts Receivable, January 1	80,000
Accounts Receivable, December 31	72,000
Allowance for Doubtful Accounts, January 1	4,000
Accounts written off during 2002	4,600

The journal entry to record bad debt expense for the period and to adjust the allowance account is to be based on an estimate of 1% of credit sales. The entry

to record the uncollectible accounts expense for 2002 would include a debit to the Bad Debt Expense account for:
a. $7,200.
b. $5,600.
c. $4,400.
d. $5,000.

Approach and Explanation: Think about the emphasis of the entry when the percentage-of-sales basis is used. This method emphasizes the income statement. Therefore, 1% times credit sales equals bad debt expense ($500,000 x 1% = $5,000). The balance of the allowance account before adjustment does **not** affect this calculation or entry. (Solution = d.)

QUESTION
6.   (L.O. 5) The following data are available for 2002:

Sales, cash	$ 200,000
Sales, credit	500,000
Accounts Receivable, January 1	80,000
Accounts Receivable, December 31	72,000
Allowance for Doubtful Accounts, January 1	4,000
Accounts written off during 2002	4,600

The journal entry to record bad debt expense for the period and to adjust the allowance account is to be based on an ageing analysis of accounts receivable. The ageing analysis of accounts receivable at December 31, 2002, reveals that $5,200 of existing accounts receivable are estimated to be uncollectible. The entry to record the uncollectible accounts expense for 2002 will involve a debit to the Bad Debt Expense account for:
a. $9,800
b. $5,800
c. $5,200
d. $4,600

Approach and Explanation: An ageing analysis is performed to determine the best figure to represent the cash (net) realizable value of the accounts receivable in the balance sheet. Thus, $5,200 is the desired balance for the allowance account at the reporting date. Determine the existing balance in the allowance account and the adjusting entry needed to arrive at the desired ending balance.

Allowance for Doubtful Accounts

Write-offs, 2002	4,600	Balance, 1/1/02	4,000	**Entry**
Balance before adjustment	600	Adjustment needed	×	←**Needed.**
		Desired balance at 12/31/02	5,200	

Solving for X: X - $600   = $5,200
                      X   = $5,200 + $600
                      X   = $5,800 (Solution = b.)

QUESTION
7.   (L.O. 5) The following data are available for 2002:

Allowance for Doubtful Accounts, January 1	$ 41,000
Writeoffs of accounts receivable during the year	35,000
Net credit sales for the year	1,300,000

Bad debts are estimated to be 3% of net credit sales. The balance of the allowance account after adjustment should be:
a. $4,000.
b. $39,000.
c. $45,000.
d. $80,000.

Approach and Explanation: Draw a T-account. Enter the data given and solve for the amount requested.

Allowance for Doubtful Accounts

		41,000	Beginning Balance
Writeoffs	35,000	39,000	Expense = 3% × $1,300,000
		45,000	Ending Balance

(Solution = c.)

QUESTION
8.   (L.O. 5) An adjusting entry is made whereby there is a debit to Sales Returns and Allowances and a credit to Allowance for Sales Returns and Allowances. The effect of this entry is to:
a.   Reduce assets and net sales.
b.   Increase assets and net sales.
c.   Reduce net sales and liabilities.
d.   Increase net sales and liabilities.

Explanation: The debit to Sales Returns and Allowances reduces net sales (and owners' equity) because of an increase in a contra sales account. The credit to Allowance for Sales Returns and Allowances increases a contra account to Accounts Receivable and thereby reduces total assets. The entry is necessary to properly match sales returns and allowances with the period in which the related sales revenue was reported. At the end of a period, an estimate is made regarding the sales made during the last few weeks of that period that may yet be subject to refunds (by way of reductions of the balances of accounts receivable) during the beginning weeks of the subsequent accounting period. (Solution = a.)

QUESTION

9.   (L.O. 6) On January 1, 2002, West Park Co. exchanged equipment for a $480,000 zero-interest-bearing note due on January 1, 2005 from Chamberlain's Health Products. Chamberlain's incremental borrowing rate at January 1, 2002 was 10%. The present value of $1 discounted at 10% for three periods is $0.75. The amount of interest revenue that should be included in West Park's income statement for the year 2003 is:

a. $0.
b. $36,000.
c. $39,600.
D. $48,000.

Explanation: The note received in exchange for equipment is an arms' length transaction and the stated interest rate is unreasonable in relation to the market rate of interest. The fair value of the equipment is not available information. Therefore, the present value of the note is to be approximated by discounting all of the future cash receipts related to the note, and the discounting is done using the market rate of interest (borrower's incremental borrowing rate). The face amount of $480,000 is discounted back three periods to yield a present value balance at January 1, 2002 of $360,000 ($480,000 X .75 = $360,000). The effective interest method is used to determine the amount of interest to report each period.

		Interest				
Present Value Balance at Beginning of Period	×	Rate Per Period	×	Time	=	Interest

$360,000 X 10% X 12/12 = $36,000 Interest for 2002

The interest for 2003 (the second year) would be calculated as follows:

$360,000	Present value, January 1, 2002
+ 36,000	Interest for 2002
396,000	Present value, December 31, 2002
(0)	Payment
396,000	Present value (carrying value), January 1, 2003
× 10%	Effective or yield rate of interest
$ 39,600	Interest for 2003 (the second year)

(Solution = c.)

QUESTION

10.   (L.O. 8) A company has a large amount of accounts receivable and a ready need for cash. The company may accelerate the receipt of cash from customers' accounts receivable through:

	Factoring	Assignment
a.	Yes	Yes
b.	Yes	No
c.	No	Yes
d.	No	No

Explanation: The company can transfer accounts receivable to a third party for cash by the assignment or factoring (sale) of the accounts receivable.   (Solution = a.)

QUESTION

11.   (L.O. 9) The accounts receivable turnover ratio measures the:
   a.   Number of times the average balance of accounts receivable is collected during the period.
   b.   Percentage of accounts receivable turnover over to a collection agency during the period.
   c.   Percentage of accounts receivable arising during certain seasons.
   d.   Number of times the average balance of inventory is sold during the period.

Approach and Explanation: Write down the components of the accounts receivable turnover ratio. Think about why it is calculated. The calculation is as follows:

$$\text{Accounts Receivable Turnover Ratio} = \frac{\text{Net Sales}}{\text{Average trade receivables (net)}}$$

Because cash sales do not go through the Accounts Receivable account, only net credit sales belong in the numerator; however, very often that information is not available. The accounts receivable ratio measures the number of times, on average, the accounts receivable balance was collected during the period. This ratio is used to assess the liquidity of the receivables. This ratio can be divided into 365 days to obtain the average days to collect accounts receivable (Solution = a.)

QUESTION

12.   (L.O. 10) The term "outstanding cheques" refers to:
   a.   Cheques that have been lost in the mail or for some other reason have been misplaced.
   b.   Depositor cheques which have been processed by the bank but have not yet been recorded by the depositor.
   c.   Customer cheques which have been returned by the bank because the customer's bank would not honour them.
   d.   Depositor cheques which have not yet cleared the banking system.

Explanation: There is a time lag between the date a cheque is issued and the date the cheque clears the banking system. During the time between these two dates, the cheques are referred to as "outstanding cheques." Cheques written by the enterprise but not mailed until **after** the balance sheet date should not be included with outstanding cheques. Rather, they should be added back to the cash balance and reported as accounts payable. (Solution = d.)

QUESTION

13.   (L.O.10) The following information pertains to Cruiser Co. at December 31, 2002:

Bank statement balance	$20,000
Chequebook balance	28,200
Deposit in transit	10,000
Outstanding cheques	2,000
Bank service charges for December	200

In Cruiser's balance sheet at December 31, 2002, cash should be reported as:
a. $18,000
b. $20,000
c. $28,000
d. $30,000

Approach and Explanation: When a question relates to data used in a bank reconciliation, you should sketch out the format for a bank reconciliation, put in the information given, and solve for the unknown piece.

Balance per bank statement	$ 20,000
Deposit in transit	10,000
Outstanding cheques	(2,000)
Correct cash balance	$ 28,000
Balance per books	$ 28,200
Bank service charges	(200)
Correct cash balance	$ 28,000

In this particular question, the completion of either the top half or the bottom half of the reconciliation using the bank-to-correct balance method would be enough to solve for the answer requested. (Solution = c.)

QUESTION

14.   (L.O.10) The following data relate to the bank account of Springfield Cleaners:

Cash balance, September 30, 2002 per bank	$ 10,000
Cash balance, October 31, 2002 per bank	21,500
Cheques paid during October by bank	5,900
Cheques written during October per books	6,800
Cash balance, October 31, 2002 per books	22,200
Bank service charges for October, not recorded on books	100
Deposits per books for October	19,000

The amount of deposits recorded by the bank in October is:

    a. $19,000
    b. $17,500
    c. $11,500
    d. $5,700

Approach and Explanation: Think about how deposits recorded by the bank affect the cash balance per bank and other items that cause that balance to change. Plug in the figures given and solve for the unknown.

Balance per bank, September 30	$ 10,000
Deposits per bank during October	X
Bank credit memoranda	-0-
Cheques paid by bank during October	(5,900)
Bank service charge for October and other bank debit memoranda	(100)
Balance per bank, October 31	$ 21,500

Solving for X:

    $10,000 + X - $5,900 - $100 = $21,500
    X = $21,500 - $10,000 + $5,900 + $100
    X = $17,500 (Solution = b.)

QUESTION

15.   (L.O.10) The following information pertains to Kimbell Corporation at December 31, 2002:

Balance per bank	$ 10,000
Deposit in transit	3,000
Outstanding cheques	8,000
Bank service charges for December	200
Bank erroneously charged Kimbell account for Franklin Co. cheque written for $700. As of Dec. 31, the bank had not corrected this error	700

Kimbell's cash balance per ledger (books) before adjustment at December 31, 2002 is:

    a. $14,100
    b. $5,900
    c. $5,500
    d. $4,100

Approach and Explanation: The balance per books (before adjustment) can easily be calculated by putting the data into the format for a bank reconciliation. Either format (balance per bank to balance per books or balance per bank to correct balance) can be used. Each approach is illustrated on the following page: (Solution = b.)

Balance per bank statement	$ 10,000
Deposit in transit	3,000
Outstanding cheques	(8,000)
Bank service charges	200
Bank error in charge for cheque	700
Balance per ledger	$ 5,900
Balance per bank statement	$ 10,000
Deposit in transit	3,000
Outstanding cheques	(8,000)
Bank error in charge for cheque	700
Correct cash balance	$ 5,700
Balance per books (ledger)	$ X
Bank service charge	(200)
Correct cash balance	$ 5,700

$$X = \underline{\$5,900}$$

CHAPTER 8

VALUATION OF INVENTORIES: A COST BASIS APPROACH

OVERVIEW

In accounting, the term inventory refers to a stock of goods held for sale in the ordinary course of business or goods that will be used or consumed in the production of goods to be sold. A number of questions regarding inventory are addressed in this chapter; these include: (1) How will the selection of a particular cost flow assumption affect the income statement and balance sheet? (2) What goods should be included in inventory? (3) How do inventory errors affect the financial statements? (4) How does a periodic inventory system differ from a perpetual system? (5) How do you calculate the various layers of inventory when the dollar-value LIFO method is used?

SUMMARY OF LEARNING OBJECTIVES

1. **Identify major classifications of inventory.** Only one inventory account, Merchandise Inventory, appears in the financial statements of a merchandising concern. A manufacturer normally has three inventory accounts: Raw Materials, Work in Process, and Finished Goods. Factory of manufacturing supplies inventory may also exist.

2. **Distinguish between the perpetual and periodic inventory systems.** Under a perpetual inventory system, a continuous record of changes in inventory is maintained in the Inventory account. That is, all purchases and transfer of goods out (issues) are recorded directly in the Inventory account as they occur. No such record is kept under a periodic system. Under the periodic inventory system, year-end inventory must be determined by a physical count upon which the amount of ending inventory and the cost of goods sold is based. Even under the perpetual system, an annual count is needed to test the records' accuracy.

3. **Identify the effects of inventory errors on the financial statements.** *If the ending inventory is misstated:* (1) inventory, retained earnings, working capital, and current ratio in the balance sheet will be misstated, and (2) the cost of goods sold and net income in the income statement will be misstated. *If purchases and inventory are misstated:* (1) the inventory, accounts payable, and current ratio will be misstated, and (2) purchases and ending inventory in the income statement will be misstated.

4. **Identify the items that should be included as inventory cost.** Product costs are directly connected with the bringing of goods to the buyer's place of business and converting such goods to a salable condition. Such charges would include freight charges on goods purchased, other direct costs of acquisition, and labour and other production costs incurred in processing the goods up to the time of sale. Manufacturing overhead costs that include indirect material, indirect labour, and such items as amortization, taxes, insurance, heat, and electricity incurred in the manufacturing process are also usually allocated to inventory, although some companies include only the costs of direct or variable overhead.

5. **Explain the difference between variable costing and absorption costing in assigning manufacturing costs to inventory.** Under variable (direct) costing, direct material, direct labour, and variable manufacturing overhead are charged to inventories and fixed manufacturing overhead is treated as a period cost. In absorption (full) costing, direct material, direct labour, and all manufacturing costs (variable and fixed) are treated as product costs and are charged to inventories.

6. **Distinguish between the physical flow of inventory and the cost flow assigned to inventory.** If the unit cost is different for various purchases, the question is which costs will be assigned to ending inventory and, as a consequence, to costs of goods sold. In accounting there is no requirement that the costs charged to goods sold be consistent with the goods' physical movement. Consequently, various cost flow methods for assigning costs to cost of goods sold and ending inventory are all generally acceptable. The primary methods are specific identification, average cost, FIFO and LIFO.

7. **Identify possible objectives for inventory valuation decisions.** The general objectives are (1) to match expenses realistically against revenues; (2) to report inventory on the balance sheet at a realistic amount; and (3) to minimize income taxes. Inevitably, tradeoffs exist between the cost flow methods and the objectives such that no one method will likely satisfy all objectives.

8. **Describe and compare the cost flow assumptions used in accounting for inventories.** (1) **Average cost** prices items in inventory on the basis of the average cost of all similar goods available during the period. (2) **First-in, first-out (FIFO)** assumes that costs are used in the order in which they are purchased. The inventory remaining must therefore represent the most recent purchases. (3) **Last-in, first-out (LIFO)** matches the cost of the last goods purchased against revenue.

9. **Evaluate LIFO as a basis for understanding the differences between the cost flow methods.** In a period of rising prices, LIFO may be viewed as providing a more realistic matching in the income statement (recent costs against revenues) and offering a greater future earnings hedge. Disadvantages include a reduction in net income and old costs for inventory on the balance sheet. In addition, it does not generally reflect physical flow, matching is destroyed when beginning inventory is liquidated, it provides an opportunity to manage (manipulate) earnings, and it is not acceptable for income tax purposes in Canada. To an extent, the advantages and disadvantages of LIFO are the disadvantages and advantages of FIFO. Average cost methods fall between these two extremes.

10. **Explain the importance of judgement in selecting an inventory cost flow method.** The only guidance provided by the *CICA Handbook* is that the method chosen should result in "the fairest matching of costs against revenues regardless of whether or not the method corresponds to the physical flow of goods." Consequently, exercise of judgement is required when choosing a cost flow method.

TIPS ON CHAPTER TOPICS

TIP: The cost of an inventory item includes all costs necessary to acquire the item and bring it to the location and condition for its intended use. This cost would include the item's purchase price, transportation-in, and any special handling charges. However, transportation-out is **not** included in the cost of inventory; it is classified as a selling expense on the income statement for the period in which the expense was incurred.

TIP: The transportation terms designate the point at which title passes. f.o.b. shipping point (or seller) means the title passes to the buyer when it leaves the seller's dock. f.o.b. destination (or buyer) means the title passes to the buyer when it arrives at the buyer's dock. Assuming that Palmer Company in Richmond Hill, Ontario sells to Woods in St. Catharines, Ontario, the following shows synonymous terms:

f.o.b. shipping point	**f.o.b. destination**
or f.o.b. seller	or f.o.b. buyer
or f.o.b. Richmond Hill, Ontario	or f.o.b. St. Catharines, Ontario

TIP: FIFO (first-in, first-out) means the cost of the first items put into inventory are used to price the first items out to cost of goods sold. Thus, the earliest acquisition prices are used to price cost of goods sold for the period, and the latest (most current) acquisition prices are used to price items in the ending inventory. LIFO (last-in, first-out) uses the most recent costs to price the units sold during the period, and it uses the oldest prices to cost the items in the ending inventory. Thus, in a period of rising prices, the method that will yield the lowest net income on the income statement and the lowest ending inventory on the balance sheet is the LIFO method.

TIP: The cost of the ending inventory determined by using the weighted-average method is an amount between the cost of the ending inventory determined by using the LIFO method and the cost of the ending inventory determined by using the FIFO method.

IP: When working a problem which requires the calculation of either ending inventory or cost of goods sold, remember that the total of the ending inventory (EI) and the cost of goods sold (COGS) should equal the total cost of goods available for sale (COGAS) during the period (beginning inventory (BI) plus the net cost of purchases), ie. BI + Purchases = COGAS – EI = COGS.

TIP: Sales revenue represents the **selling prices** of goods sold, whereas cost of goods sold expense represents the **cost price** of items sold.

TIP: The inventory pricing method selected by an entity does **not** have to correspond to the actual physical flow of goods. Thus, a company can use the LIFO method to determine the cost of ending inventory even though the first goods purchased are the first to be sold.

TIP: An understatement in ending inventory of year 1 will cause an understatement in net income for year 1 and an overstatement in net income for year 2. Thus, retained earnings and working capital at the end of year 1 are understated. However, assuming no more errors are committed at the end of year 2, retained earnings and working capital are not affected at the end of year 2.

TIP: Variable (direct) costing approach assumes that inventory cost includes only variable costs, direct material, direct labour and variable manufacturing overhead. Fixed manufacturing overhead is assumed to be a period cost (charged to the current year's income statement), in essence, the assumption is that fixed manufacturing overhead is a cost of capacity to manufacture, not a cost of inventory.

TIP: Absorption (full) costing approach assumes that all costs of manufacturing should be included in determining product cost, including direct material, direct labour, and both variable and fixed manufacturing overhead.

TIP: LIFO is not allowed for income tax purposes in Canada. The use of one method over another should be based on which method results in the "fairest matching of costs against revenues, regardless of whether or not the method corresponds to the physical flow of goods." However, In the United States, the Internal Revenue Code generally requires that if an entity selects LIFO for income tax reporting, it must also use LIFO for its general purpose financial statements.

EXERCISE 8-1

Purpose: (L.O.3) This exercise will enable you to practise identifying the effects of inventory errors on the financial statements.

The net income per books of Wacky Wicks Company was determined without knowledge of the errors indicated.

Year	Net Income Per Books	Error in Ending Inventory	
1999	$ 150,000	Overstated	$ 9,000
2000	156,000	Overstated	21,000
2001	162,000	Understated	33,000
2002	168,000	No error	

Instructions
Calculate the correct net income figure for each of the four years after taking into account the inventory errors.

Solution to Exercise 8-1

Year	Net Income Per Books	Add Over- statement Jan. 1	Deduct Under- statement Jan. 1	Deduct Over- statement Dec. 31	Add Under- statement Dec. 31	Corrected Net Income
1999	$ 150,000			$ 9,000		$ 141,000
2000	156,000	$ 9,000		21,000		144,000
2001	162,000	21,000			$ 33,000	216,000
2002	168,000		$ 33,000			135,000

Approach and Explanation: When more than one error affects a given year (such as in 2000), analyse each error separately then combine the effects of each analysis to get the net impact of the errors. The beginning inventory for 2000 (ending inventory for 1999) was overstated by $9,000. Therefore, cost of goods sold was overstated by $9,000, and net income for 2000 was understated by $9,000. The ending inventory for 2000 was overstated by $21,000. Therefore, cost of goods sold was understated, and net income for 2000 was overstated by $21,000. An understatement in net income of $9,000 and an overstatement of $21,000 in 2000 net to an overstatement of $12,000 for the net income figure reported for 2000. This overstatement of $12,000, combined with the $156,000 amount reported, yields a corrected net income figure of $144,000 for 2000.

Another way of analysing the effects of an individual error is illustrated below for the $21,000 overstatement of inventory at the end of 2000.

		Effect on 2000		Effect on 2001	
	Beginning inventory			Overstated	$21,000
+	Cost of goods purchased				
=	Cost of goods available for sale			Overstated	21,000
-	Ending inventory	Overstated	$21,000		
=	Cost of goods sold	Understated	21,000	Overstated	21,000
	Sales				
-	Cost of goods sold	Understated	21,000	Overstated	21,000
=	Gross profit	Overstated	21,000	Understated	21,000
-	Operating expenses				
=	Net income	Overstated	21,000	Understated	21,000

Thus, the previously calculated net income figure for 2000 must be reduced by $21,000 to correct for this error. Also, the net income figure for 2001 must be increased by $21,000 to correct for the same error.

TIP: The ending inventory for year 1 is the beginning inventory for year 2. Thus, when the ending inventory for year 1 is overstated, it will cause an overstatement in the net income for year 1 and an understatement in net income for year 2 for the same amount. This error will cause retained earnings at the end of year 1 to be overstated because net income for year 1 (which is overstated) is closed into retained earnings. The balance of retained earnings at the end of year 2 will be unaffected by this error because the net income for year 2 (which is understated by the same amount as the overstatement in retained earnings at the end of year 1) is closed into retained earnings; the error at this point counterbalances. Working capital at the end of year 1 is overstated (because inventory is a current asset), but working capital at the end of year 2 is unaffected because the inventory figure at the end of year 2 is determined by a physical inventory counting and pricing procedure. No new error in this process is assumed unless otherwise indicated.

EXERCISE 8-2

Purpose: (L.O.6, 8) This exercise reviews the characteristics and the effects of using various pricing methods to determine inventory costs.

Instructions

Answer each of the following questions by inserting one of these abbreviations in the space provided:

SI	(specific identification)	FIFO	(first-in-first-out)
WA	(weighted-average)	LIFO	(last-in-first-out)

_____   1.   Which inventory cost method **best** matches current costs with current revenues on the income statement?

_____   2.   Which inventory cost method yields the most realistic amount for inventory, compared to replacement cost, on the balance sheet?

_____   3.   Which method results in the most exact ending inventory valuation when inventory items of the same type are **not** homogenous?

_____   4.   Which method is based on the assumption that inventory flow is "mixed" and therefore "mixes" all acquisition prices?

During a period of **rising prices**, which method yields the:

_____   5.   lowest net income figure?

_____   6.   lowest amount for inventory on the balance sheet?

_____   7.   lowest cost of goods sold figure?

_____   8.   lowest owners' equity figure?

_____   9.   lowest income tax bill for the current year?

During a period of **declining prices**, which method yields the:

_____   10.   lowest net income figure?

_____   11.   lowest amount for inventory on the balance sheet?

_____   12.   lowest cost of goods sold figure?

_____   13.   lowest owners' equity figure?

_____   14.   best cash flow?

Solution to Exercise 8-2

1.	LIFO	4.	WA	7.	FIFO	10.	FIFO	13.	FIFO
2.	FIFO	5.	LIFO	8.	LIFO	11.	FIFO	14.	FIFO
3.	SI	6.	LIFO	9.	LIFO	12.	LIFO		

Approach: Write down a description of specific identification, weighted-average, FIFO, and LIFO cost flow assumptions. Note the relative effects of these methods on the income statement and the balance sheet in a period of rising prices.

TIP: **Inventory pricing method** is a synonymous term for **inventory costing method**.

TIP: **FIFO (first-in, first-out)** means the cost of the first items put into inventory are used to price the first items out to cost of goods sold. Thus, the earliest acquisition prices are used to price cost of goods sold for the period, and the latest (most current) acquisition prices are used to price items in the ending inventory. **LIFO (last-in, first-out)** uses the most recent costs to price the units sold during the period, and it uses the oldest prices to cost the items in ending inventory. Thus, in a period of rising prices, the method that will yield the lowest net income on the income statement **and** the lowest ending inventory on the balance sheet is the LIFO method.

TIP: In a period of rising prices:

Method	COGS	Net Income	Ending Inventory
LIFO	High	Low	Low
FIFO	Low	High	High
W/A	Always	In	Between

ILLUSTRATION 8-1
PERPETUAL VS. PERIODIC INVENTORY SYSTEMS (L.O.2)

Features of a Perpetual System

1. Purchases of merchandise for resale are debited to Inventory rather than to Purchases.
2. Freight-in, Purchase Returns and Allowances, and Purchase Discounts are recorded in Inventory rather than in separate accounts.
3. Cost of goods sold is recognized for each sale by debiting the account, Cost of Goods Sold, and crediting Inventory.
4. Inventory is a control account that is supported by a subsidiary ledger of individual inventory records. The subsidiary records show the quantity and cost of each type of inventory on hand. At any point during the accounting period (assuming all postings are up to date), the balance of the Inventory account reflects the cost of the items that should be on hand at that point in time.

Features of a Periodic System

1. Purchases of merchandise for resale are debited to Purchases.
2. The Freight-in, Purchase Returns and Allowances, and Purchase Discounts accounts are separate accounts which are used to record information about inventory acquisitions during the accounting period.
3. Cost of goods sold is recognized only at the end of the accounting period when the (1) ending inventory amount (determined by physical count, pricing, and extensions) is recorded in the Inventory account, (2) the Purchases, Freight-in, Purchase Returns and Allowances, and Purchase Discounts account balances are closed to the Income Summary account, and (3) the beginning inventory amount is transferred from the Inventory account to the Income Summary account.
4. There is no subsidiary ledger for inventory. All during the accounting period, the Inventory account reflects the cost of the inventory items on hand at the beginning of the period (beginning inventory). The Inventory account is **not** updated for acquisitions and withdrawals of inventory during the period; it is updated only at the end of the period to reflect the cost of the items on hand at the balance sheet date.

ILLUSTRATION 8-1 (Continued)

EXAMPLE	
PERPETUAL SYSTEM	**PERIODIC SYSTEM**
1. There are 8 units in beginning inventory at a cost of $2,000 each.	
The Inventory account shows the inventory on hand at $16,000.	The Inventory account shows the inventory on hand at $16,000.
2. Purchase 12 items on account at $2,000 each.	

Inventory   24,000
    Accounts Payable   24,000
	Purchases 24,000
	    Accounts Payable 24,000

3. Return one defective item for $2,000 credit.	

Accounts Payable   2,000
    Inventory   2,000
	Accounts Payable 2,000
	    Purchase Returns
	     & Allowances 2,000

4. Sell 15 items on account for $3,000 each.	

Accounts Receivable   45,000
    Sales   45,000
 	
Cost of Goods Sold   30,000
    Inventory   30,000
	Accounts Receivable 45,000
	    Sales 45,000

5. End of period entries for inventory-related accounts (4 units on hand at $2,000 each).	

No entries are necessary:
The Inventory account shows the ending balance as $8,000 ($16,000 + $24,000 - $2,000 - $30,000)
	Inventory (ending by
	   physical count) 8,000
	Purchase Returns &
	   Allowances 2,000
	Cost of Goods Sold 30,000
	    Purchases 24,000
	    Inventory
	     (beginning) 16,000

EXERCISE 8-3

Purpose: (L.O.2, 8) This exercise will allow you to practise performing calculations to determine inventory cost under each of three costing (pricing) methods, using both the periodic and the perpetual systems.

The New Brunswick Toy Company is a multi-product firm. Presented below is information concerning one of their products, Infusion-39:

Date	Transaction	Quantity	Cost
1/1	Beginning inventory	1,000	$12
2/4	Purchase	2,000	18
2/20	Sale	2,500	
4/2	Purchase	3,000	22
11/4	Sale	2,000	

Instructions

Calculate the cost of the ending inventory, assuming New Brunswick Toy uses:
(a)   Periodic system, FIFO cost method.
(b)   Perpetual system, FIFO cost method.
(c)   Periodic system, LIFO cost method.
(d)   Perpetual system, LIFO cost method.
(e)   Periodic system, average cost method.
(f)   Perpetual system, moving-average cost method.

Solution to Exercise 8-3

(a)   **Periodic-FIFO:**   Units
       Beginning inventory   1,000
       Purchases (2,000 + 3,000)   5,000
       Units available for sale   6,000
       Sold (2,500 + 2,000)   4,500
       Goods on hand (assumed)   1,500   1,500 units x $22 = $33,000

(b)   **Perpetual-FIFO:** Same as periodic: $33,000

TIP:	The use of FIFO with a perpetual system always yields the same results as the use of FIFO with a periodic system. The same does **not** hold true with the LIFO or average cost methods.

(c)   **Periodic-LIFO:**
       1,000 units x $12   = $12,000
         500 units x $18   =   9,000
       1,500 units   = $21,000

(d)   **Perpetual-LIFO:**

Date	Purchased	Sold	Balance
1/1			1,000 x $12 = $12,000
2/4	2,000 x $18 = $36,000		(2,000 x $18) + (1,000 x $12) = $48,000
2/20		(2,000 x $18) + (500 x $12) = $42,000	500 x $12 = $ 6,000
4/2	3,000 x $22 = $66,000		(3,000 x $22) + (500 x $12) = $72,000
11/4		2,000 x $22 = $44,000	(1,000 x $22) + (500 x $12) = $28,000

(e)   **Periodic-average:**

1,000 x $12	=	$ 12,000			
2,000 x $18	=	36,000			1,500 Units
3,000 x $22	=	66,000			x $19
6,000		$114,000	÷ 6,000 = $19 each		$28,500

(f)   **Perpetual-average:**

Date	Purchased	Sold	Balance
1/1			1,000 x $12 = $12,000
2/4	2,000 x $18 = $36,000		3,000 x $16[a] = $48,000
2/20		2,500 x $16 = $40,000	500 x $16 = $ 8,000
4/2	3,000 x $22 = $66,000		3,500 x $21.14[b] = $73,990
11/4		2,000 x $21.14 = $42,280	1,500 x $21.14 = $31,710

[a]
1,000 x $12 =	$12,000	
2,000 x $18 =	36,000	
3,000	$48,000	

$48,000 ÷ 3,000 = $16.00

[b]
500 x $16 =	$ 8,000	
3,000 x $22 =	66,000	
3,500	$74,000	

$74,000 ÷ 3,500 = $21.14

TIP: When using the average method and a perpetual system, a new average unit cost must be Calculated **only** after each new purchase; a sale will **not** affect the average unit cost. The average method applied to a perpetual system is often called the **moving-average** method.

TIP: Examine your solution to the exercise above and judge the reasonableness of your answers. What do you expect the relationship of the answers to be for the periodic system?

(1)   Because the trend of the acquisition costs was upward, the ending inventory calculated under LIFO should be lower than the ending inventory figure calculated under FIFO.

(2)   The cost of the ending inventory determined by using the average method should be between the amount of the ending inventory determined by using the LIFO method and the amount of the ending inventory determined by using the FIFO method.

EXERCISE 8-4

Purpose: (L.O.2) This exercise will enable you to practise determining how to handle goods in transit and other items necessary for proper inventory valuation.

Jennifer Laudermilch Company, a supplier of artworks, provided the following information from its account records for the year ended December 31, 2002.

Inventory at December 31, 2002 (at cost, based on a physical count of goods in Laudermilch's warehouse on 12/31/02)	$ 820,000
Accounts payable at December 31, 2002	460,000
Net sales (sales less sales returns)	7,000,000

Additional information is as follows:
1.   Laudermilch received goods costing $32,000 on January 2, 2003. The goods had been shipped f.o.b. shipping point on December 27, 2002, by Geoffrey Harrill Company.

2.   Laudermilch received goods costing $41,000 on January 4, 2003. The goods had been shipped f.o.b. destination on December 28, 2002 by Nanula Company.

3.   Laudermilch sold goods costing $18,000 to O'Toole Company on December 29, 2002. The goods were picked up by the common carrier on that same date and shipped f.o.b. shipping point. They were expected to arrive at the buyer's business as early as January 3, 2003. An invoice for $29,000 was recorded and mailed on December 29.

4.   Laudermilch sold goods costing $30,000 to Matheson Company on December 31, 2002. The goods were picked up by the common carrier on that same date and shipped f.o.b. destination. They were expected to arrive at the buyer's store as early as January 2, 2003. These goods were billed to the customer for $45,000 on December 31 and were not included in the physical count at December 31, 2002.

5.   Laudermilch is the consignor for a collection of prints. The prints are hanging in the showroom of The Dizzy Decorator. They cost Laudermilch $62,000 and are priced to sell at $95,000. They were not included in the physical count.

6.   Laudermilch is the consignee for some goods from Asian Collectibles. They cost the consignor $50,000 and are priced to sell for $76,000 with Laudermilch to get a commission of 10%. They were included in the ending inventory at the selling price.

7.   Included in the physical count were goods billed to a customer f.o.b. shipping point on December 31, 2002. These items had a cost of $24,000 and were billed at $38,000. The shipment was on Laudermilch's loading dock waiting to be picked up by the common carrier and was included in the physical count at December 31, 2002.

8.   Goods received from a vendor on December 26, 2002 were included in the physical count. However, the related $44,000 vendor invoice was not included in accounts payable at December 31, 2002 because the accounts payable copy of the receiving report was lost. These goods are marked to sell for $65,000.

Instructions

Using the format shown below, prepare a schedule of adjustments as of December 31, 2002 (the company's year end and physical inventory count date), to the initial amounts per Laudermilch's accounting records. Show separately the effect, if any, of each of the eight transactions on the December 31, 2002 amounts. If the transactions would have no effect on the initial amount shown, state NONE.

Adjustments increase (or decrease)	Inventory	Accounts Payable	Net Sales
Initial Amounts	$ 820,000	$ 460,000	$ 7,000,000
1.			
2.			
3.			
4.			
5.			
6.			
7.			
8.			
Total Adjustments	$	$	$
Adjusted Amounts	$	$	$

Solution to Exercise 8-4

Adjustments increase (or decrease)	Inventory	Accounts Payable	Net Sales
Initial Amounts	$ 820,000	$ 460,000	$ 7,000,000
1.	32,000	32,000	None
2.	None	None	None
3.	None	None	None
4.	30,000	None	(45,000)
5.	62,000	None	None
6.	(76,000)	None	None
7.	None	None	(38,000)
8.	None	44,000	None
Total Adjustments	48,000	76,000	(83,000)
Adjusted Amounts	$ 868,000	$ 536,000	$6,917,000

Explanation:

1. When the terms of the purchase are f.o.b. shipping point, ownership of the goods passes to the buyer when the public carrier accepts the goods from the seller. Therefore, title passed to Laudermilch on December 27, 2002, but the goods were not physically present to be included in the physical count at December 31, 2002.

2. These goods would not have been included in the physical count at December 31, 2002, and are not to be included in the inventory at that date. Title did not pass to Laudermilch until the goods were received on January 4, 2003.

3. With shipping terms of f.o.b. shipping point, title passed to the customer (O'Toole) when the goods were picked up by the common carrier on December 29, 2002. Therefore, the goods are properly excluded from the ending inventory, and the sale has been properly recorded in 2002.

4. With shipping terms of f.o.b. destination, title did not pass to Matheson (the buyer) until the goods were received by the buyer, which had to be sometime in 2003. Therefore, the sale was improperly recorded in 2002. The goods were not on the premises late December 31, 2002, so were excluded from the physical count. However, their cost should be included in ending inventory to be reported on the balance sheet.

5. Under a consignment arrangement, the holder of the goods (called the **consignee**) does not own the goods. Ownership remains with the shipper of the goods (called the **consignor**) until the goods are sold to a customer. Laudermilch, the consignor, should include merchandise held by the consignee as part of its inventory. The goods were not in Laudermilch's warehouse when the physical count was taken; however, they should be included as part of the inventory balance at December 31, 2002.

6.   Laudermilch does not own the goods which it holds on consignment. Therefore, these goods should be excluded from its inventory; they should be included in the inventory of Asian Collectibles.

7.   The $24,000 of goods on the loading dock were properly included in the physical count because they had not been released to the common carrier by the end of the day, December 31, 2002. However, the sale was improperly recorded; therefore, an adjustment is needed to reduce sales by the billing price of $38,000.

8.   The $44,000 of goods received on December 26, 2002 were properly included in the physical count of inventory; $44,000 must be added to accounts payable since the invoice was not included in the December 31, 2002 accounts payable balance.

EXERCISE 8-5

Purpose: (L.O.6, 8) This exercise will illustrate the effect on net income when the LIFO cost method rather than the FIFO cost method is used in a period of rising prices. It also requires you to examine the effect of both the beginning inventory and the ending inventory on the net income computation.

Using the FIFO cost method, Worrell Company had a beginning inventory of $24,000, ending inventory of $30,000, and net income of $80,000. If Worrell had used the LIFO cost method, the beginning inventory would have been $20,000 and the ending inventory would have been $23,000.

Instructions
Calculate what net income would have been if the LIFO cost method had been used.

Solution to Exercise 8-5

Using LIFO:
> Beginning inventory would have been less by $4,000; therefore,
>> Cost of goods sold would have been less by $4,000 and
>> Net income would have been more by $4,000, and
> Ending inventory would have been less by $7,000; therefore,
>> Cost of goods sold would have been more by $7,000 and
>> Net income would have been less by $7,000, therefore:

Net income using FIFO	$ 80,000
Decrease in beginning inventory using LIFO	4,000
Decrease in ending inventory using LIFO	(7,000)
Net income using LIFO	$ 77,000

EXERCISE 8-6

Purpose: (L.O.5) The following exercise will help you in determining what items are included in product costs using variable (direct) costing versus absorption (full) costing.

Rebelde Corporation manufactures a single product. Assume the following data for the 2003 year:

Variable Cost per unit:
Selling and administrative	$3
Production cost	$5

Fixed Cost in total:
Selling and administrative	$16,000
Production cost	$32,000

During the period, 8,000 units were produced and 7,800 units were sold (assume beginning inventory is zero).

Instructions
(a) Determine the inventoriable cost per unit under variable and absorption costing methods?
(b) Determine the ending inventory value under variable and absorption costing methods?
(c) Determine the cost of goods sold under variable and absorption costing methods?

Solution to Exercise 8-6

(a) Cost per unit	Variable	Absorption
Variable production cost	$3	$3
Fixed production cost	---	$4 ($32,000/8,000 units)
Total inventoriable cost	$3	$7

Remember that variable costing only includes variable production cost in the inventory cost and treats fixed manufacturing overhead (production) costs as a period cost.

(b) Ending Inventory   Variable   Absorption
      200 units x inventory cost $600 $1,400

The ending inventory is 200 units (8,000 produced – 7,800 units sold)

(c) Cost of Goods Sold	Variable	Absorption
Beginning Inventory	$0	$ 0
Add: current production	$24,000	$56,000
Cost of Goods Available for Sale	$24,000	$56,000
Less: Ending Inventory (from b)	600	1,400
Cost of Goods Sold	$23,400	$54,600

Proof: Variable COGS = 7,800 units sold x $3 = $23,400
        Absorption COGS = 7,800 units sold x $7 = 54,600

ANALYSIS OF MULTIPLE-CHOICE TYPE QUESTIONS

QUESTION

1. (L.O.2) At December 31, 2002, a physical count of merchandise inventory belonging to Rhoda Corp. showed $1,000,000 to be on hand. The $1,000,000 was calculated before any potential necessary adjustments related to the following:

    *   Excluded from the $1,000,000 was $80,000 of goods shipped f.o.b. shipping point by a vendor to Rhoda on December 30, 2002 and received on January 3, 2003.
    *   Excluded from the $1,000,000 was $72,000 of goods shipped f.o.b. destination to Rhoda on December 30, 2002 and received on January 3, 2003.
    *   Excluded from the $1,000,000 was $95,000 of goods shipped f.o.b. destination by Rhoda to a customer on December 28, 2002. The customer received the goods on January 4, 2003.

    The correct amount to report for inventory on Rhoda's balance sheet at December 31, 2002 is:
    a. $1,072,000
    b. $1,095,000
    c. $1,175,000
    d. $1,247,000

Explanation:
(1)   The $80,000 should be added to the $1,000,000 because f.o.b. shipping point means the title transferred to Rhoda when the goods left the seller's dock on December 30, 2002.
(2)   The $72,000 is properly excluded from the ending inventory because title did not pass to Rhoda until Rhoda received the goods on January 3, 2003.
(3)   The $95,000 should be added to the $1,000,000 because the goods belong to Rhoda until they are received by the customer (in 2003).

$1,000,000
+ 80,000
+ 95,000
$1,175,000   Amount to report for ending inventory at December 31, 2002.

(Solution = c.)

QUESTION

2.   (L.O. 2) The following amounts relate to the current year for the Rod Buckley Company:

Beginning inventory	$ 40,000
Ending inventory	56,000
Purchases	332,000
Purchase returns	9,600
Freight-out	12,000

The amount of cost of goods sold for the period is:

    a. $338,400
    b. $325,600
    c. $306,400
    d. $294,400

Approach and Explanation: Write down the calculation model for cost of goods sold. Enter the amounts given and solve for the unknown.

	$ 40,000		**B**eginning **I**nventory
+	332,000	+	**P**urchases
-	9,600	-	**P**urchase **R**eturns and **A**llowances
	0	-	**P**urchase **D**iscounts
	0	+	**F**reight-in
	362,400	=	**C**ost of **G**oods **A**vailable for **S**ale
-	56,000	-	**E**nding **I**nventory
	$306,400	=	**C**ost of **G**oods **S**old

(Solution = c.)

> **TIP:** Freight-out is classified as a selling expense, not a component of cost of goods sold. Freight-out is not a cost necessary to get the inventory item to the place and condition for sale; it is a cost incurred in the selling function.

QUESTION
3.   (L.O. 2) The accountant for the Orion Sales Company is preparing the income statement for 2002 and the balance sheet at December 31, 2002. Orion uses the periodic inventory system. The January 1, 2002 merchandise inventory balance will appear:

    a.   only as an asset on the balance sheet.
    b.   only in the cost of goods sold section of the income statement.
    c.   as a deduction in the cost of goods sold section of the income statement and as a current asset on the balance sheet.
    d.   as an addition in the cost of goods sold section of the income statement and as a current asset on the balance sheet.

Explanation: The January 1, 2002 inventory amount is the beginning inventory figure. Beginning inventory is a component of the cost of goods available for sale for the period which is a component of cost of goods sold. (Solution = b.)

> **TIP:** If the question asked about the December 31, 2002 merchandise inventory balance (ending inventory) rather than the beginning inventory balance, the correct answer would have been "c" (as a deduction in calculating cost of sales and as a current asset).

QUESTION

4.   (L.O. 3) If the beginning inventory for 2001 is overstated, the effects of this error on cost of goods sold for 2001, net income for 2001, and assets at December 31, 2002, respectively are:
a.   overstatement, understatement, overstatement
b.   overstatement, understatement, no effect
c.   understatement, overstatement, overstatement
d.   understatement, overstatement, no effect

Approach and Explanation: For questions dealing with inventory errors, assume a periodic system unless otherwise indicated. Write down the components of the cost of goods sold calculation and analyse the resulting effects on net income.

		2001	**2002**
	Beginning inventory	Overstated	No effect
+	Cost of goods purchased		↓
=	Cost of goods available for sale	Overstated	
-	Ending inventory		
=	Cost of goods sold	Overstated	
	Net income	Understated	

The inventory at the end of 2001 and the inventory at the end of 2002 are both apparently free of error because the inventory at a balance sheet date is determined by a physical count and pricing process. Assume there are no errors in this process unless otherwise indicated. (Solution = b.)

> **TIP:** The fact that the inventory at the beginning of 2001 was in error indicates that the inventory at the end of 2000 was in error because the ending inventory of one period is the beginning inventory of the next period.
>
> **TIP:** When analysing a question like this one, it is often helpful to create an example with numbers.

QUESTION

5.   (L.O.3) If beginning inventory is understated by $7,000, and ending inventory is overstated by $3,000, net income for the period will be:
a.   overstated by $10,000
b.   overstated by $4,000
c.   understated by $4,000
d.   understated by $10,000

Approach and Explanation: Each error's effect on net income should be determined separately. The effect on net income is dependent on the effect on the calculation of cost of goods sold (which is an expense affecting net income). The effects are then combined to calculate the **total** effect on net income for the period. (Solution = a.)

	First Error	Second Error	Total Effect
Beg. Inventory	Understated $7,000		Understated $7,000
+ Purchases			
= Goods Available	Understated $7,000		Understated $7,000
- Ending Inventory		Overstated $3,000	Overstated $3,000
= Cost of Goods Sold	Understated $7,000	Understated $3,000	Understated $10,000
Net Income	Overstated $7,000	Overstated $3,000	Overstated $10,000

QUESTION

6.   (L.O. 5, 9) Which inventory costing method most closely approximates current cost for each of the following:

	Ending Inventory	Cost of Goods Sold
a.	FIFO	FIFO
b.	FIFO	LIFO
c.	LIFO	FIFO
d.	LIFO	LIFO

Approach and Explanation: Write down which inventory method (LIFO or FIFO) reports current cost for ending inventory and which uses current cost to price cost of goods sold and then look for your answer combination. FIFO uses the first cost in as the first cost out, so the last (most current) costs are used to price the ending inventory. Therefore, FIFO is the answer for the first column. In contrast, LIFO uses the last cost in (current cost) as the first cost out (to cost of goods sold), so LIFO reflects the most current costs experienced in cost of goods sold. Therefore, LIFO is the answer for the second column. Answer "b" is the determined combination. (Solution = b.)

QUESTION

7.   (L.O.4) The Windsor Salt Company purchased goods with a list price of $50,000, subject to trade discounts of 20% and 10%, with a 2% cash discount allowed if payment is made within 10 days of receipt. Windsor uses the gross method of recording purchases. Windsor should record the cost of this merchandise as:
a. $34,000
b. $35,000
c. $36,000
d. $50,000
e.   None of the above

Explanation: Trade discounts are not recorded in the accounts; they are means of calculating a sales (purchase) price. Using the gross method of recording purchases, the cash discount allowed does not affect the amount recorded in the Purchases account; the cash discount allowed will be recorded if it is taken and will be recorded as a credit to Purchase Discounts. (Solution = c.)

Calculations:

List price	$ 50,000
First trade discount ($50,000 x 20%)	(10,000)
Subtotal	40,000
Second trade discount ($40,000 x 10%)	(4,000)
Purchase price	$ 36,000

TIP: A chain discount occurs when a list price is subject to several trade discounts. When a chain discount is offered, the amount of each trade discount is determined by multiplying (1) the list price of the merchandise **less** the amount of prior trade discounts by (2) the trade discount percentage.

QUESTION

8.   (L.O.4) Grennan Retail Company incurred the following costs in 2002:
Freight-in on purchases
Interest on loan to acquire inventory
Selling costs

Should the above items be included or excluded in determining Grennan's inventory valuation for its balance sheet?

	Freight-in	Interest	Selling Costs
a.	Include	Include	Include
b.	Include	Include	Exclude
c.	Include	Exclude	Exclude
d.	Exclude	Exclude	Exclude

Explanation: Freight-in is a product cost. The cost of inventory should include all costs necessary to get the inventory in the place and condition for its intended purpose (resale). Freight-in is necessary to get the merchandise to the location for resale. Interest costs should not be capitalized for inventories that are acquired by a merchandiser (because the goods do not require a period of time to ready them for sale) or inventories that are routinely manufactured or otherwise produced in large quantities on a repetitive basis. Therefore, the interest on this inventory is a period cost. Selling expenses are treated as a period cost. (Solution = c.)

QUESTION

9.   (L.O.5) For 2002, Selma Co. had beginning inventory of $75,000, ending inventory of $90,000 and net income of $120,000, using the LIFO inventory method. If the FIFO method had been used, beginning inventory would have been $85,000, ending inventory would have been $105,000 and net income would have been:
a. $125,000
b. $115,000
c. $145,000
d. $95,000

Approach and Explanation: Develop the answer by analysing the effects on the cost of goods sold calculation and resulting effects on net income. (Solution = a.)

	LIFO	FIFO	Effect on Cost of Goods Sold		Effect on Net Income	
Beginning Inventory	$ 75,000	$ 85,000	Increase	$10,000	Decrease	$10,000
+ Purchases						
= Goods Available						
- Ending Inventory	90,000	105,000	Decrease	15,000	Increase	15,000
= Cost of Goods Sold						
Net Income	120,000	?	Decrease	5,000	Increase	5,000

Net income using LIFO	$ 120,000
Increase in net income	5,000
Net income using FIFO	$ 125,000

QUESTION

10.   (L.O. 2, 5) The following facts pertain to the cost of one product carried in the merchandise inventory of the Herara Store:

Inventory on hand, January 1 200 units @ $20 =	$ 4,000
Purchase, March 18 600 units @ $24 =	14,400
Purchase, July 20 800 units @ $26 =	20,800
Purchase, October 31 400 units @ $30 =	12,000

A physical count of the inventory on December 31 reveals that 500 units are on hand. If the FIFO cost method is used with a periodic inventory system, the inventory should be reported on the balance sheet at:
a. $40,000
b. $36,600
c. $14,600
d. $11,200
e.   None of the above

Approach and Explanation: Think about what FIFO stands for: the first cost is in the first out to cost of goods sold. Therefore, ending inventory is comprised of the latest costs experienced. (Solution = c.)

400 units @ $30 =	$ 12,000
100 units @ $26 =	2,600
Ending inventory at FIFO	$ 14,600

QUESTION

11.   (L.O. 2, 5) Refer to the data in question 10 above. If the average costing method is used, the cost of goods sold for the year amounts to:
a. $38,400
b. $37,500
c. $12,800
d. $12,500

Approach and Explanation: Read the question carefully. Notice it asks for the cost of goods sold and not for the ending inventory as you might expect.

Total cost of all units available for sale:

Beginning inventory	$ 4,000
Purchases ($14,400 + $20,800 + $12,000)	47,200
Cost of goods available for sale	$ 51,200

$$
\begin{array}{rl}
& \$51,200 \quad \text{Cost of goods available for sale} \\
\div & 2,000^1 \quad \text{Units available for sale} \\
= & \$25.60 \quad \text{Average unit cost}
\end{array}
$$

$25.60 Average unit cost x 500 units = $12,800 Ending inventory
$25.60 Average unit cost x 1,500^2 units = $\underline{\$38,400}$ Cost of goods sold

^{1}200 + 600 + 800 + 400 = 2,000 units available for sale.
^{2}2,000 units available - 500 units in ending inventory = 1,500 units sold.
(Solution = a.)

QUESTION

12.   (L.O. 5) Refer to the data in question 10 above. If the LIFO costing method is used, the cost of goods sold for the year amounts to:
   - a. $40,000
   - b. $36,600
   - c. $14,600
   - d. $11,200

Approach and Explanation: Notice the question asks for the cost of goods sold rather than the cost of the ending inventory. You may approach the solution one of two ways: You may cost the items sold or calculate the cost of the ending inventory and deduct that cost from the cost of goods available for sale. Using the first of these two approaches, think of what LIFO stands for: the last cost in is the first cost out to cost of goods sold. (Solution = a.)

Units available	2,000
Units on hand at end of period	(500)
Units sold	1,500

400 units @ $30 =	12,000
800 units @ $26 =	20,800
300 units @ $24 =	7,200
1,500 units =	40,000 Cost of goods sold

TIP: The cost of the ending inventory using LIFO would be:

200 units @ $20	=	$ 4,000
300 units @ $24	=	7,200
500 units	=	$ 11,200 Ending inventory

QUESTION

13.   (L.O. 5) In a period of rising prices, which inventory flow assumption will result in the lowest amount of income tax expense?
    a.   FIFO
    b.   LIFO
    c.   Average cost
    d.   Income tax expense will be the same under all cost flow assumptions.

Explanation: Income taxes are determined by applying a tax rate to the amount of taxable income for the period. The inventory cost flow assumption yielding the highest cost of goods sold expense will yield the lowest income before tax figure. On a tax return, the cost of goods sold figure is a deduction in arriving at taxable income. The lower the taxable income, the lower the taxes due (thus, the lower the income tax expense) and the less cash required to pay taxes. In a period of rising prices, LIFO charges the highest costs experienced to cost of goods sold expense, yielding the lowest taxable income figure. (Solution = b.)

QUESTION

14.   (L.O. 5) In a period of rising prices, which of the following inventory cost flow methods will yield the largest reported amount for cost of goods sold?
    a.   Specific identification
    b.   FIFO
    c.   LIFO
    d.   Average

Explanation: In a period of rising prices, the most recent purchase prices are the highest ones experienced by the entity. Using LIFO, the latest costs (the highest ones, in this instance) are used to price cost of goods sold and the earliest ones are used to price ending inventory. FIFO would give the lowest cost of goods sold in a period of rising prices. The results of the average method would fall between the results of the LIFO and FIFO methods. The specific identification method would likely yield a cost of goods sold figure similar to FIFO (but not more than LIFO) because specific identification would use the cost of the specific items sold to price the cost of the goods sold, and the specific items sold usually follow a first-in, first-out physical flow. (Solution = c.)

QUESTION

15.   (L.O. 5) In a period of rising prices, when production exceeds sales for a given period, which method will provide the higher net income value?
    a.   absorption costing will be higher than variable costing
    b.   variable costing will be higher than absorption costing
    c.   both will yield the same value of ending inventory
    d.   there is not enough information to determine the correct answer.

Approach and Explanation: Think about the costs included in the ending inventory under each of the two methods. Absorption costing includes fixed manufacturing overhead, while variable costing treats fixed manufacturing overhead as a period cost. Thus absorption costing will have the higher inventoriable cost. Since production exceeds sales, the total number of units in ending inventory will rise for the period. Costs incurred in the current period under absorption costing will be "booked" onto the balance sheet as ending inventory, while the full fixed manufacturing overhead cost will be included in the income statement under variable costing, thus absorption costing will have a higher net income than absorption costing. Answer (a).

TIP:	When prices are rising	
	Situation	**Net Income**
	Production exceeds Sales	Absorption > Variable
	Production is less than Sales	Absorption < Variable
	Production equals Sales	Absorption = Variable

CHAPTER 9

INVENTORIES:
ADDITIONAL VALUATION ISSUES

OVERVIEW

Sometimes a business is faced with the situation where impairments in the value of its inventory are so great relative to selling prices that items cannot be sold at a normal profit. In compliance with conservatism, any impairments in value should be recognized in the current period and the inventory should be reported at the lower-of-cost-and-market (LCM) on the balance sheet. By following the LCM rule, the impairment is recognized in the period in which it occurs, rather than in the later period of disposal of the inventory. Accounting for declines in inventory value, presentation and valuation of inventories are also discussed in this chapter.

Sometimes a business may need to estimate the cost of inventory on hand at a certain date. Two estimation techniques—the gross profit and the retail method of inventory estimation—are discussed in this chapter. Although the conventional retail method yields results which are to approximate a lower-of-average-cost-and-market valuation for the inventory, the retail method also can be used to approximate FIFO cost, lower of FIFO cost or market, weighted-average cost, LIFO cost, etc. Markups and Markdowns are also discussed in relation to the retail method in this chapter.

SUMMARY OF LEARNING OBJECTIVES

1. **Recognize that the lower of cost and market basis is a departure from the historical cost principle, and understand why this is appropriate.** The lower of cost and market approach is a departure from historical cost. It is justified on the basis that assets in general, and current assets in particular, should not be reported at an amount greater than the cash expected to be realized from their use, sale, or conversion. It is also justified based on the matching principle. Any decline in an asset's utility (represented by a reduction in the future cash flows expected) should be recognized in the accounting period when the loss in utility occurs.

2. **Explain various definitions of possible market amounts that may be used when applying lower of cost and market.** Replacement cost is the amount needed to acquire an equivalent item in the normal course of business. Net realizable value is an items' estimated selling price in the ordinary course of business less reasonably predictable future costs to complete and dispose of it. Net realizable value less a normal profit margin is determined by deducting a normal profit margin from an item's net realizable value. All three are acceptable definitions of market, although net realizable value is the one used by a large majority of Canadian companies. The U.S. rules are more prescriptive and require that the middle value be chosen. Some Canadian companies follow this latter approach.

3. **Explain how LCM (lower of cost and market) works and how it is applied.** Under the lower of cost and market approach, the cost (FIFO, average cost, or LIFO) and market (replacement cost, net realizable value, or net realizable value less a normal profit margin) of inventory are

separately determined. The inventory value for the balance sheet is then the lower of the two amounts. The lower of cost and market may be determined on an item-by-item basis, major category basis, or total inventory basis. The total inventory basis is most commonly used in Canada.

4.   **Know how to account for inventory on the lower of cost and market basis.** If it is determined that market is less than cost, inventory may be directly written down to market (direct method) or the difference may be accounted for in a contra inventory allowance account (indirect or allowance method).

5.   **Identify when inventories are carried regularly at net realizable value.** Inventories are reported at net realizable value when (1) there is a controlled market with a quoted price applicable to all quantities, (2) no significant costs of disposal are involved, and (3) the cost figures are too difficult or not possible to obtain.

6.   **Explain when the relative sales value method is used to value inventories.** When a group of varying units is purchased at a single lump-sum price—a so-called basket purchase—the total purchase price may be allocated to the individual items on the basis of relative sales value. Such an allocation results in appropriately assigning a relevant cost to each item or type of inventory. This facilitates the subsequent matching of costs against revenues when an item is sold, and the reporting of an amount in the balance sheet as inventory before the item is sold.

7.   **Explain accounting issues related to purchase commitments.** Accounting for purchase commitments is controversial. Some argue that these contracts should be reported as assets and liabilities when the contract is signed; others believe that recognition at the delivery date is most appropriate. Generally, if purchase commitments are significant relative to the company's financial position and operations, they should be disclosed in a note to the financial statements. If a contract requires future payment of a price in excess of market value at the balance sheet date, the contingent loss should be recognized.

8.   **Estimate ending inventory by applying the gross profit method.** The steps to determine ending inventory by applying the gross profit method are as follows: (1) calculate the gross profit percentage on selling price; (2) calculate gross profit by multiplying net sales by the gross profit percentage; (3) calculate cost of goods sold by subtracting gross profit from net sales; (4) calculate ending inventory subtracting estimated cost of goods sold from the cost of goods available for sale.

9.   **Explain the limitations of the gross profit method.** Care must be taken in applying the gross profit method. The resulting estimate of ending inventory is only as good as the gross profit percentage is appropriate to the current period's mix of sales and operations.

10.   **Estimate ending inventory by applying the retail method.** The retail inventory method is based on multiplying the retail price of ending inventory (determined by a count or from the accounting records) by a cost-to-retail percentage (derived from information in the accounting records). To apply the retail inventory method, records must be kept of the costs and retail prices for beginning inventory, net purchases, and abnormal spoilage, as well as the retail amounts of net markups, net markdowns, and net sales. Determination of the items going into the numerator and denominator of the cost-to-retail ratio depend on the type of inventory valuation estimate desired.

11.   **Explain how inventory is reported and analysed.** Disclosure of the basis of inventory valuation and any change in the basis are required by the *CICA Handbook*. Also, it is desirable to disclose major categories of inventory, the method used to determine cost, and the definition of market applied under the lower of cost and market method. Common ratios used in the management and evaluation of inventory levels are inventory turnover and a related measure – average days to sell the inventory, often called the average age of inventory.

TIPS ON CHAPTER TOPICS

TIP: As used in the phrase "lower of cost and market," the term **market** refers to the market in which the entity buys (not the market in which it sells). The CICA is silent on the exact meaning of "market", but states it is desirable to use a specific description in lieu of the term market. Market can include replacement cost, net realizable value, and net realizable value less a normal profit margin.

TIP: The **net realizable value of inventory** is the net amount of cash expected to ultimately be received from the sale of the inventory. Thus, the net realizable value of inventory is the estimated selling price in the ordinary course of business less reasonably predictable future costs of completion and disposal. This is the term most commonly used in Canada. **Net realizable value less a normal profit margin** is determined by subtracting the normal profit margin from the net realizable value of inventory.

Ex.	Inventory—Sales Value	$1,000
	Less: estimated cost of completion and disposal	275
	Net Realizable Value	$ 775
	Less: Allowance for normal profit margin (10%)	100
	Net Realizable Value less normal profit margin	

TIP: The historical cost principle is abandoned when the asset's future utility (revenue producing ability) is no longer greater than its original cost.

TIP: In the U.S., the accounting profession has adopted a different approach than in Canada. Generally, the market is defined as "replacement cost". The lower of cost and market rule in the U.S., the market is the middle value of replacement cost, net realizable value and net realizable value less a normal profit margin.

TIP: To apply the lower of cost and market rule:
(a) determine the cost using an acceptable historical cost flow
(b) determine the market value to be used
(c) compare the cost with the market

The lower of cost and market figure is then used for inventory valuation.

TIP: If the utility of an inventory item declines prior to the period of sale (disposal), that loss of utility should be recognized in the period of decline rather than the period of disposal. Thus, if an inventory item has become obsolete, the amount of write down determined by the LCM rule should be recognized as a loss in the period of the decline in utility.

TIP: The lower of cost and market rule can be applied on an item-by-item basis, a category basis or a total inventory basis.

TIP: Two methods of recording inventory at market are acceptable. The direct method simply records the ending inventory at market. No loss is recorded on the income statement as the loss is buried in the cost of goods sold. The indirect or allowance method does not change the cost amount, but establishes a separate contra asset account and a loss account to record the write-off.

TIP: When a lump-sum purchase of inventory is made, it is necessary to split the inventory into separate components for inventory and cost of goods sold calculations. The use of relative sales prices is appropriate here.

TIP: **Gross profit** is synonymous with **gross margin**.

TIP: The gross profit percentage (expressed as a percentage of selling price) and the cost of goods sold percentage (also expressed as a percentage of selling price) are complements; that is, they sum to 100%. When the gross profit method of inventory estimation is used and the gross profit is expressed in terms of cost, the gross profit must first be expressed in terms of selling price before you can proceed with the calculations. One method of conversion is to memorize and use the following formula:

$$\text{Gross margin on selling price} = \frac{\text{Percentage markup on cost}}{100\% + \text{Percentage markup on cost}}$$

Another approach to deriving this formula is shown below. It uses the familiar formula: Sales (S) - Cost of Goods Sold (CGS) = Gross Profit (GP).

Example: If GP = 25% of cost, then cost of goods sold is 100%.
Putting this much information into our formula above: S - 100% = 25%.
Therefore S = 125%.
Expressing GP as a percentage of S we get: 25% ÷ 125% = 20%.
Thus, gross profit = 20% of sales.

Alternatively, gross profit could be determined based on cost:

$$\text{Percent of markup on cost} = \frac{\text{percent gross profit on selling price}}{100\% - \text{percent gross profit on selling price}}$$

TIP: The conventional retail method is used to approximate a lower-of-average-cost-and-market figure for inventory valuation. There are other versions of the retail method. In each application, an amount of inventory expressed in terms of retail prices is converted to a cost or to a lower-of-cost-and-market amount by multiplying the retail figure by a ratio. The components of the ratio vary depending on which version of the retail method is desired.

TIP: The conventional retail method **includes** net markups (often called net additional markups) but **excludes** net markdowns from the **ratio** calculation. The omission of the net markdowns from the ratio calculation results in a higher denominator and therefore a lower resulting ratio than what would be derived if the net markdowns were to be included in the ratio calculation. When there have been markdowns, any related writedowns in inventory should be reflected in the current income statement (from a conservative point of view). This is accomplished by reporting the inventory at a lower value which means more of the cost of goods available for sale goes to the income statement as cost of goods sold expense.

TIP:	In using the conventional retail method, the net markdowns are omitted from the ratio calculation, but they must be **included** in determining the estimated ending inventory at retail.
TIP:	The retail inventory method can be used only if sufficient information is accumulated and maintained. Purchases are recorded in the accounts at cost. Although not recorded in the accounts, the retail value of purchases and the changes in that value (markups, markup cancellations, markdowns, and markdown cancellations) must be recorded in supplemental records for use in inventory calculations utilizing the retail inventory method.

EXERCISE 9-1

Purpose: (L.O.3) This exercise reviews the steps involved in the determination of the lower-of-cost-and-market (LCM) valuation for inventory.

The Richard G. Long Company handles 10 different inventory items. The normal profit on each item is 25% of the selling price.

Instructions

From the information below, complete the blanks to calculate the value to be used for the inventory figure for financial statements if the LCM rule is applied to individual items. (Use the lowest market value in each separate case to determine market price)

		Per Unit								
Item	**No. of Units on Hand**	**Cost**	**Replace-ment Cost**	**Expected Selling Price**	**Expected Cost to Sell**	**NRV**	**NRV less profit margin**	**Market**	**LCM**	**Item Total**
1	100	$7.00	$ 7.50	$ 10.00	$ 1.00	9.00	6.50			
2	10	6.00	6.25	10.00	1.00	9.00	6.50			
3	50	5.75	9.25	10.00	1.00	9.00	6.50			
4	10	9.50	9.25	10.00	1.00	9	6.50			
5	20	5.00	6.25	10.00	1.00	9	6.50			
6	100	8.00	7.25	10.00	1.00	9	6.50			
7	30	12.00	11.50	16.00	1.00	15	11.00			
8	10	10.00	15.50	16.00	1.00	15	11.00			
9	20	14.00	11.00	20.00	2.00	18	13.00			
10	10	12.00	16.00	20.00	2.00	18	13.00			
					Grand Total					

Solution to Exercise 9-1

	Per Unit				# of Units	Item Total
Item	NRV	NRV less profit margin	Market	LCM		
1	$ 9.00	$ 6.50	$ 6.50	$ 6.50	100	$ 650.00
2	9.00	6.50	6.25	6.00	10	60.00
3	9.00	6.50	6.50	5.75	50	287.50
4	9.00	6.50	6.50	6.50	10	65.00
5	9.00	6.50	6.25	5.00	20	100.00
6	9.00	6.50	6.50	6.50	100	650.00
7	15.00	11.00	11.00	11.00	30	330.00
8	15.00	11.00	11.00	10.00	10	100.00
9	18.00	13.00	11.00	11.00	20	220.00
10	18.00	13.00	13.00	12.00	10	120.00
				Grand	Total	$ 2,582.50

Approach and Explanation: Write down the two steps involved in determining the lower of cost and market and perform the steps in order for each of the items:

Step 1: Determine the net realizable value and net realizable value less normal profit margin.

	Item 1	Item 2	Item 3	Item 4
Estimated selling price	$10.00	$10.00	$10.00	$10.00
- Cost to complete and dispose	1.00	1.00	1.00	1.00
= Net realizable value	9.00	9.00	9.00	9.00
- Normal profit margin	2.50*	2.50	2.50	2.50
= Net realizable value less normal profit margin	$ 6.50	$ 6.50	$ 6.50	$ 6.50

*$10.00 x 25% = $2.50.

Net realizable value	$ 9.00	$ 9.00	$ 9.00	$ 9.00
Net realizable value less normal profit margin	6.50	6.50	6.50	6.50
Replacement cost	7.50	6.25	9.25	9.25
Lowest of these (market)	6.50	6.25	6.50	6.50

Step 2: Compare cost with market and choose the lower.

Cost	$ 7.00	$ 6.00	$ 5.75	$ 9.50
Market (from Step 1)	6.50	6.25	6.50	6.50
Lower of cost and market	7.00	6.00	5.75	6.50

EXERCISE 9-2

Purpose: (L.O. 2) This exercise will illustrate the effects of choosing one method versus another method in applying the LCM rule.

Bava uses net realizable value less a normal profit margin in applying the lower-of-cost-and-market rule to value its inventory. At December 31, 2002, the following facts pertain to Product X-17.

Original cost	$420
Replacement cost	365
Expected selling price	400
Estimated selling expenses	50
Normal profit	25% of selling price
Quantity in ending inventory	100 units

The accountant for Bava used the replacement cost value ($365) to value Product X-17 at December 31, 2002.

Instructions

Answer the following questions:

1.   Is $365 the correct unit value for Product X-17 for balance sheet reporting at December 31, 2002? Explain.
2.   If the accountant uses the $365 replacement cost value, explain the effect of the misstatement on the following: (a) income statement for the year ending December 31, 2002, (b) balance sheet at December 31, 2002, (c) income statement for the year ending December 31, 2003, and (d) balance sheet at December 31, 2003. Assume that all of Product X-17 on hand at December 31, 2002 was sold during 2003.

Solution to Exercise 9-2

1. $365 is **not** the correct value for Product X-17 at December 31, 2002.

   Explanation: The company uses net realizable value less a normal profit margin. The CICA Handbook requires the basis of inventory valuation be consistently applied from one period to the next. If the method is changed, the effect of the change must be reported as well as disclosure of the method being used.

   Calculations:

Expected selling price	$ 400
Estimated selling expenses	(50)
Net realizable value	350
Normal profit ($400 x 25%)	(100)
Net realizable value less normal profit margin	$ 250
Cost	$ 420
Market	250
Lower of cost and market	$ 250 x 100units = $2,500

2.   (a)   Net income for 2002 is overstated by $11,150.

(b)   Assets are overstated by $11,150 and owners' equity is overstated by $11,150 at December 31, 2002.

(c)   Net income for 2003 is understated by $11,150.

(d)   No effect on the balance sheet at December 31, 2003.

Explanation:

(a) $365 - $250 = $115.
       $115 x 100 = $11,150.
       The error will cause an overstatement of ending inventory which results in an understatement of cost of goods sold expense which causes an overstatement in net income for 2002 in the amount of $11,150.

(b)   Ending inventory is overstated by $11,150, so assets at December 31, 2002 are overstated by $11,150. Owners' equity at December 31, 2002 is also overstated by $11,150 because net income for 2002 (which is overstated by $11,150) is closed into owners' equity at the end of the accounting period.

> **TIP:**   Visualize the basic accounting equation. This error will maintain balance in the basic accounting equation. If assets are overstated, then something else in the equation must be affected to keep the equation in balance. In this case, it is an overstatement of owners' equity because the error affects income (and that effect flows into owners' equity).

(c)   The inventory is all sold in 2003. Bava's accountant is using $365 as the carrying value for each of the 100 units when the correct unit value should be $250. This will cause net income for the year ending December 31, 2003 to be understated by $11,150 because cost of goods sold will be overstated by $11,150.

(d)   The inventory in question is no longer on hand at December 31, 2003, so there is no effect on assets at that date. The $11,150 understatement in income for 2003 is closed into owners' equity, which has a balance that is overstated by $11,150 at the beginning of 2003; thus, the owners' equity balance at December 31, 2003 is correct.

CASE 9-1

Purpose: (L.O. 1, 2, 3, 10) This case addresses three inventory topics: (1) inventoriable costs, (2) the LCM rule, and (3) the retail method.

Toastie Corporation, a retailer of small kitchen appliances, purchases its inventories from various suppliers.

Instructions

(a)   1.   Explain what costs will be inventoriable for Toastie.

     2.   Explain why Toastie's administrative costs would or would not be inventoriable.

(b)   1.   Toastie uses the lower of cost and market rule for its inventory. What is the theoretical justification for this rule?

     2.   The original cost of the inventory is above the net realizable value of the inventory. Explain what amount should be used to value the inventory and why.

(c)   Toastie currently uses the average cost method to determine the cost of its inventory. To simplify the procedures involved in counting and pricing its ending inventory, Toastie Corporation is considering the use of the conventional retail method. How should Toastie treat the beginning inventory and net markups in calculating the cost ratio to use to determine the ending inventory? Explain why.

Solution to Case 9-1

(a)   1.   Toastie's inventoriable costs should include all costs incurred to get the appliances ready for sale to the customer. It includes not only the purchase price of the goods but also the other associated costs incurred for the appliances up to the time they are ready for sale to the customer, for example, transportation-in.

     2.   Administrative costs are assumed to expire with the passage of time and not to attach to the product. Furthermore, administrative costs do not relate directly to inventories, but are incurred for the benefit of all functions of the business. Thus, administrative costs should be treated as period costs, not as product costs; that is, they are not inventoriable.

(b)   1.   The lower of cost and market rule is used for valuing inventories because of the conservatism principle (constraint) and because the decline in the utility of the inventories below their cost should be recognized as a loss in (and matched with) the period in which the decline took place.

     2.   The net realizable value should be used to value the inventory because market is less than cost. This indicates that there has been a decline in the utility of the inventory. The inventory should be written down and a loss recorded (assuming direct method is used). The inventory should never be valued at more than net realizable value. Apparently, not only will Toastie Corporation fail to realize a profit when it sells the inventory, it will not even recover its original cost.

(c)   Toastie's beginning inventory at cost and at retail would be included in the calculation of the cost-to-retail ratio because the conventional retail method approximates a lower of **average** cost and market valuation. An average cost method reflects all costs experienced (both from the beginning inventory and from purchases) in the ending inventory calculation. Net markups would be included in the calculation of the cost ratio. This procedure reduces the cost ratio because there is a larger denominator for the cost ratio calculation. Thus, the concept of balance sheet conservatism is being followed and a lower of cost and market valuation is approximated.

EXERCISE 9-3

Purpose: (L.O. 6) This exercise will demonstrate the use of the relative sales value method to value inventories.

Rhile Jones Corporation purchased a tract of unimproved land on Lake Sybelia for $1,000,000. Costs of subdividing and readying the land for residential lots amounted to $140,000. The lots are of two sizes and some are lakefront, so they vary in market prices as follows:

Type	No. of Lots	Sales Price per Lot
1	10	$ 60,000
2	15	80,000
3	6	100,000

Lots remaining unsold at December 31, 2002 were as follows:

Type	No. of Lots
1	4
2	9
3	2

Instructions
Calculate the value to be reported for the inventory of lots on hand on the December 31, 2002 balance sheet.

Solution to Exercise 9-3

Type	# of Lots	Sales Price per Lot	Total Sales Price	Relative Sales Price	Total Cost	Cost Allocated to Lot	Cost per Lot
1	10	$ 60,000	$ 600,000	6/24	$1,140,000	$ 285,000	$ 28,500
2	15	80,000	1,200,000	12/24	1,140,000	570,000	38,000
3	6	100,000	600,000	6/24	1,140,000	285,000	47,500
			$2,400,000			$1,140,000	

Ending Inventory:

Type	Lots Left	Cost per Lot	Total
1	4	$ 28,500	$114,000
2	9	38,000	342,000
3	2	47,500	95,000
			$551,000

Explanation: When a group of varying units is purchased (acquired) at a single lump sum price (often called a basket purchase), the total cost is allocated to the various items based on their relative sales (market) values.

EXERCISE 9-4

Purpose: (L.O. 8) This exercise will illustrate the use of the gross profit method of inventory estimation when: (1) gross profit is expressed as a percentage of cost, and (2) gross profit is expressed as a percentage of selling price.

Tim McInnes requires an estimate of the cost of goods lost by fire on April 2. Merchandise on hand on January 1 was $38,000. Purchases since January 1 were $72,000; freight-in, $3,400; and purchase returns and allowances, $2,400. Sales totalled $100,000 to April 2. Goods costing $7,700 were left undamaged by the fire; all other goods were destroyed.

Instructions
(a)   Calculate the cost of goods destroyed, assuming that the gross profit is 25% of cost.
(b)   Calculate the cost of goods destroyed, assuming that the gross profit is 25% of sales.

Solution to Exercise 9-4

(a)   Merchandise on hand, January 1 $ 38,000
       Purchases $ 72,000
       Purchase returns and allowances   (2,400)
       Net purchases   69,600
       Freight-in   3,400   73,000
       Total merchandise available for sale   111,000
       Estimated cost of goods sold*   (80,000)
       Estimated ending inventory on April 2   31,000
       Undamaged goods   (7,700)
       Estimated fire loss $ 23,300

           *Gross profit = 25% ÷ (100% + 25%) = 20% of sales.
            Therefore, cost of goods sold = 80% of sales of $100,000 = $80,000.

(b)   Gross profit is 25% of sales.
       Therefore, cost of goods sold = 75% of sales of $100,000 = $75,000.
           Total merchandise available for sale (as calculated above) $ 111,000
           Estimated cost of goods sold   (75,000)
           Estimated ending inventory at April 2   36,000
           Undamaged goods   (7,700)
           Estimated fire loss $ 28,300

TIP: It is important to understand that inventory is accounted for in terms of the **cost** of goods acquired, and the Sales account reflects the **selling prices** of goods that have been sold during the period. Therefore, the profit element must be removed from the sales amount to arrive at the cost of the goods sold.

Approach: Use these steps to perform the calculations:

(1)   **Calculate the cost of goods available for sale** for the period January 1 through April 2. This is done by combining the cost of inventory on hand at the beginning of the year (January 1) and the net cost of purchases during the period (net purchases plus freight-in).

(2)   **Determine the estimated cost of goods sold** during the period. This is done by multiplying the sales figure for the period by the cost of goods sold percentage. The cost of goods sold percentage is 100% minus the gross margin percentage. **Caution:** *The gross margin percentage used here must be stated in terms of selling price.* In part (b) of this exercise, gross profit is given in terms of sales. In part (a), however, you must convert the "25% of cost" to "20% of sales" before the cost of goods sold percentage of 80% can be applied to the sales amount.

(3)   **Calculate the estimated inventory on hand at the end of the period** (April 2, date of fire) by subtracting the estimated cost of goods sold (Step 2) from the cost of goods available for sale (Step 1).

(4)   **Determine the estimated loss** from fire by deducting the cost of the undamaged goods from the estimated cost of inventory on hand at April 2 (Step 3).

EXERCISE 9-5

Purpose: (L.O. 10) This exercise illustrates the use of the retail inventory method to value inventory.

The records of Nancy Klintworth's Baubles report the following data for the month of May.

Sales	$ 79,000
Sales returns	1,000
Markups	10,000
Markup cancellations	1,500
Markdowns	9,300
Markdown cancellations	2,800
Freight on purchases	2,400
Purchases (at cost)	48,000
Purchases (at sales price)	88,000
Purchase returns (at cost)	2,000
Purchase returns (at sales price)	3,000
Beginning inventory (at cost)	30,000
Beginning inventory (at sales price)	46,500

Instructions
(a)   Calculate the ending inventory by the conventional retail inventory method.

Solution to Exercise 9-5

	Cost		Retail
Beginning inventory	$ 30,000		$ 46,500
Purchases	48,000		88,000
Purchase returns	(2,000)		(3,000)
Freight on purchase	2,400		
Goods available for sale	78,400		131,500
Net markups:			
Markups		$ 10,000	
Markup cancellations		(1,500)	8,500
	78,400		140,000
Net markdowns:			
Markdowns		9,300	
Markdown cancellations		(2,800)	(6,500)
	$ 78,400		133,500
Net sales ($79,000 - $1,000)			(78,000)
Ending inventory, at retail			$ 55,500

(a)   Cost-to-retail ratio = $78,400 ÷ $140,000 = 56%
       Ending inventory at lower of average cost and market = 56% x $55,500 = $31,080

Approach and Explanation:
(a) Step 1: **Calculate the ending inventory at retail.** This is done by determining the retail value of goods available for sale, adjusting that figure for net markups and net markdowns, and deducting the retail value of goods no longer on hand (sales, estimated theft, etc.).

     Step 2: **Calculate the cost-to-retail ratio.** The conventional retail method approximates an average cost amount so both beginning inventory and net purchases information is used in the ratio. The conventional retail method is to approximate a lower-of-cost-and-market value so the net markups are included but the net markdowns are excluded from the ratio calculation.

     Step 3: **Determine the ending inventory at an approximate lower-of-average-cost-and-market value.** Apply the appropriate cost-to-retail ratio (Step 2) to the total ending inventory at retail (Step 1).

TIP: If prices had not been stable, additional procedures would have been required to eliminate the effects of price-level changes in order to measure the real increases in inventory, not the dollar increase.

ILLUSTRATION 9-1
HOW TO CALCULATE AND APPLY THE COST/RETAIL RATIO
FOR THE RETAIL METHOD (L.O. 10)

Method (Basis)	Cost/Retail Ratio	How to Calculate Ending Inventory
1. Conventional (Lower of Average Cost and Market).	(Beginning inventory at cost + net cost of purchases) ÷ (beginning inventory at retail + net purchases at retail + net markups).	Ending inventory at retail x ratio.

EXERCISE 9-6

Purpose: (L.O. 4)   Orishes Company is valuing their year-end inventory. The company uses the LCM rule where market is defined as net realizable value. The information compiled so far is presented below:

Item	Units	Cost	Market
Category 1			
A	100	$6	$5
B	50	4	6
C	10	9	8
Category 2			
D	50	$10	$ 9
E	100	12	14

Required: Determine the value of ending inventory using the LCM rule applied:

a) item-by-item basis
b) Category basis
c) Total inventory basis

Solution: Determine the LCM under each of the different valuation methods:

a)

Item	Units	Cost	Market	LCM		
A	100	$ 6	$ 5	$5 x 100	=	$ 500
B	50	4	6	$4 x 50	=	$ 200
C	10	9	8	$8 x 10	=	$ 80
D	50	10	9	$9 x 50	=	$ 450
E	100	12	14	$12 x 100	=	$1,200
				Total		$2,430

b)

Category 1		Total Cost	Market	LCM	
A	100	$600	$500		
B	50	200	300		
C	10	90	80		
		$890	$880		$ 880

Category 2					
D	50	$ 500	$ 450		
E	100	1,200	1,400		
		$1,700	$1,850		$1,700
				Total	$2,580

c) Using information from (b):

	Cost	Market	LCM	
Category 1	$ 890	$ 880		
Category 2	1,700	1,850		
Total	$2,590	$2,730	Total	$2,590

ANALYSIS OF MULTIPLE-CHOICE TYPE QUESTIONS

QUESTION

1.   (L.O. 4) Crosby Co. is just beginning its first year of operations. Crosby intends to use either the perpetual moving average method or the periodic weighted average method, and to apply the lower of cost and market rule either to individual items or to the total inventory. Prices of most inventory items are expected to increase throughout 2002, although the prices of a few items are expected to decrease. What inventory system should Crosby Co. select if it wants to minimize the inventory carrying amount at the end of the first year?

	Inventory Method	Cost and Market Application
a.	Perpetual	Individual items
b.	Perpetual	Total inventory
c.	Periodic	Individual items
d.	Periodic	Total inventory

Approach and Explanation: Think about the results of using the perpetual moving average method versus the results of using the periodic weighted average method. In a period of rising prices, the periodic weighted average method will yield the lower ending inventory figure (the ending weighted average unit cost for the perpetual system will be higher than the weighted average unit cost for the period for the periodic system). Then think about the results of applying the lower-of-cost-and-market rule to individual items versus the results of applying it to the total inventory. The individual item approach gives the most conservative valuation for balance sheet purposes. When categories or total inventory is used, situations caused by products whose replacement cost is higher than original cost are allowed to offset situations where replacement cost is lower than original cost. When an item-by-item approach is used, all possible declines in utility are recognized and not offset by inventory items whose replacement cost exceeds original cost. Combine the results of these analyses to get the final answer. (Solution = c.)

QUESTION

2.   (L.O. 3) Peachy Products has an item in inventory with a cost of $85. Current replacement cost is $75. The expected selling price is $100, estimated selling costs are $18, and the normal profit is $5. Using the **U. S.** lower-of-cost-smf-market rule, the item should be included in the inventory at:
a. $75
b. $77
c. $82
d. $85

Approach and Explanation: Write down the two steps in determining LCM and follow them:
(1)   Find market: Three possibilities:
                Ceiling ($100 - $18) = $82
                Floor ($82 - $5) = $77
                Replacement cost = $75
        Choose the middle value of these three: $77 = market

(2)   Compare market with cost and choose the lower.
        Market of $77 versus cost of $85. Lower = $77   (Solution = b.)

QUESTION
   3.   (L.O. 4) In applying the lower-of-cost-or-market rule to inventories at December
           31, 2002, Xavier Corporation wrote the inventory down from $500,000 to
           $420,000. This writedown should be reported:
           a.   as a prior period adjustment of $80,000.
           b.   as an operating expense in 2002.
           c.   as an extraordinary item on the 2002 income statement.
           d.   as a part of cost of goods sold expense.
           e.   immediately after cost of goods sold or immediately after gross profit on
                   the 2002 income statement.

Explanation: The $80,000 loss should be shown separately from cost of goods sold in the
income statement; it is not an extraordinary item. (Solution = e.)

QUESTION
   4.   (L.O. 7) In 2002, Lucas Manufacturing signed a contract with a supplier to
           purchase raw materials in 2003 for $700,000. Before the December 31, 2002
           balance sheet date, the market price for these materials dropped to $510,000.
           The journal entry to record this situation at December 31, 2002 will result in a
           credit that should be reported:
           a.   as a valuation account to Inventory on the balance sheet.
           b.   as a current liability.
           c.   as an appropriation of retained earnings.
           d.   on the income statement.

Approach and Explanation: Draft the entry referred to in the question. Think about the
classification of each account in the entry. Focus on the credit part addressed in the stem of the
question. The journal entry is:
            Estimated Loss on Purchase Commitments   190,000
                   Estimated Liability on Purchase Commitments   190,000
The loss would be reported on the income statement under Other Expenses and Losses. The
liability is reported as a current liability because the contract is to be executed within the year
that immediately follows the balance sheet date. (Solution = b.)

QUESTION
   5.   (L.O. 8) The following information pertains to the Godfrey Company for the six
           months ended June 30 of the current year:
                   Merchandise inventory, January 1 $ 700,000
                   Purchases   5,000,000
                   Freight-in   400,000
                   Sales   6,000,000

Gross profit is normally 25% of sales. What is the estimated amount of inventory on hand at June 30?
a. $100,000
b. $1,600,000
c. $2,100,000
d. $4,600,000

Approach and Explanation: Use the following steps to solve a gross profit inventory method question:

(1)   Calculate the cost of goods available for sale during the period:

Beginning inventory	$ 700,000
Purchases	5,000,000
Freight-in	400,000
Cost of goods available for sale	$ 6,100,000

(2)   Determine the estimated cost of goods sold during the period:

Sales	$ 6,000,000
Cost of goods sold percentage (100% - 25%)	x 75%
Estimated cost of goods sold	$ 4,500,000

TIP: This problem was simple because the gross profit percentage given in the problem is stated in terms of sales. When the gross margin percentage is expressed in terms of cost, that percentage must first be converted to the equivalent percentage of selling price before the other calculations can be performed.

(3)   Calculate the estimated inventory on hand at the end of the period:

Cost of goods available for sale	$ 6,100,000
Estimated cost of goods sold	(4,500,000)
Estimated ending inventory	$ 1,600,000
	(Solution = b.)

QUESTION

6.   (L.O. 8) The cost of goods available for sale for 2002 for Storey Corporation was $2,700,000. The gross profit rate was 20% of sales. Sales for the year amounted to $2,400,000. The ending inventory is estimated to be:
a. $0
b. $480,000
c. $540,000
d. $780,000

Explanation: Step 1:   Calculate the cost of goods available for sale during the period. Cost of goods available is given at $2,700,000.

Step 2:   Determine the estimated cost of goods sold during the period:

Sales	$2,400,000
Cost of goods sold percentage	
(100% - 20%)	x 80%
Estimated cost of goods sold	$1,920,000

Step 3:   Calculate the estimated inventory on hand at the end of the period:
Cost of goods available for sale $2,700,000

Estimated cost of goods sold	(1,920,000)
Estimated ending inventory (at cost)	$ 780,000

(Solution = d.)

QUESTION
7.   (L.O. 8) If gross profit is 25% of cost, then gross profit as a percentage of sales equals:
   a.   80%
   b.   75%
   c.   33 2/3%
   d.   20%

Explanation: Sales (S) - Cost of Goods Sold (CGS) = Gross Profit (GP)
If GP = 25% of cost, then cost of goods sold = 100%.
S - 100% = 25%.
S = 125%.
Expressing gross profit (GP) as a percentage of sales (S) we get:
       25% ÷ 125% = 20%.
Thus, gross profit = 20% of sales.

(Solution = d.)

QUESTION
8.   (L.O. 10) A company uses the retail method to estimate ending inventory for interim reporting purposes. If the retail method is used to approximate a lower-of-average-cost-or-market valuation, which of the following alternatives describe the proper treatment of net markups and net markdowns in the cost-to-retail ratio calculation?

	Net Markups	**Net Markdowns**
a.	Include	Include
b.	Include	Exclude
c.	Exclude	Include
d.	Exclude	Exclude

Approach and Explanation: First notice that the lower-of-average-cost-and-market approach to the retail method is often referred to as the conventional retail method. Recall that using a lower-of-cost-and-market figure is an application of the principle of conservatism. Also recall that the retail method involves multiplying the ending inventory at retail by a ratio. The lower the ratio, the lower the calculated inventory value. Including the net markups (increases in retail prices) but excluding the net markdowns (decreases in retail prices) gives the highest denominator possible for the ratio calculation which yields the lowest ratio possible. (Note: Net markups are often called net additional markups.) (Solution = b.)

QUESTION

9.   (L.O. 10) The following data relate to the merchandise inventory of the Hofma Company:

Beginning inventory at cost	$ 13,800
Beginning inventory at selling price	20,000
Purchases at cost	31,000
Purchases at selling price	50,000

Using the information, determine the cost to retail ratio for Hofma Company:

a.   156%
b.   145%
c.   69%
d.   64%

Explanation:

Ratio	=	Cost ÷ Retail
Ratio	=	($13,800 + $31,000) ÷ ($20,000 + $50,000)
Ratio	=	$44,800 ÷ $70,000
Ratio	=	<u>64%</u> (Solution = d.)

QUESTION

10.   (L.O. 10) The Ruffier Department Store uses the conventional retail inventory method. The following information is available at December 31, 2002:

	Cost	Retail
Beginning inventory	$ 37,800	$ 60,000
Purchases	200,000	290,000
Freight-in	7,200	
Sales		275,000

What is the estimated cost of the ending inventory?
a. $47,250
b. $52,500
c. $53,586
d. $192,500

Calculations:

	Cost	Retail	
Beginning inventory		$ 37,800	$ 60,000
Purchases		200,000	290,000
Freight-in		7,200	
Cost of goods available for sale		$ 245,000	350,000
Sales			(275,000)

Step 1: Ending inventory at retail $ 75,000
Step 2: Cost to retail ratio = $245,000 ÷ $350,000 = 70%
Step 3: Estimated cost of ending inventory = $75,000 x 70% = <u>$ 52,500</u>

Approach and Explanation: Think about how the conventional retail method of inventory estimation works. An estimate of the ending inventory at retail is made by deducting sales from the retail value of goods available for sale, and the ending inventory at retail is converted to a cost value by applying an appropriate ratio, which is an expression of the relationship between inventory cost and its retail value. Apply the following steps to calculate the amount required:

Step 1:   **Calculate the ending inventory at retail.** Deduct net sales from the retail price of all of the goods available for sale during the period. Arrive at $75,000.

Step 2:   **Calculate the cost to retail ratio.** Divide the cost of the goods available for sale ($245,000) by the retail value of those same goods ($350,000). Arrive at 70%.

Step 3:   **Determine the estimated cost of the ending inventory.** Apply the cost to retail ratio (70%) to the ending inventory at retail ($75,000). Arrive at $52,500. (Solution = b.)

QUESTION

11.   (L.O. 11) Which of the following statements is **false** regarding an assumption of inventory cost flow?

    a.   The cost flow assumption need not correspond to the actual physical flow of goods.

    b.   The assumption selected may be changed each accounting period.

    c.   The FIFO assumption uses the earliest acquired prices to cost the items sold during a period.

    d.   The LIFO assumption uses the earliest acquired prices to cost the items on hand at the end of an accounting period.

Explanation: Once a method is selected from acceptable alternative methods, the entity must consistently apply that method for successive periods. The reason for this **consistency concept** is that **comparability** of financial statements is reduced or lost if methods are changed from period to period. However, an entity may change a method if it becomes evident that another method is more appropriate. (Solution = b.)

QUESTION

12.   (L.O. 8) The Billy Dial Department Store uses a calendar year and the conventional retail inventory method. The following information is available at December 31, 2002:

	Cost	Retail
Beginning inventory	$ 37,200	$ 60,000
Purchases	200,000	290,000
Freight-in	4,000	
Net markups		30,000
Net markdowns		20,000
Sales		285,000

What is the ending inventory at cost (round to the nearest dollar)?

    a. $46,763

    b. $47,400

    c. $47,603

    d. $50,250

Calculations:

	Cost	Retail
Beginning inventory	$ 37,200	$ 60,000
Purchases	200,000	290,000
Freight-in	4,000	
Goods available for sale	241,200	350,000
Net markups		30,000
Subtotals	$ 241,200	380,000
Net markdowns		(20,000)
		360,000
Sales		(285,000)
Ending inventory at retail		$ 75,000

Cost-to-retail ratio = $\dfrac{\$241,200}{\$380,000}$ = 63.47%

Ending inventory = 63.47% x $75,000 = $47,603

Approach and Explanation: Think about how the retail method of inventory estimation works. An estimate of the ending inventory at retail is made by deducting sales from the retail value of goods available for sale and the ending inventory at retail is converted to a cost or to a lower-of-cost-and-market value by applying an appropriate ratio which is an expression of the relationship between inventory cost and its retail value. Apply the following steps to calculate the amount required:

Step 1: **Calculate the ending inventory at retail.** Arrive at $75,000.

Step 2: **Calculate the cost-to-retail ratio.** The ratio should include net markups but not net markdowns.

Step 3: **Determine the ending inventory at cost.** Multiply the cost-to-retail ratio by the ending inventory at retail (including markdowns) = $47,603. (Solution = c.)

QUESTION

13.   (L.O. 11) The inventory turnover ratio is a measure of the liquidity of the inventory. This ratio is calculated by dividing:
    a.   the cost of goods sold by 365 days.
    b.   the cost of goods sold by the average amount of inventory on hand.
    c.   net credit sales by the average amount of inventory on hand.
    d.   365 days by the cost of goods sold.

Approach and Explanation: Write down the formula to calculate the inventory turnover ratio. Think about the logic of each of the calculation's components. The formula is as follows:

$$\text{Inventory Turnover ratio} = \frac{\text{Cost of Goods Sold}}{\text{Average Inventory}}$$

The cost of goods sold figure is a cost figure whereas net credit sales is a figure reflecting the selling prices of items sold. The cost of an inventory item is reflected in the Inventory account until such time when the item is sold; then, the cost is transferred to the Cost of Goods Sold account. If an item is sold on credit, the selling price of the item is recorded in the Accounts Receivable account. Hence, the accounts receivable turnover ratio uses net credit sales and average accounts receivable balance; whereas, the inventory turnover ratio uses cost of goods sold and the average inventory balance for its calculation. A variant of the inventory turnover ratio is the **average days to sell inventory.** (Solution = b.)

QUESTION

14.   (L.O. 7) The average days to sell inventory is calculated by dividing:

a.   365 days by the inventory turnover ratio.
b.   the inventory turnover ratio by 365 days.
c.   net sales by the inventory turnover ratio.
d.   365 days by cost of goods sold.

Explanation: The **average days to sell inventory** is a variant of the inventory turnover ratio. It is calculated by dividing 365 days by the inventory turnover ratio. It measures the average number of days an item remains in inventory before it is sold. (Solution = a.)

CHAPTER 10

INVESTMENTS

OVERVIEW

Oftentimes an entity has cash that is temporarily in excess of its immediate needs. That cash should be invested wisely so that it produces income while being a ready source of funds. Sometimes an entity invests in the stocks and bonds of other entities for long-term purposes. Accounting for both short-term (temporary) and long-term investments is discussed in this chapter.

The chapter will discuss the disclosure requirements for long-term investments in debt and equity securities as well as compare the equity with the cost method for equity securities. Additional, special issues dealing with investments will also be discussed in this chapter.

SUMMARY OF LEARNING OBJECTIVES

1. **Identify the different types of investments and describe how investments are classified.** Investments are classified based primarily on management intent and to a lesser extent whether there is a ready market.

2. **Explain the nature of temporary investments and describe the accounting and reporting treatment for temporary investments.** Temporary investments are held for a short time and are generally liquidated within the year. They are valued using the lower of cost and market rule, which may be applied to the portfolio as a whole or to individual securities. Investments in affiliated companies, basis of valuation, market and carrying value, terms and conditions as well as interest rate and credit risks should be disclosed.

3. **Explain the nature of long-term investments and describe the accounting and financial reporting for these investments.** Long-term investments are normally held for a longer time and often reflect management's strategic business plan. They are recorded at cost and then the accounting treatment is a function of whether they are debt or equity securities. Debt securities are carried at amortized cost and are not written down unless there are collectibility issues. Equity investments are also recorded at cost and if the securities carry voting privileges, either the cost, equity, or consolidation methods are used to account for them. Long-term equity investments are assessed for non temporary impairment of value.

4. **Explain the equity method of accounting and compare it with the cost method for equity securities.** Under the equity method, a substantive economic relationship is acknowledged between the investor and the investee. The investment is originally, recorded at cost but is subsequently adjusted each period for changes in the investee's net assets. That is, the investment's carrying amount is periodically increased (decreased) by the investor's proportionate share of the investee's earnings (losses) and decreased by all dividends received by the investor from the investee. Under the cost method, the equity investment is reported by the

investor at cost and investment income is recognized when dividends are declared or paid to the investor. The equity method is applied to investment holdings between 20% and 50% of ownership where significant influence exists, whereas the cost method is applied to holdings below 20% where no significant influence exists.

5. **Describe the disclosure requirements for long-term investments in debt and equity securities.** The following are required: (a) basis of valuation must be disclosed, (b) investments in companies subject to significant influence, other affiliated companies and other long-term investments should be shown separately, (c) income for the items mentioned above should also be shown separately, (d) where the equity method is used, disclosure should be made of the difference between the investment cost and the underlying net book value of the investee's net assets at the date of purchase as well as the treatment of the components of the difference, and (e) fair value as well as carrying value for all marketable securities classified as portfolio investments. Similar to temporary investments, for those long-term investments categorized as financial instruments, the following must be disclosed: terms and conditions, interest rate risk, and credit risk concentrations.

*6. **Discuss the special issues that relate to accounting for investments.** The special issues that relate to investments are: recognizing dividends received in shares (share dividends and share splits); allocating cost between share and share rights; accounting for changes in the cash surrender value of life insurance; and accounting for assets set aside in special funds.
   *This material is covered in Appendix 10-A in the text.

TIPS ON CHAPTER TOPICS

TIP: An investment may be classified as a current asset (if it is a short-term investment) or as a noncurrent asset (if it is a long-term investment). For an investment in to be classified as a **current asset**: (1) it should be readily marketable, and (2) there should be a lack of management intent to hold it for long-term purposes.

TIP: Included in the long-term investment classification are the following: (1) long-term receivables, (2) long-term investments in stocks and bonds and stock rights of other entities, (3) restricted funds, (4) cash surrender value of life insurance, and (5) land held for future plant site.

TIP: When there is a price decline in a debt or equity security held as an investment, assume the decline is temporary unless otherwise indicated. Investments are valued using the lower-of-cost-and-market rule. Impairment occurs when the decline is considered other than temporary in nature. Impairment usually results from:

a) prolonged period during which market is less than carrying value
b) severe investee losses
c) continued investee losses
d) suspension of trading of investee shares
e) investee liquidy or going concern problems
f) appraised fair value of shares is less than carrying value.

TIP: The cost of an investment includes its purchase price and all other costs necessary to acquire the investment. Thus, the cost of an investment in shares or bonds is likely to include broker commissions and incidental fees.

TIP: investments can be either valued individually or collectively as a portfolio.

TIP: Although premiums and discounts on investments in debt securities classified as current assets need not be amortized (because of the immaterial effect of doing so), premiums and discounts on investments in debt securities classified as long-term (noncurrent) assets should be amortized. The **effective interest method** is the prescribed method; however, the **straight-line method** is often justifiably used based on the immaterial difference between its results and the effect of the preferable method.

TIP: In determining whether a bond discount of premium exists in the payment of the bond, consider the following table:

Market Rate of Interest	Coupon/(face) Rate of Interest	Resulting Sale
10%	9%	Discount
8%	9%	Premium
9%	9%	Par

If the company is offering 9% interest and investors can receive 10% on other similar investments, the investor will have to be induced to buy the companies bond by receiving the bond at a discount. Note, that investors will typically not set up a discount or premium account as the issuer would. Any discount or premium would be reflected in the investment account itself.

TIP: If the effective interest method of amortization is used to account for an investment in bonds, the following relationships will exist:
1.   The interest rate is constant each period.
2.   The interest revenue is an increasing amount each period if the bond is purchased as a discount (because a constant rate is applied to an increasing carrying amount each period).
3.   The interest revenue is a decreasing amount each period if the bond is purchased at a premium (because a constant rate is applied to a decreasing carrying amount each period).
4.   The amount of amortization increases each period because the difference between the effective interest revenue and the cash interest widens each period.

TIP: When the accounting period ends on a date **other** than an interest date, the amortization schedule for a bond investment is unaffected by this fact. That is, the schedule is prepared and computations are made according to the bond interest periods, ignoring the details of the accounting period. The interest revenue amounts shown in the amortization schedule are then apportioned to the appropriate accounting period(s). As an example, if the interest revenue for the six months ending April 30, 2002 is $120,000, then $40,000 of that amount would go on the income statement for the 2001 calendar year and $80,000 of it should be reflected on the income statement for the 2002 calendar year.

TIP: If an investor purchases shares of another corporation, the amount of shares will determine the method to be used:
  - Less than 20%   - Cost method
  - Between 20-50%   - Equity method
  - > 50%   - Consolidation method

TIP: A payment for an insurance premium is recorded by a credit to Cash for the amount paid, a debit to Cash Surrender Value of Life Insurance for the increase in that value during the period and a debit to Life Insurance Expense for the difference. The policy's cash surrender value only represents an asset to the company if the company is the beneficiary of the policy. If the employee or their heirs are the beneficiary, the payments for the insurance is treated similar to salary expenses.

TIP: If cash is set aside for a special purpose, Cash is reduced and a fund account (restricted cash) is increased. An appropriation of retained earnings does **not** by itself establish a fund. Regardless of the composition of the assets in the fund, the entire balance of the fund should be reported as a noncurrent asset (in the Long-term Investments section) on the balance sheet as long as the fund is earmarked for a long-term purpose.

TIP: Shares received as a result of a share split do not require a journal entry, but does require a revision in the carrying amount of a share for disposal calculations.

TIP: In a general sense, **financial assets** are defined as cash; or a contractual right to receive cash or another financial asset from another party; or a contractual right to exchange financial instruments with another party under conditions that are potentially favourable; or an equity instrument of another entity.

TIP: Equity securities acquired in exchange for nonmonetary considerations should be recorded at (1) the fair value of the consideration given or (2) the fair value of the security received, whichever is more clearly determinable.

ILLUSTRATION 10-1
SUMMARY OF INVESTMENTS IN
DEBT AND EQUITY SECURITIES (L.O. 1 THROUGH 4)

Investments in the shares of other companies are often referred to as investments in **equity securities** or share investments. Investments in the bonds of other companies are often referred to as investments in **debt securities** or debt investments.

The major categories for investments in debt and equity securities and their reporting treatments are summarized below.

Category	Balance Sheet	Income Statement
Cost method	Investments are shown at fair value. Current or long-term assets.	Interest and dividends are recognized as revenue. Gains and losses from sale are included in income.
Equity method	Investments are carried at cost, are periodically adjusted by the investor's share of the investee's earnings or losses, and are decreased by all dividends received from the investee. Classified in long-term assets.	Revenue is recognized to the extent of the investee's earnings or losses reported subsequent to the date of investment (adjusted by amortization of the difference between cost and underlying book value). Gains and losses from sale are included in income.

EXERCISE 10-1

Purpose: (L.O. 1) This exercise will quickly review the process of determining the required year-end entry to adjust the valuation account for an investment in equity securities.

Nevercrash Airlines has a portfolio of temporary marketable equity securities, the first of which was acquired in 2001. The aggregate cost and fair value of the securities contained in that investment portfolio for five balance sheet dates are as follows:

Date	Aggregate Cost	Aggregate Fair Value	Net Unrealized Gains (Losses)
12/31/01	$ 142,000	$ 138,000	$ (4,000)
12/31/02	159,000	143,000	(16,000)
12/31/03	172,000	163,000	(9,000)
12/31/04	190,000	203,000	13,000
12/31/05	190,000	184,000	(6,000)

Instructions

At each balance sheet date, determine the following:

(a)   Reported value for the portfolio.

(b)   Desired balance in the related allowance account and indicate whether the desired balance is a debit or a credit.

(c)   Amount of adjustment required to the related allowance account and indicate whether the required adjustment to the related allowance account is a debit or credit.

Solution to Exercise 10-1

	(a)		(b)		(c)	
12/31/01	$138,000	FV	$ 4,000	credit	$ 4,000	credit
12/31/02	143,000	FV	16,000	credit	12,000	credit
12/31/03	163,000	FV	9,000	credit	7,000	debit
12/31/04	190,000	FV	7,000	debit	7,000	debit
12/31/05	184,000	FV	6,000	credit	6,000	credit

Explanation: Investments in equity securities which are classified as a portfolio are initially recorded at cost, but they are to be reported at lower of cost or market at a balance sheet date. The writeup or writedown of the investment is accomplished by the use of an allowance account. The allowance is recognized when the market value of the security is lower than the original cost. Once reduced, this becomes the new value of the account for which the market will be compared. If there is an increase in valuation of the market, the allowance account will be reduced, but only up to the original cost of the portfolio.

TIP: The portfolio in this exercise may be classified as a current asset or a noncurrent asset. The responses in this exercise are not affected by whether it is a current or noncurrent classification.

EXERCISE 10-2

Purpose: (L.O. 2) This exercise will review the accounting for investments in equity securities.

At December 31, 2000, Ed & Kay Hastings Company had no investments. One equity security is purchased for $34,680 on November 15, 2001; commission costs on the purchase amount to $320. At December 31, 2001, a balance sheet date, the fair value of that security is $32,000. At December 31, 2002, the security is still held and the fair value is $34,000. The security is classified in temporary assets. On January 15, 2003, the security is sold for a price of $42,800.

Instructions

(a)   Prepare the journal entry for the purchase of the security on November 15, 2001.

(b)   Prepare the appropriate adjusting entry on December 31, 2001.

(c)   Describe what will appear on the 2001 financial statements with regard to this investment.

(d)   Prepare the appropriate adjusting entry on December 31, 2002.

(e)   Describe what will appear on the 2002 financial statements with regard to this investment.

(f)   Prepare the journal entry to record the sale of the investment on January 15, 2003.

Solution to Exercise 10-2

(a)

November 15, 2001

Temporary investments..	35,000	
Cash ($34,680 + $320)...		35,000

(b)

December 31, 2001

Loss on Investments	3,000	
Investment Allowance		3,000

(c)   The investment will be reported at a net amount of $32,000 ($35,000 - $3,000) in the current asset section of the balance sheet at December 31, 2001. The loss on investment of $3,000 is reported income (loss) at December 31, 2001. The purchase of an investment will appear as a $35,000 outflow of cash in the investing section of the statement of cash flows.

(d)

December 31, 2002

Investment Allowance	2,000	
Investment Income		2,000

(e)   The investment will be reported at the cost of $35,000 on the balance sheet at December 31, 2002. The increase in market price of $8,000 during the period will probably be reflected in a note showing the current market value of the investments. The net unrealized holding gain will show up on the companies income statement for the period.

(f)

January 15, 2003

Cash..	42,800	
Investment Allowance	1,000	
Investment Income ($42,800 - $35,000+$1,000)		8,800
Temporary Investment..		35,000

Approach: The loss incurred in the first period is charged to an allowance account for investment decline. In the subsequent year, the market value increases and the allowance is reduced. When the security is sold in 2003, the allowance account is first reduced to zero, with any subsequent gain recognized.

EXERCISE 10-3

Purpose: (L.O. 1, 2) This exercise will illustrate how to account for investments in a portfolio versus individual account valuation.

Accolades Cruise Company has three investments at the end of December 31, 2002 balance sheet date. The securities contained in these portfolios are all equity securities and were purchased during 2002, Accolades' first year of operations. None of the investments are accounted for by the equity method. No investments were sold during 2002. Details are as follows:

Trading Portfolio

December 31, 2002

	Cost	Market	Difference
Stock of ABC Co.	$100,000	$ 80,000	$(20,000)
Stock of DEF Co.	70,000	92,000	22,000
Stock of GHI Co.	60,000	50,000	(10,000)
Total	$230,000	$222,000	$(8,000)

Instructions

(a) Prepare the appropriate adjusting entry(s) at December 31, 2002 using the individual account valuation method.

(b) Prepare the appropriate adjusting entry(s) at December 31, 2002 using the portfolio valuation method.

(c) Assuming the stock of DEF Co. is sold for $94,000 on January 7, 2003 and the stock of GHI Co. is sold for $51,000 on January 8, 2003, prepare the journal entries to record these sales under each method (individual and portfolio method).

SOLUTION TO EXERCISE 10-3

(a) Loss on Investment—ABC   20,000
        Investment Allowance...   20,000

        Loss on Investment—GHI   10,000
        Investment Allowance...   10,000

Explanation: The investments are each individually subject to the lower-of-cost-or-market rule. Since DEF market value was in excess of its cost, no adjustment is necessary. (Note: This transaction could have been combined.)

(b) Loss on Investment   8,000
        Investment Allowance...   8,000

Explanation: Using the portfolio method, individual gains and losses are netted out, hence the adjustment is only a combined $8,000 loss, as the unrealized holding gain on DEF is in effect recognized here (although not directly).

(c)   **Individual Method**

                                      January 7, 2003
        Cash...   94,000
        Loss on Sale of Investment...   6,000
                Temporary Investment—ABC.....................................   100,000

January 8, 2003

Cash..	51,000	
Loss on Sale of Investment...	9,000	
Temporary Investment—GHI......................................		60,000

Portfolio Method
January 7, 2003

Cash..	94,000	
Loss on Sale of Investment...	6,000	
Temporary Investment—ABC......................................		100,000

January 8, 2003

Cash..	51,000	
Loss on Sale of Investment...	9,000	
Temporary Investment—GHI......................................		60,000

> **TIP:** The valuation account is not involved in recording the purchase or sale of securities during the period. The valuation account is adjusted **only** at the end of an accounting period.

EXERCISE 10-4

Purpose: (L.O. 1) This exercise will review the accounting procedures appropriate for an investment in debt securities held-to-maturity.

A five-year $100,000 bond with a 7% stated interest rate and a 5% yield rate is purchased on December 31, 2001 for $108,660. The bond matures on December 31, 2006. Interest is to be received at the end of each year. The following amortization schedule reflects interest to be received, interest revenue, amortization of bond premium, and amortized cost of the bond investment at year end.

Date	Cash Received	Interest Revenue	Premium Amortization	Carrying Amount
12/31/01				$108,660
12/31/02	$ 7,000	$ 5,433	$1,567	107,093
12/31/03	7,000	5,354	1,646	105,447
12/31/04	7,000	5,272	1,728	103,719
12/31/05	7,000	5,186	1,814	101,905
12/31/06	7,000	5,095	1,905	100,000
Totals	$35,000	$26,340	$8,660	

The following presents a comparison of the amortized cost and market value (assumed) of the bond at year end.

Date	Amortized Cost	Market Value	Difference
12/31/01	$108,660	$108,660	$0
12/31/02	107,093	106,000	(1,093)
12/31/03	105,447	107,500	2,053
12/31/04	103,719	105,500	1,781
12/31/05	101,905	103,000	1,095
12/31/06	100,000	100,000	0

Instructions

(a) Record the journal entries at December 31, 2001, December 31, 2002, and December 31, 2003.

(b) Describe what will be reflected in the income statement and balance sheet prepared at December 31, 2002 and December 31, 2003 with regard to this investment.

(c) Prepare the journal entry to record the sale of the investment if it is sold on January 2, 2004 for $107,250.

Solution to Exercise 10-4

(a)
December 31, 2001

Long-term Investment	108,660	
Cash		108,660

TIP: Although the issuer of the bonds sets up a separate account for premium or discount on bonds, an investor typically does **not** set up a separate account; rather, any discount or premium is reflected in the investment account.

December 31, 2002

Cash	7,000	
Interest Income		5,433
Long-term Investment		1,567

December 31, 2003

Cash	7,000	
Interest Income		5,354
Long-term Investment		1,646

(b) The bond investment would be reported in the long-term investment section of the balance sheet at amortized cost of $107,093 at December 31, 2002 and $105,447 at December 31, 2003. Interest revenue of $5,433 would be reported in the income statement for the year ending December 31, 2002 and interest revenue of $5,354 would be reported in the income statement for the year ending December 31, 2003. Interest revenue is classified as "other revenue" on a multiple-step income statement.

(c)   **January 2, 2004**

Cash.. 107,250

    Long-term Investment... 105,447[a]

    Gain on Sale of Investment (Other Income)...................... 1,803

    [a]$108,660 - ($1,567 + $1,646) = $105,447 balance

TIP: The realized gain of $1,803 from the sale of the investment will be reported in the "other revenues and gains" section of the income statement for the year ending December 31, 2004.

EXERCISE 10-5

Purpose: (L.O. 1) This exercise will review the factors involved in calculating interest revenue using the straight-line method of amortization for bonds purchased at a discount between interest payment dates.

Tenia Pumps Corporation purchased bonds to be held as a long-term investment; they are classified as held-to-maturity. Tenia uses the straight-line method of amortization, reversing entries where appropriate, and a calendar year reporting period. Other facts are as follows:

Par value of bonds	$300,000
Coupon rate of interest	10%
Purchase price	$287,960
Purchase date	March 1, 2002
Interest payment dates	January 1 and July 1
Maturity date	January 1, 2008

Instructions
(a) Calculate the interest revenue to be reported on the income statement for the year ending December 31, 2002.
(b) Calculate the interest revenue to be reported on the income statement for the year ending December 31, 2003.
(c) Calculate the interest revenue to be reported on the income statement for the year ending December 31, 2004.

TIP: Recall that the straight-line method of amortization is not a generally acceptable accounting method. It can be used and not be considered a departure from GAAP when the results of its use are not materially different from the results of using the preferable effective interest method of amortization. This problem assumes an immaterial difference exists.

Solution to Exercise 10-5

Approach: Draw a T-account. Make all the entries that would be reflected in the Interest Revenue account for the period in question.

(a)

Interest Revenue			
3/1/02	5,000	7/1/02	15,000
		12/31/02	15,000
		12/31/02	1,720
		12/31/02 Bal.	26,720

Explanation:

3/1/02   **Payment of accrued interest at date of purchase.** A purchaser of bonds must pay the seller any interest accrued between the last interest payment date and the purchase date. This amount can be debited to the Interest Revenue account or to the Interest Receivable account on the purchaser's books. This solution assumes the former.

$300,000 x 10% = $30,000 interest per year.
$30,000 ÷ 12 = $2,500 interest per month.
$2,500 x 2 = $5,000 accrued interest at 3/1/02.

7/1/02   **Receipt of interest at interest payment date.** A full six months interest is received every interest payment date. Because the accrued interest at 3/1/02 was recorded in the revenue account, the entire receipt on 7/1/02 can be credited to the revenue account.

$2,500 x 6 months = $15,000.

12/31/02   **Accrual of interest at year end.** Six months have passed since the last interest receipt.

$2,500 x 6 months = $15,000.

12/31/02   **Amortization of discount for the year.** The discount is to be amortized over the 70 months that are between the purchase date (March 1, 2002) and the maturity date (January 1, 2008). Ten months of amortization pertain to 2002 (March 1 to December 31).

$300,000 - $287,960 = $12,040 discount.
$12,040 ÷ 70 months = $172 amortization per month.
$172 x 10 months = $1,720 amortization for 2002.

(b)

Interest Revenue			
1/1/03 Reversing	15,000	1/1/03	15,000
		7/1/03	15,000
		12/31/03	15,000
		12/31/03	2,064
		12/31/03 Bal.	32,064

Explanation:

1/1/03	**Reversal of last period's accrual.** The reversal causes a debit to the Interest Revenue account.
1/1/03	**Receipt of interest at interest payment date.** $2,500 x 6 months = $15,000.
7/1/03	**Receipt of interest at interest payment date.** $2,500 x 6 months = $15,000.
12/31/03	**Accrual of interest at year end.** $2,500 x 6 months = $15,000.
12/31/03	**Amortization of discount for the year.** $172 x 12 months = $2,064.

(c) $32,064.   Same explanation and solution as for part (b) of this exercise.

EXERCISE 10-6

Purpose: (L.O.3) This exercise will illustrate (1) the calculations and journal entries for a bond investment purchased at a discount and (2) the accounting procedures required when the bond investment is sold prior to the bond's maturity date.

John and Martha Hitt Company purchased bonds to be held to maturity. The following details pertain:

Face value	$100,000.00
Coupon interest rate	7%
Yield rate	10%
Maturity date	January 1, 2005
Date of purchase	January 1, 2002
Interest receipts due	Annually on January 1
Method of amortization	Effective interest
Purchase price	$92,539.95

Instructions
(a)   Calculate the amount of purchase premium or discount.
(b)   Prepare the journal entry for the purchase of the bonds. Do not record the premium or discount separately in the accounts.
(c)   Prepare the amortization schedule for these bonds.
(d)   Prepare all of the journal entries (subsequent to the purchase date) for 2002 and 2003 that relate to these bonds. Assume the accounting period coincides with the calendar year. Assume reversing entries are not used.
(e)   Prepare the journal entry to record the sale of the bonds, assuming they are sold on January 1, 2004 for $102,000.00. Assume the sale occurs immediately after the annual interest receipt.

Solution to Exercise 10-6

(a)	Face value	$100,000.00
	Purchase price	92,539.95
	Discount on investment in bonds	$ 7,460.05

(b)
January 1, 2002

Long-term Investments	92,539.95	
Cash.		92,539.95

Explanation: The discount of $7,460.05 is reflected in the investment account because the instructions indicate the discount is not to be shown separately in the accounts.

(c)

Date	7% Cash Received	10% Interest Revenue	Discount Amortization	Carrying Value
1/1/02				$ 92,539.95
1/1/03	$ 7,000.00	$ 9,254.00	$ 2,254.00	94,793.95
1/1/04	7,000.00	9,479.40	2,479.40	97,273.35
1/1/05	7,000.00	9,726.65[a]	2,726.65	100,000.00
	$ 21,000.00	$ 28,460.05	$ 7,460.05	

[a]Includes rounding error of $.69.

Explanation: Cash received is determined by multiplying the par value ($100,000) by the contract rate of interest (7%). Interest revenue is calculated by multiplying the carrying value at the beginning of the interest period by the effective interest rate (10%). The amount of discount amortization for the period is the excess of the interest revenue over the stated interest (cash interest) amount. The carrying value at an interest receipt date is the carrying value at the beginning of the interest period plus the discount amortization for the interest period.

TIP: The amount of interest revenue of $9,479.40 appearing on the "1/1/04" receipt line is the amount of interest revenue for the interest period ending on that date. Thus, in this case, $9,479.40 is the interest revenue for the twelve months preceding the date 1/1/04 which would be the calendar year of 2003.

TIP: Any rounding error should be plugged to (included in) the interest revenue amount for the last period. Otherwise, there would be a small balance left in the Investment in Bonds account after the bonds are extinguished.

TIP: Notice that the total interest revenue ($28,460.05) over the three-year period equals the total cash interest ($21,000.00) plus the total purchase discount ($7,460.05). Thus, you can see that the purchase discount represents an additional amount of interest to be recognized over the time the bonds are held.

(d) 12/31/02

	Long-term Investments	2,254.00	
	Interest Receivable	7,000.00	
	Interest Revenue		9,254.00

Explanation: This entry records (1) the accrual of interest for twelve months, and (2) the amortization of discount for the first twelve months the bonds are held. This compound entry could be replaced with two single entries to accomplish the same objectives. The first entry would include a debit to Interest Receivable and a credit to Interest Revenue for $7,000.00. The second entry would include a debit to Long-term Investments and a credit to Interest Revenue for $2,254.00. The two entry approach is sometimes easier to employ when reversing entries are used because the first of the two single entries can be reversed, but the second of the two single entries (the one to record the amortization of discount or premium) should **never** be reversed.

1/1/03	Cash	7,000.00	
	Interest Receivable		7,000.00
12/31/03	Long-term Investments	2,479.40	
	Interest Receivable	7,000.00	
	Interest Revenue		9,479.40

(e)   1/1/04

Cash	7,000.00	
Interest Receivable		7,000.00
Cash	102,000.00	
Long-term Investments		97,273.35[a]
Gain on Sale of Securities		4,726.65[b]

[a]($92,539.95 + $2,254.00 + $2,479.40
= $97,273.35 carrying amount)
[b]($102,000.00 - $97,273.35
= $4,726.65 gain)

> **TIP:**   Gains or losses on the sale of investments are to be classified in the "other revenues, gains, expenses, and losses" section of a multiple-step income statement. They very rarely meet the criteria to be classified as an extraordinary item.

EXERCISE 10-7

Purpose: (L.O. 3) This exercise will allow you to compare the results of using the cost and equity methods of accounting for an investment in shares.

On January 1, 2002, Rocky Mountain Corporation acquired 100,000 of the 400,000 outstanding common shares of Great Plains Corporation as a long-term investment at a cost of $50 per share. The fair value and the book value of the investee's net assets were both $20,000,000 at January 1, 2002. Great Plains Corporation paid a cash dividend of $2.00 per common share on September 5, 2002 and reported net income of $1,400,000 for the year ending December 31, 2002. The market value of the Great Plains shares was $47 at December 31, 2002.

Instructions
(a)   Assuming Rocky Mountain does **not** exercise significant influence over the investee, determine the following:
   (1)   Amount to report as investment (dividend) revenue for the year ending December 31, 2002.
   (2)   Amount to report as the carrying value of the investment at December 31, 2002.
(b)   Assuming Rocky Mountain **does** exercise significant influence over the investee, determine the following:
   (1)   Amount to report as investment revenue for the year ending December 31, 2002.
   (2)   Amount to report as the carrying value of the investment at December 31, 2002.

Solution to Exercise 10-7

Approach: Mentally reconstruct the journal entries to record the transactions above. Draw T-Accounts for the investment and the investment revenue accounts. Enter the amounts as they would be posted to those accounts.

(a)   (1) $200,000.
        (2) $4,700,000.

Long-term Investment		Dividend Revenue	
1/1/02 5,000,000[1]			9/5/02 200,000[2]

[1] 100,000 shares x $50 = $5,000,000.

[2] 100,000 shares x $2 = $200,000.

Explanation: Because the investor does not exert significant influence over the investee, the investor should use the cost method (as opposed to the equity method) to account for the investment. The investment should be reported at fair value at each balance sheet date. At December 31, 2002, the market value ($47 x 100,000 = $4,700,000) is lower than the cost ($50 x 100,000 = $5,000,000) of the shares held; thus a valuation account with a $300,000 credit balance is needed.

TIP: In general, investments accounted for under the **cost method** are maintained in the investment account at acquisition cost until partially or entirely liquidated. (A writedown of cost is appropriate when [a] a dividend received represents a liquidating dividend, or [b] operating losses of the investee significantly reduce its net assets and greatly impair its earning potential.) A valuation is used to record the difference between cost and fair (market) value so that the investment in shares is reported at fair value at each balance sheet date. Cash dividends received from the investee are usually recorded as dividend revenue. However, when the dividends received by the investor in periods subsequent to the purchase exceed the investor's share of the investee's earnings for the same periods, the dividends are to be accounted for as a return of capital (liquidating dividend); thus, the investor is to record a reduction of the investment's carrying value rather than revenue.

(b)   (1) $350,000.
        (2) $5,150,000.

Investment in Great Plains Shares			Revenue From Investment	
1/1/02 5,000,000	9/5/02	200,000[3]		12/31/02 350,000[4]
12/31/02 350,000[4]				
12/31/02 Bal. 5,150,000				12/31/02 Bal. 350,000

[3]100,000 shares x $2 = $200,000.
[4]100,000 ÷ 400,000 = 25% ownership; 25% x $1,400,000 = $350,000.

Explanation: The investor should use the equity method when the investment allows the investor to exercise significant influence over the investee. The investor recognizes its proportionate share of the investee's earnings by a debit to the investment account and a credit to investment revenue. When the investee distributes earnings, the investor records an increase in cash and a decrease in the carrying value of the investment. Because the cost of the investment was equal to the carrying value of the investee's underlying net assets, there is no amortization to be considered (which would affect investment revenue and the investment account balance) in this case. The market value of the shares at the balance sheet date is not relevant when the equity method is used.

> **TIP:** Under the **equity method**, the investment is originally recorded at cost and then subsequently adjusted by the investor's **proportionate share** of the investee's earnings and dividend payments. Income earned by the investee results in investment revenue and an increase in the investment account on the books of the investor. An investee's net loss or dividend payments reduce the investment account. When the investor acquires the shares at a price unequal to the book value of the investee's underlying net assets, the investor must amortize the difference between the investor's cost and the investor's proportionate share of the underlying book value of the investee at the date of acquisition. This amortization affects investment revenue and the investment account balance.

EXERCISE 10-8

Purpose: (L.O. 3) This exercise will illustrate how to use the equity method of accounting for an investment in shares.

Delight Corporation acquired 30% of the 1,000,000 outstanding shares of Touch Corporation on January 1, 2002 for $3,240,000 when the book value of the net assets of Touch totalled $9,600,000. At January 1, 2002 Touch's plant assets, having a remaining life of ten years, had a fair value which exceeded book value by $700,000.

Touch Corporation reported net income of $1,600,000 for 2002 and $2,000,000 for 2003. Touch paid dividends of $400,000 on December 6, 2002 and $500,000 on December 5, 2003.

Instructions

(a)   Prepare all journal entries for Delight Corporation for 2002 and 2003 that relate to this investment.

(b)   Indicate the amount that should appear as investment income on Delight's income statement for (1) the year ending December 31, 2002, and (2) the year ending December 31, 2003.

(c)   Indicate the amount that should appear as the balance of Delight's investment on: (1) the balance sheet at December 31, 2002, and (2) the balance sheet at December 31, 2003.

Solution to Exercise 18-9

(a)   1/1/02   Investment in Touch Company Shares.................. 3,240,000
                    Cash   3,240,000

        12/6/02   Cash   120,000
                        Investment in Touch Company Shares.........   120,000
                        (30% x $400,000 = $120,000)

        12/31/02   Investment in Touch Company Shares.................. 480,000
                        Revenue from Investment............................   480,000
                        (30% x $1,600,000 = $480,000)

                    Revenue from Investment.....................................   21,000
                        Investment in Touch Company Shares.........   21,000
                        (30% x $700,000 = $210,000;
                        $210,000 ÷ 10 years = $21,000)

                    Revenue from Investment.....................................   3,750*
                        Investment in Touch Company Shares.........   3,750

        *Calculations:
        Total book value of net assets of investee at 1/1/02 $9,600,000
        Investor's percentage   30%
        Book value of investor's share of investee's net assets 2,880,000
        Cost of investment   3,240,000
        Excess cost over book value of underlying net assets.   360,000
        Portion attributable to excess fair value over book value
            of net identifiable assets ($700,000 x 30% = $210,000)   (210,000)
        Portion attributable to an unidentifiable asset
            (unrecorded goodwill)   150,000
                                                                                  ÷ 40 years
        Annual amortization of goodwill $ 3,750

        12/5/03   Cash   150,000
                        Investment in Touch Company Shares.........   150,000
                        (30% x $500,000 = $150,000)

12/31/03	Investment in Touch Company Shares..................		600,000	
	Revenue from Investment............................			600,000
	(30% x $2,000,000 = $600,000)			
	Revenue from Investment.......................................		21,000	
	Investment in Touch Company Shares.........			21,000
	(30% x $700,000 = $210,000;			
	$210,000 ÷ 10 years = $21,000)			
12/31/03	Revenue from Investment.......................................		3,750	
	Investment in Touch Company Shares.........			3,750
	(Same calculation for annual amortization			
	of goodwill as for 2002 above)			

Explanation: The equity method is an accrual method of accounting for an investment in shares. A portion of the investee's earnings is recorded as income by the investor in the same time period the investee earns it. Dividends received are recorded as a recovery of investment, not as income. (To record dividends as income would "double count" the amount already recorded as a share of the investee's earnings.)

The excess of the investor's cost over the carrying value of the underlying net assets on the investee's books must be determined and amortized. In this exercise, a portion ($210,000) of that excess is due to the fact that the investee has identifiable assets whose fair values are in excess of their carrying values; this portion should be amortized by the investor over the remaining life of the underlying assets (10 years in this case). The remaining excess cost over book value ($150,000) is attributed to an unidentifiable and unrecorded asset—goodwill. Because there is no indication of an amortization period to be used for goodwill, the maximum period of 40 years is assumed to be appropriate.

(b)   (1) $455,250 for the year ending December 31, 2002.
        (2) $575,250 for the year ending December 31, 2003.

Approach: Post the amounts from the entries in part (a) to a T-account to solve.

Revenue from Investment			
12/31/02	21,000	12/31/02	480,000
12/31/02	3,750		
12/31/02 To close	455,250	12/31/02 Balance	455,250
12/31/03	21,000	12/31/03	600,000
12/31/03	3,750		
		12/31/03 Balance	575,250

(c)   (1) $3,575,250 at December 31, 2002.
        (2) $4,000,500 at December 31, 2003.

Approach: Post the amounts from the entries in part (a) to a T-account to solve.

Investment in Touch Company

1/1/02	3,240,000	12/6/02	120,000
		12/31/02	21,000
12/31/02	480,000	12/31/02	3,750
12/31/02 Balance	3,575,250		
12/31/03	600,000	12/5/03	150,000
		12/31/03	21,000
		12/31/03	3,750
12/31/03 Balance	4,000,500		

EXERCISE 10-9

Purpose: (L.O. 6) This exercise will illustrate the proper accounting for the receipt of stock dividends and stock rights.

At January 1, 2002 Nickolodeon Corporation held the following securities classified as long-term investments. (Neither qualify for use of the equity method.)

	Cost
50,000 shares of Universal Corp.	$ 1,650,000
30,000 shares of Hard Rock Corp.	1,050,000

The following transactions took place during 2002:
1. January 3: Received a cash dividend of $1.00 per share from Universal.
2. May 1: Received a 10% share dividend from Universal.
3. June 5: Sold 10,000 shares of Universal for $35 per share.
4. July 1: Received one share right for every share of Hard Rock shares held. The rights stipulate that four rights and $33 can be used to purchase one new share of common stock. The market value of the shares was $37 per share and the market value of the rights was $1.50 per right at this date.
5. July 19: Sold 10,000 of the share rights received on July 1 for $1.75 per right.
6. July 30: Exercised 18,000 of the share rights received on July 1.
7. October 1: Allowed the remaining 2,000 share rights to elapse.
8. November 1: Sold 5,000 shares of Hard Rock shares for $39 per share.

Instructions
(a) Prepare the journal entries to record each of the transactions listed above.
(b) Determine the investor's book value per share of the shares acquired on July 30, 2002.

Solution to Exercise 10-9

(a)   1.   Cash 50,000
                    Dividend Revenue   50,000
                    (50,000 shares x $1 = $50,000)

2.   Memorandum entry:
Received 5,000 shares of Universal shares in connection with a 10% share dividend. This reduces the carrying value per share from $33 to $30 per share.

$$\frac{\$1,650,000 \text{ total cost}}{55,000 \text{ total shares}} = \$30 \text{ per share}$$

Explanation: If an investor in equity securities receives a **share dividend**, no income is recorded and the carrying amount of the total investment remains unchanged. However, the carrying value per share held is reduced.

3.   Cash (10,000 x $35) 350,000
                    Long-term Investments   300,000
                    Gain on Sale of Shares ($350,000 - $300,000)   50,000

4.   Long-term Investments (Share Rights) 40,908
                    Long-term Investments   40,908

$$\frac{30,000(\$1.50)}{30,000(\$1.50) \ + \ 30,000(\$37)} \text{ x } \$1,050,000 = \text{cost of rights}$$

$$\frac{\$45,000}{\$45,000 \ + \ \$1,110,000} \text{ x } \$1,050,000 =$$

3.896% x $1,050,000 = $40,908

$40,908 ÷ 30,000 rights = $1.3636 cost per right

Explanation: When an investor receives **share rights** for no consideration, the cost of the investment in share must be allocated to the rights and to the share based on the relative market values of the securities involved. The following formula can be used:

$$\frac{\text{Market Value of Rights}}{\begin{array}{c}\text{Market Value of Rights} + \\ \text{Market Value of Stock Ex - Rights}\end{array}} \text{ x } \begin{array}{c}\text{Total} \\ \text{Cost}\end{array} = \begin{array}{c}\text{Amount to} \\ \text{Allocate to Rights}\end{array}$$

5.   Cash (10,000 x $1.75) 17,500
                    Long-term Investments (Share Rights)   13,636
                    (10,000 x $1.3636)
                    Gain on Sale of Share Rights   3,864
                    ($17,500 - $13,636)
6.   Long-term Investments 173,045

Long-term Investments (Share Rights)....................	24,545	
(18,000 x $1.3636)		
Cash		148,500*

*18,000 ÷ 4 = 4,500 shares;
4,500 shares x $33 exercise price = $148,500

7.   Loss on Expiration of Share Rights 2,727
         Long-term Investments (Share Rights)..................... 2,727
         ($40,908 - $13,636 - $24,545 = $2,727)
         (or 2,000 x $1.3636 = $2,727)

8.   Cash (5,000 x $39).. 195,000
         Long-term Investments 168,182*
         Gain on Sale of Shares ($195,000 - $168,182)........ 26,818

*Initial cost of 30,000 shares	$ 1,050,000
Amount of cost allocated to share rights	(40,908)
Amount of cost allocated to 30,000 shares	1,009,092
Number of shares in first lot	÷ 30,000
Cost per share held in first lot	33.6364
Shares sold	x 5,000
Cost of shares sold	$ 168,182

(b)   Transaction 6: $173,045 cost ÷ 4,500 shares = <u>$38.4544</u> per share.

ANALYSIS OF MULTIPLE-CHOICE TYPE QUESTIONS

QUESTION

1. (L.O. 3) An investor purchased bonds with a face amount of $100,000 between interest payment dates. The investor purchased the bonds at 102, paid incidental costs of $1,500, and paid accrued interest for three months of $2,500. The amount to record as the cost of this long-term investment in bonds is:
    a. $100,000
    b. $102,000
    c. $103,500
    d. $106,000

Explanation: The cost is determined as follows:

Purchase price (102% x $100,000 par)	$ 102,000
Incidental costs to acquire	1,500
Total acquisition cost of investment	$ 103,500

The cost of an investment includes its purchase price and all incidental costs to acquire the item, such as brokerage commissions and taxes. Any accrued interest is to be recorded by a debit to Interest Receivable or by a debit to Interest Revenue; it is **not** an element of the investment's cost. Accrued interest increases the cash outlay to acquire an investment but does not increase the investment's cost. (Solution = c.)

QUESTION

2. (L.O. 3) Refer to the facts in **Question 1** above. The amount of cash outlay required to acquire the investment is:
    a. $100,000
    b. $102,000
    c. $103,500
    d. $106,000

Explanation: The amount of cash required to acquire the investment is determined as follows:

Purchase price (102% x $100,000 par)	$ 102,000
Incidental costs to acquire	1,500
Total acquisition cost of investment	103,500
Accrued interest for three months	2,500
Total cash required to acquire investment	$ 106,000

(Solution = d.)

QUESTION

3.   (L.O. 3) When an investor's accounting period ends on a date that does not coincide with an interest receipt date for bonds held as an investment, the investor must:

a.   Make an adjusting entry to debit Interest Receivable and to credit Interest Revenue for the amount of interest accrued since the last interest receipt date.

b.   Notify the issuer and request that a special payment be made for the appropriate portion of the interest period.

c.   Make an adjusting entry to debit Interest Receivable and to credit Interest Revenue for the total amount of interest to be received at the next interest receipt date.

d.   Do nothing special and ignore the fact that the accounting period does not coincide with the bond's interest period.

Approach: Think of the requirements of the accrual basis of accounting: revenues are to be recognized when they are earned and expenses are to be recognized (recorded and reported) when they are incurred. Interest is earned by the passage of time and is usually collected after the time period for which it pertains. Thus, to comply with the revenue recognition principle, an adjusting entry is necessary to record the accrued revenue (revenue earned but not yet received). (Solution = a.)

QUESTION

4.   (L.O. 1) The market value of Security A exceeds its cost, and the market value of Security B is less than its cost at a balance sheet date. Both securities are held as temporary investments in securities. How should each of these assets be reported on the balance sheet?

	Security A	**Security B**
a.	Market value	Market value
b.	Cost	Cost
c.	Cost	Market value
d.	Market value	Cost

Approach and Explanation: Mentally review the accounting requirements for temporary investments. Temporary investments utilize the lower-of-cost-and-market rule, thus Security A is above the market price and should be recorded at cost, while Security B is below the cost, and should be readjusted to the market value. (Solution =c.)

QUESTION

5.   (L.O. 2) ABC Entertainment holds four equity securities at December 31, 2002. They are all classified as long-term investments. All securities were purchased in 2002. The portfolio of securities appears as follows at December 31, 2002:

	Cost	Market Value	Difference
McKinnet Corp.	$100,000	$ 80,000	$(20,000)
Hip Corp.	220,000	230,000	10,000
Big Sea Corp.	210,000	150,000	(60,000)
Adams Corp.	140,000	145,000	5,000
Totals	$670,000	$605,000	$(65,000)

Assuming the decline in the market value of Big Sea Corp. shares is considered to be other than temporary, using the portfolio method, the amount of the loss to be realized would be:

Realized Loss
a. $60,000
b. $20,000
c. $65,000
d. $0

Explanation: A decline in fair value that is other than temporary is referred to as an **impairment**. The amount of the writedown is accounted for as a realized loss and, therefore, included in net income. The individual gains or losses are irrelevant when using the portfolio method—only the total market value is compared to the total cost of the investments, hence, unrealized gains are also recognized in this method. (Solution = c.)

QUESTION
6.   (L.O. 2) During 2001, Colquitt Company purchased 4,000 shares of Welshner Corp. common shares for $63,000 as a short-term investment. The fair value of these shares was $60,000 at December 31, 2001. Colquitt sold all of the Welshner shares for $17 per share on December 3, 2002, incurring $2,800 in brokerage commissions. Colquitt Company should report a realized gain on the sale of shares in 2002 of:
    a. $8,000
    b. $5,200
    c. $5,000
    d. $2,200

Explanation: The gain is calculated as follows:

Selling price ($17 x 4,000 shares)	$ 68,000
Cost of sale—commissions	(2,800)
Net proceeds (or net selling price)	65,200
Cost	63,000
Realized gain on sale	$ 2,200 (Solution = d.)

TIP: The valuation account balance existing at the end of 1998 would have no effect on this calculation.

QUESTION
7.   (L.O. 2) On its December 31, 2001 balance sheet, Simpson Company appropriately reported a $4,000 credit balance in its investment allowance account. There was no change during 2002 in the composition of Simpson's portfolio of marketable equity securities. The following information pertains to that portfolio:

Security	Cost	Fair value at	
		12/31/01	**12/31/02**
A	$ 50,000	$58,000	$65,000
B	40,000	39,000	38,000
C	70,000	67,000	50,000
	$160,000	$164,000	$153,000

What amount should be written off against the allowance account in the current year using the individual method?
a. $11,000
b. $22,000
c. $18,000
d. $7,000

Explanation: In 2001, the allowance account showed a balance of $4,000 correctly. During the current period security B fell an additional $1,000 below the previous cost and Security C fell an additional $17,000.

Value of Allowance Account (total)	$22,000
Amount already recorded in Allowance Account	4,000
Necessary adjustment in current year	$18,000. (Solution = c.)

QUESTION
8.   (L.O. 4) An investor has a long-term investment in shares. Regular cash dividends received by the investor are recorded as:

	Cost Method	**Equity Method**
a.	Income	Income
b.	A reduction of the investment	A reduction of the investment
c.	Income	A reduction of the investment
d.	A reduction of the investment	Income

Approach and Explanation: Write down the journal entry to record the receipt of cash dividends (other than liquidating dividends) under both the cost and equity methods. Observe the effects of the entries. Find the answer selection that correctly describes those effects.

Fair Value Method		**Equity Method**	
Cash	XX	Cash	XX
Dividend Revenue	XX	Investment in Investee Shares	XX
			(Solution = c.)

QUESTION
9.   (L.O. 4) The Higgins Corporation purchased 6,000 shares of common shares of the Barnett Corporation for $40 per share on January 2, 2002. The Barnett Corporation had 60,000 common shares outstanding during 2002, paid cash dividends of $30,000 during 2002, and reported net income of $120,000 for 2002. The Higgins Corporation should report revenue from investment for 2002 in the amount of:
a. $3,000
b. $9,000
c. $12,000
d. $15,000

Explanation: Because the Higgins Corporation owns only 10% of the outstanding common shares of the investee, it is assumed that Higgins Corporation cannot exercise significant influence over the financing and operating policies of the investee and must therefore use the cost method to account for the investment. Using the cost method, the investor will report dividend revenue equal to the amount of cash dividends received during the period. ($30,000 x 10% = $3,000). (Solution = a.)

QUESTION
10.   (L.O. 4) When the equity method is used to account for an investment in common shares of another corporation, the journal entry on the investor's books to record the receipt of cash dividends from the investee will:
       a.   include a debit to Cash and a credit to Dividend Revenue.
       b.   reduce the carrying value of the investment.
       c.   increase the carrying value of the investment.
       d.   be the same journal entry that would be recorded if the cost method were used to account for the investment.

Explanation: The journal entry will be a debit to Cash and a credit to Investment in Shares. The credit portion of this entry reduces the balance of the investment account and, therefore, it reduces the carrying value of the investment. (Solution = b.)

QUESTION
11.   (L.O. 6) A share dividend received by an investor is accounted for by:
       a.   crediting the income statement for the market value of the shares received in the dividend.
       b.   crediting the income statement for the par value of the shares received in the dividend.
       c.   crediting the investment account for the market value of the shares received.
       d.   allocating the cost of the original shares to the original investment shares plus the dividend shares.

Explanation: Shares received as a result of a share dividend or share split do not constitute revenue to the recipients, because their interest in the issuing corporation is unchanged and because the issuing corporation has not distributed any of its assets. The recipient of such additional shares requires no formal entry. The cost of the original shares purchased now constitutes the total carrying amount of both those shares plus the additional shares received. (Solution = d.)

QUESTION
12.   (L.O. 6) Zion Company pays an insurance premium of $4,000 on a $100,000 policy covering the life of the company's president, of which Zion is the beneficiary. As a result, the cash surrender value of the policy increases from $16,000 to $16,500 during the period. Which of the following is true regarding the effects of the journal entry to record the premium payment?
              I. Cash is reduced by $4,000.
              II. Assets are reduced by $3,500.

III. Shareholders' equity is reduced by $3,500.
IV. Net income is reduced by $4,000.
a. items I and IV only
b. items I, II and III only
c. items I, II, and IV only
d. items I, II, III, and IV
e. none of the above

Approach and Explanation: Prepare the journal entry to record the premium payment:

Life Insurance Expense	3,500	
Cash Surrender Value of Life Insurance	500	
Cash		4,000

Analyse the effects of each item in the entry. Expense is increased by $3,500, which reduces net income by $3,500 and, thus, causes a decrease in retained earnings (a component of shareholders' equity). The cash surrender value of life insurance is increased by $500; this item ($16,500) is reported as a long-term investment on the balance sheet. (In practice, some companies report it as an other asset.) Cash (a current asset) is reduced by $4,000. Because one asset increases by $500, and another decreases by $4,000, there is a net decrease in assets of $3,500. (Solution = b.)

QUESTION
13. (L.O. 6) A bond sinking fund is a(n):
a. investment in bonds issued by another entity.
b. savings account that is used to accumulate funds to repay bondholders when the related bonds payable mature.
c. account used to accumulate funds to be used to purchase bonds issued by other entities.
d. mutual fund for debt instruments.

Explanation: A sinking fund is cash or other assets set aside to retire debt. It is like a savings account that is used to accumulate the funds necessary to pay back bondholders when a corporation's bonds payable mature. A sinking fund makes bonds more attractive to investors because it enhances the likelihood that the bonds will be redeemed at maturity. The bond sinking fund is reported in the investment section of the balance sheet. (Solution = b.)

CHAPTER 11

ACQUISITION AND DISPOSITION OF TANGIBLE CAPITAL ASSETS

OVERVIEW

Assets that have physical existence and that are expected to be used in revenue-generating operations for more than one year or operating cycle, whichever is longer, are classified as long-term tangible assets. Some problems may arise in determining the acquisition cost of a fixed asset, such as: the initial acquisition may be the result of several expenditures, one fixed asset may be exchanged for another fixed asset, a plant asset may be obtained on a deferred payment plan, a plant asset may be constructed internally by the company, or additional expenditures may be involved subsequent to acquisition. These and other issues, and their related accounting procedures are examined in this chapter.

SUMMARY OF LEARNING OBJECTIVES

1. **Describe the major characteristics of tangible capital assets.** The major characteristics of tangible capital assets are: (1) They are acquired for use in operations and not for resale, (2) they are long-term in nature and usually subject to amortization, and (3) they possess physical substance.

2. **Identify the costs included in the initial valuation of land, buildings, and equipment.**
   Cost of land: Includes all expenditures made to acquire land and to ready it for use. Land costs typically include (1) the purchase price; (2) closing costs, such as title to the land, legal fees, and registration fees; (3) costs incurred to condition the land for its intended use, such as grading, filling, draining, and clearing; (4) assumption of any liens, mortgages or encumbrances on the property; (5) any additional land improvements that have an indefinite life.
   Cost of buildings: Includes all expenditures related directly to their acquisition or construction. These costs include (1) materials, labour and overhead costs incurred during construction and (2) professional fees and building permits.
   Cost of equipment: Includes the purchase price, freight and handling charges incurred, insurance on the equipment while in transit, cost of special foundations if required, assembling and installation costs, and costs of conducting trial runs.

3. **Describe the accounting problems associated with self-constructed assets.** The assignment of indirect costs of manufacturing creates special problems because these costs cannot be traced directly to work and material orders related to the fixed assets constructed. These costs might be handled in one of three ways: (1) assign no fixed overhead to the cost of the constructed asset, (2) assign a portion of all overhead to the construction process, or (3) allocate on the basis of lost production. The second method is used extensively in practice.

4. **Describe the accounting problems associated with interest capitalization.** Companies may choose whether to expense or capitalize interest during construction of tangible capital assets. However, only actual interest (with modifications) may be capitalized. The rationale for capitalization is that during construction, interest incurred is a cost necessary to acquire the asset, put it in place, and ready for use. Once construction is completed, the asset is ready for its intended use. Also, if the asset had been purchased fully constructed, the manufacturer's costs, such as interest, would make up a part of the costs recovered in the selling price to the buyer.

Any interest cost incurred in purchasing an asset that is ready for its intended use should be expensed.

5. **Understand accounting issues related to acquiring and valuing plant assets.** The following issues relate to acquiring and valuing plant assets: (1) *Cash discounts:* Whether taken or not, they are generally considered a reduction in the asset's cost; it's real cost is the cash or cash equivalent price of the asset. (2) *Assets purchased on long-term credit contracts:* Account for these at the present value of the consideration exchanged between the contracting parties. (3) *Lump sum or basket purchase:* Allocate the total cost among the various assets on the basis of their relative fair market values. (4) *Issuance of shares:* If the shares are being actively traded, the issued shares market value is a fair indication of the acquired property's cost. If the exchanged shares' market value is not determinable, the acquired property's fair value should be determined and used as the basis for recording the assets' cost and amount credited to the common shares. (5) *Nonmonetary Exchanges:* When assets are acquired with little or no cash or other monetary assets as part of the consideration, the new asset's cost depends on whether the assets exchanged are similar or dissimilar. If the assets are similar, it is assumed that the earnings process has not been completed, so no gain can be recognized on the disposal of the asset given up. The acquired asset's cost in this case is the carrying amount of the asset(s) given up. If the assets exchanged are not similar, the earnings process is considered completed and a gain or loss on disposal can be recognized. In this case, the acquired asset's cost is recognized as the fair value of the assets given up or those acquired, if clearer. (6) *Exchanges with a significant monetary component:* The cost of the asset acquired is determined by the fair value of the consideration given up, or the fair value of the asset acquired, if clearer, with the resulting gain or loss recognized in income. (7) *Contributions:* Contributed assets, other than from shareholders, should be recorded at the received asset's fair value with a related credit that will be taken to income over the same period as the asset contributed is used. (8) *Investment tax credits:* An immediate tax reduction benefit should be accounted for in the same manner as a government contribution.

6. **Describe the accounting treatment for costs incurred subsequent to acquisition.** The accounting treatment of costs incurred subsequent to acquisition depends on whether the cost is a capital expenditure or a revenue expenditure. In general, a capital expenditure—one that results in an increase in the asset's useful life, or in the efficiency of the output obtained from that asset— is charged to the asset account. A revenue expenditure, one that does not increase the asset's future benefits, should be expensed immediately. The specific accounting treatment depends on the circumstances. See **Illustration 10-2** for a summary of how to account for costs subsequent to acquisition.

7. **Describe the accounting treatment for the disposal of property, plant and equipment.** Regardless of the time of disposal, amortization must be taken up to the date of disposition, and then all accounts related to the retired asset should be removed. Gains or losses on the retirement of plant assets should be shown in the income statement along with other items that arise from customary business activities. Gains or losses on involuntary conversions may meet the definition of an extraordinary item. If an asset is scrapped or abandoned without any cash recovery, a loss should be recognized equal to the asset's carrying amount or book value. If scrap value exists, the gain or loss recognized is the difference between the asset's scrap value and its book value. If a tangible capital asset is donated to an organization outside the reporting entity, the donation should be reported at its fair value with a gain or loss reported.

8.* **Calculate the amount of capitalizable interest on projects involving expenditures over a period of time and borrowings from different sources at varying rates.** The amount of interest capitalized must be disclosed in the notes to the financial statements. The amount capitalized is usually based on the amount of avoidable interest during the constructional period.

   * This material is covered in Appendix-11A in the text.

TIPS ON CHAPTER TOPICS

TIP: **Tangible Capital Assets** are also referred to as **property plant and equipment**, **fixed assets** or **plant assets**. Included in this section should be long-lived tangible assets that are currently being used in operations to generate goods and services for customers. Two exceptions to this guideline are: (1) Construction of Plant in Process, and (2) Deposits on Machinery. In each of these cases, the asset is not yet being used in operations but an expenditure has been made which is to be classified in the property, plant, and equipment section of the balance sheet. Idle fixed assets are to be classified as other assets and plant assets no longer used and held for sale are to be classified either as current assets or other assets, depending on whether they are expected to be sold within the next year or not.

TIP: In determining the cost of a plant asset, keep in mind the same guideline we had for inventory. The cost includes all costs necessary to get the item to the location and condition for its intended use.

TIP: In the past, amortization of capital tangible assets was called depreciation, and amortization referred to intangible assets.

TIP: After the acquisition, additions, improvements and replacements, which add to the assets future service potential are capitalized.

TIP: In determining the cost of a plant asset, keep in mind the historical cost principle. **Cost** is measured by the cash or the fair market value of the noncash consideration given or the fair market value of the consideration received, whichever is the more clearly evident. Fair market value refers to cash equivalent value. When cash is given to acquire an asset, it is a relatively simple matter to determine the asset's cost. However, when a noncash asset is given in exchange or when a deferred payment plan is involved, more thought is required to determine the asset's cost. Pay close attention to these areas as they are often the subjects from which discriminating exam questions are derived.

TIP: The potential amount of interest to capitalize is the lesser of the actual amount of interest paid and the amount determined by multiplying the weighted-average accumulated expenditures by the weighted average interest rate.

TIP: When one noncash asset is exchanged for another noncash asset, it is important to determine if it is a dissimilar or similar asset exchange. If it is a **similar** asset exchange, the gain (if any) is to be deferred because the earning process did not culminate with the exchange. If the exchange is for **dissimilar** assets (assets that do not perform the same function), companies can recognize gains or losses on the exchange. If the exchange involves "boot" cash in excess of 10% of the fair market value of the consideration given or received, it is **not** considered a nonmonetary transaction and gains and losses should be recognized.

TIP: When a deferred payment plan is involved in the acquisition of a noncash asset, pay careful attention to whether a fair rate of interest is stated in the agreement. When an unreasonably low stated interest rate is present, interest must be imputed so that the effective amount of interest reported reflects the market rate of interest.

TIP: In the context of accounting for property, plant, and equipment, the term "capitalize" means to record and carry forward into one or more periods expenditures from which benefits or proceeds will be realized; thus, a balance sheet account is debited.

TIP: In accounting for the many expenditures related to the operation and maintenance of property, plant, and equipment, the accountant must keep in mind that expenditures benefiting the company for more than the current accounting period should be capitalized in order to properly match expenses with revenues over successive accounting periods; expenditures for items that do not yield benefits beyond the current accounting period should be expensed.

TIP: In the context of the topic of tangible capital assets, the term **carrying value** refers to the amount derived by deducting the balance in the Accumulated Amortization account from the balance in the related asset account. Synonymous terms are: **book value**, net asset value, unamortized value, and **carrying amount**. Book value may be very different from fair value. Fair value is often referred to as fair market value or market value. The calculation of book value is **not** affected by the estimated residual value or salvage value.

TIP: The net cost (cost less scrap proceeds) of tearing down an old building should be charged (debited) to the Land account if the building was someone else's old building and recently acquired along with the land as a site to be used for another structure. (The cost is charged to Land because it was necessary to get the land in the condition for its intended purpose—to provide space upon which to erect a new building.)

TIP: There are several areas in accounting that utilize the formula to allocate a single sum between two or more items based on the relative fair market values of the items involved. That formula is as follow:

$$\frac{\text{Market Value of One Item in Group}}{\text{Market Value of All Items in Group}} \times \frac{\text{Amount to be}}{\text{Allocated}} = \frac{\text{Amount to be Assigned to Item Designated in the Numerator}}{}$$

This formula is used in Chapter 11 to allocate one lump-sum amount of cost to the individual assets acquired in a **lump sum purchase** (often called a **basket purchase**). The formula will also be used to allocate the proceeds from the issuance of several classes of securities, to allocate the proceeds from the issuance of bonds with detachable warrants, to allocate the cost of certain inventory items to units based on their relative sales values, and to allocate the cost of an investment. The formula is also useful in the managerial accounting arena such as in the case where there are joint costs to be allocated to joint products.

TIP: An investment tax credit received should be treated as either a reduction in the cost of the qualified property (similar to a purchase discount) and accounted for over the same period as the related asset (cost reduction or deferral method), recommended by the Accounting Standards Board, or using the flow through method (take the full benefit of the ITC in the purchase year).

CASE 11-1

Purpose: (L.O. 2, 6) This case will review the costs to be capitalized for property, plant, and equipment.

Property, plant, and equipment generally represents a large portion of the total assets of a company. Accounting for the acquisition and usage of such assets is, therefore, an important part of the financial reporting process.

Instructions

(a) Distinguish between a revenue expenditure and a capital expenditure. Explain why its distinction is important.

(b) Identify at least six costs that should be capitalized as the cost of land. Assume that land with an existing building is acquired for cash and that the existing building is to be removed immediately in order to provide space for a new building on that site.

(c) Identify at least five costs that should be capitalized as the cost of a building.

(d) Identify at least six costs that should be capitalized when equipment is acquired for cash.

(e) Describe the factors that determine whether expenditures relating to property, plant, and equipment already in use should be capitalized.

(AICPA Adapted)

Solution to Case 11-1

(a) A **capital expenditure** is expected to yield benefits either in all future accounting periods (acquisition of land) or in a limited number of accounting periods (acquisition of buildings and equipment). Capital expenditures are capitalized, that is, recorded as assets, and, if related to assets of limited life, amortized over the periods which will be benefited. A **revenue expenditure** is an expenditure for which the benefits are **not** expected to extend beyond the current period. Hence, they benefit only the current period (recorded as an expense) or they benefit no period at all (recorded as a loss).

The distinction between capital and revenue expenditures is of significance because it involves the timing of the recognition of expense and, consequently, the determination of periodic earnings. This distinction also affects the costs reflected in the asset accounts which will be recovered from future periods' revenues.

If a revenue expenditure is improperly capitalized, net income of the current period is overstated, assets are overstated, and future earnings are understated for all the periods to which the improperly capitalized cost is amortized. If the cost is not amortized, future earnings will not be affected, but assets and retained earnings will continue to be overstated for as long as the cost remains on the books. If a nonamortizable capital expenditure is improperly expensed, current earnings are understated and assets and retained earnings are understated for all foreseeable periods in the future. If an amortizable capital expenditure is improperly expensed, net income of the current period is understated, assets and retained earnings are understated, and net income is overstated for all future periods to which the cost should have been amortized.

(b)   The cost of land may include:
   (1)   purchase price.
   (2)   survey fees.
   (3)   title search fees.
   (4)   escrow fees.
   (5)   delinquent property taxes assumed by buyer.
   (6)   broker's commission.
   (7)   legal fees.
   (8)   recording fee.
   (9)   unpaid interest assumed by buyer.
  (10)   cost of clearing, grading, landscaping, and subdividing (less salvage).
  (11)   cost of removing old building (less salvage).
  (12)   special assessments such as lighting or sewers if they are permanent in nature.
  (13)   landscaping of permanent nature.
  (14)   any other cost necessary to acquire the land and get it in the condition necessary for its intended purpose.

> **TIP:**   Typically, the cost of land includes the cost of elements that occur prior to excavation for a new building. Costs related to the foundation of the building are elements of building cost.

(c)   The cost of a building may include:
   (1)   purchase price or construction costs (including an allocation of overhead if self-constructed).
   (2)   excavation fees.
   (3)   architectural fees.
   (4)   building permit fee.
   (5)   cost of insurance during construction (if paid by property owner).
   (6)   property taxes during construction.
   (7)   interest during construction (only interest actually incurred).
   (8)   cost of temporary buildings.
   (9)   any other cost necessary to acquire the building and get it in the location and condition for its intended purpose.

(d)   The cost of equipment may include:
   (1)   purchase price (less discounts allowed).
   (2)   sales tax.
   (3)   installation charges.
   (4)   freight charges during transit.
   (5)   insurance during transit.
   (6)   cost of labour and materials for test runs.
   (7)   cost of special platforms.
   (8)   ownership search.
   (9)   ownership registration.
  (10)   breaking-in costs.
  (11)   other costs necessary to acquire the equipment and get it to the location and condition for its intended use.

(e)   The factors that determine whether expenditures relating to property, plant, and equipment already in use should be capitalized are as follows:
   (1)   Expenditures are material.
   (2)   They are nonrecurring in nature.
   (3)   They benefit future periods in some way such as by doing one of the following:
      a.   They extend the useful life of a plant asset.
      b.   They enhance the quality of existing services.
      c.   They add new asset services.
      d.   They reduce future operating costs of existing assets.
      e.   They are required to meet environmental concerns and regulations.
      f.   The quantity of units produced from the asset is increased.

Approach:
1.   Scan all requirements before you begin on the first question. Sometimes the latter requirements will help you to see more clearly what is really being requested in the earlier requirements. Sometimes the solution to one requirement appears to overlap with the solution to another part of the question.
2.   Prepare a key word outline before you begin writing detailed answers. This outline should very briefly list the concepts you want to cover in your paragraph(s). This outline will help you to organize your thoughts before you begin writing sentences.

EXERCISE 11-1

Purpose: (L.O. 2, 6) This exercise will help you identify which expenditures related to property, plant, and equipment should be capitalized and which should be expensed.

TIP: Remember that expenditures which benefit the company for more than the current accounting period should be capitalized in order to properly match expenses with revenues over successive accounting periods. Expenditures for items that do not yield benefits beyond the current accounting period should be expensed.

Instructions
Assume all amounts are material. For each of the following independent items, indicate by use of the appropriate letter if it should be:

                C = Capitalized   or   E = Expensed

_____   1.   Invoice price of drill press.

_____   2.   Sales tax on computer.

_____   3.   Costs of permanent partitions constructed in an existing office building.

_____   4.   Installation charges for new conveyer system.

_____   5.   Costs of trees and shrubs planted in front of office building.

_____   6.   Costs of surveying new land site.

_____   7.   Costs of major overhaul of delivery truck.

_____ 8. Costs of building new counters for show room.

_____ 9. Costs of powders, soaps, and wax for office floors.

_____ 10. Cost of janitorial services for office and show room.

_____ 11. Costs of carpets in a new office building.

_____ 12. Costs of annual termite inspection of warehouse.

_____ 13. Insurance charged for new equipment while in transit.

_____ 14. Property taxes on land used for parking lot.

_____ 15. Cost of a fan installed to help cool old factory machine.

_____ 16. Cost of exterminator's services.

_____ 17. Costs of major redecorating of executives' offices.

_____ 18. Cost of fertilizers for shrubs and trees.

_____ 19. Cost of labour services for self-constructed machine.

_____ 20. Costs of materials used and labour services expended during trial runs of new machine.

Solution to Exercise 11-1

1.	C	6.	C	11.	C	16.	E
2.	C	7.	C	12.	E	17.	C
3.	C	8.	C	13.	C	18.	E*
4.	C	9.	E*	14.	E	19.	C
5.	C	10.	E	15.	C	20.	C

*This answer assumes the products were consumed during the current period. Material amounts of unused supplies on hand at the balance sheet date should be reported as a prepaid expense (supplies inventory).

TIP: As used in this chapter, the term **capital expenditure** refers to an expenditure, which is expected to benefit more than one period; hence, it is initially recorded as an asset and should be expensed over the periods benefited. A **revenue expenditure** is an expenditure which is expected **not** to be of benefit to any period beyond the current period; hence, it is recorded by a debit to either an expense account or to a loss account in the period incurred.

EXERCISE 11-2

Purpose: (L.O. 2) This exercise will give you practice in identifying capital versus revenue expenditures.

Hughes Supply Company, a newly formed corporation, incurred the following expenditures related to Land, to Buildings, and to Machinery and Equipment.

Cash paid for land and dilapidated building thereon		$ 300,000
Removal of old building	$ 60,000	
Less salvage	16,500	43,500
Surveying before construction to determine best position for building		1,110
Interest on short-term loans during construction		22,200
Excavation before construction for basement		57,000
Fee for title search charged by abstract company		1,560
Architect's fees		8,400
Machinery purchased (subject to 2% cash discount, which was not taken)		165,000
Freight on machinery purchased		4,020
Storage charges on machinery, necessitated by noncompletion of building when machinery was delivered on schedule		6,540
New building constructed (building construction took 8 months from date of purchase of land and old building)		1,500,000
Assessment by city for sewers (a one-time assessment)		4,800
Transportation charges for delivery of machinery from storage to new building		1,860
Installation of machinery		6,000
Trees, shrubs, and other landscaping after completion of building (permanent in nature)		16,200

Instructions
(a)   Identify the amounts that should be debited to Land.
(b)   Identify the amounts that should be debited to Buildings.
(c)   Identify the amounts that should be debited to Machinery and Equipment.
(d)   Indicate how the costs above **not** debited to Land, Buildings, or Machinery and Equipment should be recorded.

Solution to Exercise 11-2

	(a) Land	(b) Bldgs.	(c) M&E	(d) Other
Cash paid for land & old bldg.	$300,000			
Removal of old building ($60,000 - $16,500)	43,500			
Surveying before construction		$ 1,110		
Interest on loans during construction		22,200		
Excavation before construction		57,000		
Abstract fees for title search	1,560			
Architect's fees		8,400		
Machinery purchased			$161,700	$ 3,300 Misc. Exp. (Int. Exp.)
Freight on machinery			4,020	
Storage charges caused by noncompletion of building				6,540 Misc. Exp. (Loss)
New building construction		1,500,000		
Assessment by city	4,800			
Transportation charges— machinery				1,860 Misc. Exp. (Loss)
Installation—machinery			6,000	
Landscaping	16,200			
Totals	$366,060	$1,588,710	$171,720	$11,700

> **TIP:** The purchase price of the machine is the **cash equivalent price** at the date of acquisition which is the $165,000 reduced by the 2% cash discount allowed ($3,300), whether or not the discount is taken. The additional outlay of $3,300 is due to extending the time for payment which is equivalent to interest (time value of money). The cost of the machine does **not** include the $6,540 storage charges and $1,860 transportation charges out of storage because these costs were not planned costs necessary to get the equipment to the location intended for use; rather they were caused by the lack of completing the building on schedule (hence, a loss or miscellaneous expense).

CASE 11-2

Purpose: (L.O. 5) This case will review the rules for determining a plant asset's cost when the asset is acquired on a deferred payment plan or in a nonmonetary exchange.

A company often acquires property, plant, and equipment by means other than immediate cash payment.

Instructions
(a) Explain how to determine a plant asset's cost if it is acquired on a deferred payment plan.
(b) Explain how to determine a plant asset's cost if it is acquired in exchange for a dissimilar nonmonetary asset.
(c) Explain how to determine a machine's cost if it is acquired in exchange for a similar machine and a small cash payment is also made.
(d) Explain how to determine a machine's cost if it is acquired in exchange for a similar machine and a large (greater than 10% of the fair market consideration) amount of cash is made.

Solution to Case 11-2

(a) A plant asset acquired on a deferred-payment plan should be recorded at an equivalent cash price excluding interest. If a fair rate of interest is not stated in the sales contract, an imputed interest rate should be determined. The asset should then be recorded at the contract's present value, which is calculated by discounting the payments at the stated or imputed interest rate. The interest portion (stated or imputed) of the contract price should be charged to interest expense over the life of the contract.

(b) A plant asset acquired in exchange for a dissimilar nonmonetary asset should be recorded at the fair value (cash equivalent value) of the consideration given up or the fair value of the consideration received, whichever is more clearly evident. This is an application of the historical cost principle. Any gain or loss on the exchange should be recognized because the earning process is considered complete on the old asset and the earnings process is commencing on the new asset.

(c) When exchanging an old machine and paying cash for a new machine, the new machine should be recorded at the amount of monetary consideration (cash) paid plus the unamortized cost of the nonmonetary asset (old machine) surrendered. This would reduce the recorded amount of the new machine. An experienced loss is indicated when the old asset's market value is less than its carrying value at the date of exchange; a gain is indicated if the asset's market value exceeds its carrying value, however neither should be recognized.

> **TIP:** When cash is paid in an exchange of similar assets and the market value of the asset to be exchanged is less/greater than the book value of the asset given up, a loss/gain occurs, however there is a departure from the historical cost principle in determining the cost of the new asset and the loss/gain is **not** recognized. The gain/loss is deferred because the earning process has not been culminated. The text indicates that if the market value of the asset acquired is less than the book value of the asset given up in the exchange, a loss should be recognized. This is, in fact, a culmination of two entries:
> **a.** a similar exchange in which no gain/loss is recognized, followed by,
> **b.** an impairment in the value of the asset acquired involving a write-off to market value.

(d) When the monetary component of the exchange exceeds 10% of the fair market value of the consideration given up or received, (irregardless of whether the exchange is for similar or dissimilar assets), the transaction is **not** considered a nonmonetary exchange. In this situation, the general standard of cost is applied and a resulting gain or loss is recognized in the period.

EXERCISE 11-3

Purpose: (L.O. 4) This exercise will provide an example of the capitalization of interest cost incurred during construction.

Marvel Company engaged Invention Company to construct a special purpose machine to be used in its factory. The following data pertain:

1.   The contract was signed by Marvel on August 30, 2002. Construction was begun immediately and was completed on December 1, 2002.
2.   To aid in the financing of this construction, Marvel borrowed $600,000 from Bank of X-Men on August 30, 2002 by signing a $600,000 note due in 3 years. The note bears an interest rate of 12% and interest is payable each August 30.
3.   Marvel paid Invention $200,000 on August 30, 2002, and invested the remainder of the note's proceeds ($400,000) in 5% government securities until December 1.
4.   On December 1, Marvel made the final $400,000 payment to Invention.
5.   Aside from the note payable to the Bank of X-Men, Marvel's only outstanding liability at December 31, 2002 is a $60,000, 9%, 5-year note payable dated January 1, 1999, on which interest is payable each December 31.

Instructions

(a)   Calculate the weighted-average accumulated expenditures, interest revenue, avoidable interest, total interest incurred, and interest cost to be capitalized during 2002. Round all calculations to the nearest dollar.

(b)   Prepare the journal entries needed on the books of Marvel Company at each of the following dates: August 30, 2002; December 1, 2002; and December 31, 2002.

Solution to Exercise 11-3

(a)   **Calculation of Weighted-Average Accumulated Expenditures:**

Expenditures			Capitalization		Weighted-Average	
Date	Amount	x	Period	=	Accumulated Expenditures	
August 30	$200,000		3/12		$50,000	
December 1	400,000		0		0	
					$50,000	

Interest Revenue: $400,000 x 5% x 3/12 = $5,000

Avoidable Interest: Weighted-Average
           Accumulated Expenditures x Interest Rate = Avoidable Interest
                     $50,000   12% $6,000

Total Interest Incurred: $600,000 x 12% x 4/12   = $ 24,000
                 $60,000 x 9%   =   5,400
                                               $ 29,400

Interest to be capitalized: $6,000 (lesser of avoidable interest and total interest incurred)

(b) 8/30

Cash	600,000	
Notes Payable		600,000
Machine..	200,000	
Short-term Investments	400,000	
Cash.		600,000

12/1

Cash.	405,000	
Interest Revenue		
($400,000 x 5% x 3/12)...........................		5,000
Short-term Investments		400,000
Machine..	400,000	
Cash.		400,000

12/31

Machine [calculated in part (a)]	6,000	
Interest Expense ($29,400 - $6,000).....................	23,400	
Cash ($60,000 x 9%).....................................		5,400
Interest Payable		
($600,000 x 12% x 4/12)...........................		24,000

Explanation: Paragraphs 6 and 7 of *SFAS No. 34* state:

> "The historical cost of acquiring an asset includes the costs necessarily incurred to bring it to the condition and location for its intended use. If an asset requires a period of time in which to carry out the activities necessary to bring it to that condition and location, the interest cost incurred during that period as a result of expenditures for the asset is a part of the historical cost of acquiring the asset. The objectives of capitalizing interest are (a) to obtain a measure of acquisition cost that more closely reflects the enterprise's total investment in the asset and (b) to charge a cost that relates to the acquisition of a resource that will benefit future periods against the revenues of the periods benefited."

Examples of assets that qualify for interest capitalization are: (1) assets that an enterprise constructs for its own use (such as facilities), and (2) assets intended for sale or lease that are constructed as discrete projects (such as ships or real estate projects). Interest cannot be capitalized for inventories that are routinely manufactured or otherwise produced in large quantities on a repetitive basis. Marvel's machine is a qualifying asset.

The amount to be capitalized is that portion of the interest cost incurred during the asset's acquisition period that theoretically could have been avoided (for example, by avoiding additional borrowings or by using the funds expended for the asset to repay existing borrowings) if expenditures for the asset had not been made.

Avoidable interest is determined by applying an appropriate interest rate(s) to the weighted-average amount of accumulated expenditures for the asset during the period. The appropriate rate is that rate associated with a specific new borrowing, if any. If average accumulated expenditures for the asset exceed the amount of a specific new borrowing associated with the asset, the capitalization rate to be applied to such excess shall be a weighted average of the rates applicable to other borrowings of the enterprise.

The weighted-average amount of accumulated expenditures for the asset represents the average investment tied up in the qualifying asset during the period. For Marvel, a $200,000 balance in Machine for the three-month capitalization period (date of expenditures to the date the asset is ready for use) means an equivalent (average) investment of $50,000 on an annual basis. Marvel uses only the 12% rate applicable to the specific new borrowing to calculate the avoidable interest because the specific borrowing ($600,000) exceeds the weighted-average accumulated expenditures.

The amount of interest to be capitalized is not to exceed the actual interest costs incurred. Thus, Marvel compares its avoidable interest of $6,000 and its actual interest incurred of $29,400 and chooses the lower amount to capitalize. Any interest amounts earned on funds borrowed which are temporarily in excess of the company's needs are to be reported as interest revenue rather than be used to offset the amount of interest to be capitalized. Thus, Marvel will report $5,000 as interest revenue and that $5,000 will not affect the amount of interest to be capitalized.

EXERCISE 11-4

Purpose: (L.O. 5) This exercise will give you practice in accounting for the acquisition of a plant asset on a deferred payment plan.

St. John's Fishing Inc. purchased a computer network on December 31, 2002 for $200,000, paying $50,000 down and agreeing to pay the balance in five equal instalments of $30,000 payable each December 31 beginning in 2003. An assumed interest rate of 10% is implicit in the purchase price.

Instructions (Round to the nearest cent)
(a)   Prepare the journal entry(ies) at the date of purchase.
(b)   Prepare an amortization schedule for the instalment agreement.
(c)   Prepare the journal entry(ies) at December 31, 2003, to record the cash payment and the applicable interest expense (assume the effective interest method is employed).
(d)   Prepare the journal entry(ies) at December 31, 2004, to record the cash payment and the applicable interest expense (assume the effective interest method is employed).

Solution to Exercise 11-4

(a)   Time diagram:

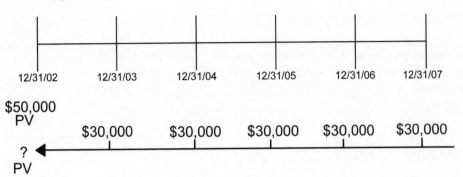

Entry:

Equipment	163,723.70*	
Discount on Notes Payable	36,276.30	
Cash.		50,000.00
Notes Payable ($30,000 x 5)		150,000.00

*PV of a $30,000 ordinary annuity @ 10% for 5 years
   ($30,000 x 3.79079) $ 113,723.70
Down payment   50,000.00
Capitalized value of equipment $ 163,723.70

(b)

Date	Cash Payment	10% Interest Expense	Reduction of Principal	Liability Balance
12/31/02				$113,723.70
12/31/03	$ 30,000.00	$ 11,372.37	$ 18,627.63	95,096.07
12/31/04	30,000.00	9,509.61	20,490.39	74,605.68
12/31/05	30,000.00	7,460.57	22,539.43	52,066.25
12/31/06	30,000.00	5,206.63	24,793.37	27,272.88
12/31/07	30,000.00	2,727.12*	27,272.88	-0-
Totals	$ 150,000.00	$ 36,276.30	$113,723.70	

*This is a plug figure, which includes a rounding error of $0.17.

(c)   **December 31, 2003**

Notes Payable	30,000.00	
Interest Expense (see schedule)	11,372.37	
Cash.		30,000.00
Discount on Notes Payable		11,372.37

(d)   **December 31, 2004**

Notes Payable..	30,000.00	
Interest Expense (see schedule)...	9,509.61	
Cash.		30,000.00
Discount on Notes Payable		9,509.61

TIP: For each entry in (c) and (d), two entries could replace the one compound entry. For example, the two equivalent entries for (c) would be:

Notes Payable...30,000.00		
Cash		30,000.00
Interest Expense	11,372.37	
Discount on Notes Payable		11,372.37

EXERCISE 11-5

Purpose: (L.O. 5) This exercise reviews the calculations involved in a lump-sum purchase of plant assets.

The Eliason Company paid $750,000 cash for a package of plant assets. The package consisted of the following:

	Seller's Book Value	Market Value
Land	$ 60,000	$ 300,000
Building	120,000	400,000
Equipment	220,000	250,000
Tools	100,000	50,000
Total	$ 500,000	$ 1,000,000

Instructions
(a)   Prepare the journal entry for Eliason to record the acquisition of these assets on the company's books.
(b)   Why must you allocate the total cost to separate accounts for the individual assets? Why can't you simply use "Plant Assets" as an account and record the total cost to that account? Explain.

Solution to Exercise 11-5

(a)	Land	225,000	
	Building	300,000	
	Equipment..	187,500	
	Tools	37,500	
	Cash		750,000

Approach and Explanation: The total cost ($750,000) is to be allocated to the individual assets based on the relative market values of these assets. The formula that can be used to accomplish this objective is as follows:

$$\frac{\text{Market Value of One Item in Group}}{\text{Market Value of All items in Group}} \times \frac{\text{Amount to be}}{\text{Allocated}} = \frac{\text{Amount to be Assigned to Item Designated in the Numerator}}{}$$

Land:	($300,000 ÷ $1,000,000) x $750,000 =	$225,000
Building:	($400,000 ÷ $1,000,000) x $750,000 =	$300,000
Equipment:	($250,000 ÷ $1,000,000) x $750,000 =	$187,500
Tools:	($50,000 ÷ $1,000,000) x $750,000 =	$37,500

TIP: Sum the four answers obtained by using the formula. They should total to the amount you set out to allocate ($750,000, in this case).

(b) The total cost must be allocated to the individual assets because land is not subject to the process of amortization, and the amortizable assets normally are subject to different service lives and maybe even different amortization methods.

ILLUSTRATION 11-1
SUMMARY OF REQUIREMENTS FOR RECOGNIZING GAINS AND LOSSES ON EXCHANGES OF NONMONETARY ASSETS (L.O. 5)

1. Calculate the total gain or loss experienced on the transaction, which is equal to the difference between the fair value of the asset given up and the book value of the asset given up. An excess of fair value over book value indicates an experienced gain; an excess of book value over fair value indicates a loss.

2. If a loss is calculated in 1,
   a) and the earning process is considered completed, the entire loss is recognized (dissimilar assets).
   (b) and the earning process is not considered completed (similar assets),
      (1) no loss is recognized.
      (2) and boot is received in excess of 10% of the fair market consideration, the loss is recognized:

3. If a gain is calculated in 1,
   (a) and the earning process is considered completed, the entire gain is recognized (dissimilar assets).
   (b) and the earning process is not considered completed (similar assets),
      (1) no gain is recognized.
      (2) and boot is received in excess of 10% of the fair market consideration, the gain is recognized:

TIP: When cash is received in a nonmonetary exchange where a gain on the old asset is evident, the amount of cash received can affect whether or not the gain is to be recognized. If the amount of cash received is 10% or more of the total fair value of the exchange, the gain is to be recognized.

TIP: "Boot" is a term used to describe monetary consideration (such as cash or a receivable which is a claim for cash) given or received in an exchange of nonmonetary assets.

TIP: Recall that it is the conservatism constraint that requires **all losses to be recognized** rather than deferred to future periods. This is why the authors indicate that the loss of a similar exchange should be realized. The *CICA Handbook* indicates that the loss of a similar asset exchange should not be realized, but if a subsequent revaluation of the asset were to take place, this is where the loss should be recognized, through an impairment transaction, and treated in a similar manner to a revision of accounting estimate.

EXERCISE 11-6

Purpose: (L.O. 5) This exercise will allow you to practise recording the exchange of similar productive assets.

Soon Yoon Company exchanged equipment used in its manufacturing operations plus $15,000 in cash for similar equipment used in the operations of Peggy Gunshanan Company. The following information pertains to the exchange:

	Soon Yoon Co.	Peggy Gunshanan Co.
Equipment (cost)	$ 84,000	$ 84,000
Accumulated amortization	66,000	30,000
Fair value of equipment	41,500	46,500
Cash given up	1,000	

Instructions
(a) Prepare the journal entries to record the exchange on the books of both companies.
(b) Prepare the journal entries to record the exchange on the books of both companies assuming cash of $15,000 is given by Soon Yoon.

Solution to Exercise 11-6

(a) **Soon Yoon Company:**

Equipment (New)	19,000	
Accumulated Amortization	66,000	
Equipment (Old)		84,000
Cash		1,000

Calculation of book value:

Cost of old asset	$ 84,000
Accumulated amortization	(66,000)
Book value of old asset	$ 18,000

Valuation of new equipment:

Book value of equipment given	$18,000
Boot given	1,000
Cost of new equipment	$19,000

Peggy Gunshanan Company:

Cash	1,000	
Equipment (New)	53,000	
Accumulated Amortization	30,000	
Equipment (Old)..		84,000

Calculation of book value:

Cost of old asset	$84,000
Accumulated amortization	(30,000)
Book value of old asset	$54,000

Calculation of loss:

Fair value of equipment received	$ 41,500	
Cash received	1,000	
Book value of equipment given	(54,000)	
Loss on old asset	$ (11,500)	(Not recognized)

Valuation of new equipment:

Book value of equipment given	$54,000
Boot received	(1,000)
Cost of new equipment	$53,000

Approach and Explanation: Refer to **Illustration 10-1** which summarizes the rules for recognizing gains and losses experienced on exchanges of nonmonetary assets.

It is an exchange of similar productive assets; hence, the earning process is not considered complete. Rather than crediting a gain, the gain is reflected in the cost of the new asset by reducing what otherwise would have been recorded as the new asset's cost. Thus, the gain is deferred and there is a departure from the historical cost principle in determining the cost of the new asset.

Peggy Gunshanan has experienced a loss. (Think about the conservatism constraint here to help you to remember this.) The loss is not recognized.

(b)   **Soon Yoon Company:**

Equipment (New)	41,500	
Accumulated Amortization	66,000	
Gain on Disposal of Plant Asset...............................		8,500
Equipment (Old)		84,000
Cash.		15,000

Calculation of gain:

Fair value of equipment given	$41,500
Boot given	(15,000)
Book value of equipment given	(18,000)
Gain experienced on old asset	$ 8,500

Valuation of new equipment:

Book value of equipment given	$18,000
Gain recognized on disposal	8,500
Boot given	15,000
Cost of new equipment	$41,500

Peggy Gunshanan Company:

Cash	15,000	
Equipment (New)	46,500	
Accumulated Amortization	30,000	
Gain on Disposal of Plant Asset...............................		7,500
Equipment (Old)		84,000

Calculation of gain:

Fair value of equipment given	$ 46,500)
Book value of equipment given	54,000
Gain experienced on old asset	$ 7,500

Valuation of new equipment:

Book value of equipment given	$ 54,000
Gain recognized on disposal	7,500
Fair value of equipment given	61,500
Boot received	(15,000)
Cost of new equipment	$46,500

Explanation: Both Soon Yoon and Peggy Gunshanan experienced gains on the disposal of their old plant assets. The gains are recognized in this case as the cash component of the exchange exceeds 10% of the fair value consideration given and received. This is not considered a nonmonetary transaction.

ILLUSTRATION 11-2
EXPENDITURES SUBSEQUENT TO ACQUISITION (L.O. 6)

A plant asset often requires expenditures subsequent to acquisition. Generally, four major types of expenditures may be incurred relative to existing plant assets; they are as follows:

- **Additions.** Increase or extension of existing assets.
- **Improvements and Replacements.** Substitution of an improved asset for an existing one.
- **Rearrangement and Reinstallation.** Movement of assets from one location to another.
- **Repairs.** Expenditures that maintain assets in condition for operation.

Costs that are incurred subsequent to acquisition are to be capitalized (by a debit to an asset account or to an accumulated amortization account, depending on the circumstances) if they are material, nonrecurring in nature, and benefit future periods in some manner such as by doing one or more of the following:

a. They extend the useful life of a plant asset.
b. They enhance the quality of existing services.
c. They add new asset services.
d. They reduce future operating costs of existing assets.
e. They are required to meet governmental regulations (such as for environmental reasons).
f. They increase the number of units produced.

The accounting treatment appropriate for various costs incurred subsequent to the acquisition of capitalized assets is summarized as follows:

ILLUSTRATION 11-2 (Continued)

Type of Expenditure	Normal Accounting Treatment
Additions	Capitalize cost of addition to asset account.
Improvements and Replacements	(a) **Carrying value of old asset known:** Remove cost of and accumulated amortization on old asset, recognizing any gain or loss. Capitalize cost of improvement/replacement. (b) **Carrying value of old asset unknown:** 1. If the asset's useful life is extended, debit accumulated amortization for cost of improvement/replacement. 2. If the quantity or quality of the asset's productivity is increased, capitalize cost of improvement/replacement to asset account.
Rearrangement and Reinstallation	(a) If original installation cost is **known**, account for cost of rearrangement/reinstallation as a replacement (carrying value known). (b) If original installation cost is **unknown** and rearrangement/reinstallation cost is **material** in amount and benefits future periods, capitalize as an asset. (c) If original installation cost is **unknown** and rearrangement/reinstallation cost is **not material or future benefit is questionable**, expense the cost when incurred.
Repairs	(a) **Ordinary:** Expense cost of repairs when incurred. (b) **Major:** As appropriate, treat as an addition, improvement, or replacement.

CASE 11-3

Purpose: (L.O. 6) This case will provide a few examples of the accounting for costs subsequent to the acquisition of fixed assets.

Hardent Resources Group has been in its plant facility for 20 years. Although the plant is quite functional, numerous repair costs are incurred to maintain it in sound working order. The company's plant asset book value is currently $750,000, as indicated below:

Original cost	$ 1,350,000
Accumulated amortization	600,000
Book value	$ 750,000

During the current year, the following expenditures were made involving the plant facility:
(a)   The entire plant was repainted at a cost of $26,000.
(b)   The roof was an asbestos cement slate; for safety purposes, it was removed and replaced with a new and better quality roof at a cost of $62,000. Book value of the old roof was $31,000.
(c)   Because of increased demands for its product, the company increased its plant capacity by building a new addition at a cost of $315,000.
(d)   The plumbing system was completely updated at a cost of $53,000. The cost of the old plumbing system was not known. It is estimated that the useful life of the building will not change as a result of this updating.
(e)   A series of major repairs were made at a cost of $50,000, because parts of the wood structure were rotting. The cost of the old wood structure was not known. These extensive repairs are estimated to increase the useful life of the building.

Instructions
Indicate how each of these transactions would be recorded in the accounting records.

Solution to Case 11-3

(a)   Expenditures that do not increase the service benefits of the asset are expensed. Painting costs are considered ordinary repairs because they maintain the existing condition of the asset or restore it to normal operating efficiency.

(b)   The approach to follow is to remove the old book value of the roof and substitute the cost of the new roof. It is assumed that the expenditure increases the future service potential of the asset. Recognize a loss equal to the book value of the old roof removed.

(c)   Any addition to plant assets is capitalized because a new asset has been created. This addition increases the service potential of the plant.

(d) Conceptually the book value of the old plumbing system should be removed. However, in practice, it is often difficult if not impossible to determine this amount. In this case, one of two approaches is followed. One approach is to capitalize the cost of the replacement on the theory that sufficient depreciation was taken on the item to reduce the carrying amount to almost zero. A second approach is to debit accumulated depreciation on the theory that the replacement extends the useful life of the asset and thereby recaptures some or all of the past depreciation. In our present situation, the problem specifically states that the useful life is not extended and therefore debiting accumulated depreciation is inappropriate. Thus, this expenditure should be added to the cost of the plant facility.

(e) See discussion in (d) above. In this case, because the useful life of the asset has increased, a debit to accumulated depreciation would appear to be the most appropriate treatment.

EXERCISE 11-7

Purpose: (L.O. 7) This exercise will (1) illustrate several different ways in which you may dispose of property, and (2) discuss the appropriate accounting procedures for each.

Presented below is a schedule of property dispositions for Friedlander Co.

Schedule of Property Dispositions

	Cost	Accumulated Amortization	Cash Proceeds	Fair Market Value	Nature of Disposition
Land	$ 80,000	---	$ 64,000	$ 64,000	Condemnation
Building	30,000	---	7,200	---	Demolition
Warehouse	130,000	$22,000	148,000	148,000	Destruction by fire
Machine	16,000	6,400	3,600	14,400	Trade-in
Furniture	20,000	15,700	---	5,600	Contribution
Automobile	16,000	6,920	5,920	5,920	Sale

The following additional information is available:

- **Land.** On January 7, a condemnation award was received as consideration for unimproved land held primarily as an investment, and on April 7, another parcel of unimproved land to be held as an investment was purchased at a cost of $70,000.

- **Building.** On May 4, land and building were purchased at a total cost of $150,000, of which 20% was allocated to the building on the corporate books. The real estate was acquired with the intention of demolishing the building, and this was accomplished during the month of August. Cash proceeds received in August represent the net proceeds from demolition of the building.

- **Warehouse.** On January 2, the warehouse was destroyed by fire. The warehouse was purchased January 2, 1995, and had been amortized $22,000. On June 15, part of the insurance proceeds was used to purchase a replacement warehouse at a cost of $130,000.

- **Machine.** On October 31, the machine was exchanged for another similar machine having a fair market value of $10,800 and cash of $3,600 was received.

- **Furniture.** On July 2, furniture was contributed to a qualified charitable organization. No other contributions were made or pledged during the year.

- **Automobile.** On December 31, the automobile was sold to Dee Dee Burgess, a shareholder.

Instructions

Indicate how these items would be reported on the income statement of Friedlander Co.

(AICPA adapted)

Solution to Exercise 11-7

The following accounting treatment appears appropriate for these items:

- **Land.** The loss on the condemnation of the land of $16,000 ($80,000 - $64,000) should be reported as an extraordinary item on the income statement. A condemnation comes about from a government unit exercising its right of eminent domain. *Eminent domain* is defined as "expropriation of assets by a government." The $70,000 land purchase has no income statement effect.

- **Building.** There is no recognized gain or loss on the demolition of the building. The entire purchase cost ($30,000), decreased by the demolition proceeds ($7,200), is allocated to land.

- **Warehouse.** The gain on the destruction of the warehouse should be reported in the "other revenues and gains" section of the income statement. A fire can happen in any environment; therefore, it is not an extraordinary item. The gain is calculated as follows:

Insurance proceeds		$148,000
Cost	$130,000	
Accumulated amortization	(22,000)	(108,000)
Realized gain		$ 40,000

Some contend that a portion of this gain should be deferred because the proceeds are reinvested in similar assets. Deferral of the gain in this situation is not permitted under GAAP.

- **Machine.** The recognized gain on the exchange would be recorded as this is not a nonmonetary transaction, regardless of whether this is a similar or dissimilar exchange. The gain is calculated as follows:

Fair market value of old machine		$14,400
Cash received		3,600
Cost	$16,000	
Accumulated amortization	(6,400)	(9,600)
Total gain experienced		$ 8,400

    This gain would probably be reported in the "other revenues and gains" section. It might be considered an unusual item, but it would usually not be infrequent. The cost of the new machine would be capitalized at $14,400:

- **Furniture.** The contribution of the furniture to a charitable organization would be reported as a contribution expense of $5,600 with a related gain on disposition of furniture of $1,300 [$5,600 - ($20,000 - $15,700)]. The contribution expense and the related gain may be netted, if desired, for reporting purposes.

- **Automobile.** The loss on sale of the automobile of $3,160 [$5,920 - ($16,000 - $6,920)] should probably be reported in the "other expenses and losses" section. This is a related party transaction; such transactions require special disclosure.

TIP: The receipt of the condemnation award (January 7) represents an **involuntary conversion of nonmonetary assets to monetary assets**. Any gain or loss related to the transaction shall be recognized even though the enterprise reinvests or is obligated to reinvest the monetary assets in replacement nonmonetary assets. The receipt of insurance proceeds due to the destruction of the warehouse is also an involuntary conversion of nonmonetary assets to monetary assets.

TIP: The sale of property, plant, and equipment for cash should be accounted for as follows:
   (1)   The carrying value at the date of the sale (cost of the property, plant, and equipment less the accumulated depreciation) should be removed from the accounts.
   (2)   The excess of cash from the sale over the carrying value removed is accounted for as a gain on the sale, while the excess of carrying value removed over cash from the sale is accounted for as a loss on the sale.

TIP: When a plant asset is disposed of, the accumulated amortization must be updated before the gain or loss can be calculated. The discussions above assume that updating has taken place.

EXERCISE 11-8

Purpose: (L.O. 2, 6) This exercise is designed to give you additional practice in analysing changes in property, plant, and equipment accounts during a period. Problems of this type frequently appear on professional exams.

At December 31, 2001, certain accounts included in the property, plant, and equipment section of the Busch Company's balance sheet had the following balances:

Land	$ 100,000
Buildings	800,000
Leasehold improvements	500,000
Machinery and equipment	700,000

During 2002 the following transactions occurred:

- Land site number 52 was acquired for $1,000,000. Additionally, to acquire the land Busch paid a $60,000 commission to a real estate agent. Costs of $15,000 were incurred to clear the land. During the course of clearing the land, timber and gravel were recovered and sold for $5,000.

- A second tract of land (site number 53) with a building was acquired for $300,000. The closing statement indicated that the land value was $200,000 and the building value was $100,000. Shortly after acquisition, the building was demolished at a cost of $30,000. A new building was constructed for $150,000 plus the following costs:

Excavation fees	$ 11,000
Architectural design fees	8,000
Building permit fee	1,000
Imputed interest on equity funds used during construction	6,000
(The company had no debt outstanding and no actual interest cost incurred.)	

  The building was completed and occupied on September 30, 2002.

- A third tract of land (site number 54) was acquired for $600,000 and was put on the market for resale.

- Extensive work was done to a building occupied by Busch under a lease agreement that expires on December 31, 2011. The total cost of the work was $125,000, which consisted of the following:

Painting of ceilings	$ 10,000	estimated useful life is 1 year
Electrical work	35,000	estimated useful life is 10 years
Construction of extension to current working area	80,000	estimated useful life is 30 years
	$ 125,000	

  The lessor paid one-half of the costs incurred in connection with the extension to the current working area.

- During December 2002, costs of $65,000 were incurred to improve leased office space. The related lease will terminate on December 31, 2004, and is not expected to be renewed.

- A group of new machines were purchased under a royalty agreement which provides for payment of royalties based on units of production for the machines. The invoice price of the machines was $75,000, freight costs were $2,000, unloading charges were $1,500, and royalty payments for 2002 were $13,000.

Instructions

(a)   Prepare a detailed analysis of the changes in each of the following balance sheet accounts for 2002:

Land	Leasehold improvements
Buildings	Machinery and equipment

Disregard the related accumulated amortization accounts.

(b)   List the items in the fact situation which were not used to determine the answer to (a) above, and indicate **where, or if,** these items should be included in Busch's financial statements.

(AICPA Adapted)

Solution to Exercise 11-8

(a)

Busch Company
ANALYSIS OF LAND ACCOUNT
for 2002

Balance at January 1, 2002		$ 100,000
Land site number 52		
Acquisition cost	$ 1,000,000	
Commission to real estate agent	60,000	
Clearing costs	$ 15,000	
Less amounts recovered	5,000	10,000
Total land site number 52		1,070,000
Land site number 53		
Land value	200,000	
Building value	100,000	
Demolition cost	30,000	
Total land site number 53		330,000
Balance at December 31, 2002		$ 1,500,000

Busch Company
ANALYSIS OF BUILDING ACCOUNT
for 2002

Balance at January 1, 2002		$ 800,000
Cost of new building constructed on land site number 53		
Construction costs	$ 150,000	
Excavation fees	11,000	
Architectural design fees	8,000	
Building permit fee	1,000	170,000
Balance at December 31, 2002		$ 970,000

Busch Company
ANALYSIS OF LEASEHOLD IMPROVEMENTS ACCOUNT
for 2002

Balance at January 1, 2002	$500,000
Electrical work	35,000
Construction of extension to current work area ($80,000 x 1/2)	40,000
Office space improvements	65,000
Balance at December 31, 2002	$640,000

Busch Company
ANALYSIS OF MACHINERY AND EQUIPMENT ACCOUNT
for 2002

Balance at January 1, 2002		$ 700,000
Cost of new machines acquired		
Invoice price	$ 75,000	
Freight costs	2,000	
Unloading charges	1,500	78,500
Balance at December 31, 2002		$ 778,500

(b)   Items in the fact situation which were not used to determine the answer to (a) above are:

- Imputed interest of $6,000 on equity funds used during construction should not be included anywhere in Busch's financial statements. Only interest actually incurred should be capitalized during construction.

- Land site number 54, which was acquired for $600,000 and held for resale, should be included in Busch's balance sheet in the investment classification.

- Painting of ceilings for $10,000 should be included as a normal operating expense in Busch's income statement.

- Royalty payments of $13,000 should be included as a normal operating expense in Busch's income statement.

ANALYSIS OF MULTIPLE-CHOICE TYPE QUESTIONS

QUESTION
1. (L.O. 2) Jacobson Manufacturing Company purchased a machine for $65,000 on January 2, 2002. At the date of purchase, Jacobson incurred the following additional costs:

Loss on sale of old machine	$ 2,000
Freight-in	900
Installation cost	1,500
Breaking-in costs	650

The amount to record for the acquisition cost of the new machine is:
a. $65,000
b. $67,400
c. $68,050
d. $69,400

Approach and Explanation: Apply the guideline: The cost of a plant asset includes all costs required to get the item to the location and condition for its intended purpose.

Purchase price	$ 65,000
Freight-in	900
Installation cost	1,500
Breaking-in costs	650
Total acquisition cost	$ 68,050

The loss on sale of the old machine should be charged to an income statement account so it will not impact the new asset's value. (Solution = c.)

QUESTION
2. (L.O. 2) Buena Vista Hotel purchases Embassy Hotel with the intention of demolishing the Embassy Hotel and building a new high-rise hotel on the site. The cost of the Embassy Hotel should be:
a. Capitalized as part of the cost of the land.
b. Capitalized as part of the cost of the new hotel.
c. Written off as a loss when it is torn down.
d. Amortized over the life of the new hotel structure.

Explanation: The cost of the land should include all costs necessary to acquire it and prepare it for its intended use by the buyer—which is to provide a site for a new building. (Solution = a.)

QUESTION
3. (L.O. 2) The Jupiter Company purchased a parcel of land to be used as the site of a new office complex. The following data pertain to the purchase of the land and the beginning of construction for the new building:

Purchase price of land	$200,000
Attorney's fees for land transaction	1,000
Title insurance cost	2,000
Survey fees to determine the boundaries of the lot	800
Excavation costs for the building's foundation	8,000
Costs of clearing and grading the land	1,400

The total acquisition cost of the land is:
a. $213,200
b. $205,200
c. $203,800
d. $202,400
e. $200,000

Approach and Explanation: Think about how the cost of land is determined: an asset's cost includes all costs necessary to acquire the asset and get it to the location and condition for its intended purpose. When land has been purchased for the purpose of constructing a building, all costs incurred up to the excavation for the new building are considered land costs. Think of the common components of land cost (refer to the listing in the **Solution to Case 10-1). The** cost is calculated as follows:

Purchase price	$200,000
Attorney's fees	1,000
Title insurance	2,000
Survey fees	800
Costs of clearing and grading	1,400
Total cost of land	$205,200

The $8,000 excavation costs for the building's foundation should be charged (debited) to the Building account. (Solution = b.)

QUESTION
4.   (L.O. 2)   The Venus Company hired an architect to design plans and a construction firm to build a new office building on a parcel of land it owns. The following data relates to the building:

Price paid to the construction firm	$320,000
Architect fees	18,000
Permit fees	1,200
Property taxes during the construction period	800
Insurance premium for first year of operations	3,000
Property taxes during the first year of operations	6,000

The total acquisition cost of the new building is:
a. $349,000
b. $340,000
c. $338,000
d. $320,000

Approach and Explanation: Think about how the cost of a building is determined: an asset's cost includes all costs necessary to acquire the asset and get it to the location and condition for its intended purpose. Think of the common components of building cost (refer to the listing in the **Solution to Case 10-1).** The cost is calculated as follows:

Price paid to construction firm	$320,000	
Architect fees	18,000	
Permit fees	1,200	
Property taxes during construction	800	
Total cost of building	$340,000	(Solution = b.)

QUESTION

5.   (L.O. 2) The Patty Company purchased a piece of office equipment to be used in operations. The following expenditures and other data relate to the equipment:

Invoice price excluding sales tax	$12,000
Sales tax	600
Delivery charges	200
Installation costs	300
Cost of a special platform	400
Cost of supplies used in testing	80
Insurance premium for first year of use	60

The total acquisition cost of this piece of equipment is:
a. $13,640
b. $13,580
c. $13,100
d. $12,700

Approach and Explanation: Apply the cost principle: the cost of equipment includes all costs necessary to acquire the equipment, transport it to the place where it will be used, and prepare it for use. Thus, all costs related to equipment incurred prior to use in regular operations are charged to the Equipment account. Recurring costs (such as for insurance and maintenance) incurred after the equipment is ready for use should be expensed in the period incurred. Refer to the list of common elements of equipment cost in the **Solution to Case 10-1**. The cost of the equipment is determined as follows:

Invoice price	$12,000
Sales tax	600
Delivery charges	200
Installation costs	300
Costs of special platform	400
Costs of supplies used in testing	80
	$13,580 (Solution = b.)

QUESTION

6.   (L.O. 3) A manufacturing company decides to build its own factory equipment. The cost of self-constructed plant assets may include which of the following:

	Materials	Labour	Mfg. Overhead
a.	Yes	Yes	Yes
b.	Yes	Yes	No
c.	Yes	No	No
d.	No	Yes	No

Explanation: In addition to the materials and labour used to build a plant asset, the manufacturer should assign a pro rata portion of the manufacturing overhead to obtain the asset's cost. However, the asset should not be recorded for more than its fair value (the total amount that would be charged by an outside independent producer). (Solution = a.)

QUESTION

7.   (L.O. 4) Herndon Inc. has a fiscal year ending October 31. On November 1, 2001, Herndon borrowed $20,000,000 at 15% to finance construction of a new plant. Repayments of the loan are to commence the month following completion of the plant. During the year ending October 31, 2002, expenditures for the partially completed structure totalled $12,000,000. These expenditures were incurred evenly through the year. Interest earned on the unexpended portion of

the loan amounted to $800,000 for the year. What amount of interest should be capitalized as of October 31, 2002?

a. $0
b. $100,000
c. $900,000
d. $2,200,000
e. $3,000,000

Explanation: The situation is one which qualifies for the capitalization of interest. The following steps should help to calculate the amount:

(1)   **Find the weighted-average accumulated expenditures** for the period:

Total expenditures at beginning of the period	$ 0
Total expenditures at end of the period	12,000,000
Sum	$ 12,000,000

$12,000,000 ÷ 2 = average of $6,000,000

(2)   **Determine the interest rate to use.** Because the amount of a specific borrowing ($20,000,000) exceeds the weighted-average accumulated expenditures ($6,000,000), use the interest rate for that specific borrowing (15%).

(3)   **Calculate the avoidable interest** by multiplying the appropriate interest rate (15% from Step 2) by the weighted-average accumulated expenditures ($6,000,000 from Step 1).

$6,000,000 x 15% = $900,000 Avoidable interest

(4)   **Determine the amount of interest to capitalize** by selecting the lower of the actual interest incurred (15% x $20,000,000 = $3,000,000) or the amount of avoidable interest ($900,000 from Step 3). The lower in this case is the $900,000 avoidable interest. (Solution = c.)

TIP: The interest earned ($800,000) is to be reported as revenue on the income statement and should not be used to offset the interest to be capitalized.

QUESTION
8.   (L.O. 5) A large plot of land was donated by the City of Kingston to the Dupont Corporation to entice the company to build a plant and provide new jobs in the community. The land should be recorded on Dupont's books at:

a.   The cost of the lawyer's fees involved in handling the transaction.
b.   The value assigned by Dupont's board of directors.
c.   The land's market value.
d.   No more than one dollar because the land was obtained for no cost.

Explanation: A donation (contribution) is a nonreciprocal transfer (value goes in only one direction rather than in both directions as happens in an exchange transaction). A nonreciprocal transfer is to be recorded at the fair value of the property, goods, or services involved. The *CICA Handbook* requires the amount received to be deferred and recognized over the period that the related assets are used (employed). This can be done as a deferred credit (either to the asset account or to deferred revenues) and reducing the donation or recognizing revenues. (Solution = c.)

QUESTION

9.   (L.O. 5) The Holstrum Corporation intends to acquire some plant assets from Bailey Corporation by issuing common shares in exchange. The cost of the assets should be measured by:
    a.   The par value of the shares.
    b.   The market value of the shares.
    c.   The book value of the shares.
    d.   Bailey's carrying value of the assets.

Explanation: Cost is measured by the fair market value (cash equivalent) of the consideration given (the shares in this case), or the fair market value of the consideration received (the plant assets in this case), whichever is the more clearly evident. If the market value of the common shares is not determinable, the fair market value of the plant assets should be used. (Solution = b.)

TIP: If treasury shares are used to acquire a new plant asset, the same rule applies: record the asset at the fair value (market value) of the treasury shares or at the fair value of the asset, whichever is the more clearly evident.

QUESTION

10.   (L.O. 5) In January 2002, Barbie Company entered into a contract to acquire a new machine for its factory. The machine, which had a cash price of $300,000, was acquired in exchange for the following:

Down payment	$ 30,000
Note payable in 24 equal monthly instalments	240,000
500 shares of Barbie common shares, with	
an agreed value of $100 per share	50,000
Total	$ 320,000

Prior to the machine's use, installation costs of $8,000 were incurred. The amount to record for the acquisition cost of the machine is:
    a. $300,000
    b. $308,000
    c. $320,000
    d. $328,000

Approach and Explanation: Any time you have a question regarding the acquisition cost of a plant asset, write down (or mentally review) the two rules regarding asset cost: (1) Cost is measured by the fair market value (cash equivalent) of the consideration given or the fair market value of the consideration received, whichever is the more clearly evident; and (2) An asset's cost includes all costs necessary to get it to the location and condition for its intended purpose. Then apply the rules to the situation given.

The cash equivalent of the machine acquired is $300,000 (cash price). The cash equivalent of the consideration given is the cash down payment of $30,000 plus the fair value of the shares ($50,000) plus the present value of the note payable (something less than $240,000). Because no information is given about the market value of the note or the appropriate interest rate for the note, but the cash equivalent price is given for the asset received, the more clearly evident figure is the $300,000. The $8,000 installation cost must be added to get the total acquisition cost. (Solution = b.)

QUESTION

11.　(L.O. 5) Two home builders agree to exchange tracts of land that each holds for purposes of development. An appraiser was hired and the following information is available:

	Batson	Beamer
Book value of land	$ 50,000	$ 72,000
Fair value of land	90,000	100,000
Cash paid	5,000	

In recording this exchange should a gain be recognized by Batson, Beamer, or both parties?

	Batson	Beamer
a.	Yes	Yes
b.	Yes	No
c.	No	Yes
d.	No	No

Approach and Explanation:

(1)　**Determine if it is an exchange of similar or dissimilar assets.** One tract of land for another to use for the same purpose is an exchange of similar assets.

(2)　**Determine if a gain or loss is experienced.** Fair value exceeds book value for both parties so both have experienced a gain.

(3)　**Determine if boot is given or received.** Batson is giving boot; Beamer is receiving boot (less than 10% of the fair market consideration given or received).

(4)　**Write down the rules for recognition of gain in a similar asset exchange.** Neither party will recognize the gain on an exchange of similar assets involving little (less than 10% of the fair market value of the consideration given or received) as the earnings process is not deemed to be complete on either plot of land. (Solution = d.)

QUESTION

12.　(L.O. 5) Refer to the facts of question 11. The amount to be recorded by Batson for the acquisition cost of the new tract of land is:

　　a.　$55,000
　　b.　$95,000
　　c.　$85,000
　　d.　$90,000
　　f.　$100,000

Approach and Explanation: When there is a similar asset exchange not involving large monetary considerations, no gain is to be recognized. The cost of the new asset is equal to the recorded value (book value) of the old asset, reduced for any impairment (minus any loss recognized), plus the boot given. There was no loss in this case; therefore, $50,000 book value + $5,000 boot = $55,000 cost. A journal entry approach can also be used (the debit to the new asset account is a plug figure): (Solution = b.)

Land (New)...	55,000		**Plug last.**
Land (Old)		50,000	**Do second.**
Cash		5,000	**Do first.**

(Solution = b.)

QUESTION

13.   (L.O. 5) The King-Kong Corporation exchanges one plant asset for a similar plant asset and gives a small amount of cash in the exchange. If a gain on the disposal of the old asset is indicated, the gain will:

a.   Be reported in the Other Revenues and Gains section of the income statement.

b.   Effectively reduce the amount to be recorded as the cost of the new asset.

c.   Effectively increase the amount to be recorded as the cost of the new asset.

d.   Be credited directly to the owner's capital account.

Explanation: The exchange of similar productive assets with only a small amount of cash does not recognize any gain on the disposal of the old asset. The gain is deferred by way of reduction (credit) to the cost of the new asset received in the exchange. The gain is thus spread over future periods by way of lower amortization charges (because of a lower cost figure for the new asset). (Solution = b.)

QUESTION

14.   (L.O. 7) A van has an original cost of $42,000 and accumulated amortization of $11,000. It is sold for $27,000 cash. The journal entry to record the sale will include a:

a.   Debit to Loss on Disposal of Plant Assets for $4,000.

b.   Credit to Gain on Disposal of Plant Assets for $4,000.

c.   Credit to Vans for $27,000.

d.   Debit to Loss on Disposal of Plant Assets for $15,000.

Approach and Explanation: Prepare the journal entry to record the sale. Begin with the cash received so debit Cash. Remove the old asset from the books; credit Vans for $42,000 and debit Accumulated Amortization for $11,000. Examine the entry and determine what is needed to balance the entry; a debit balancing figure represents a loss or a credit balancing figure represents a gain.

In this case, a debit of $4,000 is needed to balance; hence, a loss of $4,000 is recorded. (Solution = a.)

Cash	27,000
Accumulated Amortization—Vans	11,000
Loss on Disposal of Plant Assets	4,000
Vans..	42,000

QUESTION

15.   (L.O. 6) In accounting for plant assets, which of the following outlays made subsequent to acquisition should be fully expensed in the period the expenditure is made?

a.   Expenditure made to increase the efficiency or effectiveness of an existing asset.

b.   Expenditure made to extend the useful life of an existing asset beyond the time frame originally anticipated.

c.   Expenditure made to maintain an existing asset so that it can function in the manner intended.

d.   Expenditure made to add new asset services.

Explanation: If an expenditure benefits future periods, it should be capitalized (debited to a balance sheet account); if the expenditure does not yield benefits to a future period, it should be recorded by a debit to an income statement account. An expenditure made to maintain an existing asset in good working condition does not provide any benefits other than those that were in potential when the original asset was acquired; hence, it should be expensed. Answer selections "a," "b," and "d" all represent future economic benefits; hence, they should be debited to an asset account or to an accumulated amortization account, depending on whether or not an asset's life is increased by the expenditure subsequent to acquisition. (Solution = c.)

CHAPTER 12

AMORTIZATION, IMPAIRMENTS, AND DEPLETION

OVERVIEW

Expenses arise from the cost of goods or services that are consumed in the process of generating revenue. When a long-term tangible asset is acquired, it actually represents a bundle of future asset services. The total cost of these services equals the acquisition cost of the asset **minus** the asset's expected (estimated) market value at the end of its useful life. As a productive asset is used, services (benefits) are consumed to generate revenues; therefore, a portion of the original asset cost should be charged to expense in order to comply with the matching principle. The process of allocating (expensing) the cost of long-term tangible assets over the accounting periods during which the asset is used is called **amortization**. The process of allocating the costs of natural resources to inventory (and later to cost of goods sold) is called **depletion**. Amortization, impairment of capital assets and depletion are discussed in this chapter.

SUMMARY OF LEARNING OBJECTIVES

1. **Explain the concept of amortization.** Amortization is the accounting process of allocating the cost of capital assets to expense in a systematic and rational manner to those periods expected to benefit from the use of the asset. The objective is matching, not the valuation of assets at their fair values. Amortization is a generic term. The allocation of the cost of intangible capital assets is termed amortization as well, while that of property, plant and equipment is usually referred to as depreciation. The allocation of capitalized costs of natural resources is termed depletion.

2. **Identify and describe the factors that must be considered when determining amortization charges.** Three factors involved in determining amortization expense are: (1) the amount to be amortized (amortizable amount), (2) the estimated useful life, and (3) the pattern and method of cost allocation to be used.

3. **Determine amortization charges using the activity, straight-line, and decreasing-charge methods and compare the methods.** The *Activity method* assumes that the benefits provided by the asset are a function of use or productivity instead of the passage of time. The asset's life is considered in terms of either the output it provides, or an input measure such as the number of hours it works. The amortization charge per unit of activity (cost less residual value divided by estimated total units of output or input) is determined and multiplied by the units of activity produced and consumed in a period to derive amortization expense for the period. The *straight-line method* assumes that the provision of asset benefits is a function of time. As such, cost less residual value is divided by the useful economic life to determine amortization expense per period. This method is widely employed in practice because of its simplicity. The straight-line procedure is often the most conceptually appropriate when a decline in usefulness is constant from period to period. The *decreasing-charge method* provides for a higher amortization charge in the early years and lower charges in later periods. For this method, a constant rate (e.g., double the straight-line rate) is multiplied by the net book value (cost less accumulated amortization) at the start of the period to determine each period's amortization expense. The main justification for this approach is that the asset provides more benefits in the earlier periods.

4. **Explain special amortization methods.** Two special amortization methods are the *group and composite methods,* and hybrid or combination methods. The term "group" refers to a collection of assets that are similar in nature, while "composite" refers to a collection of assets that are

dissimilar in nature. The group and composite methods develop one average rate of amortization for all the assets involved and apply this rate as if they were a single asset. The hybrid or combination methods develop an amortization expense that is based on two or more approaches and that suits the specific circumstances of the assets involved.

5.   **Identify and understand reasons why amortization methods are selected.** Various amortization methods are generally acceptable. The accountant must exercise judgement when selecting and implementing the method that is most appropriate for the circumstances. Rational matching, tax reporting, simplicity, perceived economic consequences, and impact on ratios are factors that influence such judgements.

6.   **Explain the accounting issues related to asset impairment.** The Canadian standards for asset impairment are in the process (in 2001) of being harmonized with those of the FASB. The process to determine an impairment loss is as follows: (1) Review events and changes in circumstances for possible impairment. (2) If events or changes suggest impairment, determine if the sum of the undiscounted expected future net cash flows from the long-lived asset is less than the asset's carrying amount. If less, measure the impairment loss. (3) Under 2001 Canadian Standards, the impairment loss is the amount by which the asset's carrying amount exceeds its net recoverable amount, under FASB standards, the impairment loss is the amount by which the asset's carrying amount is greater than its fair value. After an impairment loss is recorded, the reduced carrying amount of the long-lived asset is now considered its new cost basis. Impairment losses may not be restored for an asset held for use. If the asset is not in use, but instead is held for sale, the impaired asset should be reported at the lower of cost or net realizable value. It is not amortized. It can be continuously revalued, as long as the write-up is never greater that the carrying amount before impairment.

7.   **Explain the accounting procedures for depletion of natural resources.** The accounting procedures for the amortization of natural resources are: (1) establishment of depletion base, and (2) write-off of resource cost. Three factors are involved in establishing the depletion base: (a) *acquisition costs*, (b) *exploration costs*, and (c) *development costs.* In the oil and gas industry, both the full cost and successful efforts method are acceptable in determining the cost to be capitalized. Amortization of the resource cost, or depletion, is normally calculated on the units of production method, which means that depletion is a function of the number of units withdrawn during the period. In this approach, the natural resource's total cost less residual value is divided by the number of units estimated to be in the resource deposit, to obtain a cost per unit of product. The cost per unit is multiplied by the number of units withdrawn in the period to calculate depletion expense. Future removal and site restoration costs are accrued and charged to income each period as well.

8.   **Explain how tangible capital assets, including natural resources, are reported and analysed.** The basis of valuation for property, plant, and equipment and natural resources should be disclosed along with pledges, liens, and other commitments related to these assets. Any liability secured by property, plant, and equipment and natural resources should be disclosed. When assets are amortized, an accumulated amortization account is credited. Companies engaged in significant oil and gas producing activities must provide special additional disclosures about these activities. Analysis may be performed to evaluate the efficiency of use of a company's investment in assets through the calculation and interpretation of the asset turnover rate, profit margin, and the rate of return on assets.

*9.   **Describe the income tax method of determining capital cost allowance.** Capital cost allowance is the term used for amortization when calculating taxable income in income tax returns. The CCA method mechanics are similar to those for the declining-balance method except that rates are specified for asset classes and the amount claimed is based on year-end balances. The half-year rule is applied to net additions in the year whereby only 50% of the normal rate is permitted. For an asset class, retirements are accounted for under specific rules that govern the determination of taxable income. Capital gains will occur if the proceeds on disposal exceed the asset's original cost. When an asset class is eliminated, a terminal loss or recapture of capital cost allowance can occur.

      *This material is covered in Appendix 12-A in the text.

TIPS ON CHAPTER TOPICS

TIP: Amortization is also called depreciation or depletion, although amortization will be used here, it is more common in the U.S. to refer to depreciation, with amortization referring to intangible assets and depletion to wasting assets such as oil and gas or forestry industries.

TIP: **Residual value** is often referred to as **salvage value**, and sometimes it is called estimated **scrap value**.

TIP: Residual value is used in the calculation of amortization for the early years of life of an asset, defined as the estimated net realizable value of a capital asset at the end of its **useful life** to an enterprise, (Assets are usually retired for either physical—casualty or economic factors—technology, supersession or obsolescence) Salvage value is **not** a factor in determining amortization for the early years of life, and is defined as the asset's estimated net realizable value at the end of its life and is normally negligible; however, salvage value can effect the amount calculated for amortization in the last year(s) of an asset's life. An asset should **not** be amortized below its salvage value. (*CICA Hhandbook,* Section 3060, pars. .14 and .31).

TIP: Three basic questions in amortization are: What is the amount to be amortized? What is the asset's useful life? What pattern and method of cost apportionment is best for this asset?

TIP: The **activity method** is often called the **variable charge** approach or the **units of output** or the **units of production method**. This is most useful when the use of the asset in producing revenue streams differs from one period to another.

TIP: The **declining-balance amortization method** applies a constant rate to a declining book value to calculate amortization. The rate used is often twice the straight-line rate, in which case the method is then referred to as the **200% declining-balance method** or the **double declining-balance method**. Another declining balance method is the sum-of-the-years'-digits, whereby the amortizable amount is multiplied by a decreasing fraction each period. This method is rarely used in practice in Canada.

TIP: The **book value** of a plant asset is determined by deducting the balance of accumulated amortization from the balance of the related asset account. The balance in the related asset account is generally the asset's original cost. Thus, the estimated residual value does not directly affect the book value calculation. Book value is often called **carrying value**, **carrying amount**, **net asset value**, or **unamortized value**. An asset's book value at a given date may be far different than its market (fair) value at the same date.

TIP: **Amortizable cost** or **amortization base** is a term that refers to the total amount to be amortized over the life of the asset. It is determined by deducting the estimated residual value from the cost of the asset.

TIP: When an asset being amortized by a group or composite amortization method is disposed of, no gain or loss is recorded; the difference between the original cost of the asset and the proceeds from disposal is charged to Accumulated Amortization. The group method is used when assets are fairly homogeneous, while the composite method is employed when assets are heterogeneous in nature.

TIP: It is not uncommon for companies to have two different sets of books as financial reporting to shareholders can employ any acceptable method under GAAP, while tax reporting requires companies to use the prescribed government method of Capital Cost Allowance (CCA) which is a form of a declining balance method.

TIP: Amortization should be recognized for only the time is in a "ready to use" form. If an asset is purchased on July 1, only ½ year's amortization should be recognized. Similarly, if an asset is sold on March 1, two months amortization should be recognized prior to disposal.

TIP: Revisions of amortization rates, due to management decisions to change estimated lives, residual values or due to capitalization of costs is done on a **proactive basis.**

TIP: Canadian standards for impairment require that when the net carrying amount of the asset, less any amount for restoration or future site removal and future income taxes, are greater than the net recoverable amount, a charge to income should occur in the period. Once an impairment has been written down, it is not subsequently increased if conditions change.

TIP: When disposing of assets for taxation purposes, it is important to determine if it is the ultimate asset in the class. Upon disposal, there is the possibility of a **recapture** into income of CCA if a negative balance occurs in the asset class. If the asset is the last asset in the class, a **terminal loss** could occur when there is a positive balance in the asset class. Regardless, if the asset is sold for more than the original cost, a **capital gain** is recognized into income.

CASE 12-1

Purpose: (L.O. 1, 2) This case examines the process of matching the cost of fixed assets with the revenues which the assets help to generate.

Plant assets provide services for two or more periods. There is a cost to the services consumed; this cost should be matched with the periods benefited.

Instructions
(a) Briefly define amortization as used in accounting.
(b) Identify the factors that are relevant in determining the annual amortization and explain whether these factors are determined objectively or whether they are based on judgement.

(AICPA Adapted)

Solution to Case 12-1

(a)   Amortization is the accounting process of allocating an asset's historical cost (recorded amount) to the accounting periods benefited by the use of the asset. It is a process of cost allocation, not valuation. Amortization is not intended to provide funds for an asset's replacement; it is merely an application of the matching principle.

(b)   The factors relevant in determining the annual amortization for an amortizable asset are the initial recorded amount (acquisition cost and any subsequent capitalized costs), estimated salvage value, estimated useful life, and amortization method.

    Assets are typically recorded at their acquisition cost, which is in most cases objectively determinable. But cost assignments in other cases—"basket purchases" and selection of an implicit interest rate in asset acquisition under deferred-payment plans—may be quite subjective and involve considerable judgement.

    The salvage value is an estimate of an amount potentially realizable when the asset is retired from service. It is initially a judgement factor and is affected by the length of the asset's useful life to the enterprise.

    The useful life is also a judgement factor. It involves selecting the "unit" of measure of service life and estimating the number of such units embodied in the asset. Such units may be measured in terms of time periods or in terms of activity (for example, years or machine hours). When selecting the life, one should select the lower (shorter) of the physical life or the economic life to the user. Physical life involves wear and tear and casualties; economic life involves such things as technological obsolescence and inadequacy.

    Selecting the amortization method is generally a judgement decision; but, a method may be inherent in the definition adopted for the units of service life, as discussed earlier. For example, if such units are machine hours, the method is a function of the number of machine hours used during each period. A method should be selected that will best measure the portion of services expiring each period. Once a method is selected, it may be applied by using a predetermined, objectively derived formula.

EXERCISE 12-1

Purpose: (L.O. 3) This exercise will give you practice in calculating amortization for three successive periods for three commonly used methods.

Red River Company purchases equipment on January 1, Year 1, at a cost of $645,000. The asset is expected to have a service life of 12 years and a salvage value of $60,000.

Instructions
(a)   Calculate the amount of amortization for each of Years 1 through 3 using the straight-line amortization method.

(b)   Calculate the amount of amortization for each of Years 1 through 3 using the sum-of-the-years'-digits method.

(c)   Calculate the amount of amortization for each of Years 1 through 3 using the double-declining balance method. (In performing your calculations, round the constant percentage to the nearest one-hundredth of a percentage point and round final answers to the nearest dollar.)

Solution to Exercise 12-1

(a) $\dfrac{\$645,000 - \$60,000}{12} = \underline{\$48,750}$ Amortization for each of years 1 through 3

(b) $\dfrac{12 \times 13}{2} = 78$

         12/78 x ($645,000 - $60,000) = $\underline{\$90,000}$ amortization Year 1
         11/78 x ($645,000 - $60,000) = $\underline{\$82,500}$ amortization Year 2
         10/78 x ($645,000 - $60,000) = $\underline{\$75,000}$ amortization Year 3

(c) $\dfrac{100\%}{12} \times 2 = 16.67\%$

         $645,000 x 16.67% = $\underline{\$107,522}$ amortization Year 1
         ($645,000 - $107,522) x 16.67% = $\underline{\$\ 89,598}$ amortization Year 2
         ($645,000 - $107,522 - $89,598)
             x 16.67% = $\underline{\$\ 74,662}$ amortization Year 3

EXERCISE 12-2

Purpose: (L.O. 5) This exercise will provide an illustration of the calculations for amortization of partial periods.

Koehn Company purchased a new plant asset on April 1, 2002, at a cost of $345,000. It was estimated to have a service life of 20 years and a salvage value of $30,000. Koehn's accounting period is the calendar year.

Instructions (Round all final answers to the nearest dollar.)
   (a) Calculate the amount of amortization for this asset for 2002 and 2003 using the straight-line method.
   (b) Calculate the amount of amortization for this asset for 2002 and 2003 using the sum-of-the-year's-digits
   (c) Calculate the amount of depreciation for this asset for 2002 and 2003 using the double-declining balance method.

Solution to Exercise 12-2

(a) $\dfrac{\$345,000 - \$30,000}{20 \text{ years}} \times 9/12 = \underline{\$11,813}$ amortization for 2002

      $\dfrac{\$345,000 - \$30,000}{20 \text{ years}} = \underline{\$15,750}$ amortization for 2003

Approach and Explanation: Write down and apply the formula for straight-line amortization. Multiply the annual amortization amount by the portion of the asset's first year of service that falls in the given accounting period.

$$\frac{\text{Cost - Salvage Value}}{\text{Estimated Service LIfe}} = \text{Amortization Charge}$$

(b) $\dfrac{20\ (20\ +\ 1)}{2} = 210$

$$
\begin{aligned}
9/12 \times 20/210 \times (\$345{,}000 - \$30{,}000) &= \underline{\$22{,}500}\ \text{amortization for 2002} \\
3/12 \times 20/210 \times (\$345{,}000 - \$30{,}000) &= \$\ 7{,}500 \\
+\ 9/12 \times 19/210 \times (\$345{,}000 - \$30{,}000) &= \underline{\ \ 21{,}375} \\
&= \underline{\$28{,}875}\ \text{amortization for 2003}
\end{aligned}
$$

Approach and Explanation: Write down and apply the formula for sum-of-the-years'-digits amortization. Apportion the amortization for the given asset year between the two accounting periods involved. The first nine months of the asset's first year of life fall in the 2002 calendar year. The last three months of the asset's first year of life and the first nine months of the asset's second year of life fall in the 2003 calendar year. There is no shortcut to the two-part calculation of amortization for 2003, as illustrated above.

Formula: $\dfrac{n\ (n\ +\ 1)}{2} = \text{Sum of the Years}$

$$\frac{\begin{array}{c}\text{No. of Years Remaining at}\\ \text{Beginning of Asset Year}\end{array}}{\text{Sum of the Years}} \times (\text{Cost - Salvage}) = \text{Amortization for Full Asset Year}$$

(c) Straight-line rate $\dfrac{100\%}{20} = 5\%$; $5\% \times 2 = 10\%$

$10\% \times \$345{,}000 = \$34{,}500$ amortization for asset's first year
$10\% \times (\$345{,}000 - \$34{,}500) = \$31{,}050$ amortization for asset's second year

$9/12 \times \$34{,}500 = \underline{\$25{,}875}$ amortization for 2002

$$
\begin{aligned}
3/12 \times \$34{,}500 &= \$\ \ 8{,}625 \\
+\ 9/12 \times \$31{,}050 &= \underline{\ \ 23{,}288} \\
&= \$\ 31{,}913 \quad \text{amortization for 2003}
\end{aligned}
$$

Approach and Explanation: Write down and apply the formula for the declining balance method. Apportion the amortization for a given **asset year** between the two accounting periods involved.

Book Value
Constant Percentage x   at Beginning   = Amortization for Asset Year
of Asset Year

An alternative approach is as follows:

After the first partial year, calculate amortization for a full **accounting year** by multiplying the constant percentage by the book value of the asset at the beginning of the accounting period.

Thus, the calculation for 2003 would be as follows:

10% x ($345,000 - $25,875) = <u>$31,913</u>.

TIP: Companies use many methods to deal with partial year amortization as long as it is applied consistently, ex. Charging a full year's amortization in the year of purchase and no amortization in the year of disposal, or ½ year in the year of acquisition and ½ year in the year of disposal.

TIP: Taxation reporting requires the use of the **½ year rule** in which a company is deemed to make all purchases on July 1, irregardless of the actual date of purchase. This is why many companies will make purchases in the later part of the year and receive a ½ years worth of CCA.

EXERCISE 12-3

Purpose: (L.O. 3) This exercise is designed to test your ability to solve for missing data by applying your knowledge regarding amortization calculations.

Dunlap Company acquired a plant asset at the beginning of Year 1. The asset has an estimated service life of 5 years. An employee has prepared amortization schedules for this asset using three different methods to compare the results of using one method with the results of using other methods. You are to assume that the following schedules have been correctly prepared for this asset using (1) the straight-line (St.-line) method, (2) Activity (AM) method, and (3) the double-declining balance (DDB) method (switching to the straight-line method after the mid-life of the asset).

Year	Straight-line	Activity	Double-declining Balance
1	$ 6,000	$ 10,000	$ 14,400
2	6,000	8,000	8,640
3	6,000	6,000	5,184
4	6,000	4,000	888
5	6,000	2,000	888
Total	<u>$ 30,000</u>	<u>$ 30,000</u>	<u>$ 30,000</u>

Instructions

Answer the following questions:
(a)   What is the cost of the asset being amortized?
(b)   What amount, if any, was used in the amortization calculations for the salvage value of this asset?
(c)   Which method will produce the highest charge to income in Year 1?
(d)   Which method will produce the highest charge to income in Year 4?
(e)   Which method will produce the highest book value for the asset at the end of Year 3?

(f)   If the asset is sold at the end of Year 3, which method would yield the highest gain (or lowest loss) on disposal of the asset?

Solution to Exercise 12-3

(a)   If there is any salvage value and the amount is unknown (as is the case here), the cost would have to be determined by looking at the data for the double-declining balance method.

$$100\% \div 5 = 20\%; \quad 20\% \times 2 = 40\%$$
$$\text{Cost} \times 40\% = \$14,400; \quad \$14,400 \div 0.40 = \underline{\$36,000} \text{ cost of asset}$$

Approach: Write down the formula for each of the amortization methods mentioned. Fill in the data given for Year 1. Examine what remains to be solved.

(Cost - Salvage Value) ÷ Estimated Service Life = St.-line Amortization
(Cost - Salvage Value) ÷ 5 = $6,000

$$\frac{\text{(Cost - Salvage Value)}}{\text{Total estimated base}} = \text{Amortization rate}$$
Amortization rate x # units per year = AM Amortization

Constant Percentage x Cost = DDB Amortization
40% x Cost = $14,400

There are two variables (cost and salvage value) unknown for each of the first two methods, and there is no way to solve for either of them. However, cost can easily be determined for the third method (DDB). Once you solve for cost, it is a simple matter to solve for salvage value.

(b) $36,000 cost (answer a) - $30,000 total amortization = $\underline{\$6,000}$ salvage value

Approach: The difference between the answer to part (a) and the total amortization per the schedule ($30,000) is the salvage value used.

(c)   The highest charge to income for Year 1 will be yielded by the double-declining balance method.

Approach: Examine the amortization schedules. Notice the method that results in the highest amortization amount for Year 1.

(d)   The highest charge to income for Year 4 will be yielded by the straight-line method.

Approach: Examine the amortization schedules given. Notice the method that results in the highest amortization amount for Year 4.

(e)   The method to yield the highest book value at the end of Year 3 would be the method that yields the lowest accumulated amortization at the end of Year 3 which is the straight-line method. Calculations:

St.-line   = $36,000 - ($6,000 + $6,000 + $6,000)
              = $18,000 book value at the end of Year 3.
AM   = $36,000 - ($10,000 + $8,000 + $6,000)

                    = $12,000 book value at the end of Year 3.
DDB   = $36,000 - ($14,400 + $8,640 + $5,184)
                    = $7,776 book value at the end of Year 3.

Approach: Write down the formula to calculate book value: Cost - Accumulated Amortization = Book Value. To obtain a high book value, you need a low accumulated amortization. Examine the amortization schedules to determine the method that would yield the lowest total amortization for the first three years.

(f)   The method that will yield the highest gain (or lowest loss) if the asset is sold at the end of Year 3 is the method which will yield the lowest book value at the end of Year 3. In this case, it is the double-declining balance method.

Approach: Write down the formula to calculate gain or loss on disposal: Selling Price - Book Value = Gain (Loss). To obtain a high gain, you need a low book value. Examine the formula for book value. To get a low book value, you need high amortization charges. Use the amortization schedules to determine the method that would yield the highest accumulated amortization balance at the end of three years.

EXERCISE 12-4

Purpose: (L.O. 4) This exercise will enable you to practise working with the composite method for calculating amortization.

Presented below is information related to the Arctic Wolf Corporation (all assets are acquired at the beginning of Year 1):

Asset	Cost	Estimated Scrap	Estimated Life (in years) x
A	$60,750	$8,250	10
B	50,400	7,200	9
C	54,000	4,800	8
D	28,500	2,250	7
E	35,250	3,750	6

Instructions
(a)   Calculate the rate of amortization per year to be applied to the plant assets under the composite method.
(b)   Calculate the composite life.
(c)   Prepare the adjusting entry necessary at the end of the year to record amortization for Year 1.
(d)   Prepare the entry at the end of Year 6 to record the sale of fixed asset D for cash of $7,500. It was used for 6 years, and amortization was recorded under the composite method.

Solution to Exercise 12-4

(a)

Asset	Cost	Estimated Scrap	Amortizable Cost	Estimated Life	Amortization Per Year
A	$ 60,750	$ 8,250	$ 52,500	10	$ 5,250
B	50,400	7,200	43,200	9	4,800
C	54,000	4,800	49,200	8	6,150
D	28,500	2,250	26,250	7	3,750
E	35,250	3,750	31,500	6	5,250
	$228,900	$26,250	$202,650		$25,200

Composite rate = $25,200 ÷ $228,900; or <u>11.009%</u>

Approach and Explanation: Steps to calculate the composite rate:

1. Calculate what would be the amount of annual straight-line amortization for each asset by dividing each asset's **amortizable cost** by its estimated service life. Sum these amounts ($25,200).

2. Calculate the composite rate by dividing the total amortization per year (results of Step 1—$25,200) by the amount of **original cost** ($228,900).

(b) Composite life = $202,650 ÷ $25,200; or <u>8.04 years</u>

Approach and Explanation: Calculate the composite life by dividing the total amortizable cost ($202,650) by the total annual amortization charge ($25,200).

(c)
End of Year 1

Amortization Expense on Plant Assets	25,200	
Accumulated Amortization on Plant Assets..............		25,200
($228,900 x 11.009% = $25,200)		

Approach and Explanation: Calculate the amortization for any given year by multiplying the balance in the asset account by the composite rate (results of Step 2). The balance in the asset account will change over time due to the acquisition of new assets and the disposal of old assets.

(d)
End of Year 6

Cash	7,500	
Accumulated Amortization on Plant Assets	21,000	
Plant Assets		28,500

Approach and Explanation: When using the group or composite method, no gain or loss on disposition is recorded. The difference between the proceeds (if any) on disposal and the original cost of the asset is debited (or credited) to the Accumulated Amortization account. Thus, if an asset is retired before, or after, the average service of the group is reached, the resulting gain or loss is buried in the Accumulated Amortization account.

EXERCISE 12-5

Purpose: (L.O. 5) This exercise will provide you with an illustration of how to account for a change in the estimated service life and salvage value of a plant asset due to an expenditure subsequent to acquisition.

The Russell Company purchased a machine on January 1, 1992 for $105,000. The machine was being amortized using the straight-line method over an estimated life span of 20 years, with a $15,000 salvage value. At the beginning of 2002, when the machine had been in use for 10 years, the company paid $25,000 to overhaul the machine. As a result of this improvement, the company estimated that the useful life of the machine would be extended an additional 5 years and the salvage value would be reduced to $10,000.

Instructions
Calculate the amortization charge for 2002.

Solution to Exercise 12-5

Cost	$ 105,000
Accumulated amortization at 1/1/02	45,000[a]
Book value at 1/1/02	60,000
Additional expenditure capitalized	25,000
Revised book value	85,000
Current estimate of salvage value	10,000
Remaining amortizable cost at 1/1/02	75,000
Remaining years of useful life at 1/1/02	÷ 15[b]
Amortization expense for 2002	$ 5,000

[a]Cost	$105,000
Original estimate of salvage value	15,000
Original amortizable cost	90,000
Original service life in years	÷ 20
Original amortization per year	4,500
Number of years used	x 10
Accumulated Amortization at 1/1/02	$ 45,000

[b]Original estimate of life in years	20
Number of years used	(10)
Additional years	5
Remaining years of useful life at 1/1/02	15

TIP: A change in the estimated useful life and/or salvage value of an existing amortizable asset is to be accounted for prospectively (in current and/or future periods). Therefore, the book value at the beginning of the period of change, less the current estimate of salvage value, is to be allocated over the remaining periods of life, using the appropriate amortization method. The book value at the beginning of the period of change is calculated using the original estimates of service life and salvage value.

TIP: The $25,000 cost of overhaul is capitalized in this case because the cost benefits future periods by extending the useful life of the machine.

Approach: Whenever you have a situation that involves a change in the estimated service life and/or salvage value of a amortizable asset, use the format shown above to calculate the remaining amortizable cost and allocate that amount over the remaining useful life using the given amortization method.

EXERCISE 12-6

Purpose: (L.O. 3) This exercise will allow you to practise using various amortization methods and it will also give you the opportunity to compare the results of using one method to the results of using another method.

On January 1, 2002, Irish Company, a machine-tool manufacturer, acquires a piece of new industrial equipment for $1,000,000. The new equipment has a useful life of 5 years and the salvage value is estimated to be $100,000. Irish estimates that the new equipment can produce a total of 40,000 units and expects it to produce 10,000 units in its first year. Production is then estimated to decline by 1,000 units per year over the remaining useful life of the equipment.
       The following depreciation methods may be used:
  • Double declining-balance
  • Straight-line
  • Sum-of-the-years'-digits
  • Units-of-output

Instructions
(a)   Identify which amortization method would result in the maximization of profits for financial statement reporting for the **three**-year period ending December 31, 2004. Prepare a schedule showing the amount of accumulated amortization at December 31, 2004, under the method selected, (Show supporting calculations in good form). Ignore present value and income tax considerations in your answer.
(b)   Identify which amortization method would result in the minimization of profits for the **three**-year period ending December 31, 2004. Prepare a schedule showing the amount of accumulated amortization at December 31, 2004, under the method selected, (Show supporting calculations in good form). Ignore present value and income tax considerations in your answer.

(AICPA Adapted)

Solution to Exercise 12-6

(a)   The straight-line method of amortization would result in the maximization of profits for financial statement reporting for the three-year period ending December 31, 2004.

Irish Company
ACCUMULATED AMORTIZATION USING STRAIGHT-LINE METHOD
December 31, 2004

(Cost - Salvage Value) ÷ Estimated Service Life

($1,000,000 - $100,000) ÷ 5 years = $180,000

Year	Amortization Expense	Accumulated Amortization
2002	$ 180,000	$ 180,000
2003	180,000	360,000
2004	180,000	540,000
	$ 540,000	

(b)   The double declining balance method of amortization would result in the minimization of profits for the three-year period ending December 31, 2004.

Irish Company
ACCUMULATED AMORTIZATION USING
DOUBLE DECLINING-BALANCE METHOD
December 31, 2004

Straight-line rate is 5 years, or 20%. Double declining-balance rate is 40% (20% x 2). Ignore salvage value.

Year	Book Value at Beginning of Year	Amortization Expense	Accumulated Amortization
2002	$1,000,000	$400,000	$400,000
2003	600,000	240,000	640,000
2004	360,000	144,000	784,000
		$784,000	

Other supporting calculations:

Irish Company
ACCUMULATED AMORTIZATION USING
SUM-OF-THE-YEARS'-DIGITS METHOD
December 31, 2004

$$[n \times (n + 1)] \div 2 = [5 \times (5 + 1)] \div 2 = 15$$

5/15 X ($1,000,000 - $100,000) = $300,000
4/15 x ($1,000,000 - $100,000) = $240,000
3/15 X ($1,000,000 - $100,000) = $180,000

Year	Amortization Expense	Accumulated Amortization
2002	$ 300,000	$ 300,000
2003	240,000	540,000
2004	180,000	720,000
	$ 720,000	

Irish Company
ACCUMULATED AMORTIZATION USING
UNITS-OF-OUTPUT METHOD
December 31, 2004

(Cost - Salvage Value) ÷ Total Units of Output =
($1,000,000 - $100,000) ÷ 40,000 =
$22.50 Amortization per Unit

10,000 x $22.50 = $225,000
9,000 x $22.50 = $202,500
8,000 x $22.50 = $180,000

Year	Amortization Expense	Accumulated Amortization
2002	$ 225,000	$ 225,000
2003	202,500	427,500
2004	180,000	607,500
	$ 607,500	

EXERCISE 12-7

Purpose: (L.O. 7) This exercise will give you practice in calculating depletion.

During 2002, Big Rock Corporation acquired a mineral mine for $2,700,000, of which $450,000 is attributable to the land value after the mineral has been removed. Engineers estimate that 15 million units of mineral can be recovered from this mine. During 2002, 1,200,000 units were extracted and 800,000 units were sold.

Instructions
Calculate the depletion for 2002.

Solution to Exercise 12-7

($2,700,000 - $450,000) ÷ 15,000,000 = $.15

$.15 x 1,200,000 = $180,000 Depletion for 2002

Approach and Explanation: Write down the formula to calculate depletion, enter the data given, and solve.

Acquisition Cost + Costs to Explore and Develop
- Residual Value of Land +

$$\frac{\text{Costs to Restore Land to Alternative Use}}{\text{Number of Units to be Extracted}} = \frac{\text{Depletion Cost Per}}{\text{Recoverable Unit}}$$

Depletion Cost Per Recoverable Unit	x	Units Extracted During Period	=	Depletion for the Period

TIP: The depletion charge for the period is the amount to be removed from the property, plant, and equipment classification ($180,000 in this case). It is based on the units **extracted** from the earth during the period. The portion of this $180,000, which gets to the income statement is dependent upon the number of units **sold**. When the number of units extracted exceed the number sold, as in this exercise, a portion of the depletion costs goes into the Inventory account on the balance sheet.

EXERCISE 12-8

Purpose: (L.O. 9A) This exercise will give you practice in calculating CCA.

Westcoast Fishing purchased equipment for their boat (class 8—20%), valued at $60,000 in March of 2002. The Unamortized Capital Cost at the beginning of 2002 was $240,000. In 2003, the company sold a boat valued for $25,000 for which they had originally paid $40,000. In 2004, the company sold an asset for $150,000, which had originally cost $325,000. This was the last asset in the class. Calculate the CCA for each of years 2002, 2003 and 2004. Determine if there was any recapture, terminal losses or capital gains for the company?

Solution to Exercise 12-8

Draw up a chart to recognize the CCA and UCC for the year. Remember the ½ year rule is in effect for equipment purchases. Since there is already an opening balance in the UCC, two separate calculations will need to be done to recognize the CCA in the period.

Class 8-20%	CCA	UCC
December 31,2001		$240,000
Additions less disposals, 2002		
— Equipment ($60,000)		$60,000
		$300,000
CCA, 2002		
$240,000 x 20% = $48,000		
$60,000 x ½ x 20% = 6,000	$54,000	(54,000)
		$246,000
December 31, 2002		
Additions less disposals, 2003		
—Equipment (lesser of original cost $40,000		
And proceeds of disposal $25,000)		(25,000)
		$221,000
CCA, 2003: $221,000 x 20%	$44,200	(44,200)

December 31, 2003 $176,800
Additions less disposals, 2004
   —Equipment (lesser of original cost $325,000
   and proceeds of disposal $150,000) $150,000
                                                                                                                    $26,800

Terminal Loss, 2004 $26,800   (26,800)
                                                                                                                    $0

The company experienced a terminal loss in 2004 as the disposal of this asset represented the last asset in the class. Once disposed of, there was a positive balance left in the account which would be written off against current income. (In essence, the company did not amortize enough during the life of the asset.)

ILLUSTRATION 12-1
ACCOUNTING FOR IMPAIRMENTS (L.O. 6)

A summary of the key concepts in accounting for impairments is presented below:

A **recoverability test** is used to determine whether an impairment has occurred: If the sum of the expected future net undiscounted cash flows (from the use of the asset and its eventual disposition) is less than the carrying amount of the asset, the asset has been impaired.

If the recoverability test indicates that an impairment has occurred, a loss is calculated. The impairment loss is the amount by which the carrying amount of the asset exceeds its fair value. The fair value of an asset is measured by its market value (if an active market exists) or by the present value of expected future net cash flows (if an active market does not exist). If an asset is to be disposed of instead of held for use, the asset's net realizable value (fair value less cost to sell) is used as a measure of the net cash flows that will be received from this asset.

Subsequent to recognizing the loss from impairment, the following guidelines are to be followed:
1. If the asset is to be held for use, it will be amortized based on the new cost basis.
2. If the asset is to be sold, no more amortization is taken once the asset is no longer used.
3. Restoration of the impairment loss is not permitted for an asset which is held for use.
4. Restoration of the impairment loss is allowed for an asset held for sale. Because assets held for disposal will be recovered through sale rather than through use in operations, they are continually revalued. Each period they are reported at the lower of cost or net realizable value. Thus, an asset held for disposal can be written up or down in future periods, as long as the write-up does not produce a new carrying value greater than the carrying amount of the asset before an adjustment was made to reflect a decision to dispose of the asset.

TIP: Losses or gains related to impaired assets should be reported as part of income from continuing operations. Thus, they are **not** classified as extraordinary items.

ANALYSIS OF MULTIPLE-CHOICE TYPE QUESTIONS

QUESTION
1.   (L.O. 2) The term "amortizable cost," or "amortizable base," as it is used in accounting, refers to:
   a.   The total amount to be charged (debited) to expense over an asset's useful life.
   b.   Cost of the asset less the related amortization recorded to date.
   c.   The estimated market value of the asset at the end of its useful life.
   d.   The acquisition cost of the asset.

Approach and Explanation: Write down a definition of amortizable cost **before** you read any of the answer selections. **Amortizable cost** or **amortizable base** is the total amount of asset cost that can be expensed over the life of the asset; thus, it is original cost less estimated residual (salvage) value. Answer selection "b" describes the term book value. Answer selection "c" describes salvage value or residual value. Selection "d" represents the total cost of the asset. (Solution = a.)

QUESTION
2.   (L.O. 2) A machine is purchased by the Dunnagin Company for $18,000. Dunnagin pays $6,000 in cash and gives a note payable for $12,000 that is payable in instalments over a four-year period. Dunnagin estimates that the machine could physically last for 12 years, even though Dunnagin expects to use it in its business for only 9 years. The period of time to be used by Dunnagin for amortization purposes is:
   a.   4 years
   b.   5 years
   c.   9 years
   d.   12 years

Approach and Explanation: Think about the objective of the amortization process—to allocate an asset's cost to the periods benefited. The asset should be amortized over its useful life, which is the length of time the asset will be of service to the entity using it. (Solution = c.)

QUESTION
3.   (L.O. 3) A machine with an estimated service life of 5 years and an expected salvage value of $5,000 was purchased on January 1, 2002 for $50,000. The amount to be recorded for amortization for 2002, 2003, and 2004, respectively, using the sum-of-the-years'-digits method will be:
   a. $20,000; $12,000; $7,200
   b. $16,667; $13,333; $10,000
   c. $15,000; $12,000; $9,000
   d. $15,000; $8,000; $4,400

Approach and Explanation: Write down the formula to calculate SYD depreciation. Enter the data given and solve.

$$\frac{n\,(n\,+\,1)}{2} = \text{Sum of the Years} \qquad\qquad \frac{5\,(6)}{2} = 15$$

$$\frac{\text{\# of Years Life Remaining at Beginning of Asset Year}}{\text{Sum of the Years}} \times (\text{Cost - Salvage}) = \text{Amortization for Full Asset Year}$$

2002:	($50,000 - $5,000) x 5/15 =	$ 15,000
2003:	($50,000 - $5,000) x 4/15 =	$ 12,000
2004:	($50,000 - $5,000) x 3/15 =	$ 9,000 (Solution = c.)

QUESTION
4.   (L.O. 3) A machine with an estimated service life of 5 years and an expected salvage value of $5,000 was purchased on January 1, 2002, for $50,000. The amount to be recorded for amortization for years 2002, 2003, and 2004, respectively, using the 200% declining-balance method will be:
   a. $20,000; $12,000; $7,200.
   b. $18,000; $10,800; $6,480.
   c. $16,667; $13,333; $10,000.
   d. $10,000; $8,000; $6,400.

Approach and Explanation: Write down the formula for the declining-balance method. Enter the data given and solve.

Book Value at Beginning of Year x Constant Percentage = Amortization

Constant Percentage = 2 x (100% ÷ Life) = 2 x (100% ÷ 5) = 40%

2002:	$50,000 x 40% =	$20,000
2003:	($50,000 - $20,000) x 40% =	$12,000
2004:	($50,000 - $20,000 - $12,000) x 40% =	$ 7,200

(Solution = a.)

QUESTION
5.   (L.O. 3) Salvage (residual) value may or may not be used in calculating amortization expense in the early years of an asset's life. Net income is understated if, in the first year, estimated salvage value is excluded from the amortization calculation when using the:

	Units of Output Method	Double-Declining Balance Method
a.	Yes	Yes
b.	No	No
c.	No	Yes
d.	Yes	No

Approach and Explanation: Before looking at the methods addressed directly in the question, think about how salvage value affects the amortization calculation under various methods. In considering the common amortization methods such as straight-line, activity methods, and declining-balance methods. The declining-balance methods are the only methods that do not use the residual value in calculating amortization in the early years of the asset's life. However, the residual value may affect the calculations with the declining-balance method in the latter years of the asset's life because the asset should not be amortized below its residual value. The units-of-output method is an activity method. (Solution = d.)

QUESTION

6.   (L.O. 3, 5) A machine was purchased for $8,000,000 on January 1, 2002. It has an estimated useful life of 8 years and a residual value of $800,000. Amortization is being calculated using the double-declining method. What amount should be shown for this machine, net of accumulated amortization, in the company's December 31, 2003 balance sheet?
a. $4,000,000
b. $4,500,000
c. $6,000,000
d. $6,125,000

Approach and Explanation: Write down the formula to calculate book value and the formula to calculate amortization using the double-declining balance method. Fill in the data from the scenario at hand and solve. Be careful that you don't get so involved with the calculation for amortization that you lose sight of the question—and that is, to calculate the book value of the equipment. It would be helpful to underline the middle of the last sentence of the stem of the question in order to keep your focus on what is being asked.

Cost - Accumulated Depreciation = Book Value

Constant Percentage x Book Value at Beginning of the Year = Amortization
$100\% \div 8 \times 2 = 25\%$

Year	BV beginning	Rate	Amortization Expense	Balance of Accumulated Amortization	NBV (End of year)
1	$8,000,000	25%	$2,000,000	$2,000,000	$6,000,000
2	$6,000,000	25%	$1,500,000	$3,500,000	$4,500,000

(Solution = b.)

QUESTION

7.   (L.O. 3, 5) Tammy Corporation purchased a machine on July 1, 2002 for $900,000. The machine has an estimated life of 5 years and a salvage value of $120,000. The machine is being amortized by the 150% declining-balance method. What amount of amortization should be recorded for the year ended December 31, 2003?
a. $229,500
b. $198,900
c. $189,000
d. $163,800

Approach and Explanation: Write down the formula to use for the declining-balance approach. (Notice the facts indicate there is a partial period for the first year (2002) and the question asks for the amortization for the 2003 reporting period.) Calculate the rate that is 150% of the straight-line rate. Apply the formula to the facts given. Remember that salvage value is not used with this method in calculating amortization in the early years of the asset's life.

Constant Percentage x Book Value at Beginning of the Year = Amortization

$$\frac{100\%}{\text{Life}} = \frac{100\%}{5 \text{ years}} = 20\% \qquad 20\% \times 150\% = 30\% \text{ constant percentage}$$

30% x $900,000 = $270,000 First year of life
30% x (900,000 - $270,000) = $189,000 Second year of life
   1/2 x $270,000 = $135,000 for 2002
   (1/2 x $270,000) + (1/2 x $189,000) = <u>$229,500 for 2003</u>
OR
   30% x ($900,000 - $135,000) = <u>$229,500 for 2003</u>   (Solution = a.)

QUESTION

8.   (L.O. 3, 5) A plant asset with a five-year estimated useful life and no salvage value is sold during the second year of the asset's life. How would the use of the straight-line method of amortization instead of an accelerated amortization method affect the amount of gain or loss on the sale of the plant asset?

	Gain	Loss
a.	Increase	Decrease
b.	Decrease	Increase
c.	No Effect	Increase
d.	No Effect	No Effect

Approach and Explanation: An accelerated method would result in more accumulated amortization and, therefore, a lower book value. In contrast, the straight-line method results in less accumulated amortization and a higher book value. This means a lower gain or a higher loss is calculated if the asset is sold and the straight-line method is in use. One way you can prove this to yourself is to make up a set of facts (cost, service life, accelerated method to use) and assume the asset is sold for a given amount at the end of the second year. Compare that gain or loss with the gain or loss that would result if the straight-line method is used. (Solution = b.)

QUESTION

9.   (L.O. 4) Roberts Truck Rental uses the group amortization method for its fleet of trucks. When it retires one of its trucks and receives cash from a salvage company, the carrying value of property, plant, and equipment will be decreased by the:
a.   Original cost of the truck.
b.   Original cost of the truck less the cash proceeds.
c.   Cash proceeds received.
d.   Cash proceeds received and original cost of the truck.

Approach and Explanation: Write down the journal entry to record the disposal of the truck and analyse its effect. Remember that no gain or loss is recorded on the disposal when the group or composite method is used.

Cash	....	Proceeds
Accumulated Amortization	....	**Plug**
Truck	....	Original Cost

In analyzing the entry's net effect on the book value (carrying amount) of property, plant, and equipment we find the following: (1) The decrease in Truck will reduce PP&E by the truck's original cost. (2) The debit to Accumulated Amortization will increase PP&E by the excess of the truck's original cost over the proceeds from disposal. (3) Therefore, the net effect is to decrease PP&E by the amount of the cash proceeds from the sale. (Solution = c.)

QUESTION

10.   (L.O. 4) Which of the following uses a straight-line amortization calculation?

	Group Amortization	Composite Amortization
a.	Yes	Yes
b.	Yes	No
c.	No	Yes
d.	No	No

Explanation: Both the group and composite amortization methods use a straight-line method calculation. Both methods perform one calculation for a group of assets. The group method is used for a collection of similar assets; whereas, the composite method is used for a group of dissimilar assets. Each method involves the calculation of a total amortizable cost for all the assets included in one asset account and of an estimated weighted-average useful life. (Solution = a.)

QUESTION

11.   (L.O. 5) The Schoen Company purchased a piece of equipment at the beginning of 1992 for $60,000. The equipment was being amortized using the straight-line method over an estimated life of 20 years, with no salvage value. At the beginning of 2002, when the equipment had been in use for 10 years, the company paid $10,000 to overhaul the equipment. As a result of this improvement, the company estimates that the useful life of the equipment will be extended an additional 5 years. What should be the amortization expense for this equipment in 2002?

a. $2,000
b. $2,667
c. $3,000
d. $1,867

Approach and Explanation: Write down the model or format to calculate amortization whenever there has been a change in the estimated service life and/or salvage value. Fill in the data of the case at hand and solve.

Cost	$ 60,000
Accumulated amortization at 1/1/02	30,000[a]
Book value (before overhaul) at 1/1/02	30,000
Additional expenditure capitalized (if any)	10,000
Revised book value (after overhaul)	40,000
Current estimate of salvage value	0
Remaining amortizable cost at 1/1/02	40,000
Remaining years of useful life at 1/1/02	÷ 15[b]
Amortization expense for 2002	$ 2,667

(Solution = b.)

[a]Cost	$ 60,000
Original estimate of salvage	0
Original amortizable cost	60,000
Original service life in years	÷ 20
Original amortization per year	3,000
Number of years used	x 10
Accumulated amortization at 1/1/02	$ 30,000

[b]Original estimate of life in years	20
Number of years used	(10)
Additional years	5
Remaining years of useful life at 1/1/02	15

> **TIP:** Be careful when calculating the length of time between two dates. The length of time between the beginning of 1992 and the beginning of 2002 is 10 years; whereas, the length of time between the end of 1992 and the beginning of 2002 is nine years. It is a common mistake to deduct one year from the other (2002 - 1992 = 10 years). As you can see from the foregoing, that will not always work. It is wise to write down the years that fall between the two dates and then count those years on your list. For example, the length of time between the end of 1999 and the beginning of 2002 is two years and is determined as follows:
>
>   2000   1
>   2001   2

QUESTION

12.   (L.O. 6) As the result of certain changes in circumstances indicating that the carrying amount of plant assets may not be recoverable, Timberlake Company reviewed the assets at the end of 2002 for impairment. The company estimates that it will receive net future cash inflows of $85,000 (undiscounted) as a result of continuing to hold and use these assets. The fair value of the assets at December 31, 2002 is estimated to be $75,000. The assets were acquired two years ago at a cost of $500,000 and have been amortized using the straight-line method and a five-year service life. The loss from impairment to be reported at the end of 2002 is:

a. $0
b. $215,000
c. $225,000
d. $300,000

Explanation: The carrying amount of the asset at the end of 2002 is $300,000 [$500,000 cost less (2 years × $500,000 × 20%)], but the recoverable amount is only $85,000. Thus, the test for recognition of an impairment loss has been met. The impairment loss is measured by the excess of the carrying amount ($300,000) over the fair value ($75,000). Therefore, Timberlake should recognize a loss of $225,000 ($300,000 - $75,000 = $225,000). (Solution = c.)

QUESTION
13.   (L.O. 8) The book value of a plant asset is:
    a.   The fair market value of the asset at a balance sheet date.
    b.   The asset's acquisition cost less the total related amortization recorded to date.
    c.   Equal to the balance of the related accumulated amortization account.
    d.   The assessed value of the asset for property tax purposes.

Approach and Explanation: Write down the definition for the term book value: **book value** is the asset's original cost (acquisition cost) less accumulated amortization. Look for the answer selection that agrees with your definition. (Solution = b.)

QUESTION
14.   (L.O. 8) The rate of return on total assets can be calculated by which of the following calculations?

1. $$\frac{\text{Net income}}{\text{Net sales}}$$

2. $$\frac{\text{Net sales}}{\text{Average total assets}}$$

3. Profit margin on sales x Asset turnover

4. $$\frac{\text{Net income}}{\text{Average total assets}}$$

    a.   Formula 1.
    b.   Formula 2.
    c.   Formula 3.
    d.   Formula 4.
    e.   Formula 3 or 4.

Explanation: Formula 1 above measures the rate of return on sales (profit margin on sales ratio). Formula 2 calculates the asset turnover ratio. Formula 3 is one of two ways to calculate the rate of return on total assets; Formula 4 is the second of two ways to calculate the rate of return on total assets. (Solution = e.)

QUESTION

15. (L.O. 9) Pantanges Inc. has just sold the last asset in class 8 for $20,000. The original cost of the asset was $18,000. The UCC prior to the disposal was valued at $35,000. Pantages would report:

    a.   recapture of $15,000
    b.   capital gain of $15,000
    c.   terminal loss of $15,000
    d.   terminal loss of $2,000

Solution: Think about the definitions of the terms listed. Recapture occurs when the last asset of a class is disposed of and, after the disposal, the asset class has a negative balance. The amount would be added to income. A capital gain occurs when a company sells an asset for more than they paid for the asset (not the case here). A terminal loss occurs when the last asset of a class is disposed of and, after the disposal, the asset class has a positive balance as is the case here. (answer = c).

CHAPTER 13

INTANGIBLE ASSETS

OVERVIEW

The balance sheet classification for intangible assets is used to report assets that lack physical existence and are not properly classifiable elsewhere. For instance (1) bank deposits and accounts receivable both are intangible by a legal definition but are properly classified as current assets for accounting purposes, and (2) investment in stock is intangible in nature but should be classified as either a current asset or a long-term investment for accounting purposes. Assets such as patents, trademarks, copyrights, and franchises are intangible in nature and are classified in the intangible asset section of a balance sheet. Intangible assets derive their value from the rights and privileges granted to the company using the assets and are discussed in this chapter.

SUMMARY OF LEARNING OBJECTIVES

1. **Describe the characteristics of intangible assets.** Intangible assets have two main characteristics: (1) they lack physical existence and (2) they are not financial instruments. Intangibles may be subdivided on the basis of the following characteristics: (1) *Identifiability:* separately identifiable or lacking specific identification. (2) *Manner of acquisition:* acquired singly, in groups, or in business combinations, or developed internally. (3) *Expected period of benefit:* limited by law or contract, related to human or economic factors, or indefinite or indeterminate duration. (4) *Separability from the enterprise:* rights transferable without title, salable, or inseparable from the enterprise.

2. **Discuss the recognition and measurement issues of acquiring intangibles.** Intangibles,like other assets, are recorded at cost. When several intangibles, or a combination of intangibles and tangibles, are bought in a "basket purchase," the cost should be allocated on the basis of relative fair values. Costs incurred to develop an intangible internally are generally expensed immediately because of the uncertainty of the future benefits, and the inability to relate the costs with specific intangible assets. Deferred charges are permitted in restricted circumstances where the future benefits associated with the costs incurred can be identified. When acquired in a business combination, it is necessary that any identifiable intangibles be recognized separately from the goodwill component. Only those that can be exchanged or whose future benefits can be controlled through contractual or other legal means should be recognized separately as identifiable intangibles.

3. **Explain how specifically identifiable intangibles are valued subsequent to acquisition.** An intangible with a finite useful life should be amortized over its useful life to the entity. Except in unusual and specific circumstances, the residual value is assumed to be zero. An intangible with an indefinite life should not be amortized until its life is determined to be no longer indefinite. The carrying values of the intangibles are subsequently tested for impairment. The test for intangibles that are amortized is against the net recoverable amount, while the test for those not amortized is against their fair value.

4. **Identify the types of specifically identifiable intangible assets.** The major identifiable intangible assets are: (1) **Patents:** gives the holder exclusive right to use, manufacture, and sell a product or process for a period of 20 years without interference or infringement by others. (2) **Copyrights:** a federally granted right that all authors, painters, musicians, sculptors, and other artists have in their creations and expressions. (3) **Trademarks and trade names:** a word,

phrase, or symbol that distinguishes or identifies a particular enterprise or product. (4) **Leaseholds:** a contractual understanding between a lessor (owner of property) and a lessee (renter or property) that grants the lessee the right to use specific property, owned by the lessor, for a specific period of time in return for stipulated, and generally periodic, cash payments. (5) **Franchises and licences:** a contractual arrangement under which the franchisor grants the franchisee the right to sell certain products or services, to use certain trademarks or trade names, or to perform certain functions, usually within a designated geographical area.

5.   **Explain the conceptual issues related to goodwill.** Goodwill is unique because unlike receivables, inventories, and patents that can be sold or exchanged individually in the marketplace, goodwill can be identified only with the business as a whole. Goodwill is a "going-concern" valuation and is recorded only when an entire business is purchased. Goodwill generated internally is not capitalized in the accounts, because measuring the components of goodwill is simply too complex and associating any costs with future benefits too difficult. The future benefits of goodwill may have no relationship to the costs incurred in the development of that goodwill. Also, goodwill may exist even in the absence of specific costs to develop it.

6.   **Describe the accounting procedures for recording goodwill at acquisition and subsequently.** To calculate goodwill, the fair value of the identifiable assets acquired and liabilities assumed is compared with the purchase price of the acquired business. The residual is goodwill—the excess of cost over fair value of the identifiable net assets acquired. Goodwill is sometimes identified on the balance sheet as the excess of cost over the fair value of the net assets acquired. Subsequent to acquisition, goodwill is tested annually for impairment, and, at other times, is tested on an events and circumstances basis. When the implied fair value of goodwill is less than its carrying value, an impairment loss is recognized.

7.   **Differentiate between research and development expenditures and describe and explain the rational for the accounting for each.** R & D costs are not in themselves intangible assets, but research and development activities frequently result in the development of something that is patented or copyrighted. Research is planned investigation undertaken with the hope of gaining new scientific or technical knowledge and understanding. Development is the translation of research findings or other knowledge into a plan or design for new or substantially improved products or processes prior to commercial production or use. The difficulties in accounting for R & D expenditures are (1) identifying the costs associated with particular activities, projects, or achievements; and (2) determining the magnitude of the future benefits and length of time over which such benefits may be realized. Accounting practice requires that all research expenditures be expensed, and that all development costs be expensed except in prescribed circumstances. The circumstances require reasonable assurance of realization of future benefits.

8.   **Identify other examples of deferred charges and the accounting requirements for them.** Other deferred charges include long-term prepayments, debt discount and issue costs, pre-operating costs, organization costs, and advertising costs. In general, only costs determined to have specific future benefits may be deferred. They are charged to income on the same basis that the future benefits are recognized.

9.   **Indicate the disclosure requirements for intangible, including deferred charges.** Similar to tangible capital assets, the cost and any accumulated amortization must be reported on the balance sheet, with separate disclosure of the amortization expense amount on the income statement. For intangibles that are not amortized, companies must indicate the amount of any impairment losses recognized as well as information about the circumstances requiring the writedown. Goodwill is required to be separately reported.

*10.   **Explain various approaches to valuing goodwill.** One method of valuing goodwill is the excess earnings approach. Using this approach, the total expected future earnings the company is expected to generate is calculated. The next step is to calculate "normal earnings" by determining and applying the normal rate of return on assets in that industry. The difference between what the firm earns and what the industry earns is referred to as the excess earnings. This excess earning power indicates that there are unidentifiable underlying asset values that result in the higher than average earnings. Finding the value of goodwill is a matter of discounting these excess future earnings to their present value. The number of years method of valuing goodwill, which simply multiples the excess earnings by the number of years of expected excess earnings, is used to provide a rough measure of goodwill. Another method of valuing goodwill is the discounted free cash flow method, which projects the future operating cash that will be generated over and above the amount needed to maintain current operating levels. The present value of the free cash flows is today's value of the firm.

   * This material appears in Appendix 13-A of the text.

TIPS ON CHAPTER TOPICS

TIP: As the book goes to print, accounting for intangibles are changing in Canada. There is a move to harmonize with U.S. standards, thus the book will use the proposed changes for this chapter.

TIP: Research and development (R & D) costs are to be expensed in the period incurred, except for very specific prescribed situations where the economic benefit realizable is assured for development cost capitalization to occur. All research costs are to be expensed as the future economic benefit is too difficult to ascertain.

TIP: Intangible assets have three main characteristics which are:
   1.   **They lack physical existence.** Unlike tangible assets such as property, plant, and equipment, intangible assets derive their value from the rights and privileges granted to the company using them.
   2.   **They are not a financial instrument.** Assets such as bank deposits, accounts receivable, and long-term investments in bonds and stocks lack physical substance, but are not classified as intangible assets. These assets are financial instruments and derive their value from the right (claim) to receive cash or cash equivalents in the future.
   3.   **They are long-term in nature and subject to amortization.** Intangible assets provide services over a period of years. Investments in these assets are normally assigned to future periods through periodic amortization charges. They are not current items and exclude non-capital assets.

   The most common types of intangibles reported are patents, copyrights, franchises or licences, trademarks or trade names, and goodwill. Intangible assets are often further subdivided on the basis of the following characteristics:

   1.   **Identifiability.** Separately identifiable or lacking specific identification.
   2.   **Manner of Acquisition.** Acquired singly, in groups, or in business combinations, or developed internally.
   3.   **Expected Period of Benefit.** Limited by law or contract, related to human or economic factors, or indefinite or indeterminate duration.
   4.   **Separability from an Entire Enterprise.** Rights transferable without title, saleable, or inseparable from the enterprise or a substantial part of it.

   These subdivisions provide insight into how the reporting requirements for intangibles have developed.

TIP: A corporation's intangible items such as quality of management, customer loyalty, information infrastructure, trade secrets, knowledge, intellectual capital, and computer programming know-how often provide more value to a corporation than its "hard" assets (like buildings and equipment), and yet they are normally not reported on the company's balance sheet. These "soft" assets are all part of goodwill if and when they are purchased by another corporation as a part of the whole business in a business combination.

TIP: The guidelines used in determining the cost of an intangible asset are similar to those for determining the cost of inventory and property, plant, and equipment items. The **cost of an intangible asset** includes all costs of acquisition and expenditures necessary to make the intangible asset ready for its intended use—for example, purchase price, legal fees, and other incidental costs. The cost of the intangible is measured by the fair market value, (cash equivalent value) of the consideration given or by the fair market value of the intangible asset received, whichever is more clearly evident. When several intangibles, or a combination of intangibles and tangibles are bought in a "basket purchase," the total cost should be allocated to the individual items on the basis of their fair market values of the items. Thus, essentially the accounting treatment for purchased intangibles closely parallels that followed for purchased tangible assets.

TIP: The costs incurred to create intangibles are generally expensed as incurred. The only internal costs capitalized are direct costs incurred in obtaining the intangible, such as legal costs.

TIP: The systematic allocation of the cost of intangible assets to expense over the periods benefited is called **amortization.** Usually the straight-line method is employed. **Prior to 2001,** each intangible should be amortized over its useful life; however, the amortization period should not exceed 40 years, (even if the asset has an indefinite life such as goodwill). (The new proposed changes would limit the amortization period to 20 years for most intangible assets.). The greater the uncertainty regarding an asset's useful life, the shorter is the amortization period. If an intangible becomes impaired or worthless, the asset should be written down or written off immediately to expense (or loss).

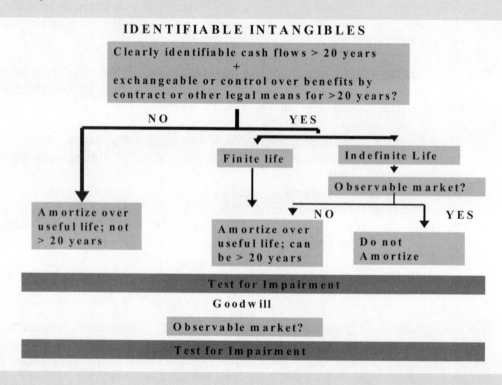

TIP: When an intangible asset is amortized, the charge (debit) should be reported as an expense and the credit is made to the appropriate asset account. A separate accumulated amortization account may be used but usually the asset account is credited directly.

TIP: An observable market is one in which intangible assets are bought and sold from which a market price can be observed to estimate the fair value of a similar asset.

TIP: Patents have a granted life of 20 years from the date of application. An average time from application to granting of the patent is 3 years, thus the useful life is a maximum of 17 years generally.

TIP: To record goodwill when a business is acquired, the total fair market value of the net tangible and identifiable intangible assets is compared with the purchase price of the acquired business. The difference is considered goodwill, which is why goodwill is sometimes referred to as a "master valuation" account. Goodwill is the residual: the excess of cost over fair value of the identifiable net assets acquired.

TIP: Negative goodwill occurs when the fair value of the identifiable assets acquired is higher than the purchase price paid. The excess should be used to reduce the amounts assigned to given assets acquired and, if any remains, the remainder should be treated as an extraordinary gain.

TIP: To capitalize earnings means to discount or calculate the present value of the projected future earnings of an asset or business. Calculating goodwill (appendix 13A) uses various methods to determine benefit of acquisition. In each case, it is assumed that the benefit (goodwill) is represented by excess earnings over and above the norm for the industry, with the view that any excess earnings is due to the purchased goodwill. The methods used are the excess earnings approach, number of years method and discounted free cash flow method.

TIP: Goodwill should be recorded on a company's books as an asset and only reduced if it is found to be impaired (test for impairment, based on a regular, (annual or interim basis) testing), or if associated assets are sold or disposed of. Impairment losses are recognized separately before extraordinary items and discontinued operations on the income statement. The credit part of the journal entry should be to accumulated amortization, goodwill, thus bringing down the carrying value of the goodwill.

EXERCISE 13-1

Purpose: (L.O. 2, 7) This exercise will give you practice in identifying items that are to be classified as costs associated with various intangible assets.

The Hatchling Fish Corporation incurred the following costs during January 2002:
1. Attorneys' fees in connection with organization of the corporation.
2. Meetings of incorporators, filing fees, and other organization costs.
3. Improvements to leased offices prior to occupancy.
4. Costs to design and construct a prototype.
5. Testing of prototype.

6. Troubleshooting breakdowns during commercial production.
7. Fees paid to engineers and lawyers to prepare patent application; patent granted January 22.
8. Payment of six months rent on leased facilities.
9. Stock issue costs.
10. Payment for a copyright.
11. Materials purchased for future research and development projects; materials have alternative future use.
12. Costs to advertise new business.

Instructions
(a) For each item above, identify what account should be debited to record the expenditure.
(b) Indicate in which classification the related account will be reported in the financial statements.

Solution to Exercise 13-1

(a) Account Debited	(b) Classification
1. Organization Cost	Intangible Asset
2. Organization Cost	Intangible Asset
3. Leasehold Improvements	Property, Plant, and Equipment (or Intangible Asset)
4. Research and Development Expense	Operating Expense
5. Research and Development Expense	Operating Expense
6. Factory Overhead	Allocated to Inventory and Cost of Goods Sold
7. Patent	Intangible Asset
8. Prepaid Rent	Current Asset
9. Organizational Costs	Intangible Asset
10. Copyright	Intangible Asset
11. Raw Materials Inventory	Current Asset
12. Advertising Expense	Operating Expense

TIP: Many companies will charge off organization costs to expense due to materiality and the short time period over which they will be deemed to have future economic benefits. If capitalized, they will usually be up to 5 years.

CASE 13-1

Purpose: (L.O. 1) This case will review examples of various types of intangible assets.

Although companies are permitted to capitalize certain costs to develop specifically identifiable intangible assets such as patents and copyrights, the amounts capitalized are generally not significant. Material amounts of intangible assets are recorded, however, when companies purchase (rather than internally develop) intangible assets, particularly in situations involving the purchase of another business (often referred to as a business combination).

Instructions
Give at least two examples of each of the six types of intangible assets listed below:
1. Intangible assets that relate to customers or market factors of the business.
2. Intangible assets that have a fixed or definite life.
3. Intangible assets that relate to innovation or technological advances within the business.
4. Intangible assets with statutorily established useful lives.
5. Intangible assets that relate to the value of the established employees or workforce of a business.
6. Intangible assets that relate to the organizational structure of the company.

Solution to Case 13-1

1. **Intangible assets that relate to customers or market factors of the business:**
    Lists (advertising, customers, mailing and so forth)   Production backlog
    Customer routes   Retail shelf space
    Trademarks and brand names   Delivery system

2. **Intangible assets that have a fixed or definite life:**
    Agreements (consulting, income, royalty, manufacturing)
    Covenants not to compete
    Licences (liquor, for example)
    Permits (construction, for example)
    Rights (broadcasting, gas allocation, landing, and so forth)

3. **Intangible assets that relate to innovation or technological advances within the business:**
    Computer software   Technological know-how
    Internet domain names and portals   Databases
    Secret formulas and processes

4. **Intangible assets with statutorily established useful lives:**
    Patents   Franchises
    Copyrights   Trademarks or tradenames

5. **Intangible assets that relate to the value of the established employees or workforce of a business:**
    Assembled workforce, trained staff   Technical expertise
    Strong labour relations   Ongoing training program

6. **Intangible assets that relate to the organizational structure of the company:**
    Favourable financial arrangements   Favourable governmental relations
    Easy access to capital markets   Outstanding credit rating

---

TIP: It is extremely difficult not only to identify certain types of intangibles but also to assign a value to them in a business combination. As a result, the approach followed is to record identifiable intangible assets that can be reliably measured. Other intangible assets that are difficult to identify or measure are recorded as goodwill.

EXERCISE 13-2

Purpose: (L.O. 2, 4) This exercise will review the accounting guidelines related to three types of intangible assets—patent, franchise, and trademark.

Information concerning Linda Heckenmueller Corporation's intangible assets follows:

1.   Heckenmueller incurred $85,000 of experimental and development costs in its laboratory to develop a patent which was granted on January 2, 2002. Legal fees and other costs associated with registration of the patent totalled $16,000. Heckenmueller estimates that the useful life of the patent will be 8 years.

2.   On January 1, 2002, Heckenmueller signed an agreement to operate as a franchisee of Cluck-Cluck Fried Chicken, Inc. for an initial franchise fee of $150,000. Of this amount,

$30,000 was paid when the agreement was signed and the balance is payable in four annual payments of $30,000 each, beginning January 1, 2003. The agreement provides that the downpayment is not refundable and no future services are required of the franchisor. The present value at January 1, 2002, of the four annual payments discounted at 14% (the implicit rate for a loan of this type) is $87,400. The agreement also provides that 5% of the revenue from the franchise must be paid to the franchisor annually. Heckenmueller's revenue from the franchise for 2002 was $1,800,000. Heckenmueller estimates the useful life of the franchise to be 10 years.

3.   A trademark was purchased from Wolfe Company for $64,000 on July 1, 1999. Expenditures for successful litigation in defence of the trademark totalling $16,000 were paid on July 1, 2002. Heckenmueller estimates that the useful life of the trademark will be 20 years from the date of acquisition.

Instructions

(a)   Prepare a schedule showing the intangible asset section of Heckenmueller's balance sheet at December 31, 2002. Show supporting calculations in good form.

(b)   Prepare a schedule showing all expenses resulting from the transactions that would appear on Heckenmueller's income statement for the year ended December 31, 2002. Show supporting calculations in good form.

(AICPA adapted)

Solution to Exercise 13-2

(a)
Linda Heckenmueller Corporation
INTANGIBLE ASSETS
December 31, 2002

Patent, net of accumulated amortization of $2,000 (Schedule 1)	$ 14,000
Franchise, net of accumulated amortization of $11,740 (Schedule 2)	105,660
Trademark, net of accumulated amortization of $11,671 (Schedule 3)	68,329
Total intangible assets	$ 187,989

Schedule 1: Patent

Cost of securing patent on 1/2/02	$ 16,000
2002 amortization ($16,000 x 1/8)	(2,000)
Cost of patent, net of amortization	$ 14,000

Schedule 2: Franchise

Cost of franchise on 1/1/02 ($30,000 + $87,400)	$ 117,400
2002 amortization ($117,400 x 1/10)	(11,740)
Cost of franchise, net of amortization	$ 105,660

Schedule 3: Trademark

Cost of trademark on 7/1/99	$ 64,000
Amortization, 7/1/99 to 1/1/02 ($64,000 x 1/20 x 2.5)	(8,000)
Book value on 1/1/02	56,000
Cost of successful legal defence on 7/1/02	16,000
Book value after legal defence	72,000
Amortization, 1/1/02 to 12/31/02 (Schedule 4)	(3,671)
Cost of trademark, net of amortization	$ 68,329

(b)

Linda Heckenmueller Corporation
EXPENSES RESULTING FROM SELECTED INTANGIBLES TRANSACTIONS
For the Year Ended December 31, 2002

Interest expense ($87,400 x 14%)	$ 12,236
Patent amortization (Schedule 1)	2,000
Franchise amortization (Schedule 2)	11,740
Franchise fee ($1,800,000 x 5%)	90,000
Trademark amortization (Schedule 4)	3,671
Total expenses	$119,647

> **TIP:**   The $85,000 of research and development costs incurred in developing the patent would have been expensed prior to 2002.

Schedule 4: Trademark Amortization

Amortization of original cost ($64,000 x 1/20)	$ 3,200
Amortization of legal fees ($16,000 x 1/17 x 6/12)	471
Total trademark amortization	$ 3,671

Approach: The ideal approach would be to prepare the journal entries associated with the facts given and post them to T-accounts to determine the balances to be reported on the income statement for the year ending December 31, 2002 and on the balance sheet at December 31, 2002. Under some circumstances (such as exam conditions), time may not permit these additional steps. You should at least think about and visualize the flow of the information through the accounts. This will greatly aid the successful completion of the schedules required.

Explanation:

1.   Research and development costs are to be expensed in the period incurred. Thus, the $85,000 of experimental and development costs incurred in developing the patent would have been expensed prior to 2002. Legal fees and other costs associated with obtaining the patent should be matched with each of the 8 years estimated to be benefited; therefore, the $16,000 of legal fees and registration costs should be capitalized and amortized.

2.   The franchise rights will benefit future periods. Therefore, the costs associated with obtaining those rights should be capitalized and amortized over future periods. The acquisition cost is determined by the cash given (down payment of $30,000) and the cash equivalent of the related payable (present value of the four annual payments at 14%—$87,400). The fact that "the down payment is not refundable and no future services are required of the franchisor" has no impact on how the franchisee accounts for the franchise. The provision in the agreement which calls for the franchisee to pay 5% of the annual revenue from the franchise to the franchisor does not initially require any accounting treatment; an expense accrues as revenues are earned from use of the franchise. The capitalized franchise costs are to be amortized over the useful period of

10 years. The interest expense resulting from deferred payment is to be recognized annually by applying the implicit interest rate of 14% to the outstanding payable balance.

3.   The purchase price of the trademark ($64,000) was capitalized in mid-1999 when the trademark was acquired. That cost is being amortized over the 20-year useful life. (Note that only one-half year of amortization was recorded in 1999.) Expenditures of $16,000 for successful litigation in defence of the trademark rights are to be charged to the Trademark account because such a suit establishes the legal rights of the holder of the trademark (which benefits future periods). Because the litigation was settled in the middle of 2002, only one-half year of amortization of these legal costs is recorded for 2002. The $16,000 is to be amortized over the remaining useful life of the trademark (17 years in this case).

EXERCISE 13-3

Purpose: (L.O. 4) This exercise reviews the subject of leasehold improvements.

On January 1, 2002, Mr. Howard Anderson's Prize Paints entered into a lease contract with the Regency Mall Corp. The agreement provides for a 10-year lease on store space in a suburban mall. Mr. Anderson is leasing the space for his wholesale paint business. In order to prepare the facilities for his purpose, Mr. Anderson constructed several partitions at a cost of $3,200 and lowered the ceiling at a cost of $1,400. The partitions and ceiling revert to the owner of the property at the end of the lease term. Mr. Anderson assumes they will last as long as the building, which he estimates to have a 20-year life. The company uses a calendar year reporting period.

Instructions
(a)   Prepare the journal entry to record the payment to the builder who put in the partitions and ceiling.
(b)   Identify the period of time over which the improvements should be amortized. Explain why.
(c)   Prepare the related adjusting entry (if any) at December 31, 2002.
(d)   Explain how the improvements would appear on the balance sheet at the end of the third year of the lease.

Solution to Exercise 13-3

(a)   Leasehold improvements ($3,200 + $1,400).................................   4,600

          Cash   4,600

(b)   Leasehold improvements are to be amortized over their useful life or the remaining term of the lease, whichever is less. In this scenario, the remaining term of the lease is 10 years, which is less than the 20-year useful life of the improvements. The 10-year period should be used.

(c)   The adjusting entry to amortize the improvements at December 31, 2002, would be:

          Amortization of Leasehold Improvements Expense.........................   460

            Leasehold Improvements ($4,600 ÷ 10 years = $460)...............   460

(d)   Leasehold Improvements would most likely appear in the property, plant, and equipment section of Prize Paints' balance sheet at an amount of $3,220 [$4,600 - (3 x $460) = $3,220] at the end of the third year of the lease, although some accountants would prefer to report this item in the intangible asset classification.

EXERCISE 13-4

Purpose: (L.O. 6, 7) This exercise will give you practice in identifying activities that constitute R & D activities.

Listed below are four independent situations involving research and development costs:

1.   During 2002 Bebe Co. incurred the following costs:

Research and development services performed by Way Co. for Bebe	$ 325,000
Testing for evaluation of new products	300,000
Laboratory research aimed at discovery of new knowledge	375,000
Research and development services performed by Bebe for Elway Co.	220,000

How much should Bebe report as research and development expense for the year ended December 31, 2002?

2.   Holly Corp. incurred the following costs during the year ended December 31, 2002:

Design, construction, and testing of preproduction prototypes & models	$ 220,000
Routine, on-going efforts to refine, enrich, or otherwise improve upon the qualities of an existing product	250,000
Quality control during commercial production including routine testing of products	300,000
Laboratory research aimed at discovery of new knowledge	360,000
Conceptual formulation and design of possible product alternatives	100,000

What is the total amount to be classified and expensed as research and development for 2002?

3. Polanski Company incurred costs in 2002 as follows:
    Equipment acquired for use in various R & D projects
      (current and future) $ 890,000
    Amortization on the equipment above   135,000
    Materials used in R & D   300,000
    Compensation costs of personnel in R & D   400,000
    Outside consulting fees for R & D work   150,000
    Indirect costs appropriately allocated to R & D   260,000

    What is the total amount of research and development expense that should be reported in Polanski's 2002 income statement?

4. Liverpool Inc. incurred the following costs during the year ended December 31, 2002:
    Laboratory research aimed at discovery of new knowledge $ 175,000
    Routine design of tools, jigs, molds, and dies   60,000
    Radical modification to the formulation of a chemical product   125,000
    Research and development costs reimbursable under a contract
      to perform R & D for Johnathon King, Inc.   350,000
    Testing for evaluation of new products   275,000

    What is the total amount to be classified and expensed as research and development for 2002?

Instructions

Provide the correct answer to each of the four situations.

Solution to Exercise 13-4

1. Research and development services performed by Way Co. for Bebe $ 325,000
    Testing for evaluation of new products   300,000
    Laboratory research aimed at discovery of new knowledge   375,000
            Total R & D expense $ 1,000,000

TIP:	R & D costs related to R & D activities conducted for other entities are classified as a receivable (because of the impending reimbursement).

2. Design, construction and testing of preproduction prototypes and models $ 220,000
    Laboratory research aimed at discovery of new knowledge   360,000
    Conceptual formulation and design of possible product alternatives   100,000
            Total R & D expense $ 680,000

TIP:	routine, ongoing efforts to refine, enrich or improve an existing product is not considered R&D., similarly, quality control is a regular operating expense of production.

3.	Amortization on the equipment acquired for use in	
	various R & D projects	$ 135,000
	Materials used in R & D	300,000
	Compensation costs of personnel in R & D	400,000
	Outside consulting fees for R & D work	150,000
	Indirect costs appropriately allocated to R & D	260,000
	Total R & D expense	$ 1,245,000

> **TIP:** Equipment, facilities, and purchased intangibles that have **alternative future uses** (in other R & D projects or otherwise) are to be **capitalized**; the **related amortization are to be classified as R & D**.

4.	Laboratory research aimed at discovery of new knowledge	$ 175,000
	Radical modification to the formulation of a chemical product	125,000
	Testing for evaluation of new products	275,000
	Total R & D expense	$ 575,000

Approach: Read the requirement of each situation before you begin detailed work on the first one. Notice that all four items deal with research and development costs. Therefore, review in your mind the definitions of the words "research" and "development." Recall what you can from the list of activities considered to be R & D and the list of activities which are **not** considered to be R & D. Think of why the items logically appear on a particular list. It is important to think about these items **before** you dig into the questions because details in the situations may mislead you. To minimize confusion, organize your thoughts and recall what you know about the subject before you begin to process the data at hand.

Explanation: To differentiate research and development costs from other similar costs:

> **Research** is planned search or critical investigation undertaken with the hope of gaining new scientific or technical knowledge and understanding. Such investigation may or may not be directed toward a specific practical aim or application.

> **Development** is the translation of research findings or other knowledge into a plan or design for a new or substantially improved materials, devices, products, processes, systems, or services prior to the commencement of commercial production or use. *CICA Handbook, Section 3450, par. .02.*

Many costs have characteristics similar to those of research and development costs, for instance, costs of relocation and rearrangement of facilities, start-up costs for a new plant or new retail outlet, marketing research costs, promotion costs of a new product or service, and costs of training new personnel. To distinguish between R & D and those other similar costs, the following schedule provides (1) examples of activities that typically would be **included** in research and development, and (2) examples that typically would be **excluded** from research and development.

1.	**R & D Activities**	**2.**	**Activities Not Considered R & D**
(a)	Laboratory research aimed at discovery of new knowledge.	(a)	Engineering follow-through in an early phase of commercial production.
(b)	Searching for applications of new research findings.	(b)	Quality control during commercial production including routine testing.

(c) Conceptual formulation and design of possible product or process alternatives.

(d) Testing in search for or evaluation of product or process alternatives.

(e) Modification of the design of a product or process.

(f) Design, construction, and testing of preproduction prototypes and models.

(g) Design of tools, jigs, molds, and dies involving new technology.

(h) Design, construction, and operation of a pilot plant not useful for commercial production.

(i) Engineering activity required to advance the design of a product to the manufacturing stage.

(c) Trouble-shooting breakdowns during commercial production.

(d) Routine, on-going efforts to refine, enrich, or improve the qualities of an existing product.

(e) Adaptation of an existing capability to a particular requirement or customer's need.

(f) Periodic design changes to existing products.

(g) Routine design of tools, jigs, molds, and dies.

(h) Activity, including design and construction engineering related to the construction, relocation, rearrangement, or startup of facilities or equipment.

(i) Legal work on patent applications, sale, licencing, or litigation.

TIP: Disclosure should be made in the financial statements (generally in the notes) of the total R & D costs charged to expense each period for which an income statement is presented.

CASE 13-2

Purpose: (L.O. 7) This case is designed to give you practice in differentiating expenditures which are classified as research and development costs and expenditures which are not included with R & D.

Instructions

Various types of expenditures are listed below. Indicate the accounting treatment appropriate for each type of expenditure listed.

Type of Expenditure	Accounting Treatment
1. Construction of long-range research facility for use in current and future projects (three storey, 400,000-square-foot building).	
2. Acquisition of R & D equipment for use on current project only.	
3. Acquisition of machinery to be used on current and future R & D projects.	
4. Purchase of materials to be used on current and future R & D projects.	
5. Salaries of research staff designing new laser bone scanner.	

6. Research costs incurred under contract with another corporation and billable to that company monthly.
7. Material, labour, and overhead costs of prototype laser scanner.
8. Costs of testing prototype and design modifications.
9. Legal fees to obtain patent on new laser scanner.
10. Executive salaries.
11. Cost of marketing to promote new laser scanner.
12. Engineering costs incurred to advance the laser scanner to full production stage.
13. Cost of successfully defending patent on laser scanner.
14. Commissions to sales staff marketing new laser scanner.

SOLUTION TO CASE 13-2

Type of Expenditure	Accounting Treatment
1. Construction of long-range research facility for use in current and future projects (three storey, 400,000-square-foot building).	Capitalize and amortize as R & D expense.
2. Acquisition of R & D equipment for use on current project only.	Capitalize and amortize as R & D expense.
3. Acquisition of machinery to be used on current and future R & D projects.	Capitalize and amortize as R & D expense.
4. Purchase of materials to be used on current and future R & D projects.	Inventory and allocate to R & D projects; expense as consumed.
5. Salaries of research staff designing new laser bone scanner.	Expense immediately as R & D.
6. Research costs incurred under contract with another corporation and billable to that company monthly.	Expense as operating expense in period of related revenue recognition
7. Material, labour, and overhead costs of prototype laser scanner.	Capitalize as development costs if all criteria are met, otherwise expense
8. Costs of testing prototype and design modifications.	Capitalize as development costs if all criteria are met, otherwise expense
9. Legal fees to obtain patent on new laser scanner.	Capitalize as patent and amortize to overhead as part of cost of goods manufactured as used.
10. Executive salaries.	Expense as operating expense (general and administrative).
11. Cost of marketing to promote new laser scanner.	Expense as operating expense (selling).
12. Engineering costs incurred to advance the laser scanner to full production stage.	Capitalize as development costs if all criteria are met, otherwise expense

13. Cost of successfully defending patent on laser scanner.	Capitalize as patent and amortize to overhead as part of cost of goods manufactured as used.
14. Commissions to sales staff marketing new laser scanner.	Expense as operating expense (selling).

TIP: **Development costs** must be expensed unless **all of the following criteria are met:**
1. The product or process is clearly defined and the costs attributable to it can be identified.
2. The technical feasibility of the product or process has been established.
3. The enterprise management has indicated its intention to produce and market or use the product or process.
4. The future market for the product or process is clearly defined or, if it is to be used internally rather than sold, its usefulness to the enterprise has been established.
5. Adequate resources exist or are expected to be available to complete the project. Furthermore, the total amount of development costs deferred must be limited to the extent that their recovery can reasonably be regarded as assured.
CICA Handbook, Section 3450, par. .13.

TIP: Refer to Item 6 above. Sometimes one enterprise conducts R & D activities for other entities under a contractual arrangement. In this case, the contract usually specifies that all direct costs, certain specific indirect costs, plus a profit element, should be reimbursed to the enterprise performing the R & D work. Because reimbursement is expected, such R & D costs should be recorded as a receivable. It is the company for whom the work has been performed that reports these costs as R & D and expenses them as incurred.

ILLUSTRATION 13-1
DETERMINATION OF GOODWILL AND PURCHASE PRICE, (EXCESS EARNINGS APPROACH), (L.O. 10)

Step 1: **Determine normal earnings.** Multiply *the industry average rate of return on net assets* times *the fair market value of the identifiable net assets* of the company.

Step 2: **Determine an estimate of future average annual earnings.** This is usually done by calculating the adjusted (normalized) average net earnings of the company in the past, (usually 6 years). Adjust for accounting changes, extraordinary items, and other such special items.

Step 3: **Determine excess earnings.** This is the average earnings from Step 2 less the normal earnings from Step 1.

Step 4: **Determine the value of goodwill.** This can be done by using an appropriate discount rate and choosing the number of periods for which the excess earnings will be maintained. It could be treated as a perpetuity by capitalizing the excess earnings (dividing excess earnings by an appropriate capitalization rate). Alternatively, the number of years method could be used.

Step 5: **Determine purchase price.** This will be the sum of the value of goodwill and the fair value of identifiable net assets of the firm.

EXERCISE 13-5

Purpose: (L.O. 10) This exercise illustrates the steps in estimating the value of goodwill.

Mr. Lastman is contemplating the sale of his business, Classic Vettes. The following data are available:

Book value of tangible and identifiable intangible assets less liabilities	$ 185,000
Market value of tangible and identifiable intangible assets less liabilities	$ 200,000
Estimated average future annual income for Classic Vettes	$ 28,000
Normal rate of return for the industry	10%

Instructions
(a)   Calculate the estimated value of goodwill if excess income is capitalized at a 10% rate.
(b)   Calculate the estimated value of goodwill if excess income is capitalized at a 25% rate.

Solution to Exercise 13-5

(a) $200,000 x 10% = $20,000 normal earnings
$28,000 - $20,000 = $8,000 excess earnings
$8,000 ÷ 10% = $80,000 goodwill

Approach and Explanation: Perform the applicable steps described in **Illustration 12-1**:

Step 1:   Determine normal earnings. Multiply the industry average rate of return times the fair market value of the identifiable net assets of the firm.
10% x $200,000 = $20,000 Normal earnings

Step 2:   Determine an estimate of future average annual earnings. This is given data in the exercise at hand—$28,000.

Step 3:   Determine excess earnings. Deduct normal earnings from future average annual earnings.
$28,000 - $20,000 = $8,000 Excess earnings

Step 4:   Determine the value of goodwill. Capitalize excess earnings by dividing excess earnings by the chosen capitalization rate.
$8,000 ÷ 10% = $80,000 goodwill

(b) $200,000 x 10% = $20,000 normal earnings
$28,000 - $20,000 = $8,000 excess earnings
$8,000 ÷ 25% = $32,000 goodwill

TIP: The higher the capitalization rate, the lower the resulting value for goodwill.

TIP: Excess earnings are often referred to as superior earnings.

TIP: Net identifiable assets are determined by deducting total liabilities from total identifiable (tangible and intangible) assets.

> **TIP:** Fair value, market value, and fair market value are terms which are often used interchangeably.

EXERCISE 13-6

Purpose: (L.O. 10) This exercise will provide an example of how to use the present value method to estimate the value of goodwill.

As president of Winnie Audio Corp., you are considering purchasing Winkle Video Corp., whose balance sheet is summarized as follows:

Current assets	$ 400,000	Current liabilities	$ 400,000
Fixed assets (net of		Long-term liabilities	500,000
amortization)	800,000	Common shares	300,000
Other assets	200,000	Retained earnings	200,000
Total	$1,400,000	Total	$ 1,400,000

The fair market value of current assets is $700,000. The normal rate of return on net assets for the industry is 15%. The average expected annual earnings projected for Winkle Video Corp. is $160,000.

Instructions
Assuming that the excess earnings continue for 5 years, determine the value for goodwill by use of the present-value method.

Solution to Exercise 13-6

Step 1:	Fair market value of net assets	$ 800,000*
	Normal rate of return	15%
	Normal earnings	$ 120,000

Step 2: Average expected annual earnings are $160,000 (data given).

Step 3:	Expected earnings	$ 160,000
	Normal earnings	(120,000)
	Excess earnings	$ 40,000

Step 4:	Excess earnings	$ 40,000
	Present value of an annuity of 1 factor, 5 years @ 15%	3.35216
	Estimated goodwill	$ 134,086.40

*Book value of total assets	$ 1,400,000
Excess fair market value over book value of current assets	300,000**
Fair value of total assets	1,700,000
Total liabilities ($400,000 + $500,000)	900,000
Fair market value of net identifiable assets of Winkle	$ 800,000

**Fair market value of current assets	$ 700,000
Book value of current assets	400,000
Excess fair market value over book value of current assets	$ 300,000

Approach: Apply the steps listed in **Illustration 13-1**.

TIP:	You should also be able to calculate the purchase price that would result if both parties agree with the estimated goodwill figure calculated above. The fair value of the net identifiable assets ($800,000) plus the value of the unidentifiable asset (goodwill of $134,086) equals a total fair value of $934,086 for Winkle Video Corp.
TIP:	You should also be able to record the purchase of Winkle Video Corp. if Audio Corp. pays $934,086 to purchase it. The identifiable assets would be recorded at their fair values ($1,700,000), Goodwill would be debited for $134,086, the liabilities would be recorded at their fair values ($900,000) and Cash would be credited for $934,086.

ANALYSIS OF MULTIPLE-CHOICE TYPE QUESTIONS

QUESTION

1.   (L.O. 2) Innoventions Inc. acquired a patent from Whizkid Inc. on January 1, 2002, in exchange for $7,000 cash and an investment security that had been acquired in 1998. The following facts pertain:

Original cost of investment	$ 14,000
Carrying value of patent on books of Whizkid Inc.	4,500
Fair market value of the investment security on January 1, 2002	23,000

The cost of the patent to be recorded by Innoventions Inc. is:
a. $7,000
b. $11,500
c. $21,000
d. $30,000
e.   None of the above

Approach and Explanation: Recall the guideline for determining the cost of any intangible asset. The cost of an intangible asset includes all costs incurred to acquire the asset. The historical cost principle dictates that cost be measured by the fair market value (i.e., cash equivalent value) of the consideration given or by the fair market value of the consideration received, whichever is the more objectively determinable. Innoventions Inc. gave $7,000 cash plus the investment security with a fair market value of $23,000 at the date of the exchange. The cost of the patent is, therefore, $30,000. (Solution = d.)

QUESTION

2.   (L.O. 4) The adjusted trial balance of the Laventhal Corporation as of December 31, 2002 includes the following accounts:

Trademark	$ 30,000
Discount on bonds payable	37,500
Organization Costs	12,500
Excess of cost over fair value of identifiable net assets of acquired business	175,000
Advertising costs (to promote goodwill)	20,000

What should be reported as total intangible assets on Laventhal's December 31, 2002 balance sheet?
a. $205,000
b. $230,000
c. $217,500
d. $275,000

Approach and Explanation: Identify the classification of each item listed. Sum the ones you identify as being intangible assets.

Trademark	$ 30,000
Organization Costs	12,500
Excess of cost over fair value of identifiable net assets of acquired business	175,000
Total intangible assets	$ 217,500

Discount on bonds payable is to be classified as a contra liability. Advertising costs incurred are to be reported as an expense on the income statement. The costs to develop, maintain, or restore goodwill are not to be capitalized. Only the costs to acquire goodwill with a going business can be recorded as goodwill. The "excess of cost over fair value of net identifiable net assets of acquired business" is a technical term referring to goodwill. (Solution = c.)

QUESTION

3.   (L.O. 4) A patent with a remaining legal life of 12 years and an estimated useful life of 8 years was acquired for $288,000 by Bradley Corporation on January 2, 1998. In January 2002, Bradley paid $18,000 in legal fees in a successful defence of the patent. What should Bradley record as patent amortization for 2002?

   a. $24,000
   b. $36,000
   c. $38,250
   d. $40,500

Approach and Explanation: Analyse the Patent account. Use the data given to calculate the amounts reflected therein and the resulting amortization for 2002.

Cost at beginning of 1998	$ 288,000
Amortization for 1998–2001	(144,000)*
Book value at beginning of 2002	144,000
Legal fees capitalized	18,000
Revised book value, beginning of 2002	162,000
Remaining years of life	÷ 4
Amortization for 2002	$ 40,500 (Solution = d.)

*Beginning of 1998, patent cost	$ 288,000
Estimated years of service life	÷ 8
Annual amortization for 1998–2001	36,000
Number of years used	4
Total amortization 1998–2001	$ 144,000

QUESTION

4.   (L.O. 4) On January 1, 2002, Teeple Corporation acquired a patent for $30,000. Due to the quickly changing technology associated with the patent, Teeple is amortizing the cost of the patent over 5 years. What portion of the patent cost will Temple defer to years subsequent to 2002?

   a. $0
   b. $6,000
   c. $24,000
   d. $30,000

Explanation: $30,000 ÷ 5 yrs. = $6,000 amortization per year.
If $6,000 is amortized, then the amount to defer is calculated as follows:

Total patent cost	$ 30,000
Amount amortized in 2002	(6,000)
Amount to defer to subsequent periods	$ 24,000 (Solution = c.)

> **TIP:** Note the importance of reading the question carefully. An intermediate step—the calculation of the $6,000 amortization amount for 2002—is one of the distracters. You should read the last sentence of the question stem first to understand the essence of the problem. It is wise to write down the essential calculation to keep your focus:
>
> Total Patent Cost
> <u>- Amount to Amortize in 2002</u>
> = Amount to Defer

QUESTION
5. (L.O. 4) The legal life of a patent is:
    a. 17 years
    b. 20 years
    c. 40 years
    d. The life of the inventory plus 50 years.

Explanation: A patent offers its holder an exclusive right to use, manufacture, and sell a product or process over a period of 20 years without interference or infringement by others. It is not subject to renewal. (Solution = b.)

QUESTION
6. (L.O. 4) The cost of permits and licences are material to the entity for whom you are accounting. The cost of these items should be:
    a. expensed in the period acquired.
    b. expensed over the useful life of the items, but not more than 40 years.
    c. charged against paid-in capital.
    d. capitalized but not amortized.

Explanation: Licenses and permits offer the holder certain rights. Like all other intangible assets, the cost of these items should be matched with the periods benefited. To comply with the matching principle, the cost of an intangible asset is to be amortized over its useful life; however, the amortization period is not to exceed 20 years. (Solution = b.)

QUESTION
7. (L.O. 2) The costs of intangible assets which are internally created are typically:
    a. capitalized but not amortized.
    b. capitalized and amortized over a long period of time.
    c. capitalized and amortized over a short period of time.
    d. expensed as incurred.

Explanation: The following is helpful to keep in mind:

	Manner Acquired	
Type of Intangible	Purchased	Internally Created
Specifically identifiable intangibles	Capitalize	Expense, except certain costs
Goodwill-type intangibles	Capitalize	Expense
Deferred Charges	Capitalize	Capitalize restricted amounts

If you purchase a patent from an inventor or an owner, the cost of that patent is capitalized. If you develop (internally generate) a product yourself, the research and development costs related to the development of the product or idea that is subsequently patented must be expensed unless the specified criteria are met. However, other costs incurred in connection with securing a patent, as well as attorney's fees and other unrecovered costs of a successful legal suit to protect the patent, can be capitalized as a part of the patent cost. (Solution = d.)

QUESTION

8.   (L.O. 7) A development stage enterprise should use the same generally accepted accounting principles that apply to established operating enterprises for:

	Recognition of Revenue	Recognition of Expenses
a.	Yes	Yes
b.	No	No
c.	No	Yes
d.	Yes	No

Explanation: The Emerging Issue Committee of the CICA, in EIC-27, indicates that pre-operating costs should be expensed unless all three of the following criteria are met:
1. It relates directly to placing the new business into service.
2. It is incremental in nature, and would not have been incurred in the absence of the new business.
3. It is probable that the expenditure is recoverable from the future operations of the new business.(Solution = d.)

QUESTION

9.   (L.O. 8) The costs of organizing a corporation include legal fees, fees paid for incorporation, fees paid to underwriters, and the costs of meetings for organizing the underwriters. These costs are said to benefit the corporation for the entity's entire life. These costs should be:
a.   capitalized and never amortized.
b.   capitalized and amortized over 40 years.
c.   capitalized and amortized over 5–10 years.
d.   expensed as incurred.

Explanation:. Although it is difficult to exactly determine the length of benefit, costs incurred in establishing an organization are deferred as organization costs. Amortization costs are normally short (5–10 years) as a conservative approach.(Solution = c.)

QUESTION

10.   (L.O. 8) Windsor Corporation was organized in 2001 and began operations at the beginning of 2002. Prior to the start of operations, the following costs were incurred in 2001:

Attorneys' fees for assistance in obtaining corporate charter and drafting related documents	$ 33,000
Meetings of incorporators	14,000
Improvements to leased office space prior to occupancy	48,000
Fees to underwriters to help locate buyers for Windsor's common shares	21,000
	$116,000

What should be the balance of the Organization Cost account based on the above?

a. $21,000
b. $33,000
c. $68,000
d. $116,000
e.   None of the above.

Approach and Explanation: Before reading through the list of costs incurred, define "organization costs" and think of the most common examples. **Organization costs** are costs incurred in the formation of a corporation such as fees to underwriters, legal fees, federal fees of various sorts, and certain promotional expenditures. They are to be deferred. Windsor should charge the following to Organization Cost:

Attorneys' fees for incorporation	$ 33,000
Meetings of incorporators	14,000
Fees to promoters	21,000
Total organization costs	$ 68,000

(Solution = c.)

TIP: The $48,000 of improvements to leased office space prior to occupancy should be recorded in the Leasehold Improvements account.

QUESTION

11.   (L.O. 7) Motts Corporation purchased the following items at the beginning of 2002:

Materials to be used in R & D activities; these materials have alternative future uses and they remain unused at the end of 2002.	$ 50,000
Materials to be used in R & D activities; these materials do not have alternative future uses and $12,000 of them remain unused at the end of 2002.	33,000
Equipment to be used in R & D activities; this equipment was used in one R & D project during 2002 and is expected to be used in other R & D projects to be undertaken over the next 5 years. It has no residual value. Motts normally uses the straight-line amortization method for equipment.	100,000
Total	$ 183,000

Based on the above information, Motts should report R & D expenses for 2002 of:
a. $183,000
b. $103,000
c. $53,000
d. $21,000
e. None of the above.

Approach and Explanation: Mentally review the proper accounting treatment for materials and equipment acquired for use in R & D activities. The cost of materials acquired for use in R & D activities should be expensed in the period acquired unless the items have alternative future uses (in R & D projects or otherwise); then they should be carried as inventory and allocated to R & D expense as used. The cost of equipment and facilities acquired for use in R & D activities should be expensed in the period acquired unless the items have alternative future uses (in R & D projects or otherwise); then they should be capitalized and amortized as used (the resulting amortization should be classified as R & D expense). Thus, Motts would have the following R & D expense for 2002: (Solution = c.)

Materials acquired, no future alternative use	$ 33,000
Amortization on equipment used in R & D activities	
($100,000 ÷ 5 years)	20,000
Total R & D expense for 2002	$ 53,000

QUESTION
12.   (L.O. 3) Which one of the following is not a condition of an intangible with an indefinite useful life which should not be amortized:
a. has a useful economic life that is not limited.
b. is exchangeable or control over the benefits is through contractual or other legal rights extending for more than 20 years.
c. generates clearly identifiable cash flows exceeding 20 years.
d. does not have an observable market.

Explanation: An intangible with an indefinite useful life should not be amortized, such as goodwill, until it is impaired. If the conditions are not met, the intangible should be amortized over a period not exceeding 20 years. The CICA Accounting Standards Board concluded in 2001 that an intangible that has clearly identifiable cash flows exceeding 20 years, has exchangeable or control over benefits by contract or other legal means for over 20 years and has an observable market (one in which intangible assets are separately bought and sold and from which a market price can be observed to use in estimating the fair value of similar assets), should not be amortized. These are, however, subject to tests for impairment as are all other intangible assets. (Solution = d).

QUESTION
13.   (L.O. 4) The total amount of patent cost amortized to date is usually:
   a.   shown in a separate Accumulated Patent Amortization account which is shown contra to the Patent account.
   b.   shown in the current income statement.
   c.   reflected as credits in the Patent account.
   d.   reflected as a contra property, plant and equipment item.

Explanation: In accounting for intangible assets, the amortization of an asset is usually credited directly to the Accumulated Amortization, Patent contra asset account.

QUESTION
14.   (L.O. 7) Gates Inc. develops computer software to be sold to the general public. The costs incurred in creating a new piece of software should be:
   a.   charged to R & D expenses.
   b.   capitalized and amortized.
   c.   charged to R & D expense when incurred until technological feasibility has been established for the product; the costs incurred after this point are to be capitalized.
   d.   charged to cost of goods sold expense.

Explanation: Costs incurred in creating computer software to be sold to external parties should be charged to research and development expense when incurred until technological feasibility has been established for the product (which occurs upon completion of a detailed program design or working model). Costs incurred subsequent to this point are to be capitalized and amortized to current and future periods. (Solution = c.)

QUESTION
15.   (L.O. 10) The owners of Tellmart Shoe Store are contemplating selling the business to new interests. The cumulative earnings for the past 5 years amounted to $750,000, including extraordinary gains of $25,000. The annual earnings based on an average rate of return on investment for this industry would have been $115,000. If excess earnings are to be capitalized at 15%, then implied goodwill should be:
   a. $175,000
   b. $233,334
   c. $200,000
   d. $725,000

Approach and Explanation: Follow the steps in **Illustration 12-1**.
Step 1:   Normal earnings = $115.000.

Step 2:	Cumulative earnings over the past 5 years	$ 750,000
	Extraordinary gains included in above	(25,000)
	Total earnings excluding extraordinary items	725,000
	Number of years included above	÷ 5
	Average earnings in past 5 years assumed to be average annual earnings	$ 145,000

Step 3:	Expected average earnings	$ 145,000
	Normal earnings	(115,000)
	Excess earnings	$ 30,000
Step 4:	Excess earnings	$ 30,000
	Capitalization rate	÷ 15%
	Estimated value of goodwill	$ 200,000

(Solution = c.)

NOTES